Basic Facts about the United Nations

Basic Facts
about the
United Nations
42nd Edition

United Nations Department of Public Information
New York

NO LOAN
PER
UNI
DPI
B12

Basic Facts about the United Nations

Published by the United Nations Department of Public Information
New York, New York 10017, United States of America

Forty-second edition
Copyright © 2017 United Nations
All rights reserved. First edition 1947.

All queries on rights and licenses, including subsidiary rights,
should be addressed to: United Nations Publications,
300 East 42nd Street, New York, NY 10017, United States of America;
e-mail: order@un.org; website: shop.un.org.

ISBN: 978-92-1-101350-4
eISBN: 978-92-1-058490-6
United Nations publication
Sales No. E.17.I.2

Printed in the United States of America

FOREWORD

The United Nations remains an indispensable pillar of the international system, working around the world, around the clock, for peace, sustainable development and human rights. At a time when challenges are increasingly global, and our fates are inexorably intertwined, understanding the United Nations itself—its aims, workings and ideals—is more important than ever.

Published since 1947, *Basic Facts about the United Nations* provides a comprehensive and authoritative overview of the Organization. This latest edition describes the history and structure of the United Nations system, how it functions and its continuing efforts to serve the world's people.

Significant progress has been made over recent decades to improve human well-being. Yet, many issues, including violent conflict, mass migration, humanitarian crises, terrorism, poverty, youth unemployment, intolerance and inequality, have grown in complexity. Climate change is a growing threat, amplifying the impact of natural disasters and putting global water and food security at risk.

All these issues demonstrate the urgent need for multilateral cooperation that recognizes the links between peace and security, human rights and sustainable development. The venue for that cooperation is the United Nations—the world's unique universal forum where States can come together to address shared problems and seize common opportunities. Recent cooperation is chronicled in this volume, including three transformative international agreements endorsed in 2015: the Paris Agreement on climate change, the Addis Ababa Action Agenda on Financing for Development and the 2030 Agenda for Sustainable Development. These landmark plans provide a blueprint for peace, prosperity and dignity for all on a healthy planet.

At this time of challenge and opportunity for the human family, I am committed to reforming the United Nations to ensure that the Organization delivers meaningful results for the world's people. This volume provides a window into that work, and I hope that anyone interested in the United Nations will find it a useful resource, as well as a call to action as we strive to realize the objectives of the Organization's founding *Charter*.

António Guterres
Secretary-General of the United Nations
New York, March 2017

CONTENTS

LIST OF ACRONYMS

CEB	United Nations System Chief Executives Board for Coordination
CTBTO	Preparatory Commission for the Comprehensive Nuclear-Test-Ban Treaty Organization
DESA	Department of Economic and Social Affairs
DFS	Department of Field Support
DGACM	Department for General Assembly and Conference Management
DM	Department of Management
DPA	Department of Political Affairs
DPI	Department of Public Information
DPKO	Department of Peacekeeping Operations
DSS	Department of Safety and Security
ECA	Economic Commission for Africa
ECE	Economic Commission for Europe
ECLAC	Economic Commission for Latin America and the Caribbean
ECOSOC	Economic and Social Council
ESCAP	Economic and Social Commission for Asia and the Pacific
ESCWA	Economic and Social Commission for Western Asia
FAO	Food and Agriculture Organization of the United Nations
IAEA	International Atomic Energy Agency
IASC	Inter-Agency Standing Committee
IBRD	International Bank for Reconstruction and Development
ICAO	International Civil Aviation Organization
ICC	International Criminal Court
IDA	International Development Association
IDPs	Internally displaced persons
IFAD	International Fund for Agricultural Development
IFC	International Finance Corporation
ILO	International Labour Organization
IMF	International Monetary Fund
IMO	International Maritime Organization
IOM	International Organization for Migration
IPCC	Intergovernmental Panel on Climate Change
ITC	International Trade Centre
ITU	International Telecommunication Union
MDGs	Millennium Development Goals
NEPAD	New Partnership for Africa's Development

NGOs	non-governmental organizations
OCHA	Office for the Coordination of Humanitarian Affairs
ODA	Office for Disarmament Affairs
OHCHR	Office of the United Nations High Commissioner for Human Rights
OIOS	Office of Internal Oversight Services
OLA	Office of Legal Affairs
OPCW	Organisation for the Prohibition of Chemical Weapons
PBSO	Peacebuilding Support Office
SDGs	Sustainable Development Goals
UNAIDS	Joint United Nations Programme on HIV/AIDS
UNCDF	United Nations Capital Development Fund
UNCTAD	United Nations Conference on Trade and Development
UNDP	United Nations Development Programme
UNEP	United Nations Environment Programme
UNESCO	United Nations Educational, Scientific and Cultural Organization
UNFPA	United Nations Population Fund
UN-Habitat	United Nations Human Settlements Programme
UNHCR	Office of the United Nations High Commissioner for Refugees
UNICEF	United Nations Children's Fund
UNICRI	United Nations Interregional Crime and Justice Research Institute
UNIDIR	United Nations Institute for Disarmament Research
UNIDO	United Nations Industrial Development Organization
UNISDR	United Nations Office for Disaster Risk Reduction
UNITAR	United Nations Institute for Training and Research
UNODC	United Nations Office on Drugs and Crime
UN-OHRLLS	Office of the High Representative for the Least Developed Countries, Landlocked Developing Countries and Small Island Developing States
UNOP	United Nations Office for Partnerships
UNOPS	United Nations Office for Project Services
UNRISD	United Nations Research Institute for Social Development
UNRWA	United Nations Relief and Works Agency for Palestine Refugees in the Near East
UNSSC	United Nations System Staff College
UNU	United Nations University
UNV	United Nations Volunteers
UN-Women	United Nations Entity for Gender Equality and the Empowerment of Women
UNWTO	World Tourism Organization
UPU	United Nations Postal Union
WFP	World Food Programme
WHO	World Health Organization
WIPO	World Intellectual Property Organization
WMO	World Meteorological Organization
WTO	World Trade Organization

ABOUT THIS EDITION

B asic Facts about the United Nations, published regularly since 1947, serves as the definitive introduction to the UN and its family of related institutions and agencies. Over the years, Basic Facts has expanded the scope and depth of its coverage as the Organization has broadened its commitment to meet the urgent needs of an ever more populous and complex world. At the same time, the book has remained true to its roots as a comprehensive yet concise guide to this leading world body. Continuing that tradition, this forty-second edition outlines the current structure of the UN system and explains how each individual part contributes to achieving key international goals.

Basic Facts begins by recounting the origins of the United Nations and providing an overview of the wider system of UN institutions and agencies. Published in a year that began with the ninth Secretary-General taking office, it also explains the selection process. Successive chapters describe the Organization's efforts to advance international peace and security; enhance economic and social development in an environmentally sustainable manner; protect human rights and eliminate discrimination; provide humanitarian relief to refugees, displaced persons and those affected by natural and man-made disasters; and develop and standardize international law. These chapters portray an Organization unique in its ability to mobilize collective action to meet the challenges facing our world.

Also functioning as a practical handbook, Basic Facts includes appendices providing essential information on UN membership; current and former UN peacekeeping missions; and the observance of UN decades, years, weeks and days. It also contains contact information for UN information centres, services and offices, and lists selected UN websites.

This edition has been updated to reflect significant recent developments in the world and within the UN itself. Photographs illustrate how various UN system bodies have partnered with local institutions, governments, civil society—and local people—to help save and improve lives everywhere. Coverage has been streamlined to provide a more focused picture of today's dynamic and effective UN. Developments concerning new and continuing peacekeeping and peacebuilding missions are discussed, but situations in states or regions in which the UN has ended its security presence or mandate are no longer treated. Likewise, details concerning past UN programmes and conferences have been replaced by information on newer entities such as the high-level political forum on sustainable development, and on action taken such as the adoption of the Paris Agreement on climate change and the launch of the 2030 Agenda on Sustainable Development and its 17 sustainable development goals. This edition covers the work completed by the Trusteeship Council as a principal UN organ, however, as the Council's operations have been suspended, coverage has been condensed and consolidated in the chapter on peace and security.

Although officially produced by the UN Department of Public Information, this forty-second edition of *Basic Facts about the United Nations* incorporates material provided by UN system offices, programmes, agencies and institutions throughout the world. Their input has been essential in bringing *Basic Facts* to diplomats, researchers, students and the public at large, and they deserve thanks for their contributions to this book and for their efforts to strengthen the United Nations and improve the lives of the world's poorest and most vulnerable people.

All data presented in this book are current as at 31 January 2017 unless otherwise noted. Web addresses have been included for access to the latest information on the related topic. For other UN activities throughout the world, please visit:

- the official website of the United Nations (www.un.org);
- the UN News Centre (www.un.org/news);
- the *Yearbook of the United Nations* (unyearbook.un.org), the Organization's authoritative reference work, providing an in-depth and historical presentation of UN goals and activities; and
- the *UN Chronicle* magazine (unchronicle.un.org), providing a thematic perspective on issues of global concern.

UN Secretariat staff mark the occasion of the 70th anniversary of the United Nations by joining in a formation which reads "What R U Doing 4 Peace" around the circle in front of the Secretariat Building at Headquarters in New York (17 September 2015, UN Photo/Rick Bajornas).

The United Nations System

UN PRINCIPAL ORGANS

GENERAL ASSEMBLY

SECURITY COUNCIL

ECONOMIC AND SOCIAL COUNCIL

SECRETARIAT

INTERNATIONAL COURT OF JUSTICE

TRUSTEESHIP COUNCIL[6]

Subsidiary Organs

- Main Committees
- Disarmament Commission
- Human Rights Council
- International Law Commission
- Joint Inspection Unit (JIU)
- Standing committees and ad hoc bodies

Funds and Programmes[1]

UNDP United Nations Development Programme
- **UNCDF** United Nations Capital Development Fund
- **UNV** United Nations Volunteers

UNEP[8] United Nations Environment Programme

UNFPA United Nations Population Fund

UN-Habitat[8] United Nations Human Settlements Programme

UNICEF United Nations Children's Fund

WFP World Food Programme (UN/FAO)

Subsidiary Organs

- Counter-Terrorism Committee
- International Tribunal for the former Yugoslavia (ICTY)
- International Residual Mechanism for Criminal Tribunals
- Military Staff Committee

Functional Commissions

- Crime Prevention and Criminal Justice
- Narcotic Drugs
- Population and Development
- Science and Technology for Development
- Social Development
- Statistics
- Status of Women
- United Nations Forum on Forests

Regional Commissions[8]

ECA Economic Commission for Africa

ECE Economic Commission for Europe

ECLAC Economic Commission for Latin America and the Caribbean

ESCAP Economic and Social Commission for Asia and the Pacific

ESCWA Economic and Social Commission for Western Asia

Departments and Offices[9]

EOSG Executive Office of the Secretary-General

DESA Department of Economic and Social Affairs

DFS Department of Field Support

DGACM Department for General Assembly and Conference Management

DM Department of Management

DPA Department of Political Affairs

DPI Department of Public Information

DPKO Department of Peacekeeping Operations

DSS Department of Safety and Security

OCHA Office for the Coordination of Humanitarian Affairs

ODA Office for Disarmament Affairs

OHCHR Office of the United Nations High Commissioner for Human Rights

OIOS Office of Internal Oversight Services

OLA Office of Legal Affairs

OSAA Office of the Special Adviser on Africa

PBSO Peacebuilding Support Office

SRSG/CAAC Office of the Special Representative of the Secretary-General for Children and Armed Conflict

SRSG/SVC Office of the Special Representative of the Secretary-General on Sexual Violence in Conflict

SRSG/VAC Office of the Special Representative of the Secretary-General on Violence Against Children

UNISDR United Nations Office for Disaster Risk Reduction

UNODC[1] United Nations Office on Drugs and Crime

Research and Training

UNIDIR United Nations Institute for Disarmament Research
UNITAR United Nations Institute for Training and Research
UNSSC United Nations System Staff College
UNU United Nations University

Other Entities

ITC International Trade Centre (UN/WTO)
UNCTAD[1,8] United Nations Conference on Trade and Development
UNHCR[1] Office of the United Nations High Commissioner for Refugees
UNOPS[1] United Nations Office for Project Services
UNRWA[1] United Nations Relief and Works Agency for Palestine Refugees in the Near East
UN-Women[1] United Nations Entity for Gender Equality and the Empowerment of Women

Related Organizations

CTBTO Preparatory Commission Preparatory Commission for the Comprehensive Nuclear-Test-Ban Treaty Organization
IAEA[1,3] International Atomic Energy Agency
ICC International Criminal Court
IOM[1] International Organization for Migration
ISA International Seabed Authority
ITLOS International Tribunal for the Law of the Sea
OPCW[3] Organization for the Prohibition of Chemical Weapons
WTO[1,4] World Trade Organization

Peacebuilding Commission

HLPF High-level political forum on sustainable development

- Peacekeeping operations and political missions
- Sanctions committees (ad hoc)
- Standing committees and ad hoc bodies

Specialized Agencies[1,5]

FAO Food and Agriculture Organization of the United Nations
ICAO International Civil Aviation Organization
IFAD International Fund for Agricultural Development
ILO International Labour Organization
IMF International Monetary Fund
IMO International Maritime Organization
ITU International Telecommunication Union
UNESCO United Nations Educational, Scientific and Cultural Organization
UNIDO United Nations Industrial Development Organization
UNWTO World Tourism Organization
UPU Universal Postal Union
WHO World Health Organization
WIPO World Intellectual Property Organization
WMO World Meteorological Organization
WORLD BANK GROUP[7]
  - **IBRD** International Bank for Reconstruction and Development
  - **IDA** International Development Association
  - **IFC** International Finance Corporation

Other Bodies

- Committee for Development Policy
- Committee of Experts on Public Administration
- Committee on Non-Governmental Organizations
- Permanent Forum on Indigenous Issues

UNAIDS Joint United Nations Programme on HIV/AIDS
UNGEGN United Nations Group of Experts on Geographical Names

Research and Training

UNICRI United Nations Interregional Crime and Justice Research Institute
UNRISD United Nations Research Institute for Social Development

UNOG United Nations Office at Geneva
UN-OHRLLS Office of the High Representative for the Least Developed Countries, Landlocked Developing Countries and Small Island Developing States
UNON United Nations Office at Nairobi
UNOP[2] United Nations Office for Partnerships
UNOV United Nations Office at Vienna

Notes:
1 Members of the United Nations System Chief Executives Board for Coordination (CEB).
2 UN Office for Partnerships (UNOP) is the UN's focal point vis-a-vis the United Nations Foundation, Inc.
3 IAEA and OPCW report to the Security Council and the General Assembly (GA).
4 WTO has no reporting obligation to the GA, but contributes on an ad hoc basis to GA and Economic and Social Council (ECOSOC) work on, inter alia, finance and development issues.
5 Specialized agencies are autonomous organizations whose work is coordinated through ECOSOC (intergovernmental level) and CEB (inter-secretariat level).
6 The Trusteeship Council suspended operation on 1 November 1994, as on 1 October 1994 Palau, the last United Nations Trust Territory, became independent.
7 International Centre for Settlement of Investment Disputes (ICSID) and Multilateral Investment Guarantee Agency (MIGA) are not specialized agencies in accordance with Articles 57 and 63 of the Charter, but are part of the World Bank Group.
8 The secretariats of these organs are part of the UN Secretariat.
9 The Secretariat also includes the following offices: The Ethics Office, United Nations Ombudsman and Mediation Services, Office of Administration of Justice and the Office on Sport for Development and Peace

This Chart is a reflection of the functional organization of the United Nations System and for informational purposes only. It does not include all offices or entities of the United Nations System.

Published by the United Nations Department of Public Information   DPI/2470 rev.5 —17-00023—March 2017

Chapter I

UN CHARTER, STRUCTURE AND SYSTEM

MINUSTAH conducts a patrol in Port-au-Prince as Hurricane Matthew makes landfall in Haiti. In other affected areas, military and police contingents were providing assistance, especially in cleaning blocked roads (4 October 2016, UN Photo/Igor Rugwiza).

The struggle for peace is an enduring one. More than a century ago, in 1899, the first International Peace Conference was held in The Hague to elaborate multilateral instruments for settling crises peacefully, preventing wars and codifying rules of warfare. It adopted the *Convention for the Pacific Settlement of International Disputes* and established the Permanent Court of Arbitration, which began its work in 1902. Subsequently, in 1919, the League of Nations, conceived during the First World War, was established under the *Treaty of Versailles* "to promote international cooperation and to achieve peace and security". While the League of Nations ceased activities after failing to prevent the Second World War, the need for peaceful resolution of conflicts through international collaboration and dialogue continued to grow.

The term "United Nations" was coined by United States President Franklin D. Roosevelt during the Second World War. It first appeared in the *Declaration by United Nations* of 1 January 1942, which put forth a pledge by 26 nations to fight together against the Axis powers. Following deliberations held in Washington, D.C., in 1944 among representatives from China, the Soviet Union, the United Kingdom and the United States, delegates from 50 countries met in San Francisco in 1945 at the United Nations Conference on International Organization. There, with a firm commitment to end "the scourge of war", they drew up the *Charter of the United Nations*, signed on 26 June 1945.

Headquartered in New York, the United Nations officially came into existence on 24 October 1945 with the ratification of the *Charter* by China, France, the Soviet Union, the United Kingdom, the United States and a majority of other signatories. In commemoration of this historic pledge for world peace, **United Nations Day** is celebrated on 24 October each year. Despite the sharp divisions from which it arose in the Second World War and those of the ensuing cold war that marked many of its deliberations, the UN continues to grow in remaining true to this pledge—one all the more relevant in the face of conflicts becoming more complex, the emergence of new threats such as global terrorism and the need for a world forum for negotiations to address them.

THE CHARTER OF THE UNITED NATIONS

The *Charter of the United Nations* (www.un.org/en/charter-united-nations/) is the constitutive instrument of the UN, setting out the rights and obligations of member states, and establishing its principal organs and procedures. An international treaty, the *Charter* codifies basic tenets of international relations—from the sovereign equality of states to prohibition of the use of force in any manner inconsistent with the purposes of the United Nations.

The *Charter* consists of a Preamble and 111 articles grouped into 19 chapters. Of these, Chapter 1 sets forth the purposes and principles of the United Nations; Chapter 2 establishes the criteria for UN membership; Chapter 3 names the six principal UN organs; Chapters 4–15 define the functions and powers of these organs; Chapters 16–17 relate the United Nations to existing international law; and Chapters 18–19 define the amendment and ratification of the *Charter*.

The Preamble to the *Charter* expresses the shared ideals and common aims of all the peoples whose governments joined together to form the United Nations:

We the peoples of the United Nations determined

to save succeeding generations from the scourge of war, which twice in our lifetime has brought untold sorrow to mankind, and

to reaffirm faith in fundamental human rights, in the dignity and worth of the human person, in the equal rights of men and women and of nations large and small, and

to establish conditions under which justice and respect for the obligations arising from treaties and other sources of international law can be maintained, and

to promote social progress and better standards of life in larger freedom,

and for these ends

to practice tolerance and live together in peace with one another as good neighbours, and

to unite our strength to maintain international peace and security, and

to ensure, by the acceptance of principles and the institution of methods, that armed force shall not be used, save in the common interest, and

to employ international machinery for the promotion of the economic and social advancement of all peoples,

have resolved to combine our efforts to accomplish these aims

Accordingly, our respective Governments, through representatives assembled in the city of San Francisco, who have exhibited their full powers found to be in good and due form, have agreed to the present *Charter of the United Nations* and do hereby establish an international organization to be known as the United Nations.

Purposes and principles

As set forth in the *Charter*, the purposes of the United Nations are to:

- maintain international peace and security;
- develop friendly relations among nations based on respect for the principle of equal rights and self-determination of peoples;
- cooperate in solving international economic, social, cultural and humanitarian problems and in promoting respect for human rights and fundamental freedoms;
- be a centre for harmonizing the actions of nations in attaining these common ends.

In turn, the United Nations acts in accordance with the following principles:

- it is based on the sovereign equality of all its members;
- all members are to fulfil in good faith their *Charter* obligations;

- they are to settle their international disputes by peaceful means and without endangering international peace and security and justice;
- they are to refrain from the threat or use of force against any other state;
- they are to give the United Nations every assistance in any action it takes in accordance with the *Charter*;
- nothing in the *Charter* is to authorize the United Nations to intervene in matters which are essentially within the domestic jurisdiction of any state.

Amendments to the Charter

The *Charter* may be amended by a vote of two thirds of the members of the General Assembly and ratification by two thirds of the members of the United Nations, including the five permanent members of the Security Council. So far, four Articles of the *Charter* have been amended, one of them twice:

- In 1965, the membership of the Security Council was increased from 11 to 15 states (Article 23) and the number of affirmative votes needed for a decision was increased from seven to nine, including the concurring vote of the five permanent members for all matters of substance rather than procedure (Article 27).
- In 1965, the membership of the Economic and Social Council was increased from 18 to 27 states, and again in 1973 from 27 to 54 states (Article 61).
- In 1968, the number of votes required in the Security Council to convene a General Conference to review the *Charter* was increased from seven to nine (Article 109).

Membership and official languages

Membership in the United Nations is open to all peace-loving nations that accept the obligations of the *Charter* and are willing and able to carry out these obligations. The General Assembly admits new member states on the recommendation of the Security Council. The *Charter* provides for the suspension or expulsion of a member for violation of the principles of the *Charter*, but no such action has ever been taken. While the *Charter* was equally authentic in Chinese, English, French, Russian and Spanish, the languages of the General Assembly, the Security Council and the Economic and Social Council have expanded over time to six languages (Arabic, Chinese, English, French, Russian and Spanish). Of these, French and English are the working languages of the Secretariat and the official languages of the International Court of Justice.

UN STRUCTURE

The *Charter* establishes six principal organs of the United Nations: the General Assembly, the Security Council, the Economic and Social Council, the Trusteeship Council, the International Court of Justice and the Secretariat. The United Nations family, however, is much larger, encompassing 15 specialized agencies, numerous funds and programmes, as well as other entities.

General Assembly

The **General Assembly** (www.un.org/ga) is the chief deliberative, policymaking and representative organ of the United Nations. It is composed of representatives of all member states, each of which has one vote. Decisions on important questions (such as those on peace and security, admission of new members and budgetary matters) require a two-thirds majority. Decisions on other questions take place by simple majority.

Functions and powers

Under the *Charter*, the General Assembly may:

- discuss any question or matter within the scope of the *Charter* or affecting the powers and functions of any UN organ, except where a dispute or situation is being discussed by the Security Council, and make recommendations on it;
- discuss and, with the same exception, make recommendations on any question relating to international peace and security;
- consider and make recommendations on the general principles of cooperation in the maintenance of international peace and security, including those governing disarmament and arms regulation; and
- make recommendations for the peaceful adjustment of any situation, regardless of origin, which might impair friendly relations among nations.

The *Charter* also assigns the General Assembly to:

- initiate studies and make recommendations to promote international political cooperation, the progressive development and codification of international law, the realization of human rights and fundamental freedoms for all, and international cooperation in the economic, social, cultural, educational and health fields;
- receive and consider annual and special Security Council reports, and reports from other UN organs;
- consider and approve the UN budget and apportion the contributions among members; and
- elect the non-permanent members of the Security Council, the members of the Economic and Social Council and additional members of the Trusteeship Council (when necessary); elect jointly with the Security Council the judges of the International Court of Justice; and, on the recommendation of the Security Council, appoint the Secretary-General.

Under the "Uniting for peace" resolution, adopted by the General Assembly in November 1950, the Assembly may take action if the Security Council, because of lack of unanimity of its permanent members, fails to act where there appears to be a threat to international peace, a breach of the peace or an act of aggression. The Assembly shall consider the matter immediately with a view to making recommendations to members for collective measures, including, in the case of a breach of the peace or an act of aggression, the use of armed forces when necessary to maintain or restore international peace and security.

Sessions

The General Assembly's regular session begins each year on Tuesday in the third week of September, counting from the first week that contains at least one working day. The election of the President of the Assembly, as well as its 21 Vice-Presidents and the Chairpersons of its six Main Committees, takes place at least three months before the start of the regular session. To ensure equitable geographical representation, the presidency of the Assembly rotates each year among five groups of states: African, Asian, Eastern European, Latin American and Caribbean, and Western European and other states. In addition, the Assembly may meet in special sessions at the request of the Security Council; a majority of member states; or one member if the majority of members concur. The twenty-ninth and thirtieth special sessions of the Assembly (UNGASS) were held respectively, on population and development (2014) and on the world drug problem (2016). Emergency special sessions may be called within 24 hours of a request by the Security Council on the vote of any nine Council members; a majority of UN members; or one member if the majority of members concur. At the beginning of each regular session, the Assembly holds a general debate—often addressed by heads of state and government—in which member states express their views on the most pressing international issues.

Year-round, the work of the United Nations derives largely from the mandates given by the General Assembly—that is to say, the will of the majority of the members as expressed in the resolutions and decisions adopted by the Assembly. That work is carried out by committees and other bodies established by the Assembly to study and report on specific matters such as disarmament, peacekeeping, development and human rights; through international conferences called for by the Assembly; and by the Secretariat of the United Nations—the Secretary-General and his staff of international civil servants.

Most questions are discussed in one of the six **Main Committees** of the Assembly:

- First Committee (Disarmament and International Security);
- Second Committee (Economic and Financial);
- Third Committee (Social, Humanitarian and Cultural);
- Fourth Committee (Special Political and Decolonization);
- Fifth Committee (Administrative and Budgetary);
- Sixth Committee (Legal).

While some issues are considered directly in plenary meetings, most are allocated to one of these committees. Resolutions and decisions, including those recommended by the committees, may be adopted—with or without a vote—in plenary meetings, usually before the recess of the regular session in December.

The Assembly normally adopts its resolutions and decisions by a majority of members present and voting. Important questions—including recommendations on international peace and security, the election of members to some principal organs, and budgetary matters—must be decided by a two-thirds majority. Voting may be conducted as a recorded vote, a show-of-hands or a roll-call vote. While the decisions of the Assembly have no legally binding force for governments, they carry the weight of world opinion and the moral authority of the world community.

Security Council

The **Security Council** (www.un.org/en/sc) of the United Nations has primary responsibility, under the *Charter*, for the maintenance of international peace and security. It has 15 members: 5 permanent (China, France, the Russian Federation, the United Kingdom and the United States) and 10 elected by the General Assembly for two-year terms. These currently consist of Egypt, Japan, Senegal, Ukraine and Uruguay (with terms ending in 2017); and Bolivia, Ethiopia, Italy, Kazakhstan and Sweden (with terms ending in 2018). Each member has one vote. Decisions on procedural matters are made by an affirmative vote of at least 9 of the 15 members. Decisions on substantive matters require nine votes and the absence of a negative vote (veto) by any of the five permanent members. All five permanent members have exercised the right of veto at one time or another. If a permanent member does not fully agree with a proposed resolution but does not wish to cast a veto, it may choose to abstain, thus allowing the resolution to be adopted if it obtains the required number of nine favourable votes. The presidency of the Council is held by each of the members in turn for one month, following alphabetical order.

The composition of the Council as well as its procedures are the subject of a working group of the General Assembly considering Security Council reform, especially the addition of permanent seats or enlargement of non-permanent membership. At issue is the notion of the equitable representation of member states in addressing matters of global consequence. Over 60 UN member states have never sat on the Council. All members of the United Nations, however, agree to accept and carry out the decisions of the Security Council. While other organs of the United Nations make recommendations to member states, only the Security Council has the power to make decisions that member states are then obligated to implement under the *Charter*.

Functions and powers

Under the *Charter*, the functions and powers of the Security Council include:

- maintain international peace and security in accordance with the principles and purposes of the United Nations;
- investigate any dispute or situation that might lead to international friction, and recommend methods of adjustment or terms of settlement;
- call on the parties to a dispute to settle it by peaceful means;
- formulate plans for establishing a system to regulate armaments;
- determine the existence of a threat to the peace or act of aggression and recommend what action should be taken;
- call on the parties concerned to comply with such provisional measures as it deems necessary or desirable to prevent an aggravation of the situation;
- call on members of the United Nations to apply sanctions and other measures not involving the use of armed force to give effect to the Council's decisions;
- resort to or authorize the use of force to maintain or restore international peace and security;
- encourage the peaceful settlement of local disputes through regional arrangements and use such regional arrangements for enforcement under its authority;
- recommend to the General Assembly the appointment of the Secretary-General and, together with the Assembly, elect the judges of the International Court of Justice (ICJ);
- request the ICJ to give an advisory opinion on any legal question; and
- recommend to the General Assembly the admission of new members to the United Nations.

The Security Council is organized in such a way that it can function continuously. A representative of each of its members must be present at all times at UN Headquarters. The Council may meet elsewhere: in 1972 it held a session in Addis Ababa, Ethiopia; in 1973 it met in Panama City, Panama; in 1990 it met in Geneva; and in 2004 in Nairobi.

When a complaint concerning a threat to peace is brought before it, the Council's first action is usually to recommend that the parties try to reach agreement by peaceful means. The Council may set forth principles for such an agreement. In some cases, the Council itself undertakes investigation and mediation. It may dispatch a mission, appoint special envoys or request the Secretary-General to use his good offices to achieve a pacific settlement of the dispute.

When a dispute leads to hostilities, the Council's primary concern is to bring them to an end as soon as possible. It may issue ceasefire directives that can help prevent an escalation of the conflict. The Council may also dispatch military observers or a peacekeeping force to help reduce tensions, separate opposing forces and establish a calm in which peaceful settlements may be sought. Beyond this, the Council may opt for enforcement measures, including economic sanctions, arms embargoes, financial penalties and restrictions, and travel bans; severance of diplomatic relations; blockade; or even collective military action. A chief concern is to focus action on those responsible for the policies or practices condemned by the international community, while minimizing the impact of the measures taken on other parts of the population and economy.

The Council established the Counter-Terrorism Committee as a subsidiary organ following the terrorist attacks on the United States on 11 September 2001. The Peacebuilding Commission, established by the Council in 2005, supports peace efforts in countries emerging from conflict.

On military action, the Security Council may rely on the Military Staff Committee (www.un.org/sc/suborg/en/subsidiary/msc), a subsidiary organ established by the *Charter*, to advise on military requirements for the maintenance of international peace and security, the employment and command of forces placed at its disposal, the regulation of armaments, and possible disarmament.

Tribunals and courts

In the 1990s, the Security Council established, as subsidiary organs, two ad hoc, international criminal tribunals to prosecute serious alleged crimes committed in the territories of the former Yugoslavia and in Rwanda and its neighbouring states. In 2010, the Council established, also as a subsidiary organ, a judicial institution to continue the jurisdiction, rights and essential functions of these two ad hoc Tribunals, following the completion of their mandates. Three "hybrid" courts have been established by Cambodia, Lebanon and Sierra Leone, respectively, with substantial help from the United Nations. These are not permanent courts and will cease to exist once their business draws to a close; the court in Sierra Leone completed its mandate in December 2013.

International Criminal Tribunal for Rwanda (ICTR)

Created by the Security Council in 1994, the International Criminal Tribunal for Rwanda (unictr.unmict.org) was mandated to prosecute persons responsible for genocide and other serious violations of international humanitarian law committed in Rwanda during 1994, as well as Rwandan citizens responsible for such violations committed in the territory of neighbouring states. ICTR indicted 93 individuals for genocide and other serious violations of humanitarian law committed in 1994, concluded proceedings for 85 of the accused, and transferred 8 cases to other jurisdictions. ICTR completed its mandate in December 2015 and its residual functions have been taken over by the Mechanism for International Criminal Tribunals (MICT).

International Tribunal for the former Yugoslavia (ICTY)

Established by the Security Council in 1993, the International Tribunal for the former Yugoslavia (www.icty.org) is mandated to prosecute persons responsible for genocide, war crimes and crimes against humanity committed in the former Yugoslavia since 1991. Its organizational components are its Chambers, Registry and the Office of the Prosecutor. As at 13 October 2016, ICTY had seven permanent judges, one ad hoc judge and a staff of 393, representing 62 nationalities. Its 2016–2017 regular budget was $113.6 million. The Tribunal has indicted 161 persons accused of crimes committed from 1991 to 2001 against members of various ethnic groups in Bosnia and Herzegovina, Croatia, Kosovo, Serbia and The former Yugoslav Republic of Macedonia. Those indicted include heads of state, prime ministers, army chiefs-of-staff, interior ministers and many other high- and mid-level political, military and police leaders from various parties to the Yugoslav conflicts. By holding individuals accountable regardless of their position, the ICTY has substantially contributed to dismantling impunity for war crimes.

President: Judge Carmel Agius (Malta)
Prosecutor: Serge Brammertz (Belgium)
Registrar: John Hocking (Australia)
Headquarters: Churchillplein 1, 2517 JW The Hague, The Netherlands
Tel.: +31 70 512 5000 | **Fax:** +31 70 512 5355
Twitter: @ ICTYnews | **Facebook:** www.facebook.com/ICTYMKSJ

Mechanism for International Criminal Tribunals (MICT)

Established by the Security Council in 2010, the Mechanism for International Criminal Tribunals (www.unmict.org) is mandated to continue the jurisdiction, rights, obligations and essential functions of ICTR and ICTY, following the completion of their respective mandates. MICT is responsible for locating, arresting and ensuring the trial of the eight ICTR accused still at large; handling appeals proceedings originating from ICTR, ICTY and MICT cases; conducting retrials of ICTR, ICTY and MICT cases; protecting ICTR, ICTY and MICT victims and witnesses; supervising the enforcement of ICTR, ICTY and MICT sentences; providing assistance to national jurisdictions; and preserving and managing ICTR, ICTY and MICT archives. MICT consists of three organs—the Chambers, the Office of the Prosecutor and the Registry—and has two branches: one in Arusha, Tanzania, which commenced operations on 1 July 2012, and one in The Hague, the Netherlands, which commenced operations on 1 July 2013. The President, the Prosecutor, and the Registrar are common to both branches. MICT has a roster of 25 independent judges who, apart from the President, serve on an as-needed basis and are only present at the seats of the branches as required by the President. In so far as possible, the judges carry out their functions remotely. As at June 2016, MICT had 331 staff members representing 63 nationalities. Its budget in 2016–2017 amounts to $137.4 million gross. MICT is currently seized of the appeals in the *Karadžić* and *Šešelj* cases and the retrial in the *Stanišić and Simatović* case, among other matters.

President: Judge Theodor Meron (United States)
Prosecutor: Serge Brammertz (Belgium)
Registrar: Olufemi Elias (Nigeria)
Headquarters: P.O. Box 6016, Arusha, Tanzania
Tel.: +31 70 512 5000 | **Fax:** +31 70 512 5355
Twitter: @un_mict | **Facebook:** www.facebook.com/unitednations.mict

Residual Special Court for Sierra Leone (RSCSL)

The Residual Special Court for Sierra Leone (www.rscsl.org) was set up jointly by the Government of Sierra Leone and the United Nations in August 2010, to oversee the continuing legal obligations of the **Special Court for Sierra Leone**—the world's first hybrid international criminal tribunal. In December 2013, the Special Court for Sierra Leone became the first international criminal tribunal since Nuremberg to complete its judicial mandate. The Residual Special Court commenced its operations on 1 January 2014 and is mandated to protect and support witnesses and victims; supervise the enforcement of sentences; preserve and manage archives; provide legal aid; conduct contempt of court and review proceedings; and assist national authorities pursuant to requests for information. The Residual Special Court is funded on the basis of voluntary contributions from member states. During 2016, however, the Residual Special Court received a UN subvention due to inadequate voluntary contributions received during that year. The Residual

Special Court has contributed to the development of international criminal law in a variety of ways, including through the establishment of conditional early release of persons convicted of war crimes and crimes against humanity. Moinina Fofana, former leader of the Civil Defence Forces, was the first convicted person granted conditional early release in August 2014.

President: Justice Renate Winter (Austria)
Prosecutor: Brenda J. Hollis (United States)
Registrar: Binta Mansaray (Sierra Leone)
Principal Defender: Ibrahim Yillah (Sierra Leone)
Interim Seat: Churchillplien 1, 2517 JW, The Hague, The Netherlands
Tel.: +31 70 512 8481 | **E-mail:** info@rscsl.org | **Twitter:** @SpecialCourt

Extraordinary Chambers in the Courts of Cambodia (ECCC)

The Extraordinary Chambers in the Courts of Cambodia for the Prosecution of Crimes Committed during the Period of Democratic Kampuchea (www.eccc.gov.kh), is a national court established in 2006 pursuant to an agreement between Cambodia and the United Nations to bring to trial senior leaders of Democratic Kampuchea (Khmer Rouge regime) and those who were responsible for the crimes and serious violations committed during the period from 17 April 1975 to 6 January 1979. UN support is organized through the United Nations Assistance to Khmer Rouge Trials (UNAKRT) and constitutes the international side of ECCC. The assistance is provided by international staff recruited by the UN to work with their Cambodian counterparts. The Pre-Trial and Trial Chambers are each composed of five judges, three of whom are Cambodian, including the President. The Supreme Court Chamber has seven judges, four of whom are Cambodian, including the President. International judges are appointed by the Supreme Council of Magistracy of Cambodia upon nomination by the UN Secretary-General.

Pre-Trial Chamber President: Judge Prak Kimsan (Cambodia)
Trial Chamber President: Judge Nil Nonn (Cambodia)
Supreme Court Chamber President: Judge Kong Srim (Cambodia)
Headquarters: National Road 4, Chaom Chau Commune, Porsenchey District, P.O. Box 71, Phnom Penh, Cambodia
Tel.: +855 0 23 861 500 | **Fax:** +855 0 23 861 555
E-mail: info@eccc.gov.kh | **Twitter:** @KRTribunal

Special Tribunal for Lebanon (STL)

The Special Tribunal for Lebanon (www.stl-tsl.org) was established by the Security Council in 2007, as requested by the Lebanese government in 2005, to prosecute those responsible for the 14 February 2005 attack in Beirut that killed the former Lebanese Prime Minister Rafik Hariri and 21 others. The Tribunal, which opened on 1 March 2009, also has jurisdiction over other attacks in Lebanon between 1 October 2004 and 12 December 2005 if they are determined to be connected to the 14 February 2005 attack because of their gravity or nature. In 2015, the Tribunal's mandate was extended through 28 February 2018. Its main case, *Prosecutor v. Ayyash et al.*, started on 16 January 2014 and concerns five individuals allegedly involved in the February 2005 attack. In July 2016, one of the accused was determined to be deceased and the indictment was amended. Two contempt trials have been held in relation to the publication of alleged confidential witness information. The Prosecution continues its investigation into three connected cases to determine if additional indictments can be filed and its analysis of other terrorist attacks that may fall under the Tribunal's mandate.

President: Ivana Hrdličková (Czech Republic)
Prosecutor: Norman Farrell (Canada)
Registrar: Daryl Mundis (United States of America)
Headquarters: Dokter van der Stamstraat 1, 2265 BC, Leidschendam, The Netherlands
Tel.: +31 0 70 800 3400 | **E-mail:** stl-pressoffice@un.org
Twitter: @STLebanon | **Facebook:** www.facebook.com/STLebanon

Economic and Social Council (ECOSOC)

The *Charter of the United Nations* establishes the **Economic and Social Council** (www.un.org/ecosoc) as the principal organ to coordinate the economic, social and related work of the United Nations and the specialized agencies and other bodies. Reforms over the last decade have strengthened the Council's leading role in identifying emerging challenges, promoting innovation, and achieving a balanced integration of the three dimensions of sustainable development—economic, social and environmental.

Building on its coordination role within the UN system, the Council is a gateway for UN partnership and participation by the rest of the world. It offers a unique global meeting point for productive dialogues among policymakers, parliamentarians, academics, foundations, businesses, youth and non-governmental organizations. Each year, the Council structures its work around an annual theme of global importance to sustainable development. This ensures focused attention, among the Council's array of partners, and throughout the UN development system.

The 54 members of the Council serve for three-year terms. Seats on the Council are allocated based on geographical representation, with 14 allocated to African states, 11 to Asian states, 6 to Eastern European states, 10 to Latin American and Caribbean states, and 13 to Western European and other states. Voting in the Council is by simple majority, with each member having one vote.

Functions and powers

ECOSOC is tasked with:

- serving as the central forum for discussing international economic, social and environmental issues, and for formulating policy recommendations addressed to member states and the United Nations system;
- helping achieve a balanced integration of the three dimensions of sustainable development;
- making or initiating studies and reports and making recommendations on international economic, social, cultural, educational, health and related matters;
- assisting in preparing and organizing major international conferences in the economic, social and related fields, and promoting a coordinated follow-up to these conferences;
- reviewing trends and progress in international development cooperation to bring greater coherence in policies and activities; and
- coordinating the activities of the specialized agencies through consultations with and recommendations to them, as well as to the General Assembly.

Through its discussion of international economic and social issues and its policy recommendations, ECOSOC plays a key role in fostering international cooperation for development and in setting priorities for action throughout the UN system.

Sessions and subsidiary bodies

The Council normally holds several short sessions and many preparatory meetings, round tables and panel discussions throughout the year with members of civil society dealing with the organization of its work. It also holds a high-level segment in July attended by cabinet ministers and other officials, to discuss major economic, social and environmental issues. The segment includes the annual ministerial meeting of the high-level political forum and the biennial high-level Development Cooperation Forum. The Council's substantive sessions also include the humanitarian affairs, integration, and operational activities for development segments, as well as coordination and management meetings. The Council's annual integration segment makes full use of its multidisciplinary network of specialized bodies. The Council also cooperates with, and to a certain extent coordinates the work of, United Nations programmes (such as UNDP, UNEP, UNFPA, UN-Habitat and UNICEF) and the specialized agencies (such as FAO, ILO, WHO and UNESCO), all of which report to the Council and make recommendations for its substantive sessions.

The year-round work of the Council is carried out in its subsidiary and related bodies. These include:

- eight functional commissions—deliberative bodies whose role is to consider and make recommendations on issues in their areas of responsibility and expertise: the Statistical Commission, Commission on Population and Development, Commission for Social Development, Commission on the Status of Women, Commission on Narcotic Drugs, Commission on Crime Prevention and Criminal Justice, Commission on Science and Technology for Development, and the United Nations Forum on Forests;
- five regional commissions: Economic Commission for Africa (Addis Ababa, Ethiopia), Economic and Social Commission for Asia and the Pacific (Bangkok, Thailand), Economic Commission for Europe (Geneva), Economic Commission for Latin America and the Caribbean (Santiago, Chile), and Economic and Social Commission for Western Asia (Beirut, Lebanon);
- three standing committees: Committee for Programme and Coordination, Committee on Non-Governmental Organizations, Committee on Negotiations with Intergovernmental Agencies;
- expert bodies on such topics as development cooperation, geographical names, geospatial information management, public administration, international cooperation in tax matters, the transport of dangerous goods and economic, social and cultural rights; and
- other bodies, including the Permanent Forum on Indigenous Issues, the International Narcotics Control Board, and the high-level political forum on sustainable development.

Regional commissions

The regional commissions of the United Nations report to ECOSOC and are funded under the regular UN budget; their secretariats are under the authority of the Secretary-General. Their mandate is to promote the economic development of each region, and strengthen the economic relations of the countries in that region, both among themselves and with other countries of the world.

Economic Commission for Africa (ECA)

Established in 1958, the Economic Commission for Africa (www.uneca.org) promotes the economic and social development of its 54 member states, fosters intraregional integration, and promotes international cooperation for Africa's development. ECA serves a dual role as a regional arm of the United Nations and as a key component of the African institutional landscape. To enhance its impact, the Commission places a special focus on promoting policy consensus; providing capacity development; providing advisory services in key thematic fields; and collecting up-to-date and original regional statistics in order to ground its policy research and advocacy on clear objective evidence.

Executive Secretary: Vera Songwe (Cameroon)
Address: P.O. Box 3001, Addis Ababa, Ethiopia
Tel.: +251 11 551 7200 | **Fax:** +251 11 5510365 | **E-mail:** ecainfo@uneca.org
Twitter: @eca_official | **Facebook:** www.facebook.com/economiccommissionforafrica

Economic Commission for Europe (ECE)

Created in 1947, the Economic Commission for Europe (www.unece.org) is the forum at which the countries of North America, Europe (including Israel) and Central Asia forge the tools of their economic cooperation. ECE has 56 member countries. Priority areas include environment, statistics, sustainable energy, trade, economic cooperation and integration, housing and land management, population, forestry and timber, and transport. It pursues its goals primarily through policy analysis, as well as conventions, regulations and standards. Such instruments help facilitate trade in the region and with the rest of the world. All help countries achieve the sustainable development goals. ECE contributes to their implementation by providing technical assistance, in particular to countries with economies in transition.

Executive Secretary: Olga Algayerova (Slovakia)
Address: Palais des Nations, CH-1211 Geneva 10, Switzerland
Tel.: +41 22 917 4444 | **Fax:** +41 22 917 0505 | **E-mail:** info.ece@unece.org
Twitter: @unece | **Facebook:** www.facebook.com/unecepage

Economic Commission for Latin America and the Caribbean (ECLAC)

The Economic Commission for Latin America and the Caribbean (www.cepal.org) coordinates policies for promoting sustainable economic and social development in the region. Established in 1948 as the Economic Commission for Latin America (ECLA), the scope of the Commission's work was later broadened to include the countries of the Caribbean. The 33 countries of Latin America and the Caribbean are members of ECLAC, together with 12 North American, Asian and European nations that have historical, economic and cultural ties with the region. Thirteen non-independent Caribbean territories are associate members of the Commission. Its work areas include economic development; international trade and integration; gender affairs; population and development; social development; natural resources and infrastructure; sustainable development and human settlements; statistics; and production, productivity and management, including agriculture and rural development, foreign direct investment, and innovation science and technology. ECLAC maintains subregional headquarters in Mexico City and Port of Spain, Trinidad and Tobago.

Executive Secretary: Alicia Bárcena Ibarra (Mexico)
Address: Avenida Dag Hammarskjöld 3477, Casilla 179-D, Santiago de Chile
Tel.: +56 2 2471 2000 | **Fax:** +56 2 208 0252
Twitter: @eclac_un | **Facebook:** www.facebook.com/eclac

Economic and Social Commission for Asia and the Pacific (ESCAP)

Created in 1947, the Economic and Social Commission for Asia and the Pacific (www.unescap.org) has the mandate to address the economic and social issues of the region. ESCAP is the only multi-sectorial intergovernmental forum for all the countries of Asia and the Pacific. Its 53 member states and 9 associate member states represent some 60 per cent of the world's population. ESCAP assists governments in capacity building for social and economic development. This assistance takes the form of advisory services to governments, training, and information-sharing through publications and intercountry networks. The Commission supports its member states in achieving the 2030 Agenda for Sustainable Development in order to improve socioeconomic conditions and help build the foundations of modern society in the region. Four subregional offices and six research and training institutions—for agricultural development, sustainable agricultural machinery, statistics, technology transfer, information technology for development, and disaster information management—operate under its auspices. Priority areas are financing for development, poverty reduction, sustainable development, disaster risk reduction and emerging social issues.

Executive Secretary: Shamshad Akhtar (Pakistan)
Address: United Nations Building, Rajadamnern Nok Avenue, Bangkok 10200, Thailand
Tel.: +66 2 288 1234 | **Fax:** +66 2 288 1000 | **E-mail:** escap-registry@un.org
Twitter: @unescap | **Facebook:** www.facebook.com/unescap

Economic and Social Commission for Western Asia (ESCWA)

Established in 1973, the Economic and Social Commission for Western Asia (www. escwa.un.org) facilitates concerted action for the economic and social development of the countries of the region by promoting economic cooperation and integration. Comprising 18 member states, ESCWA serves as the main general economic and social development forum for Western Asia in the UN system. Its focal areas are sustainable development and productivity; social development; economic development and globalization; information and communication technology; statistics; women's empowerment; and conflict-related issues.

Executive Secretary: Mohamed Ali Alhakim (Iraq)
Address: P.O. Box 11-8575, Riad el-Solh Square, Beirut, Lebanon
Tel.: +961 1 978800 or (via New York) +1 212 963 9731 | **Fax:** +961 1 98 1510
Twitter: @escwaciu | **Facebook:** www.facebook.com/unescwa

Relations with non-governmental organizations

Non-governmental organizations (NGOs) are regarded by the United Nations as important partners and valuable links to civil society. Consulted regularly on matters of mutual concern in policy and programme, NGOs in growing numbers around the world collaborate daily with the UN community to help achieve its objectives. Indeed, under the *Charter of the United Nations*, the Economic and Social Council may consult not only with member states, but also with NGOs concerned with matters within its competence. As at September 2016, some 4,665 NGOs had consultative status with the Council. The Council recognizes that these organizations should have the opportunity to express their views, and that they possess special experience or technical knowledge valuable for its work.

The Council classifies NGOs into three categories: *general* organizations are those concerned with most of the Council's activities; *special* organizations are those offering competence in particular areas corresponding to the concerns of the Council; and *roster* organizations are those that can contribute to the Council when consulted on an ad hoc basis. NGOs with consultative status may send observers to meetings of the Council and its subsidiary bodies and may submit written statements relevant to its work.

International Court of Justice

The **International Court of Justice** (www.icj-cij.org) is the principal judicial organ of the United Nations. Located at The Hague, the Netherlands, it is the only one of the six principal organs not located in New York. It began work in 1946, when it replaced the Permanent Court of International Justice. Also known as the "World Court", ICJ is the only court of a universal character with general jurisdiction. The Statute of the Court is an integral part of the *Charter of the United Nations*.

President: Judge Ronny Abraham (France)
Registrar: Philippe Couvreur (Belgium)
Headquarters: Peace Palace, Carnegieplein 2, 2517 KJ The Hague, The Netherlands
Tel.: +31 70 302 23 23 | **Twitter:** @CIJ_ICJ

Mission

The Court has a twofold role: first, to settle, in accordance with international law, legal disputes submitted to it by states (ICJ judgments have binding force and are without appeal for the parties concerned); and, second, to give advisory opinions on legal questions referred to it by duly authorized United Nations organs and agencies of the UN system. Contentious cases have represented 80 per cent of the work of ICJ since its creation, and it has delivered over a hundred judgments on disputes concerning, for example, international boundaries and territorial sovereignty, violations of international humanitarian law, and diplomatic relations. The Court has also rendered nearly 30 advisory opinions.

Jurisdiction

The Court is open to all states that are parties to its Statute, which includes all members of the United Nations. Only states may be parties in contentious cases before the Court and submit disputes to it. The Court's jurisdiction covers all questions referred to it by states and all matters provided for in the *Charter* or in international treaties and conventions. States may bind themselves in advance to accept the jurisdiction of the Court, either by signing a treaty or convention that provides for referral to the Court or by making a declaration to that effect. Such declarations accepting compulsory jurisdiction often contain reservations excluding certain classes of disputes. The Court decides in accordance with international treaties and conventions in force, international custom, the general principles of law and, as subsidiary means, judicial decisions and the teachings of the most highly qualified international law experts.

Judges

The Court is composed of 15 judges elected for a nine-year term by the General Assembly and the Security Council, voting independently. Five posts are renewed every three years and judges can be re-elected for further terms of nine years. The members of the Court must each be from a different country. They do not represent their countries: they are independent magistrates. The composition of the Court has also to reflect the main forms of civilization and the principal legal systems of the world. For a number of years, the composition of the Court has maintained the following geographical balance, corresponding to the current membership of the Security Council: five seats on the bench are occupied by judges from Western Europe and other western countries; three judges are from Africa; three from Asia; two from Eastern Europe and two from Latin America. Although no country is entitled to a seat, there has always been one judge from each of the five permanent members of the Security Council. If, in a particular case, the Court does not have a judge of the nationality of each of the states parties to the case, those states can each appoint what is called an ad hoc judge. Such judges have the same rights and duties as elected judges.

Budget

The annual budget of the ICJ is adopted by the General Assembly. For the biennium 2016–2017, it amounts to some $22 million annually.

Trusteeship Council

The **Trusteeship Council** (www.un.org/en/decolonization/trusteeship) was originally established by the *Charter* to provide international supervision for 11 Trust Territories placed under the administration of seven member states, and to ensure that adequate steps were taken to prepare the Territories for self-government or independence. It carried out this work for forty-nine years. By a 1994 resolution, the Council amended its rules of procedure to drop the obligation to meet annually and agreed to meet as occasion required—by its decision or the decision of its President, or at the request of a majority of its members or the General Assembly or the Security Council. Subsequently, on 1 November 1994, the Trusteeship Council suspended operation following the independence of Palau, the last remaining UN Trust Territory, on 1 October of that year.

Secretariat

The UN Secretariat (www.un.org/en/sections/about-un/secretariat/index.html)—consisting of staff representing all nationalities working in duty stations around the world—carries out the diverse day-to-day work of the Organization. Calling upon some 41,000 staff members worldwide, the Secretariat services the other principal organs of the United Nations and administers the programmes and policies established by them. Organized along departmental lines, each department or office of the Secretariat has a distinct area of action and responsibility. At its head is the Secretary-General, who is appointed by the General Assembly on the recommendation of the Security Council.

The United Nations is headquartered in New York, and maintains three regional headquarter offices—in Geneva, Vienna and Nairobi. Each centre serves as a representative office of the Secretary-General and provides administrative, common or other support services to UN entities located at the office. The United Nations Office at Geneva (UNOG) (www.unog.ch), the second largest duty station outside of New York, is a centre for conference diplomacy and a forum for disarmament and human rights. The United Nations Office at Vienna (UNOV) (www.unov.org) manages the programme on the peaceful uses of outer space and is the headquarters for the office on drugs and crime. The United Nations Office at Nairobi (UNON) (www.unon.org) facilitates cooperation between the UN and regional organizations and is the headquarters for the environment and the human settlements programmes.

The duties carried out by the Secretariat are wide-ranging. These extend from administering peacekeeping operations, mediating international disputes and organizing humanitarian relief programmes to surveying economic and social trends, preparing studies on human rights and sustainable development, and laying the groundwork for international agreements. Secretariat staff also inform the world—the media, governments, NGOs, research and academic networks and the general public—about the work of the United Nations. They organize international conferences on issues of global significance; interpret speeches and translate documents into the Organization's official languages; and establish clearing houses of information.

As international civil servants, staff members and the Secretary-General answer to the United Nations alone for their activities, not to any member state or other organization, even as they serve the community of nations. They pledge not to seek or receive instructions from any government or outside authority. In turn, under the *Charter*, each member state undertakes to respect the exclusively international character of the responsibilities of the Secretary-General and staff members, and to refrain from seeking to influence them improperly.

Secretary-General

The Executive Office of the Secretary-General, comprising the Secretary-General and his senior advisers, establishes general policies and provides overall guidance to the Organization. Equal parts diplomat, advocate, civil servant and manager, the Secretary-General (www.un.org/sg) is a symbol of UN ideals and a spokesperson for the interests of the world's peoples. The ninth Secretary-General, Mr. António Guterres (Portugal), took office on 1 January 2017.

Under the *Charter of the United Nations*, the Secretary-General is appointed for a five-year renewable term by the General Assembly upon the recommendation of the Security Council. Mr. Guterres' predecessors were Ban Ki-moon (Republic of Korea), 2007–2016; Kofi A. Annan (Ghana), 1997–2006; Boutros Boutros-Ghali (Egypt), 1992–1996; Javier Pérez de Cuéllar (Peru), 1982–1991; Kurt Waldheim (Austria), 1972–1981; U Thant (Burma, now Myanmar), November 1961, when he was appointed acting Secretary-General (he was formally appointed Secretary-General in November 1962) to December 1971; Dag Hammarskjöld (Sweden), who served from April 1953 until his death in a plane crash on mission in Africa in September 1961—the only Secretary-General to die in office; and Trygve Lie (Norway), the first Secretary-General, who held office from February 1946 until his resignation in November 1952.

The 2016 selection process for Secretary-General began with candidates informally expressing their intention to run within their country's delegation. Regional distribution of the position to date has included Africa, Asia, Western Europe, and Latin America and the Caribbean. No Secretary-General has hailed from Eastern Europe and a female candidate has never been selected. Traditionally, candidates from the five permanent members of the Security Council are not considered for the position. In December 2015, in a joint invitational letter calling for member states to nominate candidates, the General Assembly President, Mogens Lykketoft, and the Security Council President, Samantha Power, laid out the procedure for candidates to participate in informal dialogues or meetings with the members of their respective bodies. The selection process (April to October 2016) was more open than previous ones, with public nominations being sought and candidates taking part in the first-ever globally televised town hall event. Following private discussions of each candidate's nomination, the Security Council votes and issues a recommendation, once nine members have voted affirmatively for a candidate and no permanent member has issued a veto. On 6 October 2016, among thirteen candidates, Mr. Guterres was recommended for the appointment for a term of office from 1 January 2017 to 31 December 2021.

The *Charter* describes the Secretary-General as "chief administrative officer" of the Organization, who acts in that capacity and performs such other functions as are entrusted to him or her by the Security Council, General Assembly, Economic and Social Council and other UN organs. The *Charter* also empowers the Secretary-General to

Secretary-General designate António Guterres takes the oath of office—administered by Peter Thompson, President of the 71st session of the General Assembly—on the *Charter of the United Nations* (12 December 2016, UN Photo/Eskinder Debebe).

bring to the attention of the Security Council any matter that in his opinion might threaten the maintenance of international peace and security. These guidelines both define the functions and powers of the office and grant it considerable leeway for action. The Secretary-General must take account of the needs and concerns of individual member states while upholding the values and moral authority of the United Nations, and speaking and acting independently for peace—even at the risk of disagreeing with or challenging those same member states. One of the most vital roles played by the Secretary-General is the use of his good offices—steps taken publicly and in private, drawing on his impartiality—to prevent and resolve international disputes.

In his inauguration speech on 12 December 2016, Mr. Guterres stressed the need for greater emphasis on conflict prevention and on addressing the root causes of conflict, stating that, "prevention is not a novel concept—it is what the founders of the UN asked us to do. It is the best way to save lives and alleviate human suffering". He expressed his intention to undertake major reforms in three main areas: the UN peace and security architecture; the UN development system; and the Organization's internal management. He also pledged to achieve gender parity across the UN system and to promote a culture of accountability in the work of the UN.

Deputy Secretary-General. Louise Fréchette of Canada was appointed as the first Deputy Secretary-General in 1998. She was succeeded in 2006 by Mark Malloch Brown (United Kingdom); in 2007 by Asha-Rose Migiro (Tanzania); and in 2012 by Jan Eliasson (Sweden). The current Deputy Secretary-General is Amina J. Mohammed of Nigeria, who began her term in 2017.

UN Deputy Secretary-General Amina J. Mohammed (1 January 2017, UN Photo/Mark Garten)

Departments and offices

Department of Economic and Social Affairs (DESA)
Under-Secretary-General: Wu Hongbo (China)

The mission of the Department of Economic and Social Affairs (https://www.un.org/development/desa/) is to promote and support international cooperation in the pursuit of sustainable development for all. DESA's work addresses a range of cross-cutting issues that affect peoples' lives and livelihoods, such as social policy, poverty eradication, employment, social inclusion, inequalities, population, indigenous rights, macroeconomic policy, development finance and cooperation, public sector innovation, forest policy, climate change and sustainable development. To this end, DESA:

- analyses, generates and compiles a wide range of data and information on development issues;
- brings together the international community at conferences and summits to address economic and social challenges;
- supports the formulation of development policies, global standards and norms;
- supports the implementation of international agreements, including the 2030 Agenda for Sustainable Development; and
- assists states in meeting their development challenges through a variety of capacity-development initiatives.

In carrying out its work, DESA engages with a variety of stakeholders around the world, NGOs, civil society, the private sector, research and academic organizations, philanthropic foundations and intergovernmental organizations, as well as partner organizations in the UN system.

Department of Field Support (DFS)
Under-Secretary-General: Atul Khare (India)

The Department of Field Support (www.un.org/en/peacekeeping/about/dfs) provides services for international peace operations including peacekeeping, special political and other field operations. Working with UN and non-UN partners, it plans, mobilizes and sustains these operations through support solutions that are rapid, effective, efficient and responsible. DFS core services address matters ranging from budget, finance, personnel, procurement, logistics, technology and infrastructure, to supply chain and asset management. In 2016–2017, DFS supported 36 UN and non-UN peacekeeping operations in over 30 countries with nearly 168,000 authorized personnel and a combined budget of about $8.5 billion to help create the conditions for lasting peace and stability. Of the 14,520 authorized field support personnel worldwide, 13,200 were assigned to field missions, over 900 to global and shared service centres, and 420 staff worked in DFS in New York.

Department for General Assembly and Conference Management (DGACM)
Under-Secretary-General: Catherine Pollard (Guyana)

The Department for General Assembly and Conference Management (www.un.org/depts/DGACM/) provides technical and secretariat support services to the General Assembly, the Security Council, the Economic and Social Council, their committees and other subsidiary bodies, as well as to conferences held at and away from UN Headquarters. It is responsible for processing and issuing all official documents in the official languages of the Organization, and providing interpretation services for these languages to inter-governmental meetings. In addition, it produces the official records of the United Na-tions, including summary and verbatim records of meetings. Responsible for UN confer-ence management policies and parliamentary procedure, the Under-Secretary-General of DGACM advises the General Assembly President on all matters relating to the work of the Assembly and coordinates the overall implementation of multilingualism Secretariat-wide.

Department of Management (DM)

Under-Secretary-General: YUKIO TAKASU (Japan)

The Department of Management (www.un.org/en/hq/dm) provides services and opera-tions for the global UN Secretariat in the areas of finance, human resources, and sup-port services. These fall under the purview of the offices of Programme Planning, Budget and Accounts; Human Resources Management; Central Support Services; Information Communication Technology (ICT); and Umoja-Enterprise Resource Planning. DM also services the General Assembly Fifth Committee (Administrative and Budgetary) and the Committee for Programme and Coordination. The head of the Department represents the Secretary-General on matters relating to human resources, ICT, preparation and oversight of UN budgets, procurement of goods and services, accounting and financial manage-ment, travel and transportation, and facilities management; and provides support for the UN internal justice system. DM is leading many of the ongoing efforts to transform the UN Secretariat from a primarily Headquarters-oriented organization into a global, nim-ble and more efficient one. Initiatives include the implementation of international public sector accounting standards, the deployment of a new enterprise resource planning solu-tion, and the release of a strategy on the management of ICT across the organization.

Department of Political Affairs (DPA)

Under-Secretary-General: JEFFREY FELTMAN (United States)

The Department of Political Affairs (www.un.org/depts/dpa) plays a central role in the efforts of the United Nations to prevent and resolve conflict around the world and to consolidate and sustain peace in the aftermath of conflict. To that end, DPA:

- monitors, analyses and assesses political developments throughout the world;
- identifies potential or actual conflicts the United Nations could play a useful role in forestalling or resolving;
- recommends to the Secretary-General appropriate action in such cases and executes the approved policy;
- assists the Secretary-General in carrying out political activities decided by him, the General Assembly and the Security Council in the areas of preventive diplomacy, peacemaking and peacebuilding;
- advises the Secretary-General on requests for electoral assistance received from mem-ber states and coordinates programmes established in response to such requests;
- coordinates the Organization's work to prevent terrorism and violent extremism;
- advises and supports the Secretary-General in the political aspects of his relations with member states; and
- services the Security Council and its subsidiary bodies, as well as the Committee on the Exercise of the Inalienable Rights of the Palestinian People and the Special Com-mittee of 24 on Decolonization.

The head of the Department also undertakes consultations and negotiations relating to peaceful settlement of disputes, and is the focal point for UN electoral assistance activities.

Department of Public Information (DPI)

Acting Under-Secretary-General: MAHER NASSER (State of Palestine)

The Department of Public Information (www.un.org/dpi) promotes global awareness and greater understanding of the work of the United Nations; interacts and partners with diverse audiences; and builds support for peace, development and human rights. It pursues these ends using various communication tools, including radio, television, print, the Internet, videoconferences, outreach programmes, information campaigns, and social media platforms. DPI organizes exhibits, concerts, seminars and other events to mark occasions of international importance. It also provides library and knowledge-sharing services. In addition to its staff at UN Headquarters, DPI has 59 UN information centres (UNICs) worldwide (unic.un.org), including services, offices as well as a regional information centre (UNRIC) in Brussels (www.unric.org).

The Department consists of three divisions:

- Its Strategic Communications Division develops communication strategies and campaigns to promote UN priorities, manages the UNICs and produces information on peace and security, development, Palestine, and Africa, including the magazine *Africa Renewal* (www.un.org/africarenewal).
- The News and Media Division produces and distributes UN news items, including daily press briefings and statements by the Office of the Spokesperson for the Secretary-General, UN websites, radio broadcasts and live TV feeds (www.unmultimedia.org/tv/unifeed).
- The Outreach Division, which includes the Dag Hammarskjöld Library, publishes books—notably the *Yearbook of the United Nations*—and the *UN Chronicle* magazine; works with NGOs and educational institutions; engages the public through guided tours, special events and exhibitions on priority issues; and offers an annual training programme for journalists from developing countries. It also develops partnerships with the private and public sector to advance UN goals.

Since 1997, distinguished individuals have been appointed by successive Secretaries-General to serve as **UN Messengers of Peace** and **UN Goodwill Ambassador** (outreach.un.org/mop) for an initial period of two years. These prominent personalities—carefully selected from the fields of art, literature, music and sports—volunteer their time, talent and passion to help focus worldwide attention on UN work. On 11 April 2017, Nobel Peace Prize winner Malala Yousafzai was named the youngest ever UN Messenger of Peace, with a special focus on girls' education. The Pakistani activist became known around the world after she was shot by the Taliban in 2012. The **Holocaust and the United Nations Outreach Programme** (www.un.org/en/holocaustremembrance) seeks to remind the world of the lessons to be learned from the Holocaust, in order to help to prevent acts of genocide. The UN **Remember Slavery Programme** (www.un.org/en/events/slaveryremembranceday) honours the memory of the victims of slavery.

Department of Peacekeeping Operations (DPKO)

Under-Secretary-General: JEAN-PIERRE LACROIX (France)

The Department of Peacekeeping Operations (www.un.org/en/peacekeeping) is responsible for assisting member states and the Secretary-General in their efforts to maintain, achieve and sustain international peace and security. It does this by planning, preparing and conducting United Nations peacekeeping operations, in accordance with mandates provided by member states.

To this end, DPKO:

- undertakes contingency planning for possible new peacekeeping operations;
- secures, through negotiations with member states, the civilian, military and police personnel, and equipment and services required to accomplish the mandate;
- provides political and executive guidance, direction and support to peacekeeping operations;
- maintains contact with parties to conflicts and with members of the Security Council on the implementation of Council resolutions;
- manages integrated operational teams to direct and supervise all peacekeeping operations;
- advises the Security Council and member states on key peacekeeping issues, including security sector reform, the rule of law, and the disarmament, demobilization and reintegration of former combatants;
- analyses emerging policy questions and best practices related to peacekeeping, and formulates policies, procedures and general peacekeeping doctrine; and
- coordinates all UN activities related to landmines, and develops and supports mine-action programmes in peacekeeping and emergency situations.

The head of the Department directs peacekeeping operations on behalf of the Secretary-General; formulates policies and guidelines for operations; and advises the Secretary-General on all matters relating to peacekeeping and mine action.

Department of Safety and Security (DSS)

Under-Secretary-General: PETER T. DRENNAN (Australia)

The mission of the United Nations Department of Safety and Security (www.un.org/undss), formally established on 1 January 2005, is to provide professional safety and security services to enable the United Nations to deliver its programmes globally. DSS is responsible for providing leadership, operational support and oversight of the UN security management system to enable the safe and secure delivery of mandated programmes and activities of the UN system worldwide. DSS functions include ensuring a coherent and timely response to all security-related threats and other emergencies, managing security risks through the establishment of a coordinated and system-wide security threat and risk assessment mechanism, developing best-practice security policies, standards and operational procedures across the UN system and supporting and monitoring their implementation, and ensuring the most cost-effective provision and employment of security personnel. Efforts are under way to integrate the safety and security resources of field missions overseen by the Department of Political Affairs (DPA), the Department of Field Services (DFS) and the Department of Peacekeeping Operations (DPKO) under the overall management and authority of DSS with the goal to achieve one Department that will provide security services to all clients at Headquarters and in the field with a single effective chain of management authority, responsibility and accountability, and a mobile and global Secretariat security workforce.

Office for the Coordination of Humanitarian Affairs (OCHA)

Under-Secretary-General for Humanitarian Affairs and Emergency Relief Coordinator: STEPHEN O'BRIEN (United Kingdom)

The Office for the Coordination of Humanitarian Affairs (www.unocha.org) mobilizes and coordinates humanitarian action in partnership with national and international actors to ensure that assistance reaches the people most in need when conflict or natural disaster causes humanitarian emergencies. OCHA advocates—both publicly and privately—for the rights of people in need, promotes preparedness and prevention, ensures that global information management tools and platforms are in place to support humanitarians, develops and coordinates humanitarian policy to guide operations, and facilitates the implementation of sustainable solutions to humanitarian problems. OCHA also coordinates global humanitarian financing to ensure funds for humanitarian response. Its mandate is governed by four core humanitarian principles:

- *Humanity*: human suffering must be addressed wherever it is found;
- *Neutrality*: humanitarian actors must not take sides in hostilities;
- *Impartiality*: humanitarian action must be carried out on the basis of need alone; and
- *Independence*: humanitarian action must be autonomous from political, economic, military or other objectives.

As at June 2016, OCHA had 2,300 staff located in over 60 countries. The annual budget is under $300 million, of which 6 per cent is funded by the regular UN budget and 94 per cent is voluntarily funded by over 40 donor governments. In 2015, OCHA spent 71 per cent of its budget on field activities and 29 per cent on headquarters and global coordination work.

Office for Disarmament Affairs (ODA)

High Representative for Disarmament Affairs: Izumi Nakamitsu (Japan)

The Office for Disarmament Affairs (www.un.org/disarmament) promotes: nuclear disarmament and non-proliferation; strengthening of the disarmament regimes in respect to other weapons of mass destruction; and disarmament efforts in the area of conventional weapons, especially small arms and light weapons. It also promotes disarmament and confidence-building measures in the conflict-prevention and post-conflict peacebuilding efforts of the UN system.

ODA provides substantive and organizational support for norm-setting in the area of disarmament through the work of the General Assembly and its First Committee, the Disarmament Commission, the Conference on Disarmament and other bodies. It fosters disarmament measures through dialogue, transparency and confidence-building on military matters, and encourages regional disarmament efforts, including those of the UN Register of Conventional Arms and regional forums.

The Office also provides objective, impartial and up-to-date information on multilateral disarmament issues and activities to UN member states, states parties to multilateral agreements, intergovernmental organizations and institutions, departments and UN system agencies, research and educational institutions, and civil society, especially non-governmental organizations, the media and the general public.

Office of the United Nations High Commissioner for Human Rights (OHCHR)

High Commissioner: Zeid Ra'ad Al Hussein (Jordan)

The United Nations High Commissioner for Human Rights is the official with principal responsibility for UN human rights activities, and is mandated, along with the Office of the High Commissioner for Human Rights (www.ohchr.org), to promote and protect all human rights for all people. OHCHR is the leading UN entity in human rights. It provides assistance, including technical expertise and capacity-development, to support the implementation of international human rights standards on the ground. The Office also assists governments, which bear the primary responsibility for the protection of human rights, to fulfil their obligations; supports individuals to claim their rights; and speaks out objectively on human rights violations. OHCHR's 2016 budget requirement was $318.6

million—$101.3 million from the UN regular budget and $217.3 million from voluntary contributions. OHCHR, with some 1,165 staff (44 per cent based in the field), is organized into three divisions.

The Human Rights Council (HRC) and Treaty Mechanisms Division includes the Human Rights Treaties Branch, which supports 10 human rights treaty bodies. It assists independent experts in monitoring implementation of treaty obligations, processes communications on alleged human rights violations, and follows-up on treaty-body recommendations and decisions. The Human Rights Council Branch supports the HRC, and its mechanisms. The Universal Periodic Review Branch supports the review of the human rights records of all 193 UN member states every 4.5 years, capacity-building activities, and various trust and voluntary funds.

The Thematic Engagement, Special Procedures and Right to Development Division codifies lessons learned from human rights action, develops policy positions and strategies on thematic human rights issues, produces tools and learning packages on human rights themes and mainstreams human rights in the work of the UN system. The development of indicators in the context of the 2030 Agenda has been a key aspect of OHCHR efforts to mainstream human rights. The Division also assists in the implementation of mandated activities on specific themes; conducts studies, writes reports and organizes panels and expert workshops on human rights issues; and supports the theme-based independent special procedures appointed by the HRC.

The Field Operations and Technical Cooperation Division oversees and supports the work of OHCHR at the country and regional levels, including through advisory services and technical cooperation. OHCHR works with national counterparts to strengthen national protection systems and support the implementation of measures to overcome obstacles to the realization of human rights. It also responds to deteriorating human rights situations and early signs of emerging crises through the rapid deployment of monitoring missions or additional surge capacity for UN operations on the ground in the context of humanitarian emergencies. At the end of 2016, OHCHR was running 60 field presences and providing support to other members of the UN system in response to emerging situations across regions.

Office of Internal Oversight Services (OIOS)
Under-Secretary-General: HEIDI MENDOZA (Philippines)

The Office of Internal Oversight Services (oios.un.org) provides independent, professional and timely internal audit, inspection, evaluation and investigation services. It promotes responsible administration of resources, a culture of accountability and transparency, and improved programme performance. OIOS assists the Organization and member states in protecting UN assets and ensuring the compliance of programme activities with regulations, rules and policies, as well as a more efficient and effective delivery of UN activities; and detecting fraud, waste, abuse, malfeasance or mismanagement. The Under-Secretary-General is appointed by the Secretary-General and approved by the General Assembly for one five-year term without possibility of renewal.

Office of Legal Affairs (OLA)
Under-Secretary-General: MIGUEL DE SERPA SOARES (Portugal)

The Office of Legal Affairs (legal.un.org/ola) is the central legal service of the Organization. It also contributes to the progressive development and codification of international public and trade law. Among its chief responsibilities, OLA:

- provides legal advice to the Secretary-General, Secretariat departments and offices and principal and subsidiary organs of the United Nations in the field of public and private international law;
- performs substantive and secretariat functions for legal organs involved in public international law, the law of the sea and international trade law; and
- carries out the functions conferred on the Secretary-General as depositary of multilateral treaties.

In other activities, OLA deals with legal questions relating to international peace and security; the status, privileges and immunities of the United Nations; and the credentials and representations of member states. It also prepares drafts of international conventions, agreements, rules of procedure of UN organs and conferences, and other legal instruments; and provides legal services and advice on issues of international private and administrative law, and on UN resolutions and regulations.

Office of the Special Adviser on Africa (OSAA)

Under-Secretary-General and Special Adviser: MAGED ABDELFATAH ABDELAZIZ (Egypt)

The Office of the Special Adviser on Africa (www.un.org/en/africa/osaa) was established in May 2003. OSAA enhances international support for Africa's development and security through its advocacy, reporting, monitoring and analytical work and assists the Secretary-General in improving coherence and coordination of UN system support to Africa. Among its key responsibilities, OSAA:

- facilitates intergovernmental deliberations on Africa at the global level, in particular relating to the New Partnership for Africa's Development (NEPAD);
- takes the lead in the preparation of Africa-related reports on causes of conflict, NEPAD and critical issues affecting Africa;
- convenes an Interdepartmental Task Force on African Affairs to ensure a coordinated approach for UN support to Africa, and the Regional Coordination Mechanism for Africa to form partnerships with the African Union (AU) and other regional organizations in the implementation of the 2030 Agenda for Sustainable Development and the AU Agenda 2063;
- monitors commitments made toward Africa's sustainable development and produces the Secretary-General's biennial UN Monitoring Mechanism report; and
- organizes high-level ministerial and expert group meetings on key and emerging issues related to peace, security and sustainable development.

OSAA also annually organizes "Africa Week" to showcase the continent's advancements in social, economic, political and environmental development, and to mobilize support for Africa. In 2016, Africa Week, held from 10 to 14 October, took place in the context of the first year of implementation of the 2030 Agenda for Sustainable Development and the AU 2063 Agenda. The theme was "Strengthening Partnerships for Inclusive Sustainable Development, Good Governance, Peace and Stability in Africa".

Peacebuilding Support Office (PBSO)

Assistant Secretary-General: OSCAR FERNANDEZ-TARANCO (Argentina)

The Peacebuilding Support Office (www.un.org/en/peacebuilding/pbso), established in 2005, helps to sustain peace in conflict-affected countries by garnering international support for nationally-owned and -led peacebuilding efforts. PBSO supports the Peacebuilding Commission with strategic advice and policy guidance, administers the Peacebuilding

Fund and assists the Secretary-General in developing peacebuilding policies for the UN system and in coordinating UN entities in their peacebuilding efforts.

Office of the Special Representative of the Secretary-General for Children and Armed Conflict (SRSG/CAAC)

Special Representative: VIRGINIA GAMBA (Argentina)

The Special Representative of the Secretary-General for Children and Armed Conflict (childrenandarmedconflict.un.org) serves as the leading UN advocate for the protection and well-being of children affected by armed conflict. The mandate was created in 1996 by General Assembly resolution 51/77 following the publication of *Impact of Armed Conflict on Children,* a report providing a comprehensive picture of child soldiers, highlighting the disproportionate impact of war on children and identifying them as the primary victims of armed conflict. The Special Representative strengthens the protection of children affected by armed conflict; raises awareness; promotes the collection of information about the plight of children affected by war; reports annually to the General Assembly and the Human Rights Council; and raises challenges faced by children in war to political bodies, such as the Security Council and relevant governments. In March 2014, the Office launched the *Children, Not Soldiers* campaign (childrenandarmedconflict.un.org/children-not-soldiers) with UNICEF to end and prevent the recruitment and use of children by government forces in conflict.

Office of the Special Representative of the Secretary-General on Sexual Violence in Conflict (SRSG/SVC)

Special Representative: PRAMILA PATTEN (Mauritius)

The Special Representative of the Secretary-General on Sexual Violence in Conflict (www.un.org/sexualviolenceinconflict) serves as the UN spokesperson and political advocate on conflict-related sexual violence, and is the chair of the Stop Rape Now-UN Action against Sexual Violence in Conflict (www.stoprapenow.org), a network of focal points from 13 UN agencies that amplify programming and advocacy on this issue in the wider UN agenda. The six priorities of the Office are to end impunity for sexual violence in conflict; protect and empower civilians who face sexual violence in conflict, in particular women and girls who are targeted disproportionately by this crime; mobilize political ownership; increase recognition of rape as a tactic and consequence of war; harmonize the UN response by leading UN Action Against Sexual Violence in Conflict; and emphasize greater national ownership.

Office of the Special Representative of the Secretary-General on Violence Against Children (SRSG/VAC)

Special Representative: MARTA SANTOS PAIS (Portugal)

The Special Representative of the Secretary-General on Violence Against Children (srsg.violenceagainstchildren.org/) promotes dissemination of and ensures the effective follow-up to the recommendations of the Secretary-General's 2006 in-depth study on violence against children, carried out by an independent expert, in collaboration with OHCHR, UNICEF and WHO. A global effort to paint a detailed picture of the nature, extent and causes of violence against children, the study addressed violence against children in five settings: the family; schools; alternative care institutions and detention facilities; places where children work; and communities. The Special Representative chairs the UN Inter-Agency Working Group on Violence against Children and collaborates with a wide range of partners, within and beyond the UN system. UNICEF has established a trust account in order to facilitate financial contributions in support of the mandate.

United Nations Office at Geneva (UNOG)

Director-General: MICHAEL MØLLER (Denmark)

The United Nations Office at Geneva (www.unog.ch/) serves as the representative office of the Secretary-General at Geneva and performs liaison functions with permanent missions, the host Government and other governments, intergovernmental and non-governmental organizations, research and academic institutions, as well as other UN system organizations at Geneva. UNOG services more than 8,000 meetings annually, making it one of the busiest conference centres in the world. With more than 1,600 staff, it is the largest duty station outside of UN headquarters in New York. The Office provides financial and support services to more than 20 Geneva-based organizations and departments, as well as entities located in Bonn, Germany, and Turin, Italy.

Office of the High Representative for the Least Developed Countries, Landlocked Developing Countries and Small Island Developing States (UN-OHRLLS)

Under-Secretary-General and High Representative for the Least Developed Countries, Landlocked Developing Countries and Small Island Developing States: FEKITAMOELOA KATOA 'UTOIKAMANU (Tonga)

Established by the General Assembly in 2001, UN-OHRLLS (www.un.org/ohrlls) helps to mobilize and coordinate international support for implementation and follow-up to the 10-year programmes of action for the least-developed countries (LDCs), landlocked developing countries (LLDCs) and small island developing states (SIDS). It also works to ensure linkages between the follow-up of these programmes and the review arrangements of the 2030 Agenda for Sustainable Development and the 2015 Addis Ababa Action Agenda on financing for development. The Office provides support to LDCs, LLDCs and SIDS in the context of formulation of common positions and effective participation in global intergovernmental negotiations. OHRLLS also promotes global awareness on issues affecting these countries in partnership with UN entities, other international and regional organizations, civil society, the media, academia and foundations.

United Nations Office at Nairobi (UNON)

Director-General: SAHLE-WORK ZEWDE (Ethiopia)

The United Nations Office at Nairobi (www.unon.org), the UN headquarters in Africa, established in 1996, serves as the representative office of the Secretary-General in Nairobi and performs liaison functions with permanent missions, the host country and other governments, and organizations in Nairobi, as well as other UN system organizations in Kenya. It facilitates UN-regional organization cooperation; provides administrative and support services to UNEP and UN-Habitat; manages and implements the programmes of administration, conference services and public information; and provides security and safety services for UN staff and UNON facilities.

United Nations Office at Vienna (UNOV)

Director-General: YURY FEDOTOV (Russian Federation)

The United Nations Office in Vienna (www.unov.org), established in January 1980, as the third UN Headquarters after New York and Geneva, performs representation and liaison functions with UN missions, the host Government and intergovernmental and non-governmental organizations in Vienna. It also manages the UN programme on the peaceful uses of outer space; provides common services for organizations located at the Vienna International Centre; and shares common services, as well as financial, human resources and information technology and communication services with the UNODC.

Budget

The regular budget of the United Nations is approved by the General Assembly for a two-year period. The budget is initially submitted by the Secretary-General and then reviewed by the Advisory Committee on Administrative and Budgetary Questions. The Advisory Committee consists of 16 experts, nominated by their governments and elected by the Assembly, who serve in their personal capacity. Programmatic aspects of the budget are reviewed by the Committee for Programme and Coordination, which is made up of 34 experts who are elected by the Assembly and represent the views of their governments. The budget reflects the main priorities of the Organization, as set out in its strategic framework for each biennium. During the biennium, the approved budget can be adjusted by the General Assembly to reflect changing circumstances.

Contributions of member states are the main source of funds for the budget. These are assessed on a scale approved by the Assembly on the recommendation of the Committee on Contributions, made up of 18 experts serving in their personal capacity and selected by the Assembly on the recommendation of its Fifth (Administrative and Budgetary) Committee. The scale is based on the capacity of countries to pay. This is determined by considering their relative shares of total gross national product, adjusted to take into account a number of factors, including per capita income. The Committee reviews the scale every three years in light of the latest national income statistics in order to ensure that assessments are fair and accurate. There is a fixed maximum of 22 per cent of the budget for any one contributor. New rates of assessment went into effect on 1 January 2016.

Budget of the United Nations for the biennium 2016–2017

Main categories of expenditure	US dollars
1. Overall policymaking, direction and coordination	735,550,200
2. Political affairs	1,382,135,000
3. International justice and law	94,821,600
4. International cooperation for development	464,597,500
5. Regional cooperation for development	542,599,900
6. Human rights and humanitarian affairs	364,098,600
7. Public information	188,021,900
8. Common support services	589,587,900
9. Internal oversight	40,213,800
10. Jointly financed administrative activities and special expenses	164,693,000
11. Capital expenditures	97,091,100
12. Safety and security	234,295,400
13. Development account	28,398,800
14. Staff assessment	482,614,800
Total	5,408,719,500

The regular budget approved for the biennium 2016–2017 amounts to $5.408 billion, including provisions for special political missions expected to be extended or approved during the course of the biennium. The budget for such missions—mandated by the Security Council and/or the General Assembly—stood at $575.8 million in 2016–2017. The budget also covers the costs of UN programmes in areas such as development, public information, human rights and humanitarian affairs. The overall financial position of the Organization as at 8 December 2016 was generally sound. Some 138 member states had paid their regular budget assessments for the current and previous years in full. Unpaid assessments amounted to $532 million.

The regular budget does not cover peacekeeping operations or international tribunals. For those budgets, member states are separately assessed. Peacekeeping budgets are approved by the General Assembly for a one-year period beginning on 1 July. The Assembly apportions the costs based on a special scale of assessment applicable to peacekeeping. This scale takes into account the relative economic wealth of member states, with the permanent members of the Security Council paying a larger share because of their special responsibility for the maintenance of international peace and security. Global approved peacekeeping resources stood at $7.4 billion in 2016–2017. The UN mission in the Democratic Republic of the Congo, the hybrid United Nations-African Union mission in Darfur and the UN mission in the Republic of South Sudan together account for $3.3 billion—nearly 45 per cent—of the 2016–2017 peacekeeping budget.

Outstanding assessed contributions for peacekeeping operations in December 2016 totalled $2.05 billion. Non-payment of assessed contributions delays reimbursements to those member states that contribute troops, equipment and logistical support. Assessed contributions in the amount of $50 million were outstanding for the international tribunals.

UN programmes, funds and offices have separate budgets. The bulk of their resources are provided by governments on a voluntary basis, but a portion also comes from individuals and institutions. UN specialized agencies also have separate budgets supplemented through voluntary state contributions.

UN SYSTEM

The United Nations system (www.unsystem.org/directory) consists of the UN family of organizations. It includes the Secretariat, the UN funds and programmes, the specialized agencies, and other related organizations. The funds, programmes and offices are subsidiary bodies of the General Assembly. The specialized agencies are linked to the United Nations through individual agreements and report to the Economic and Social Council and/ or the Assembly. Related organizations—including IAEA, IOM and the World Trade Organization—have their own legislative bodies and budgets. Together, the members of the UN system address all areas of cultural, economic, scientific and social endeavour.

The United Nations System Chief Executives Board for Coordination (CEB) (www. unsystem.org) is the UN system's longest-standing and highest-level coordinating mechanism. Chaired by the Secretary-General, its members are the leaders of the main parts of the UN system. CEB meets twice a year and is supported in its work by the High-level Committee on Programmes, the High-level Committee on Management and the United Nations Development Group (UNDG) (undg.org). Its 31 members include the United Nations, FAO, IAEA, ICAO, IFAD, ILO, IMF, IMO, IOM, ITU, UNCTAD, UNDP, UNEP, UNESCO, UNFPA, UN-Habitat, UNHCR, UNICEF, UNIDO, UNODC, UNOPS, UNRWA, UN-Women, UNWTO, UPU, WFP, WHO, WIPO, WMO, World Bank and WTO.

Other UN system entities (www.unsystem.org/other-entities), which are not members of CEB, include the regional commissions, research and training institutes and jointly financed bodies, such as the Joint Inspection Unit (JIU), the only independent external oversight body mandated to conduct evaluations, inspections and investigations system-wide; and the International Civil Service Commission (ICSC), whose mandate covers all facets of staff employment conditions.

UN and the Nobel Peace Prize. The United Nations family and its associates have been awarded the Nobel Peace Prize numerous times in recognition of their contributions to the cause of world peace (www.un.org/en/sections/nobel-peace-prize/index. html). UN-related Nobel Peace Prize laureates since the establishment of the Organization include:

- Cordell Hull—United States Secretary of State instrumental in establishing the United Nations (1945);
- John Boyd Orr—founding Director-General of the Food and Agriculture Organization of the United Nations (1949);
- Ralph Bunche—UN Trusteeship Director and principal secretary of the UN Palestine Commission, leader of mediation efforts in the Middle East (1950);
- Léon Jouhaux—a founder of the International Labour Organization (1951);
- Office of the United Nations High Commissioner for Refugees (1954);
- Lester Bowles Pearson—General Assembly President in 1952 honoured for trying to end the Suez conflict and solve the Middle East question through the UN (1957);
- Secretary-General Dag Hammarskjöld—one of only two posthumous awards (1961);
- United Nations Children's Fund (1965);
- International Labour Organization (1969);
- Seán MacBride—UN Commissioner for Namibia and promoter of human rights (1974);
- Office of the United Nations High Commissioner for Refugees (1981);
- United Nations Peacekeeping Forces (1988);
- United Nations and Secretary-General Kofi A. Annan (2001);
- International Atomic Energy Agency and its Director General Mohamed El-Baradei (2005);
- Intergovernmental Panel on Climate Change and former United States Vice-President Albert Arnold (Al) Gore, Jr. (2007); and
- Organisation for the Prohibition of Chemical Weapons (2013).

This list does not include the many Nobel laureates who have worked closely with the United Nations or at common purpose with it in making their contribution to peace.

Funds and programmes, research and training institutes, and other entities

International Trade Centre (ITC)

The International Trade Centre (www.intracen.org) is the joint agency of the World Trade Organization and the United Nations. Established in 1964, ITC supports the internationalization of small- and medium-sized enterprises, which are proven to be major job creators and engines of inclusive growth. ITC works with developing countries and economies in transition to achieve "trade impact for good" and contribute to the achievement of the SDGs through trade. ITC provides knowledge such as trade and market intelligence, technical support and practical capacity-building to policymakers, the private sector and trade and investment support institutions, as well as linkages to markets. Economic empowerment of women, young entrepreneurs and support of poor communities, as well as fostering sustainable and green trade are also priorities.

The ITC budget has two parts: the regular budget, which is provided equally by WTO and the UN; and extrabudgetary funds, which are provided by funders as voluntary contributions. ITC's annual regular budget is around $37 million and its extrabudgetary funds amount to $50 million. ITC has a headquarters staff of around 300, as well as some 600 consultants and individual contractors providing technical expertise.

Executive Director: Arancha González (Spain)
Headquarters: Palais des Nations, CH-1211 Geneva 10, Switzerland
Tel.: +41 22 730 0111 │ **Fax:** +41 22 733 4439 │ **E-mail:** itcreg@intracen.org
Twitter: @itcnews │ **Facebook:** www.facebook.com/internationaltradecentre

Joint United Nations Programme on HIV/AIDS (UNAIDS)

Active since 1996, UNAIDS (www.unaids.org) is the UN entity that advocates for comprehensive and coordinated global action against the HIV/AIDS epidemic. It plays a vital role in reducing new HIV infections, reducing AIDS-related deaths since the peak of the epidemic and ensuring that HIV infection is no longer a death sentence, but a manageable, chronic, condition. UNAIDS leads and inspires the world to achieve its shared vision of zero new HIV infections, zero discrimination and zero AIDS-related deaths. The Programme unites the efforts of 11 UN organizations—UNHCR, UNICEF, WFP, UNDP, UNFPA, UNODC, UN-Women, ILO, UNESCO, WHO and the World Bank—and works closely with global and national partners to end the AIDS epidemic by 2030 as part of the SDGs.

Executive Director: Michel Sidibé (Mali)
Headquarters: 20 Avenue Appia, CH-1211 Geneva 27, Switzerland
Tel.: +41 22 791 3666 │ **Fax:** +41 22 791 4187 │ **E-mail:** communications@unaids.org
Twitter: @unaids │ **Facebook:** www.facebook.com/unaids

United Nations Conference on Trade and Development (UNCTAD)

Established in 1964 as a permanent intergovernmental body and subsidiary of the General Assembly, the Geneva-based United Nations Conference on Trade and Development (unctad.org) is the UN focal point for the integrated treatment of trade and development and related issues of finance, investment, technology and sustainable development. UNCTAD's main goal is to help developing countries and transition economies use trade and investment as an engine for development, poverty reduction and integration into the world economy. It works in three main areas: research and analysis; consensus-building through intergovernmental deliberations; and technical cooperation projects carried out with various partners. It also contributes to international debate on emerging issues related to developing countries and the world economy through major reports, policy briefs and contributions to international meetings.

UNCTAD's highest decision-making body is its ministerial conference, at which the organization's 194 member states debate international economic issues and set UNCTAD's mandate. The theme of the fourteenth conference in 2016 (UNCTAD 14) was "From decision to action: moving toward an inclusive and equitable global economic environment for trade and development". In 2015, UNCTAD had 489 staff members and an annual regular budget of $74 million. Its technical cooperation activities, financed from extrabudgetary resources, amounted to more than $39.5 million, with some 229 technical assistance projects ongoing in 145 countries. UNCTAD's main publications are: the *Trade and Development Report, World Investment Report, Economic Development in Africa Report, Least Developed Countries Report, UNCTAD Handbook of Statistics, Information Economy Report,* and *Review of Maritime Transport.*

Secretary-General: Mukhisa Kituyi (Kenya)
Headquarters: Palais des Nations, 8–14, Av. de la Paix, 1211, CH-1211 Geneva 10, Switzerland
Tel.: +41 22 917 1234 | **Fax:** +41 22 917 0057 | **E-mail:** info@unctad.org
Twitter: @unctad | **Facebook:** www.facebook.com/unctad

United Nations Development Programme (UNDP)

The United Nations Development Programme (www.undp.org) leads the UN global development network. With activities in 170 countries, UNDP works throughout the developing world helping countries achieve their development goals. Its mandate is to work with countries to reduce poverty, promote democratic governance, prevent and recover from crises, protect the environment and combat climate change. The UNDP network seeks to ensure that developing countries have access to resources and knowledge to meet the Sustainable Development Goals.

UNDP is governed by a 36-member Executive Board representing both developing and developed countries. Its flagship publication, the annual *Human Development Report*, focuses on key development issues and provides measurement tools, innovative analysis and policy proposals. UNDP is funded entirely by voluntary contributions from member states; its annual budget is around $5 billion.

Administrator: Achim Steiner (Germany)
Headquarters: 1 UN Plaza, New York, NY 10017, USA
Tel.: +1 212 906 5000 | **Fax:** +1 212 906 5364
Twitter: @undp | **Facebook:** www.facebook.com/undp

United Nations Capital Development Fund (UNCDF)

The United Nations Capital Development Fund (www.uncdf.org) is the UN capital investment agency for the world's 49 least developed countries. It creates new opportunities for poor people and their businesses by increasing access to microfinance and investment capital. UNCDF focuses on Africa, with a special commitment to countries emerging from conflict or crisis. It provides seed capital (grants and loans) and technical support to help microfinance institutions reach more poor households and small businesses. It also helps local governments finance the capital investments—water systems, roads, schools, irrigation schemes—that improve the lives of the poor. Over 65 per cent of the clients of UNCDF-supported microfinance institutions are women. All UNCDF support is provided via national systems, in accordance with the *2005 Paris Declaration on Aid Effectiveness*. UNCDF programmes are designed to catalyse larger investment flows from the private sector, development partners and national governments. Established by the General Assembly in 1966 and headquartered in New York, UNCDF is an autonomous UN organization affiliated with UNDP. In 2012, total revenue of the Fund was approximately $57 million. UNCDF employs 150 staff.

Executive Secretary: Judith Karl (United States)
Headquarters: 2 UN Plaza, New York, NY 10017, USA
Tel.: +1 212 906 6565 | **Fax:** +1 212 906 6479 | **E-mail:** info@uncdf.org
Twitter: @uncdf | **Facebook:** www.facebook.com/uncdf

United Nations Volunteers (UNV)

The United Nations Volunteers programme (www.unv.org) is the UN organization that contributes to peace and development through volunteerism worldwide. UNV works with partners to integrate qualified, highly motivated and well-supported UN Volunteers into development programming. UNV mobilizes nearly 7,000 volunteers every year in over 120 countries. More than 80 per cent of UNVs come from developing countries, and more than 30 per cent volunteer in their own countries. Volunteers assist UN organizations in advancing progress towards the Sustainable Development Goals. They support the delivery of basic social services, as well as efforts in the field of sustainable environment and climate change, crisis prevention and recovery, humanitarian assistance and peacebuilding. In addition, 12,000 online volunteers conduct assignments via the Internet to bolster the peace and development activities of UN agencies, governments and civil society organizations.

Created by the General Assembly in 1970, UNV is administered by UNDP and reports to the UNDP Executive Board. Its financial volume decreased to $402 million in 2014–2015, compared to $430 million in the previous biennium. UNV funding comes from UNDP, partner agencies and contributions to the UNV Special Voluntary Fund.

Executive Coordinator: Olivier Adam (France)
Headquarters: UN Campus, Platz der Vereinten Nationen 1, 53113 Bonn, Germany
Tel.: +49 228 815 2000 | **Fax:** +49 228 815 2001 | **E-mail:** information@unv.org
Twitter: @unvolunteers | **Facebook:** www.facebook.com/unvolunteers

United Nations Environment Programme (UNEP)

Founded in 1972, the United Nations Environment Programme (web.unep.org) provides leadership and encourages partnerships in caring for the environment, enabling nations and peoples to improve their quality of life without compromising that of future generations. As the principal UN body in the field of the environment, UNEP sets the global environmental agenda, assists policymakers, promotes implementation of the environmental dimension of sustainable development in the UN system, and serves as an authoritative advocate of the global environment.

During 2014–2017, UNEP work focused on seven priorities:

- climate change: strengthening the ability of countries—in particular developing countries—to integrate climate change responses into national development processes;
- ecosystem management: ensuring that countries manage land, water and living resources in a manner conducive to conservation and sustainable use;
- environmental governance: ensuring that environmental governance and interactions at the country, regional and global levels are strengthened to address environmental priorities;
- chemicals, waste and air quality: minimizing their impact on the environment and people;
- disasters and conflicts: minimizing threats to human well-being from the environmental causes and consequences of natural and man-made disasters;
- resource efficiency: ensuring that natural resources are produced, processed and consumed in a more environmentally sustainable way; and
- environment under review: empowering stakeholders at global, regional and national levels by providing open web platforms and access to timely, substantiated knowledge about the environment and emerging issues.

UNEP's mandate and focus are determined by its governing body, the United Nations Environment Assembly (UNEA), which succeeded the 58-member Governing Council. The first session of UNEA, held in June 2014, tackled major issues such as the illegal trade in wildlife, air quality, environmental rule of law, financing the green economy, and the SDGs. The second session, in May 2016, was held under the theme "Delivering on the environmental dimension of the 2030 Agenda for Sustainable Development".

UNEP's 2016–2017 approved budget is $672.9 million, including $118.37 million in funding from the Global Environment Facility (GEF). Its main voluntary funding mechanism is the Environment Fund. Additional funds are provided by the UN regular budget, as well as those mobilized by UNEP in the form of trust funds and earmarked contributions. UNEP has a global staff of approximately 840.

Executive Director: Erik Solheim (Norway)
Headquarters: United Nations Avenue, Gigiri, P.O. Box 30552, 00100, Nairobi, Kenya
Tel.: +254 20 762 1234 | **Fax:** +254 20 762 4489/4490 | **E-mail:** unepinfo@unep.org
Twitter: @unep | **Facebook:** www.facebook.com/unep

United Nations Population Fund (UNFPA)

Established in 1967 at the initiative of the General Assembly and operational in 1969, the United Nations Population Fund (www.unfpa.org) is the largest internationally funded source of population assistance to developing countries and those with economies in transition. It helps countries improve reproductive health and family planning services on the basis of individual choice. It is a subsidiary organ of the General Assembly and has the same Executive Board as UNDP. With headquarters in New York and a global network of 132 offices, UNFPA supports the development priorities of 155 countries, territories and areas. In 2015, the Fund's revenue totalled $992 million, including $548 million in voluntary contributions from governments and private donors. UNFPA provided $477 million in assistance for reproductive health—including safe motherhood, family planning and sexual health—to refine approaches to adolescent reproductive health; reduce maternal disabilities such as obstetric fistula; address HIV/AIDS; and provide assistance in emergencies. UNFPA also devoted $113 million to gender equality and women's empowerment, $104 million to evidence-based population and development strategies, and $60 million to adolescents and youth. In 2015, UNFPA had a regular staff of more than 2,600.

Executive Director: Dr. Babatunde Osotimehin (Nigeria)
Headquarters: 605 Third Avenue, New York, NY 10158, United States
Tel.: +1 212 297 5000 | **Fax:** +1 212 370 0201 | **E-mail:** hq@unfpa.org
Twitter: @unfpa | **Facebook:** www.facebook.com/unfpa

United Nations Human Settlements Programme (UN-Habitat)

The United Nations Human Settlements Programme (www.unhabitat.org), established in 1978, promotes sustainable human settlements development through advocacy, policy formulation, capacity-building, knowledge creation and the strengthening of partnerships between governments and civil society. As the focal point on sustainable urbanization and human settlements development, UN-Habitat coordinates implementation, follow-up and review of the New Urban Agenda (NUA) in collaboration with other UN entities. UN-Habitat and other stakeholders generate evidence-based and practical guidelines for the implementation of NUA and the urban dimension of the SDGs. UN-Habitat also coordinates the development of standards and capacity development tools for effective implementation and monitoring of NUA. Its technical programmes and projects focus on slum upgrading, urban poverty reduction, post-disaster reconstruction, the provision of urban water and sanitation and the mobilization of domestic financial resources for shelter delivery.

UN-Habitat is governed by a 58-member Governing Council. Expenditures of $483.1 million were approved for 2016–2017, of which $440.3 million (91 per cent) was reserved for programme activities and $42.8 million for support activities and management functions. The organization produces the *World Cities Report* (wcr.unhabitat.org/main-report).

Executive Director: Joan Clos (Spain)
Headquarters: P.O. Box 30030, GPO, Nairobi, 00100, Kenya
Tel.: +254 20 762 3120 | **Fax:** +254 20 762 3477 | **E-mail:** infohabitat@unhabitat.org
Twitter: @unhabitat | **Facebook:** www.facebook.com/unhabitat

Office of the United Nations High Commissioner for Refugees (UNHCR)

The Office of the United Nations High Commissioner for Refugees (www.unhcr.org) —established on 1 January 1951 to help more than 1 million people still uprooted after the Second World War—was initially given a three-year mandate, which was later extended by successive five-year terms until 2003, when the General Assembly declared the continuation of the mandate "until the refugee problem is solved". The primary purpose of UNHCR is to protect and safeguard the rights of refugees and asylum- seekers, returnees, stateless people and the forcibly internally displaced, and ensure that no person is returned involuntarily to a country where he or she has reason to fear persecution. It monitors government compliance with international law, advocates for refugee rights, and provides emergency and material assistance to those under its care, collaborating with a variety of partners: governments, NGOs, civil society, faith-based groups and other UN organizations. It seeks long-term solutions for refugees through voluntary repatriation, integration in countries where they first sought asylum, or resettlement in third countries. In recent years, conflicts and persecution, often compounded by the impact of climate change and competition for scarce resources have resulted in unprecedented forcible displacement. At the end of 2015, some 65.3 million people—or one person in 113—around the world were displaced.

In October 2016, there were 10,700 UNHCR staff members working in 128 countries across 461 locations. Some 87 per cent were field-based, protecting the most vulnerable victims of displacement, 7 per cent worked at Geneva headquarters, and the remaining 6 per cent worked in the Global Service Centres located in Budapest, Hungary; Copenhagen, Denmark; and Amman, Jordan. The UNHCR Executive Committee is composed of 98 member states. UNHCR is funded almost entirely by voluntary contributions, with 86 per cent coming from governments and the European Union; 6 per cent from other intergovernmental organizations and pooled funding mechanisms; and 6 per cent from the private sector. The Office receives a limited subsidy (2 per cent) from the UN regular budget for administrative costs. UNHCR also accepts "in-kind" contributions, including relief items such as tents, medicine, trucks and air transport. Its initial proposed budgets for 2016 and 2017 were $6.5 billion and $6.4 billion, respectively.

High Commissioner: Filippo Grandi (Italy)
Headquarters: Case Postale 2500, 1211 Geneva 2, Switzerland
Tel.: +41 22 739 8111 | **Fax:** +41 22 739 7377
Twitter: @refugees | **Facebook:** www.facebook.com/unhcr

United Nations Children's Fund (UNICEF)

The United Nations Children's Fund (www.unicef.org) was created by the General Assembly in 1946 to provide emergency food and health care to children in countries that had been ravaged by World War II. The Fund provides long-term humanitarian and developmental assistance to children and mothers in developing countries. It has evolved from an emergency fund to a development agency, committed to protecting the rights of every child to survival, protection and development. UNICEF works in partnership with governments, civil society, and other international organizations to protect the rights of every child, focusing on the most disadvantaged and excluded children, families and communities. UNICEF advocates for a protective environment for children, especially in emergencies, and advances efforts to prevent and respond to violence, exploitation and abuse. UNICEF is guided by the *Convention on the Rights of the Child*, ratified by 196 states parties.

UNICEF is governed by an Executive Board composed of delegates from 36 UN member states. It has over 12,000 regular employees working in more than 150 countries and territories. The Fund is supported entirely by voluntary contributions; its programme expenditures in 2015 totalled $4.5 billion. Total income was $5 billion, with $3.5 billion received from the public sector, including contributions from 136 governments.

UNICEF also received $1.46 billion from the private sector and NGOs, including more than $5.3 million from regular donors who give through and from 34 national committees. Its flagship publication, *The State of the World's Children*, appears annually.

Executive Director: Anthony Lake (United States)
Headquarters: UNICEF House, 3 United Nations Plaza, New York, NY 10017, United States
Tel.: +1 212 326 7000 | **Fax:** +1 212 888 7465 | **E-mail:** www.unicefusa.org/about/contact
Twitter: @unicef | **Facebook:** www.facebook.com/unicef

United Nations Interregional Crime and Justice Research Institute (UNICRI)

The United Nations Interregional Crime and Justice Research Institute (www.unicri.it) supports countries worldwide in preventing crime and facilitating criminal justice. Established in 1965, it formulates and implements policies in the field of justice, crime prevention and control. UNICRI works across the continuum of crime prevention, justice, security governance, counter-terrorism and social cohesion. The Institute contributes to the 2030 Agenda for Sustainable Development by conducting research and field activities, building technical assistance capacity, and supporting policy formulation on issues of social concern, including emerging and transnational forms of crime. It also develops practical models and systems to contribute to socioeconomic development, increased security and the protection of human rights. UNICRI is financed exclusively from voluntary contributions and does not receive funds from the UN regular budget.

Director: Cindy J. Smith (United States)
Headquarters: Viale Maestri del Lavoro, 10, 10127 Turin, Italy
Tel.: +39 011 6537 111 | Fax: +39 011 6313 368 | **E-mail:** publicinfo@unicri.it
Twitter: @unicri | **Facebook:** www.facebook.com/unicri.it

United Nations Institute for Disarmament Research (UNIDIR)

Established in 1980, the United Nations Institute for Disarmament Research (www.unidir.org) is an autonomous think tank that generates knowledge and promotes action to improve disarmament and security policies, programmes and practices. UNIDIR fills a critical niche with new ideas on emerging issues, thought leadership through fact-based analysis, and its role as a facilitator in multilateral disarmament-related matters. The Institute is mandated to consider both current and future security issues and examines topics as varied as tactical nuclear weapons, nuclear risk, cyberconflict, autonomous weapon systems, space security, explosive weapons, and weapons and ammunition management. It convenes expert-level meetings and discussions, conducts research and analysis, and publishes books, reports and papers. In 2015, UNIDIR conducted 22 individual projects, held 34 conferences and seminars, and issued 21 publications. The Institute relies predominantly on voluntary contributions from governments and private funders. It received nearly $3 million in 2015. UNIDIR's staff of 15 is based in Geneva and is supplemented by visiting fellows and consultants.

Director: Jarmo Sareva (Finland)
Headquarters: Palais des Nations, 1211 Geneva 10, Switzerland
Tel.: +41 22 917 1234 | **Fax:** +41 22 917 0176 | **E-mail:** unidir@unog.ch
Twitter: @unidir | **Facebook:** www.facebook.com/unidirgeneva

United Nations International Strategy for Disaster Risk Reduction (UNISDR)

The United Nations International Strategy for Disaster Risk Reduction (www.unisdr.
org), also known as the UN Office for Disaster Risk Reduction, was created by the General Assembly in 1999 and serves as the focal point for coordinating disaster risk reduction activities of the UN system and regional organizations. UNISDR supports the implementation and review of the Sendai Framework for Disaster Risk Reduction 2015–2030, which succeeded the Hyogo Framework for Action 2005–2015. The Sendai Framework is a 15-year voluntary agreement that maps out a broad, people-centred approach to disaster risk reduction. UNISDR campaigns to create global awareness of disaster risk reduction; advocates for greater investments in risk reduction; and informs and connects people and stakeholders by providing guidance and tools. It publishes the UN flagship study of the state of disaster risk reduction, the biennial *Global Assessment Report*, and hosts the biennial Global Platform for Disaster Risk Reduction, a biennial multi-stakeholder global forum for deliberations and strategic guidance on disaster risk reduction. Led by the Special Representative of the Secretary-General for Disaster Risk Reduction, UNISDR is headquartered in Geneva and has regional offices around the world.

Special Representative of the Secretary-General: Robert Glasser (Australia)
Headquarters: 9–11 Rue de Varembé, CH1202, Geneva, Switzerland
Tel.: +41 22 917 8907 8 | **Fax:** +41 22 917 8964 | **E-mail:** isdr@un.org
Twitter: @unisdr | **Facebook:** www.facebook.com/unisdr

United Nations Institute for Training and Research (UNITAR)

An autonomous UN body established in 1963, the United Nations Institute for Training and Research (www.unitar.org) has the mandate to enhance the effectiveness of the UN through diplomatic training, and to increase the impact of national actions through public awareness-raising, education and training of public policy officials. UNITAR provides training and capacity development to assist mainly developing countries with special attention to least developed countries, small island developing states, and other groups and communities that are most vulnerable. It also conducts research on innovative learning approaches, methods, and tools, as well as applied research to address critical issues. In 2015, UNITAR delivered 487 activities, including training, learning and knowledge-sharing events benefiting close to 40,000 participants—almost 80 per cent of whom were from developing countries. Seventy-eight per cent of the Institute's activities is delivered face-to-face, while 22 per cent are delivered via UNITAR's e-learning platform. UNITAR activities are conducted from its headquarters in Geneva, as well as through its offices in New York and Hiroshima. Most of the activities take place at the country level. UNITAR is governed by a Board of Trustees. The Institute is financed entirely from voluntary contributions from governments, UN entities, international and intergovernmental organizations, foundations, NGOs and the private sector. Its 2016–2017 revised budget amounted to $51.3 million. UNITAR has 40 regular staff members and 19 remunerated fellows.

Executive Director: Nikhil Seth (India)
Headquarters: International Environment House, Chemin des Anémones 11–13, 1219 Châtelaine, Geneva, Switzerland
Tel.: +41 22 917 8400 | **Fax:** +41 22 917 8047
Twitter: @unitar | **Facebook:** www.facebook.com/unitarhq

United Nations Office on Drugs and Crime (UNODC)

Established in 1997, the United Nations Office on Drugs and Crime (www.unodc.org) is a global leader in tackling illicit drugs and transnational organized crime. It is committed to achieving health, security and justice for all, and to delivering legal and technical assistance to prevent terrorism. With the aim of building concerted international action to further the rule of law, the Office's mission involves research and analysis to produce authoritative reports; technical assistance to states in ratifying and implementing international treaties on drugs, crime and terrorism; developing domestic legislation consistent with these treaties; and training judicial officials. Other focus areas include prevention, treatment and reintegration, along with the creation of sustainable alternative livelihoods for drug-crop farmers. These measures aim at reducing incentives for illicit activities and addressing drug use, the spread of HIV and AIDS and drug-related crime.

UNODC has over 1,600 staff and personnel working through a network of more than 60 field and project offices, as well as liaison offices in New York and Brussels. In its two-year budget for 2016–2017, the General Assembly allocated $38.2 million to UNODC, accounting for 6.6 per cent of total UNODC income. In 2015, voluntary contributions were pledged in the amount of $238.7 million. Overall voluntary funding for the two-year budget period 2014–2015 totalled $526.5 million.

Executive Director: Yury Fedotov (Russian Federation)
Headquarters: Vienna International Centre, Wagramerstrasse 5, P.O. Box 500, 1400 Vienna, Austria
Tel.: +43 1 26060 | **Fax:** +43 1 263 3389 | **E-mail:** unodc@unodc.org
Twitter: @unodc | **Facebook:** www.facebook.com/unodc

United Nations Office for Project Services (UNOPS)

The mission of the United Nations Office for Project Services (www.unops.org) is to help people build better lives and countries to achieve sustainable development. UNOPS envisions a world where people can live full lives supported by appropriate, sustainable and resilient infrastructure and by the efficient, transparent use of public resources in procurement and project management. With 5,000 employees and experience working in more than 130 countries over the last 20 years, UNOPS supports partners in the implementation of more than $1 billion worth of projects annually. The Office delivers products and services of the highest quality and assists countries in establishing new kinds of partnerships and accessing innovative funding sources. UNOPS functions as a fully self-financing organization working in development, humanitarian and peacekeeping contexts with a variety of partners, including governments, NGOs and the private sector. The management budget estimate for the 2016–2017 biennium is $125.6 million.

Executive Director: Grete Faremo (Norway)
Headquarters: Marmorvej 51, PO Box 2695, 2100 Copenhagen, Denmark
Tel.: +45 4533 7500 | **Fax:** +45 4533 7501 | **E-mail:** info@unops.org
Twitter: @unops | **Facebook:** www.facebook.com/unops.org

United Nations Research Institute for Social Development (UNRISD)

The United Nations Research Institute for Social Development (www.unrisd.org) works to ensure that social equity, inclusion and justice are central to development thinking, policy and practice. Established in 1963, UNRISD is an autonomous institution within the UN system dedicated to interdisciplinary research and policy analysis on the social dimensions of contemporary development issues in the areas of gender, social policy and sustainable development. UNRISD carries out research, communications and policy engagement activities in collaboration with a global network of individuals and institutions to co-create and share knowledge, and to shape and shift policy within and beyond the UN system. UNRISD relies entirely on voluntary contributions for financing its activities and has an average annual operating budget of approximately $3 million. Responsibility for approving the research programme and budget of the Institute is vested in a board of independent experts nominated by the UN Commission for Social Development and confirmed by ECOSOC.

Director: Paul Ladd (United Kingdom)
Headquarters: Palais des Nations, 1211 Geneva 10, Switzerland
Tel.: +41 22 917 3020 │ **Fax:** +41 22 917 0650 │ **E-mail:** info@unrisd.org
Twitter: www.twitter.com/unrisd │ **Facebook:** www.facebook.com/unrisd

United Nations Relief and Works Agency for Palestine Refugees in the Near East (UNRWA)

The United Nations Relief and Works Agency for Palestine Refugees in the Near East (www.unrwa.org) was established by the General Assembly in 1949 to carry out direct relief and works programmes for Palestine refugees. It began operations on 1 May 1950. In the absence of an agreed solution to the refugee problem, its mandate has been periodically renewed; it was most recently extended until 30 June 2017. The Agency provides essential services to a population of over 5 million registered Palestine refugees in the Middle East, including more than 1.5 million in 58 refugee camps in Jordan, Lebanon and Syria, as well as the Gaza Strip and the West Bank, including East Jerusalem. The Agency's services encompass education, health care, relief and social services, camp infrastructure and improvement, microfinance and emergency assistance, including in times of armed conflict. UNRWA has been providing emergency humanitarian assistance to mitigate the effects of the ongoing crisis on the most vulnerable refugees in Gaza and the West Bank since 2000. It has also responded to the emergency needs of conflict-affected refugees in Lebanon since 2006. In response to the situation in Syria, the Agency has been providing emergency and regular services to refugees inside Syria, as well as to those who have fled to Lebanon and Jordan.

UNRWA's operations are supported by its two headquarters in Gaza and Amman, Jordan. The Commissioner-General, who reports to the General Assembly, is assisted by the 27-member Advisory Commission composed of Australia, Belgium, Brazil, Canada, Denmark, Egypt, Finland, France, Germany, Ireland, Italy, Japan, Jordan, Kuwait, Lebanon, Luxembourg, the Netherlands, Norway, Saudi Arabia, Spain, Sweden, Switzerland, Syria, Turkey, the United Arab Emirates, the United Kingdom and the United States. The European Union, the League of Arab States and Palestine are observers. UNRWA's employs around 30,000 area staff and 170 international staff. UNRWA's 2016–2017 programme budget amounted to $2.4 billion, including $884.6 million for projects. The Agency depends almost entirely on voluntary contributions from donor states. Less than 3 per cent of its current biennium budget requirements are met by the UN regular budget. Most voluntary contributions are in cash, but some are in kind—mostly food for needy refugees.

Commissioner-General: Pierre Krähenbühl (Switzerland)
Headquarters (Amman, Jordan): Bayader Wadi Seer, P.O. Box 140157, Amman 11814, Jordan
Tel.: +962 6 580 8100 │ **Fax:** +962 6 580 8335
Headquarters (Gaza): Gamal Abdul Nasser Street, Gaza City, P.O. Box 371 Gaza City
Tel.: +972 8 288 7701 │ **Fax:** +972 8 288 7699
Twitter: @unrwa │ **Facebook:** www.facebook.com/unrwa

United Nations University (UNU)

The United Nations University (www.unu.edu), established in 1975 in Tokyo, is an international community of academics engaged in research, policy study, and institutional and individual capacity development, as well as the dissemination of knowledge to further the UN aims of peace and progress. UNU has a worldwide network of 14 research and training centres and programmes. Its aim is to contribute to solving the pressing global problems of human survival, development and welfare. The University is financed entirely by voluntary contributions from states, agencies, foundations and individual donors. Receiving no funds from the United Nations budget, its annual income for operating expenses comes from investment income derived from its Endowment Fund. UNU's estimated budget for the 2016–2017 biennium amounts to $117.6 million. UNU personnel, numbering 652 staff members, represent both developing and developed countries. The University's governing board—the UNU Council—is composed of 12 members who serve for three- or six-year terms; the University Rector; and three ex-officio members: the Secretary-General, the UNESCO Director-General and the UNITAR Executive Director.

Rector: David M. Malone (Canada)
Headquarters: 5-53-70 Jingumae, Shibuya-ku, Tokyo 150-8925, Japan
Tel.: +81 3 5467 1212 | **Fax:** +81 3 3499 2828 | **E-mail:** mbox@hq.unu.edu
Twitter: @ununiversity | **Facebook:** www.facebook.com/unitednationsuniversity

United Nations Entity for Gender Equality and the Empowerment of Women (UN-Women)

The General Assembly created the United Nations Entity for Gender Equality and the Empowerment of Women (UN-Women) (www.unwomen.org) in 2010 by consolidating the existing mandate and functions of four UN agencies and offices: the United Nations Development Fund for Women, the Division for the Advancement of Women, the Office of the Special Adviser on Gender Issues, and the International Research and Training Institute for the Advancement of Women. UN-Women aims to accelerate progress in realizing the rights and meeting the needs of women and girls worldwide, as well as achieving the 2030 Agenda for Sustainable Development. The entity supports the Commission on the Status of Women and other intergovernmental bodies in devising policies, and member states in implementing global standards and commitments on gender equality and women's empowerment. It also holds the UN system accountable for its own work on gender equality and the empowerment of women, including regular monitoring of system-wide progress.

Executive Director: Phumzile Mlambo-Ngcuka (South Africa)
Headquarters: 220 East 42nd Street, New York, NY 10017, USA
Tel.: +1 646 781 4400 | **Fax:** +1 646 781 4444
Twitter: @un_women | **Facebook:** www.facebook.com/unwomen

World Food Programme (WFP)

The World Food Programme (www.wfp.org) is the leading humanitarian organization fighting hunger worldwide, delivering food assistance in emergencies and working with communities to improve nutrition and build resilience. Each year, WFP assists some 80 million people in around 80 countries. Two thirds of WFP's work is in conflict-affected countries where people are three times more likely to be undernourished than those living in countries without conflict. On an average day, WFP has 20 ships, 70 planes and 5,000 trucks moving and delivering food and other assistance to those in need. In 2015, WFP provided school meals, snacks or take-home rations to 17.4 million school children. It provided food assistance to 6.1 million refugees, 16.4 million IDPs and 1.3 million returnees. Increasingly, WFP meets people's food needs through cash-based transfers that allow them to choose and shop for their own food locally. Some 9.6 million people received food assistance through, for example, electronic cards, banknotes, vouchers or credit on their mobile phones. In addition to providing food assistance, WFP supported 1.8 million people who were trained in areas of nutrition and food security or smallholder farmers who were connected to food markets. WFP is funded entirely by voluntary donations. In 2015, WFP raised close to $5 billion. More than 90 per cent of its 14,000 staff are based in the countries where the agency provides assistance. WFP is governed by a 36-member Executive Board. It works closely with its two Rome-based sister organizations, the Food and Agriculture Organization of the United Nations and the International Fund for Agricultural Development. The Programme also partners with more than 1,000 NGOs to provide food assistance and tackle the underlying causes of hunger.

Executive Director: David Beasley (United States)
Headquarters: Via Cesare Giulio Viola 68, Parco de' Medici, 00148, Rome, Italy
Tel.: +39 06 65131 | **Fax:** +39 06 6590632 | **E-mail:** wfpinfo@wfp.org
Twitter: @wfp | **Facebook:** www.facebook.com/worldfoodprogramme

Specialized agencies and related organizations

Food and Agriculture Organization of the United Nations (FAO)

The Food and Agriculture Organization of the United Nations (www.fao.org) is the lead agency in the UN system for food security and nutrition; agriculture—including crops, livestock, forestry, fisheries and aquaculture; and rural development. World Food Day, observed annually on 16 October, marks the founding of FAO in 1945 and promotes the themes of food and agriculture. FAO supports its 194 member nations in their efforts to eradicate hunger and poverty and ensure the sustainable use of natural resources. FAO's work centres on five objectives closely aligned with the Sustainable Development Goals of the 2030 Agenda: help eliminate hunger, food insecurity and malnutrition; make agriculture, forestry and fisheries more productive and sustainable; reduce rural poverty; enable inclusive and efficient agricultural and food systems; and increase the resilience of livelihoods to threats and crises. Present in over 130 countries, FAO provides policy and planning advice to governments, collects and disseminates information, and acts as an international forum for debate on food and agriculture issues. Special programmes help countries prepare for emergency food crises and provide relief assistance. Partnerships are at the heart of FAO's mission to help build consensus for a world without hunger. In 2016, FAO managed 1,942 field projects, with a total value of $3.4 billion; 92.5 per cent of that amount was funded by voluntary contributions through trust funds. Every year FAO mobilizes approximately $850 million in new voluntary contributions, accounting for over 60 per cent of its budget.

FAO is governed by its Conference of member nations. Its 49-member elected Council serves as the governing body between sessions of the Conference. FAO has a staff of 11,000 working at headquarters and in the field. Its regular programme budget for 2016–2017 is $1 billion.

Director-General: José Graziano da Silva (Brazil)
Headquarters: Viale delle Terme di Caracalla, 00153 Rome, Italy
Tel.: +39 06 57051 | **Fax:** +39 06 570 53152 | **E-mail:** FAO-HQ@fao.org
Twitter: @unfao | **Facebook:** www.facebook.com/unfao

International Civil Aviation Organization (ICAO)

The International Civil Aviation Organization (www.icao.int) promotes the safe and orderly development of international civil aviation throughout the world. It sets standards and develops regulations necessary for aviation safety, security, efficiency and regularity, as well as for environmental protection. To achieve safe, secure and sustainable development of civil aviation, it relies on the cooperation of its 191 member states. ICAO has an Assembly—its policymaking body—comprising delegates from all contracting states, and a Council of representatives of 36 nations elected by the Assembly. The Council is the executive body, and carries out Assembly directives.

President of the Council: Dr. Olumuyiwa Benard Aliu (Nigeria)
Secretary General: Dr. Fang Liu (China)
Headquarters: 999 Robert Bourassa Boulevard, Montreal, Quebec H3C 5H7, Canada
Tel.: +1 514 954 8219 | **Fax:** +1 514 954 6077 | **E-mail:** icaohq@icao.int
Twitter: @icao | **Facebook:** www.facebook.com/internationalcivilaviationorganization/

International Fund for Agricultural Development (IFAD)

The International Fund for Agricultural Development (www.ifad.org) is dedicated to enabling poor rural people to improve their food and nutrition security, increase their incomes and strengthen their resilience. IFAD mobilizes resources from its 176 member countries to provide low-interest loans and grants to finance rural development. It gives grants instead of loans to poor countries unable to sustain debt to ensure that essential financial assistance does not cause undue financial hardship for those most in need. IFAD works in partnership with governments, other UN agencies, bilateral and multilateral development agencies, international agricultural research centres and the private sector. It maintains strong relationships with civil society organizations, particularly those of smallholder farmers and rural people, as well as NGOs, policy research institutes and universities. The Fund is financed by voluntary contributions from governments, special contributions, loan repayments and investment income. From its inception until the end of 2016, IFAD mobilized $26.1 billion and contributed an additional $18.5 billion for agriculture and rural development. As at 31 December 2016, IFAD was supporting 209 programmes and projects in 96 countries. IFAD's investments reduce poverty by 5.6–9.9 per cent, compared with 3–7 per cent for cash transfer programmes. IFAD's Governing Council is made up of all member states. The Executive Board, which consists of 18 members and 18 alternates, oversees operations and approves loans and grants.

President: Gilbert F. Houngbo (Togo)
Headquarters: Via Paolo di Dono 44, 00142 Rome, Italy
Tel.: +39 06 54 591 | **Fax:** +39 06 504 3463 | **E-mail:** ifad@ifad.org
Twitter: @ifadnews | **Facebook:** ww.facebook.com/ifad

International Labour Organization (ILO)

The International Labour Organization (www.ilo.org) promotes rights at work, encourages decent employment opportunities, enhances social protection and strengthens dialogue on work-related issues. Established in 1919, it was founded on the premise that universal, lasting peace can be established only if it is based on social justice. It became the first specialized agency of the United Nations in 1946. ILO sets labour standards, develops policies and devises programmes promoting decent work for all women and men. Its *International Labour Standards* serve as guidelines for national authorities to put labour policies into action. Extensive technical cooperation programmes help governments make these policies effective, while ILO training, education and research help advance these efforts. ILO is unique among world organizations in that representatives of workers and employers have an equal voice with those of governments in formulating its policies. It is composed of three bodies:

- the International Labour Conference, which brings together government, employer and worker delegates from member countries every year. It sets international labour standards and acts as a forum where social and labour questions of importance to the entire world are discussed;
- the Governing Body, which directs ILO operations, prepares the programme and budget, and examines cases of non-observance of ILO standards; and
- the International Labour Office, which is the permanent secretariat of ILO.

In addition, opportunities for study and training are offered at the International Training Centre in Turin, Italy. ILO publishes cutting-edge research on key labour policy areas and is the world's leading provider of labour statistics. ILO employs 2,700 staff at its Geneva headquarters and in 40 field offices around the world. Its budget for the 2016–2017 biennium amounted to $797.4 million.

Director-General: Guy Ryder (United Kingdom)
Headquarters: 4 route des Morillons, CH-1211, Genève 22, Switzerland
Tel.: +41 22 799 6111 | **Fax:** +41 22 798 8685 | **E-mail:** ilo@ilo.org
Twitter: @ilo | **Facebook:** www.facebook.com/ilo.org

International Monetary Fund (IMF)

Established at the Bretton Woods Conference in 1944, the International Monetary Fund (www.imf.org) facilitates international monetary cooperation; promotes exchange rate stability and orderly exchange arrangements; assists in the establishment of a multilateral system of payments and the elimination of foreign exchange restrictions; and assists members by temporarily providing financial resources to correct maladjustments in their balance of payments. IMF has authority to create and allocate to its members international financial reserves in the form of Special Drawing Rights—IMF's unit of account. The Fund's financial resources consist primarily of the subscriptions ("quotas" determined by a formula based principally on the relative economic size of the members) of its 189 member countries and bilateral arrangements with various members, which totalled $668 billion as at September 2016. A core responsibility of IMF is to provide loans to countries experiencing balance-of-payment problems. This financial assistance enables such countries to rebuild their international reserves, stabilize their currencies, continue paying for imports, and restore conditions for strong economic growth. In return, members borrowing from the Fund agree to undertake policy reforms to correct the problems that underlie these difficulties. The amounts that IMF members may borrow are limited in proportion to their quotas. The Fund also offers concessional assistance to low-income member countries.

The IMF Board of Governors includes all member states. Its day-to-day work is led by its 24-member Executive Board. IMF has a staff of approximately 2,700 from over 148 countries, headed by a Managing Director selected by the Executive Board. The administrative budget for the financial year 2016 was $1.05 billion, and the capital budget was about $42.1 million. IMF publishes the *World Economic Outlook* and the *Global Financial Stability Re*port, along with a variety of other studies.

Managing Director: Christine Lagarde (France)
Headquarters: 700 19th Street NW, Washington, D.C. 20431, USA
Tel.: +1 202 623 7000 | **Fax:** +1 202 623 6220 | **E-mail:** publicaffairs@imf.org
Twitter: @imfnews | **Facebook:** www.facebook.com/imf

International Maritime Organization (IMO)

The International Maritime Organization (www.imo.org), which began functioning in 1959, is responsible for the safety and security of shipping in international trade and for preventing marine and atmospheric pollution from ships. IMO is the global standard-setting authority for the safety, security and environmental performance of international shipping. Its main role is to create a regulatory framework for the shipping industry that is fair and effective, universally adopted and globally implemented. IMO also facilitates the flow of commerce through shipping. Some 50 conventions and agreements and more than 1,000 codes and recommendations have been adopted by IMO. In 1983, it established the World Maritime University in Malmö, Sweden, which provides advanced training for administrators, educators and others involved in shipping at the senior level. The IMO International Maritime Law Institute (Valletta, Malta) was established in 1989 to train lawyers in international maritime law. The Assembly—IMO governing body—consists of all 171 member states and three associate members. It elects the 40-member Council, IMO executive organ. The IMO budget for 2016 totalled £32,618,000. It has a staff of about 300.

> **Secretary-General:** Kitack Lim (Republic of Korea)
> **Headquarters:** 4, Albert Embankment, London SE1 7SR, United Kingdom
> **Tel.:** +44 207 735 7611 | **Fax:** +44 207 587 3210 | **E-mail:** info@imo.org
> **Twitter:** @imohq | **Facebook:** www.facebook.com/IMOHQ

International Telecommunication Union (ITU)

The International Telecommunication Union (www.itu.int) is the specialized agency for information and communication technologies (ICTs). It allocates global radio frequency spectrum and satellite orbits, develops the technical standards that ensure networks and technologies seamlessly interconnect, and strives to improve access to ICTs to underserved communities worldwide. Through its work, ITU protects and supports everyone's fundamental right to communicate. ICTs help manage and control emergency services, water supplies, power networks and food distribution chains. They also support health care, education, government services, financial markets, transportation systems, e-commerce platforms and environmental management. Founded in Paris in 1865 as the International Telegraph Union, ITU took its present name in 1932 and became a UN specialized agency in 1949. It has a membership of 193 countries and more than 700 sector members and associates, including scientific and industrial bodies, public and private companies, regional and international organizations, civil society organizations and academic institutions. ITU governing body, the Plenipotentiary Conference, elects its senior officials, as well as the 48-member ITU Council representing all regions of the world. Based in Geneva, ITU has 700 staff members representing 116 nationalities. For the 2016–2017 biennium it had a budget of CHF 321 million.

> **Secretary-General:** Houlin Zhao (China)
> **Headquarters:** Place des Nations, 1211 Geneva 20, Switzerland
> **Tel.:** +41 22 730 5111 | **Fax:** +41 22 733 7256 | **E-mail:** itumail@itu.int
> **Twitter:** @itu | **Facebook:** www.facebook.com/itu

United Nations Educational, Scientific and Cultural Organization (UNESCO)

Created in 1946, the United Nations Educational, Scientific and Cultural Organization (en.unesco.org) works to create the conditions for dialogue among civilizations, cultures and peoples, based upon respect for commonly shared values and geared towards sustainable development, a culture of peace, observance of human rights and the alleviation of poverty. Within its areas of work, specific concerns include achieving education for all; promoting natural and social science research; supporting the expression of cultural identities; protecting the world's natural and cultural heritage; promoting the free flow of information and press freedom; and strengthening the communication capacities of developing countries. The Organization also has two global priorities, namely Africa and gender equality. In May 2015, following the adoption of the *Incheon Declaration* at the World Education Forum in Korea, UNESCO took on a new role leading the coordination and monitoring of the global *Education 2030* agenda, which is encapsulated in Sustainable Development Goal 4.

UNESCO maintains a system of 199 national commissions and is supported by some 4,000 UNESCO associations, centres and clubs in more than 100 countries. It enjoys official relations with hundreds of NGOs and a range of foundations and similar institutions. It also works with a network of over 10,000 schools worldwide and 700 higher education and research institutions in 128 countries. UNESCO's governing body—the General Conference—is made up of its 195 member states. The Executive Board, consisting of 58 members elected by the Conference, is responsible for supervising the programme adopted by the Conference. UNESCO has a staff of more than 2,000 from some 170 countries. Over 700 of those staff members work in 65 field offices, institutes and centres worldwide. Its approved budget ceiling for 2016–2017 is $667 million.

>**Director-General:** Irina Bokova (Bulgaria)
>**Headquarters:** 7, place de Fontenoy, 75007 Paris 07-SP, France
>**Tel.:** +33 14568 1000 | **Fax:** +33 14567 1690 | **E-mail:** info@unesco.org
>**Twitter:** @unesco | **Facebook:** www.facebook.com/unesco

United Nations Industrial Development Organization (UNIDO)

The United Nations Industrial Development Organization (www.unido.org) promotes industrial development for poverty reduction, inclusive globalization and environmental sustainability. Established by the General Assembly in 1966, it became a UN specialized agency in 1985. UNIDO's mission as described in the *Lima Declaration* adopted at the General Conference in 2013, is to promote and accelerate inclusive and sustainable industrial development (ISID) in developing countries and economies in transition. The relevance of ISID is recognized by the 2030 Agenda for Sustainable Development and the related Sustainable Development Goals (SDGs), including SDG-9, to build resilient infrastructure, promote inclusive and sustainable industrialization and foster innovation. UNIDO focuses on three thematic priorities: creating shared prosperity; advancing economic competitiveness; and safeguarding the environment. It collaborates with governments, the private sector, business associations and other stakeholders to meet complex challenges in industrial development. UNIDO's resource pool includes specialist staff in Vienna working in the fields of engineering, industrial and economic policy, technology and the environment, as well as professional staff in its network of Investment and Technology Promotion Offices, International Technology Centres, and National Cleaner Production Centres in 56 countries.

UNIDO's 170 member states meet at its General Conference to approve its budget and work programme. The Industrial Development Board, comprising 53 member states, makes recommendations relating to the planning and implementation of the programme and budget. In 2015, UNIDO employed more than 663 staff members working at headquarters in Vienna and worldwide in 47 regional and country offices. In 2015, funds available for future implementation amounted to $476 million and the value of technical cooperation delivery rose to $174.7 million.

>**Director General:** Li Yong (China)
>**Headquarters:** Vienna International Centre, Wagramerstrasse 5, P.O. Box 300, 1400 Vienna, Austria
>**Tel.:** +43 1 26026 0 | **Fax:** +43 1 269 2669 | **E-mail:** unido@unido.org
>**Twitter:** @unido.com | **Facebook:** www.facebook.com/unido.hq

World Tourism Organization (UNWTO)

The World Tourism Organization (www.unwto.org) promotes sustainable and universally accessible tourism. Established in 1975, UNWTO became a UN specialized agency in 2003. As the leading international organization in the tourism field, UNWTO promotes tourism as a driver of economic growth, inclusive development and environmental sustainability and offers leadership and support to the sector in advancing knowledge and tourism policies worldwide. It encourages the implementation of the Global Code of Ethics for Tourism, endorsed by the UN General Assembly in 2001, to maximize tourism's socioeconomic contribution, while minimizing its possible negative impacts. UNWTO is committed to promoting tourism as an instrument in achieving the Sustainable Development Goals. UNWTO generates market knowledge; promotes competitive and sustainable tourism policies and instruments; fosters tourism education and training; and works to make tourism an effective tool for development through technical assistance projects in over 100 countries around the world. Its membership includes 163 countries and associate members, two permanent observers and over 500 affiliate members, including local governments, educational institutions, tourism associations and private sector firms. In 2015, the UN General Assembly proclaimed 2017 the International Year of Sustainable Tourism for Development (IY2017) and mandated UNWTO to facilitate its implementation.

UNWTO's General Assembly—its supreme body, made up of full, associate and affiliate members—approves the organization's budget and programme of work, and debates major topics of importance to the tourism sector. The Executive Council, its governing board, is composed of 32 full members elected by the Assembly, and a permanent member, Spain (the host country of UNWTO headquarters). For the 2016–2017 biennium, UNWTO had a staff of 106 and a budget of €27 million.

Secretary-General: Taleb Rifai (Jordan)
Headquarters: Calle Capitán Haya 42, 28020 Madrid, Spain
Tel.: +34 91 567 8100 | **Fax:** +34 91 571 3733 | **E-mail:** omt@unwto.org
Twitter: @unwto | **Facebook:** www.facebook.com/worldtourismorganization

Universal Postal Union (UPU)

The Universal Postal Union (www.upu.int), an intergovernmental organization with 192 member countries, is mandated to ensure universal access to affordable public postal services of the highest standard. Established in 1874, it became a UN specialized agency in 1948. In addition to maintaining a universal network—with physical, financial and electronic dimensions—the UPU establishes the rules for international mail exchanges among its member countries and makes recommendations to modernize products and services, stimulate mail volume growth and improve the quality of service for customers. The global postal network is a formidable infrastructure through which essential public services are provided to millions of citizens and businesses. This enables the postal sector to play a critical role in fueling countries' social and economic development. Postal operators also provide financial, logistics and e-commerce services to countless customers to meet their evolving needs. The Universal Postal Congress is the supreme authority of the UPU, whose annual budget is approximately $37 million. Some 250 staff, drawn from 60 countries, work at the UPU International Bureau in Berne, Switzerland.

Director-General: Bishar A. Hussein (Kenya)
Headquarters: Weltpoststrasse 4, Case Postale 312, 3000 Berne 15, Switzerland
Tel.: +41 31 350 3111 | **Fax:** +41 31 350 3110 | **E-mail:** info@upu.int
Twitter: @universalpostal | **Facebook:** www.facebook.com/universalpostalunion

World Health Organization (WHO)

Established in 1948, the World Health Organization (www.who.int) is the directing and coordinating authority within the UN system for health. WHO is responsible for providing leadership on global health matters; shaping the health research agenda; setting norms and standards; articulating evidence-based policy options; providing technical support to countries; and monitoring and assessing health trends. Its decision-making body is the World Health Assembly, which meets annually and is attended by delegations from all 194 member states. The Executive Board is composed of 34 members technically qualified in the health field. Some 7,000 people from more than 150 countries work for WHO in 150 country offices, its headquarters in Geneva, and its six regional offices in Brazzaville, Congo; Washington, D.C.; Cairo, Egypt; Copenhagen, Denmark; New Delhi, India; and Manila, the Philippines. The programme budget for the biennium 2016–2017 was over $4.5 billion, of which $929 million was financed by the assessed contributions from member states (regular budget), with the remainder coming from voluntary contributions.

Director-General: Dr. Margaret Chan (China)
Headquarters: Avenue Appia 20, 1211 Geneva 27, Switzerland
Tel.: +41 22 791 21 11 | **Fax:** +41 22 791 31 11 | **E-mail:** www.who.int/about/contact_form
Twitter: @who | **Facebook:** www.facebook.com/who

World Intellectual Property Organization (WIPO)

The World Intellectual Property Organization (www.wipo.int) is the global forum for intellectual property services, policy, information and cooperation. Its mission is to lead the development of a balanced and effective international intellectual property (IP) system that enables innovation and creativity for the benefit of all. Established in 1970, WIPO became a UN specialized agency in 1974. It has 189 member states, and administers 26 international treaties. WIPO works with its member states to help governments, businesses and society realize the benefits of IP. It provides a policy forum where governments negotiate and shape international IP rules to meet society's changing needs; global services to protect IP across borders and to resolve disputes; technical infrastructure to make IP systems more efficient and to share knowledge; cooperation and capacity-building programs to enable all countries to use IP for economic, social and cultural development; the world reference source for IP information; and public-private partnerships to address global challenges, such as public health and climate change. WIPO is unusual among UN organizations in that it is almost entirely self-financing. Approximately 94 per cent of WIPO's budget of CHF 707 million for the 2016–2017 biennium came from income generated by services WIPO provides to users of its international IP filing systems (the PCT, Madrid, Hague and Lisbon Systems).

Director-General: Francis Gurry (Australia)
Headquarters: 34 chemin des Colombettes, 1211 Geneva 20, Switzerland
Tel.: +41 22 338 9111 | **Fax:** +41 22 733 5428
Twitter: @wipo | **Facebook:** www.facebook.com/worldipday

World Meteorological Organization (WMO)

The World Meteorological Organization (public.wmo.int), a UN specialized agency since 1951, provides authoritative scientific information on weather, climate and water. WMO coordinates international cooperation in observing and monitoring the state and behaviour of the Earth's atmosphere, its interaction with the land and oceans, the weather and climate it produces, and the resulting distribution of water resources. The national meteorological and hydrological services of WMO's 191 member states and territories work year round to provide daily weather forecasts, as well as, early and reliable warnings of high-impact weather and climate events. These warnings help to save countless lives, protect property and the environment, support planning and decision-making, and minimize the harm that weather, climate and water hazards can cause to socioeconomic development. WMO has a staff of around 300. Its budget for 2016–2019 is CHF 266.2 million.

Secretary-General: Petteri Taalas (Finland)
Headquarters: 7 bis, Avenue de la Paix, Case postale 2300, 1211 Geneva 2, Switzerland
Tel.: +41 22 730 8111 | **Fax:** +41 22 730 8181 | **E-mail:** wmo@wmo.int | **Twitter:** @wmo

Intergovernmental Panel on Climate Change (IPCC)

The Intergovernmental Panel on Climate Change (www.ipcc.ch) is the leading body for the assessment of climate change. It was established by UNEP and WMO to provide a clear scientific view on the state of climate change and its potential environmental and socioeconomic consequences. IPCC reviews and assesses scientific, technical and socio-economic information produced worldwide that is relevant to the understanding of the global climate. It does not conduct its own scientific research, nor does it monitor data. The IPCC secretariat is hosted by WMO at its Geneva headquarters and has a staff of 13. IPCC is open to all UN and WMO member countries; 195 countries are IPCC members. Its Bureau and Chair are elected in plenary sessions.

Chair: Hoesung Lee (Republic of Korea)
Head of Secretariat: Abdalah Moksitt (Morroco)
Secretariat: c/o World Meteorological Organization, 7 bis, Avenue de la Paix, C.P. 2300, 1211 Geneva 2, Switzerland
Tel.: +41 22 730 8208 | **Fax:** +41 22 730 8025 | **E-mail:** IPCC-Sec@wmo.int
Twitter: @ipcc_CH | **Facebook:** www.facebook.com/ipcc

World Bank Group

The World Bank Group (www.worldbank.org/) consists of five institutions:

- the International Bank for Reconstruction and Development (IBRD, founded in 1944);
- the International Finance Corporation (IFC, 1956);
- the International Development Association (IDA,1960);
- the International Centre for Settlement of Investment Disputes (ICSID, 1966); and
- the Multilateral Investment Guarantee Agency (MIGA,1988).

The term "World Bank" refers specifically to two of the five institutions: IBRD and IDA. The goal of the Bank is to reduce poverty around the world by strengthening the economies of poor nations and improving people's living standards by promoting economic growth and development. In 2015, for the first time ever, the World Bank Group forecast that the global percentage of people living in extreme poverty fell under 10 per cent. The Bank has set two goals for the world to achieve by 2030: end extreme poverty by decreasing the percentage of people living on less than $1.90 a day to no more than 3 per cent; and promote shared prosperity by bolstering the income growth of the bottom 40 per cent for every country. The Bank orients its lending and capacity-building activities on two pillars for development: building a climate for investment, jobs, and sustainable growth; and investing in poor people and empowering them to participate in development.

The World Bank Group is owned by its 189 member countries, which constitute its Board of Governors. General operations are delegated to a smaller group, the Board of Executive Directors, with the President of the Bank serving as Chairman of the Board. At the end of fiscal year 2016, the institutions of the World Bank Group together had a full-time staff of about 11,000 professionals and administrative personnel from some 174 countries. In fiscal year 2016, the World Bank Group provided $64.2 billion in loans, grants, equity investments, and guarantees to partner countries and private businesses. As at 31 January 2017, lending projects the Bank had been involved in since its inception totalled 12,773 in 173 countries. Among its major publications are the annual *World Development Report* and *Doing Business*.

President: Jim Yong Kim (United States)
Headquarters: 1818 H Street NW, Washington, D.C. 20433, USA
Tel.: +1 202 473 1000 | **Fax:** +1 202 477 6391 | **E-mail:** pic@worldbank.org
Twitter: @worldbank | **Facebook:** www.facebook.com/worldbank

International Bank for Reconstruction and Development (IBRD)

The International Bank for Reconstruction and Development (www.worldbank.org/en/about/what-we-do/brief/ibrd)—the original institution of the World Bank Group—seeks to reduce poverty in middle-income and creditworthy poorer countries by promoting sustainable development through loans, guarantees, risk management products, and analytical and advisory services. IBRD is structured like a cooperative owned and operated for the benefit of its 189 member countries. It raises most of its funds on the world's financial markets. The income that the Bank has generated over the years has allowed it to fund development activities and ensure its financial strength, which enables it to borrow at low cost and offer good borrowing terms to its clients. The amount paid in by countries when they join the Bank constitutes about 5 per cent of IBRD's subscribed capital, which has been used to fund hundreds of billions of dollars in development loans since the Bank was established. In fiscal year 2016, IBRD's new loan commitments amounted to $29.7 billion, covering 114 operations.

International Development Association (IDA)

The International Development Association (ida.worldbank.org) is the World Bank's fund for the poorest. One of the world's largest sources of aid, IDA, with 173 member states, provides support for health and education, infrastructure and agriculture, and economic and institutional development to 77 of the world's poorest countries, 39 of which are in Africa. With IDA's help, hundreds of millions of people have escaped abject poverty through the creation of jobs, access to clean water, food security, schools, roads, and electricity. IDA lends money on concessional terms, with credits of zero or very low interest charge and repayments stretched over 25 to 40 years, including a 5- to 10-year grace period. It also provides grants to countries at risk of debt distress, as well as significant levels of debt relief. Since its establishment in 1960, IDA has provided $312 billion for investments in 112 countries. In fiscal year 2016, new IDA commitments amounted to $16.2 billion for 161 operations, including $14.4 billion in credits, $1.3 billion in grants, and $500 million in guarantees. IDA is replenished every three years by both developed and developing country donors, as well as by two other World Bank Group organizations—the International Bank for Reconstruction and Development and the International Finance Corporation.

International Finance Corporation (IFC)

The International Finance Corporation (www.ifc.org) is the largest global development institution focused on the private sector in developing countries. It helps developing countries achieve sustainable growth by financing private sector investment, mobilizing capital in international financial markets, and providing advisory services to businesses and governments. IFC, which has 184 member countries, joins in an investment only when it can make a special contribution that complements the role of market investors.

It also plays a catalytic role by helping introduce innovative solutions to development challenges; helping influence development policies and raise environmental and social standards; demonstrating that investments in challenging markets can be profitable; and improving lives. In fiscal year 2016, IFC long-term investment commitments totalled $18.8 billion, including $7.7 billion mobilized from investment partners. IFC investments in fragile and conflict-affected areas climbed to nearly $1 billion, an increase of more than 50 per cent over the previous year.

Multilateral Investment Guarantee Agency (MIGA)

The mandate of the Multilateral Investment Guarantee Agency (www.miga.org) is to promote foreign direct investment in developing countries by providing guarantees (political risk insurance) to investors and lenders. Its subscribed capital comes from its 181 member countries. In fiscal year 2016, MIGA issued a record $4.3 billion in political risk and credit enhancement guarantees underpinning various investments, with 45 per cent of its active portfolio in IDA-eligible countries and 10 per cent in countries affected by conflict and fragility.

International Centre for Settlement of Investment Disputes (ICSID)

The International Centre for the Settlement of Investment Disputes (icsid.worldbank. org), which has 153 member countries, aims to foster increased flows of international investment by providing a neutral international forum for the resolution of disputes between governments and foreign investors. ICSID administers procedures for the settlement of such disputes where both the host and the home country of the investor are ICSID members, and upon request by the parties or the tribunals involved in other dispute-settlement proceedings. It appoints arbitrators and administers proceedings conducted under the Arbitration Rules of the UN Commission on International Trade Law. ICSID also maintains a publications programme in the area of foreign investment law.

Preparatory Commission for the Comprehensive Nuclear-Test-Ban Treaty Organization (CTBTO)

The Comprehensive Nuclear-Test-Ban Treaty (CTBT) was adopted and opened for signature in 1996. It prohibits all nuclear explosions everywhere, by anyone and for all times. As at September 2016, 183 states had signed the *Treaty* and 166 had ratified it. Of the 44 nuclear-technology-holding States whose ratification is needed for the *Treaty*'s entry into force, eight have yet to ratify: China, the Democratic People's Republic of Korea (DPRK), Egypt, India, Iran, Israel, Pakistan and the United States. India, the DPRK and Pakistan have also yet to sign the *Treaty*. The Vienna-based Preparatory Commission for the Comprehensive Nuclear-Test-Ban Treaty Organization (CTBTO) (www.ctbto.org) is tasked with building up the Treaty verification regime so that it will be fully operational when the *Treaty* enters into force. Its mandate also includes promoting the signature and ratification of the *Treaty*. The CTBT verification regime consists of a globe-spanning network of 337 facilities monitoring the Earth for signs of a nuclear explosion; an International Data Centre for processing and analysis; and on-site inspections to collect evidence on the ground in the case of a suspicious event. The organization has an annual budget of around $130 million. It employs over 270 staff from more than 80 countries.

Executive Secretary: Lassina Zerbo (Burkina Faso)
Headquarters: Vienna International Centre, P.O. Box 1200, 1400 Vienna, Austria
Tel.: +43 1 26030 6200 | **Fax:** +43 1 26030 5823 | **E-mail:** info@ctbto.org
Twitter: @ctbto_alerts | **Facebook:** www.facebook.com/ctbto

International Atomic Energy Agency (IAEA)

The International Atomic Energy Agency (www.iaea.org) is the world's centre for coop-eration in the nuclear field, working to prevent the spread of nuclear weapons and to help all countries—especially those in the developing world—benefit from the peaceful, safe and secure use of nuclear science and technology. IAEA also serves as the global platform for strengthening nuclear safety and security. IAEA verifies states' compliance with their non-proliferation obligations and in 2015, its inspectors conducted 2,118 in-field verifica-tions in over 1,200 sites in 181 states to verify that nuclear material was not being diverted from peaceful purposes. IAEA helps transfer knowledge and expertise to its 168 member states to ensure greater access to energy, improve human health, increase food production, improve access to clean water and protect the environment. The Agency was established in 1957 as an autonomous entity under the aegis of the United Nations.

IAEA's governing bodies include the General Conference, which meets annually and consists of all member states, and the 35-member Board of Governors, which meets quarterly and makes major policy decisions. The Director General oversees a secretariat of over 2,500 staff, with headquarters in Vienna, Austria. IAEA's regular budget, €361 million in 2016, is funded primarily by annual assessments. These are augmented by voluntary contributions, which finance also the Technical Cooperation Fund, and had a target of €84.5 million in 2016.

Director General: Yukiya Amano (Japan)
Headquarters: P.O. Box 100, Wagramerstrasse 5, 1400 Vienna, Austria
Tel.: +43 1 2600 0 │ **Fax:** +43 1 2600 7 │ **E-mail:** Official.Mail@iaea.org
Twitter: @iaeaorg │ **Facebook:** www.facebook.com/iaeaorg

International Organization for Migration (IOM)

Established in 1951, the International Organization for Migration (www.iom.int) is the leading intergovernmental organization in the field of migration and is committed to the principle that humane and orderly migration benefits migrants and society. IOM provides services and advice to governments and migrants and works with its partners in the inter-national community to assist in meeting the growing operational challenges of migration; advance understanding of migration issues; encourage social and economic development through migration; and uphold the well-being and human rights of migrants. IOM has 166 member states, eight states with observer status and offices in over 100 countries. In 2015, the number of international migrants worldwide—people residing in a country other than their country of birth—was the highest ever recorded, having reached 244 million.

Director General: William Lacy Swing (United States)
Headquarters: 17, Route des Morillons, CH-1211 Geneva 19, Switzerland
Tel.: +41 22 717 9111 │ **Fax:** +41 22 798 6150 │ **E-mail:** hq@iom.int
Twitter: @unmigration │ **Facebook:** www.facebook.com/unmigration

Organisation for the Prohibition of Chemical Weapons (OPCW)

The Organisation for the Prohibition of Chemical Weapons (www.opcw.org) is an in-dependent international organization in close working relationship with the United Nations. It monitors the implementation of the *Convention on the Prohibition of the Development, Production, Stockpiling and Use of Chemical Weapons and on their De-struction*. The *Convention*, which entered into force in 1997, is the first multilateral disarmament and non-proliferation agreement that provides for the global elimination of an entire category of weapons of mass destruction in accordance with a stringent international verification regime.

OPCW is composed of 192 member states. Since 1997, member states have verifiably destroyed more than 67,000 metric tons of chemical agents—approximately 93 per cent of the total declared quantity of more than 72,000 metric tons. OPCW inspectors have conducted over 6,194 inspections on the territory of over 86 states parties. These missions ensure that chemical weapons production facilities are deactivated and destroyed or verifiably converted to permitted purposes, and prevent the re-emergence of chemical weapons. Inspectors also verify the destruction of chemical weapons through their presence at destruction facilities. All OPCW member states are obliged to assist one another if they are threatened or attacked with chemical weapons. To handle such a contingency, OPCW regularly tests and enhances its capacity to coordinate a swift and effective international response aimed at protecting lives, as well as to efficiently investigate allegations of the use of chemical weapons or toxic chemicals used as weapons. OPCW also has a range of international cooperation programmes to facilitate the peaceful uses of chemistry. The OPCW Technical Secretariat, based in The Hague, the Netherlands, has a staff of over 450, representing some 70 nationalities. Its budget for 2016 was around €67 million.

Director-General: Ahmet Uzümcü (Turkey)
Headquarters: Johan de Wittlaan 32, 2517 JR, The Hague, The Netherlands
Tel.: +31 70 416 3300 | **Fax:** +31 70 306 3535 | **E-mail:** media@opcw.org
Twitter: @opcw | **Facebook:** www.facebook.com/opcwonline/

World Trade Organization (WTO)

The World Trade Organization (www.wto.org) is the only international organization dealing with global trade rules between nations. Established in 1995, its aim is to help trade flow as smoothly as possible in a system based on multilateral rules agreed to by all its members, settle trade disputes between governments, review trade policy of individual members, as well as globally, and provide a forum for trade negotiations. At its heart are the WTO agreements, negotiated and signed by the bulk of the world's trading nations, which provide the legal ground rules for international commerce. The principles on which these agreements are based include non-discrimination, transparency, more open trade, encouraging competition, and special provisions for less developed countries.

WTO is the forum for negotiations among its members to achieve reform of the international trading system through lower barriers and revised trade rules. Significant reforms in the global trading system include, the Trade facilitation Agreement, the Information Technology Agreement and a deal to abolish export subsidies in agriculture, which delivered on a key target of the UN Sustainable Development Goals. Meanwhile, negotiations known as the Doha Development Agenda, launched in 2001, are ongoing. WTO also continues to oversee implementation of the agreements reached in the 1986–1994 Uruguay Round of world trade talks. Since 1995, over 500 trade disputes have been brought to WTO's dispute settlement mechanism.

WTO has 164 members. Its governing body is the Ministerial Conference; the General Council carries out the day-to-day work. WTO's budget for 2016 was CHF 197 million. WTO employs some 647 staff.

Director-General: Roberto Azevêdo (Brazil)
Headquarters: Centre William Rappard, Rue de Lausanne 154, 1211 Geneva 21, Switzerland
Tel.: +41 22 739 5111 | **Fax:** +41 22 731 4206 | **E-mail:** enquiries@wto.org
Twitter: @wto | **Facebook:** www.facebook.com/worldtradeorganization

A female military police officer from the Nepalese contingent
at the MINUSCA ceremony commemorating International Peacekeepers Day
(29 May) in the Central African Republic. As at February 2017,
there were 4,097 women serving in UN peace operations worldwide
(28 May 2016, UN Photo/Nektarios Markogiannis).

One of the primary purposes of the United Nations is the maintenance of international peace and security. Since its creation, the UN has been called upon to prevent disputes from escalating into war, persuade opposing parties to use peaceable means rather than force of arms to settle disputes, or help restore peace when armed conflict does break out. Over the decades, the UN has helped prevent or end numerous conflicts and foster reconciliation, including in Cambodia, Colombia, El Salvador, Guatemala, Guinea, Liberia, Mozambique, Namibia, Nepal, Sierra Leone, Tajikistan and Timor-Leste. While the Security Council is the primary organ for dealing with issues of international peace and security, the General Assembly and the Secretary-General also play important, complementary roles. UN activities cover the principal areas of conflict prevention, peacemaking, peacekeeping, enforcement and peacebuilding (www.un.org/en/sections/what-we-do/maintain-international-peace-and-security).

New global threats have emerged in the 21st century. Civil conflicts have raised complex issues regarding the adequate response of the international community, including how best to protect civilians in conflicts. The United Nations has revitalized the use of preventive diplomacy; reshaped and strengthened its peacekeeping capacity to meet new challenges; enhanced its partnerships with regional and sub-regional organizations; expanded the use of political missions mandated to prevent and resolve conflicts or facilitate political transitions; and enhanced its post-conflict peacebuilding capacities. In addressing civil conflicts, the Security Council has authorized complex and innovative peacekeeping and political missions. These have provided the time and space for building the foundations of sustainable peace, enabled millions of people in dozens of countries to participate in free and fair elections, and helped disarm half a million ex-combatants in the past decade alone.

At the end of the 1990s, continuing crises in the Central African Republic, the Democratic Republic of the Congo, Kosovo, Sierra Leone and Timor-Leste led the Council to establish five new missions. The surge in peacekeeping reached an apex in 2009–2010, when more than 100,000 UN peacekeepers—known as "blue helmets"—were deployed globally. Recurring conflicts over recent years have brought the United Nations to focus increasingly on conflict prevention and peacebuilding, with targeted efforts to reduce a country's risk of lapsing or relapsing into conflict. Lasting peace depends on pulling together all resources to help countries foster economic development, social justice, respect for human rights, accountable political and security institutions, and good governance. No other institution has the global legitimacy, multilateral experience, competence, coordinating ability and impartiality that the United Nations brings in support of these tasks. The United Nations has established special political missions and offices in a number of countries, including Afghanistan, Burundi, Colombia, Cyprus, Guinea-Bissau, Iraq, Lebanon, Libya, Somalia, Syria and Yemen. Regional missions have also been deployed to Central Africa, Central Asia, and West Africa and the Sahel region.

UN efforts to maintain international peace and security are also directed towards the challenges and dangers of international terrorism and weapons of mass destruction. Member states, through the General Assembly and the Security Council, are coordinating counter-terrorism efforts through activities delivered through UN system programmes, offices and agencies. The Organization has placed a high priority on multilateral disarmament. Through sustained efforts, the world community has achieved numerous multilateral agreements on disarmament and arms limitation. These include treaties and protocols on reducing and eliminating nuclear weapons, destroying chemical weapons, prohibiting biological weapons and halting the proliferation of small arms and light weapons. The scope of these negotiations continues to change as the international environment evolves, bringing further new security challenges.

ROLE OF PRINCIPAL ORGANS

Security Council

The *Charter of the United Nations*—an international treaty—obligates member states to settle their disputes by peaceful means, in such a manner that international peace, security and justice are not endangered. They are to refrain from the threat or use of force against any state, and may bring any dispute before the Security Council: the UN organ with primary responsibility for maintaining peace and security. Under the *Charter*, member states are obliged to accept and carry out its decisions. Recommendations of other UN bodies do not have the mandatory force of Security Council decisions, but can influence situations by expressing the opinion of the international community.

When a dispute is brought to its attention, the Security Council usually urges the parties to settle it peacefully. The Council may make recommendations to the parties for a peaceful settlement, appoint special representatives, ask the Secretary-General to use his good offices, or undertake investigation and mediation. When a dispute leads to fighting, the Council seeks to bring it to an end as quickly as possible. Often the Council has issued ceasefire directives that have been instrumental in preventing wider hostilities. In support of a peace process, the Council may deploy military observers or a peacekeeping force to an area of conflict.

Under Chapter VII of the *Charter*, the Security Council is empowered to take measures to enforce its decisions. It can impose embargoes and sanctions, or authorize the use of force to ensure that mandates are fulfilled. In some cases, the Council has authorized the use of military force by a coalition of member states or by a regional organization or arrangement. However, the Security Council takes such action only as a last resort, when peaceful means of settling a dispute have been exhausted, and after determining that a threat to the peace, a breach of the peace or an act of aggression actually exists. Many of the recently established peacekeeping operations have been authorized by the Council in this way, meaning that the peacekeepers may use force if needed to implement their mandates. Also under Chapter VII of the *Charter*, the Security Council has established international tribunals to prosecute those accused of gross violations of human rights and serious breaches of international humanitarian law, including genocide.

General Assembly

Article 11 of the *Charter of the United Nations* empowers the General Assembly to "consider the general principles of cooperation in the maintenance of international peace and security" and "make recommendations ... to the Members or to the Security Council or to both". The Assembly offers a means for finding consensus on difficult issues, providing a forum for the airing of grievances and diplomatic exchanges. To foster the maintenance of peace, it has held special sessions or emergency special sessions on such issues as disarmament, the question of Palestine and the situation in Afghanistan. The General Assembly considers peace and security issues in its First Committee (Disarmament and International Security Committee) and in its Fourth Committee (Special Political and Decolonization Committee). Over the years, the Assembly has helped promote peaceful relations among nations by adopting declarations on peace, the peaceful settlement of disputes and international cooperation.

The Assembly in 1980 approved the establishment in San Jose, Costa Rica, of the **University for Peace** (www.upeace.org), an international institute for study, research and dissemination of knowledge on peace-related issues. The Assembly has designated 21 September each year as the **International Day of Peace**.

CONFLICT PREVENTION

The opening words of the *Charter* "To save succeeding generations from the scourge of war" have never appeared as urgent or as challenging. Long-simmering disputes have escalated or relapsed into wars, while new conflicts have emerged in countries and regions once considered stable. Violent crises are drawing unprecedented levels of international engagement. United Nations special political missions and peacekeeping operations today deploy more than 128,000 people in 39 missions—more than at any time in their history. However, the proliferation of conflict is outpacing UN efforts. Missions are struggling to cope with the spread and intensity of conflicts, and unity among member states is more important than ever.

The 2015 report of the High-level Independent Panel on Peace Operations provided a solid foundation upon which the UN could tackle such profound challenges. It calls for peaceful political settlement to be restored to the centre of UN efforts to prevent and resolve conflicts and protect civilians. It emphasizes partnerships with regional organizations, host governments and local communities to achieve these goals and stresses the need for new approaches to prevent conflicts and mediate disputes before violence erupts.

The prevention of conflict is at the heart of the mission of the United Nations. Preventive diplomacy is the cornerstone of UN action to forestall conflict or keep confrontations from escalating, under the Secretary-General's good offices mandate, and may take the form of mediation, conciliation or negotiation. Early warning is an essential component of prevention, and the UN carefully monitors developments worldwide to detect threats to international peace and security, thereby enabling the Security Council and the Secretary-General to carry out preventive action. Envoys and special representatives of the Secretary-General, including the heads of many special political missions, are engaged in mediation and preventive diplomacy throughout the world. The presence of a skilled envoy can often help prevent the escalation of tension. This work is often undertaken in cooperation with regional or sub-regional organizations.

The Secretary-General plays a central role in peacemaking, both personally and by dispatching special envoys or missions for specific tasks, such as negotiation or fact-finding. Under the *Charter*, the Secretary-General may bring to the attention of the Security Council any matter that might threaten the maintenance of international peace and security. The UN Department of Political Affairs (www.un.org/undpa) is the principal support structure for those efforts, planning and supporting the work of peace envoys, providing conflict analysis and overseeing more than a dozen field-based political missions that serve as key platforms for preventive diplomacy. The UNITAR Peacemaking and Conflict Prevention Programme (unitar.org/pmcp), which delivers innovative training in negotiation and mediation, also enhances the effectiveness of UN efforts in conflict prevention and resolution.

In partnership with UN development actors, including UNDP and UN Resident Coordinators on the ground, DPA works to ensure that UN programmatic activities in the field are conflict sensitive and contribute to the development of national capacities for conflict prevention. To ensure the inclusion and participation of women in its work related to conflict prevention and resolution, DPA has taken on fifteen specific women, peace and security agenda commitments, including those relating to mediation, women's political participation and addressing conflict-related sexual violence.

PEACEKEEPING

United Nations peacekeeping operations (www.un.org/en/peacekeeping) are a vital instrument employed by the international community to advance peace and security. While not specifically envisaged in the *Charter of the United Nations*, the UN pioneered peacekeeping in 1948 with the establishment of the United Nations Truce Supervision Organization in the Middle East. Since then, it has established a total of 71 operations, 16 of which were active at the end of December 2016.

Peacekeeping operations are deployed with the authorization of the Security Council and the consent of the host government and/or the main parties to the conflict. Peacekeeping was originally a primarily military model of observing ceasefires and the separation of forces after inter-state wars. Today, it has evolved into a complex model of many elements—military, police and civilians—working together to help lay the foundations of a sustainable peace.

In recent years, the Council has introduced the practice of invoking the enforcement provisions in Chapter VII of the *Charter* when authorizing the deployment of certain UN peacekeeping operations, or mandating them to perform tasks which may require the use of force, such as the protection of civilians under imminent threat of physical violence. Originally, UN peacekeepers could only use their weapons in self-defence, but the more "robust" mandates under Chapter VII enable them to use force in the exercise of their mandates, for example, their mandate to protect civilians.

The United Nations has no military force of its own. The military personnel of peacekeeping operations are provided voluntarily and financed by member states. Operations are directed by the Secretary-General, usually through a special representative. Depending on the mission, a Force Commander is responsible for the operation's military aspects, but military contingents answer to their own national defence entities. They wear their country's uniform with a UN blue helmet or beret and a badge. Civilian staff of missions is recruited or volunteer from around the world.

Peacekeeping operations are financed through the peacekeeping budget and include troops from many countries. Member states are assessed under the budget, and troop-contributing states are compensated at a standard rate. The approved peacekeeping budget for 2016–2017 was approximately $7.9 billion—which represents less than 0.5 per cent of global military spending. This worldwide "burden-sharing" can offer extraordinary efficiency in human, financial and political terms.

Current peacekeeping operations. As at 31 December 2016, 100,376 military and police personnel from 125 countries were serving in the following 16 peacekeeping operations:

- United Nations Truce Supervision Organization (UNTSO, est. 1948), in the Middle East (148 military observers; 234 civilians);
- United Nations Military Observer Group in India and Pakistan (UNMOGIP, est. 1949) (44 military observers; 72 civilians);
- United Nations Peacekeeping Force in Cyprus (UNFICYP, est. 1964) (862 troops; 67 police; 151 civilians);
- United Nations Disengagement Observer Force (UNDOF, est. 1974), in the Syrian Golan Heights (787 troops; 140 civilians);

- United Nations Interim Force in Lebanon (UNIFIL, est. 1978) (10,497 troops; 848 civilians);
- United Nations Mission for the Referendum in Western Sahara (MINURSO, est. 1991) (23 troops; 193 military observers; 241 civilians; 4 UN Volunteers);
- United Nations Interim Administration Mission in Kosovo (UNMIK, est. 1999) (8 military observers; 7 police; 328 civilians; 19 UN Volunteers);
- United Nations Mission in Liberia (UNMIL, est. 2003) (1,171 troops; 62 military observers; 570 police; 1,159 civilians; 138 UN Volunteers);
- United Nations Operation in Côte d'Ivoire (UNOCI, est. 2004) (2,601 troops; 142 military observers; 759 police; 961 civilians; 93 UN Volunteers);
- United Nations Stabilization Mission in Haiti (MINUSTAH, est. 2004) (2,360 troops; 2,326 police; 1,245 civilians; 83 UN Volunteers);
- African Union-United Nations Hybrid Operation in Darfur (UNAMID, est. 2007) (13,608 troops; 162 military observers; 3,293 police; 3,412 civilians; 141 UN Volunteers);
- United Nations Organization Stabilization Mission in the Democratic Republic of the Congo (MONUSCO, est. 2010) (16,797 troops; 475 military observers; 1,392 police; 3,470 civilians; 364 UN Volunteers);
- United Nations Interim Security Force for Abyei (UNISFA, est. 2011) (4,403 troops; 128 military observers; 15 police; 202 civilians; 30 UN Volunteers);
- United Nations Mission in South Sudan (UNMISS, est. 2011) (12,099 troops; 188 military observers; 1,454 police; 2,002 civilians; 404 UN Volunteers);
- United Nations Multidimensional Integrated Stabilization Mission in Mali (MINUSMA, est. 2013) (10,358 troops; 39 military observers; 1,295 police; 1,246 civilians; 145 UN Volunteers);
- United Nations Multidimensional Integrated Stabilization Mission in the Central African Republic (MINUSCA, est. 2014) (10,242 troops; 149 military observers; 2,022 police; 760 civilians; 154 UN Volunteers).

Since 1948, 3,520 peacekeepers have lost their lives in the line of duty.

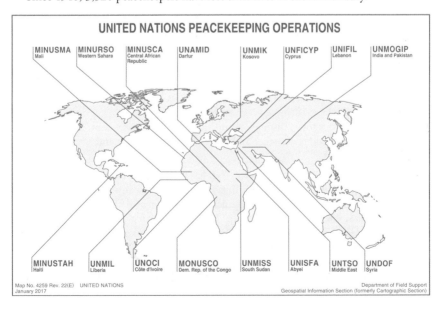

UNITED NATIONS PEACEKEEPING OPERATIONS

MINUSMA Mali · MINURSO Western Sahara · MINUSCA Central African Republic · UNAMID Darfur · UNMIK Kosovo · UNFICYP Cyprus · UNIFIL Lebanon · UNMOGIP India and Pakistan

MINUSTAH Haiti · UNMIL Liberia · UNOCI Côte d'Ivoire · MONUSCO Dem. Rep. of the Congo · UNMISS South Sudan · UNISFA Abyei · UNTSO Middle East · UNDOF Syria

Map No. 4259 Rev. 22(E)   UNITED NATIONS
January 2017

Department of Field Support
Geospatial Information Section (formerly Cartographic Section)

With 65 million people forcibly displaced, armed conflict today is impacting the lives of a record number of people. An estimated 30 to 40 per cent of political violence is directed against civilians, affecting a disproportionate number of children and women. The tripling of civil wars between 2007 and 2014, particularly in the Middle East and in West Africa, has resulted in a surge of global, conflict-related fatalities. In these environments, a new generation of armed groups has gained strength from instability. Operating independently of each other, but within networks that straddle borders and draw on transnational organized crime, these groups defy traditional state-based responses. Achieving durable political settlements in these settings will be an enduring challenge for the international community, and in particular for UN peacekeeping operations.

The regionalization of conflict continues to pose significant challenges, in conflicts both new and old. The spill-over of conflict across borders is abetted by information technology and is often linked to criminal networks. Recent conflicts have involved a deadly mix of civil strife and the illegal import/export of resources, such as diamonds, cultural artifacts and arms. The response must be equally multifaceted. International unity around a common strategy to resolve or manage conflict, with regional and global actors pursuing conflicting interests, has been elusive in environments such as South Sudan or Syria. Greater efforts are also required to develop and implement regional strategies that respond to the fluidity and mobility of transnational threats. In the case of illegally trafficked conflict minerals, for example, the Kimberley Process Certification Scheme (KPCS) (www.kimberleyprocess.com/en/about) was introduced by the General Assembly in 2000 to prevent diamond sales from financing conflict and human rights violations. KPCS aims at preventing "blood diamonds" from entering the mainstream market.

United Nations operations, because of their universality, offer unique legitimacy as a means of addressing conflicts. Peacekeepers from outside a conflict can foster discussion among warring parties while focusing global attention on local concerns, opening doors that would otherwise remain closed for collective peace efforts. Prerequisites for the success of an operation include a genuine desire on the part of the opposing forces to resolve their differences peacefully, a clear peacekeeping mandate, strong political support by the international community, and the provision of the financial, uniformed and human resources necessary to achieve the operation's objectives. Most importantly, peacekeeping must accompany a political process; it cannot substitute for one.

Peacekeeping operations continuously evolve in light of changing circumstances. The tasks discharged by peacekeepers over the years have included:

- maintaining ceasefires and separation of forces;
- protecting humanitarian operations;
- implementing a comprehensive peace settlement;
- leading states or territories through a transition to stable government, based on democratic principles, good governance and economic development; and
- protecting civilians.

High-level panel on peace operations. The changing and increasingly complex roles of peacekeeping operations, and the increasingly dangerous and austere environments into which they are deployed, have posed considerable challenges for the Organization in executing mandates safely and effectively. In 2014 the Secretary-General commissioned a High-Level Independent Panel on Peace Operations (HIPPO) (un.org/en/peacekeeping/operations/reform.shtml) to undertake a thorough review of UN peace operations, including peacekeeping operations and special political missions. The Panel's June 2015 report laid the groundwork for UN peacekeeping to become more effective, efficient and responsive to the needs of the populations served by missions. It presented four essential shifts to:

- *the primacy of politics* and that political solutions must guide all UN peace operations;
- *responsive operations* and that UN missions should be tailored to context;
- *stronger partnerships* and the need for a more resilient global and regional architecture for international peace and security; and
- *field-focused and people-centered* operations with UN Headquarters focusing more on enabling field missions and UN personnel renewing their resolve to serve and protect the people.

The report strengthened a number of ongoing reform agendas, including efforts to improve the performance of peacekeeping operations, make better use of technology, improve efforts to protect civilians and strengthen community engagement. It also renewed efforts to strengthen management and accountability for the conduct and discipline of UN personnel.

The Panel's report is recognized as a document which resets the direction of UN peace operations, peacekeeping and special political missions. The Panel's call for a renewed collective commitment to delivering a people-centered approach to peace operations, mindful that political solutions must be at the core of the UN peace and security strategies, has resonated across the international community. In that connection, the agenda for action contained in the Secretary-General's September 2015 report to implement the HIPPO recommendations continues to be carried out by DPKO and DFS, in collaboration with partners across the UN system. The Secretariat's work is focused on three themes: prevention, partnerships and improving the planning and conduct of peace operations.

Cooperation with regional and collective security organizations. In line with Chapter VIII of the *Charter*, the United Nations has increasingly cooperated with regional organizations and mechanisms in geographic and thematic areas of peacekeeping. It works closely with the African Union (www.au.int), the European Union (europa.eu), the North Atlantic Treaty Organization (www.nato.int), the Organization for Security and Co-operation in Europe (www.osce.org), and the Organization of American States (www.oas.org), to name a few. The UN has strengthened its partnership with such organizations in a broad range of thematic issues, including rapid response, security sector reform, training and exercises, modern technologies, logistics support, women, peace and security, and many others. As global demand for peace operations currently outstrips the capacity of any single actor, including the UN, the development of partnerships continues to gain significance. The UN has also established dedicated liaison offices based in Brussels, Vienna and Addis Ababa to support and strengthen partnership efforts and streamline UN Secretariat presences in the headquarters of regional organizations.

ENFORCEMENT

Under Chapter VII of the *Charter*, the Security Council can take enforcement measures to maintain or restore international peace and security. Such measures range from economic sanctions to international military action.

Sanctions

Sanctions measures, adopted under Chapter VII (Article 41) of the *Charter*, encompass a broad range of enforcement options that do not involve the use of force (www.un.org/sc/suborg/en/sanctions). Since 1968, the Security Council has established 30 sanctions committees to oversee its sanctions regimes, of which 13 remain ongoing, with respect to: the Central African Republic; the Democratic People's Republic of Korea; the Democratic Republic of the Congo; Guinea-Bissau; Iraq; ISIL (Da'esh) & Al-Qaida and associated individuals, groups, undertakings and entities; events in Lebanon; Libya; Somalia and Eritrea; South Sudan; the Sudan; the Taliban; and Yemen.

UN sanctions have taken a number of different forms. The measures have ranged from comprehensive economic and trade embargoes to specific commodity bans and arms embargoes, as well as measures targeting designated individuals and entities, such as travel bans and asset freezes. The Security Council has applied sanctions to support peaceful transitions, deter non-constitutional changes of government, counter terrorism, protect human rights and promote non-proliferation. Contrary to the assumption that sanctions are punitive, many sanctions regimes are part of a comprehensive strategy encompassing peacekeeping, peacebuilding and peacemaking and are designed to support governments and regions working towards peaceful transition.

Concerns about the adverse impact of comprehensive economic sanctions on the most vulnerable segments of the civilian population have led to improvements in the design and application of sanctions. Since 2003, all new sanctions regimes have been targeted. Measures are applied with respect to specifically designated individuals and entities. Similarly, trade restrictions imposed since that time have been limited to specific commodities.

The Council applies sanctions with ever-increasing cognizance of the importance of due process for those targeted and the need to ensure that fair and clear procedures are in place for the imposition and lifting of sanctions measures and for the granting of humanitarian exemptions. The establishment of a focal point for de-listing, and the Office of the Ombudsperson to the ISIL (Da'esh) & Al-Qaida Sanctions Committee are examples of this approach in practice.

Authorizing military action

When peacemaking efforts fail, stronger action by member states may be authorized under Chapter VII of the *Charter*. The Security Council has authorized coalitions of member states to use "all necessary measures", including military action to deal with conflict—as it did to restore the sovereignty of Kuwait after its invasion by Iraq (1991); to establish a secure environment for humanitarian relief operations in Somalia (1992); to restore the democratically elected government in Haiti (1994); to protect humanitarian operations in Albania (1997); to restore peace and security in East Timor (1999 and 2006); and to protect civilians in Libya (2011). These actions, although authorized by the Security Council, were entirely under the control of the participating states. They were not UN peacekeeping operations, which are established by the Council and directed by the Secretary-General.

PEACEBUILDING

For the United Nations, peacebuilding includes a range of measures targeted to reduce the risk of violent conflict—by strengthening national capacities at all levels for conflict management—and to lay the foundation for sustainable peace and development. The UN focuses on a country's own ability to overcome the forces that may lead to violent conflict. While the exact nature of peacebuilding depends on the different circumstances in each country, efforts generally include strengthening safety, security, justice and public administration; supporting dialogue and reconciliation; providing basic services; and revitalizing the economy. Peacebuilding involves action by the General Assembly, Security

Council, and Economic and Social Council, as well as a wide array of UN system organizations and offices, including field operations, specialized agencies and international financial institutions. There are three types of political and peacebuilding missions: field-based; special envoys; and sanctions panels and monitoring groups of the Security Council.

Peacebuilding has played a prominent role in UN operations in Afghanistan, Bosnia and Herzegovina, Cambodia, El Salvador, Guatemala, Iraq, Liberia, Libya, Mozambique and Sierra Leone. Inter-state peacebuilding was guided by the UN Mission in Ethiopia and Eritrea.

Peacebuilding architecture

The UN peacebuilding architecture comprises the Peacebuilding Commission, an intergovernmental advisory body; the Peacebuilding Fund, a unique financing mechanism; and the Peacebuilding Support Office, an analytical and coordinating capacity.

The **Peacebuilding Commission** (www.un.org/peacebuilding) is a 31-member intergovernmental advisory body of the United Nations dedicated to helping countries build peace. It brings together all relevant peacebuilding actors, including international donors and financial institutions, governments, troop-contributing countries and representatives of civil society; proposes integrated strategies for peacebuilding and recovery; helps ensure predictable financing for early recovery activities and sustained financial investment; extends the period of attention by the international community; and develops good practices on issues that require collaboration among political, military, humanitarian and development actors.

The **Peacebuilding Fund** (www.unpbf.org) is a multi-year standing fund for peacebuilding supported by voluntary contributions. The Fund supports more than 120 projects in over 25 countries and acts as an investor of first resort in countries emerging from conflict. It delivers immediate aid when other funds are not yet available to countries at risk of descending into violent conflict. Its specialists also provide guidance to ensure well-coordinated, conflict-sensitive and politically-astute programming. Contributions to the Fund in 2015 totalled $53.5 million; the Fund had a cumulative total of $732.4 million in commitments in January 2017.

The **Peacebuilding Support Office** (www.un.org/en/peacebuilding/pbso) supports the Peacebuilding Commission, administers the Peacebuilding Fund and assists the Secretary-General in developing peacebuilding policies for the UN system and in coordinating UN entities in their peacebuilding efforts.

Current political and peacebuilding missions. As at 31 January 2017, there were 4,823 personnel serving in the following 11 field-based political and peacebuilding missions:

- Office of the United Nations Special Coordinator for the Middle East Peace Process (UNSCO, est. 1999) (58 civilians);
- United Nations Office for West Africa and the Sahel (UNOWAS, est. 2001) (63 civilians; 2 military advisers);
- United Nations Assistance Mission in Afghanistan (UNAMA, est. 2002) (1,618 civilians; 12 military advisers; 5 police advisers; 66 UN Volunteers);
- United Nations Assistance Mission for Iraq (UNAMI, 2003) (staff based in Iraq, Jordan and Kuwait: 873 civilians; 245-member guard unit; 5 military advisers; 4 police advisers);
- Office of the United Nations Special Coordinator for Lebanon (UNSCOL, est. 2007) (82 civilians);

- United Nations Regional Centre for Preventive Diplomacy for Central Asia (UNRCCA, est. 2007) (32 civilians);
- United Nations Integrated Peacebuilding Office in Guinea-Bissau (UNIOGBIS, est. 2010) (137 civilians; 2 military advisers; 13 police; 6 UN Volunteers);
- United Nations Office for Central Africa (UNOCA, est. 2011) (38 civilians; 2 military advisers; 1 police adviser);
- United Nations Support Mission in Libya (UNSMIL, est. 2011) (197 civilians; 7 police; 3 UN Volunteers);
- United Nations Assistance Mission in Somalia (UNSOM, est. 2013) (265 civilians; 530-member guard unit);
- United Nations Mission in Colombia (est. 2016) (280 unarmed military observers, set to rise to 450; 277 civilians)

For a list of previous political and peacebuilding missions, visit the DPA website (www.un.org/undpa/en/past-political-missions).

ELECTORAL ASSISTANCE

Electoral assistance is one of the most high profile and politically sensitive activities (www.un.org/undpa/en/elections) of the UN. The UN currently assists approximately 70 member states, 8 of which are under a Security Council mandate. More than 100 countries have requested and received election assistance since 1991 when the General Assembly created the current institutional and policy framework, which includes the Under-Secretary-General for Political Affairs as the UN system focal point for electoral assistance. UN assistance can involve a wide range of activities, but usually takes the form of technical assistance, that is, the provision of advice and assistance on the legal, technical, administrative, and human rights aspects of conducting democratic

Following presidential elections on 20 November 2016, MINUSTAH Chilean peacekeepers collect election materials from Anjou, a small town in the mountains above Haiti's capital, Port au Prince (22 November 2016, UN Photo/Nektarios Markogiannis).

elections. Assistance can also entail financial or material support, as well as logistical, security and transportation support, the latter typically in a peacekeeping context.

UN entities involved in electoral assistance include DPA, DPKO, OHCHR, UNDP, UNOPS, UN-Women and the UN Volunteers programme. UN assistance is provided at the request of member states or on the basis of a legislative mandate only. The decision if, and how, to provide assistance, is made by the focal point, on the basis of a needs assessment carried out by the **Electoral Assistance Division in the Department of Political Affairs**. Such assessments also serve as a political risk management tool.

UN electoral assistance respects the sovereignty of member states, recognizes the diversity of democratic practices, and views an election as a mechanism to arrive at a legitimate representation of the people. The UN rarely undertakes electoral observation, and only with a mandate from the General Assembly or Security Council. Demand for UN assistance is strong and evolving.

During the 1990s, the UN organized or observed landmark elections and popular consultations in Cambodia, El Salvador, Mozambique, South Africa and Timor-Leste. More recently, it has provided crucial technical and logistical assistance in milestone elections in Afghanistan, Burundi, the Democratic Republic of the Congo, Iraq, Nepal, Sierra Leone and the Sudan. Most UN member state elections are peaceful and produce results which are broadly accepted.

BUILDING PEACE THROUGH DEVELOPMENT

Healthy and balanced development is the best form of conflict prevention. The United Nations aims to consolidate peace through development assistance. Organizations including UNDP, UNICEF, UNHCR and WFP play key roles in the recovery stage, which is crucial for providing opportunities for displaced persons and restoring confidence in national and local institutions. The United Nations can help repatriate refugees, clear landmines, repair infrastructure, mobilize resources and stimulate economic recovery.

ACTION FOR PEACE

United Nations peacekeeping, political and peacebuilding missions are underway throughout the world—in Africa, Asia and the Pacific (including the Middle East), the Americas and Europe. Current operations are described below in their historical context. For a full list of past and present peacekeeping missions, see p. 253.

Africa

Africa is an area of major focus and action for the United Nations (www.un.org/en/africa/osaa). The Organization has addressed the challenges posed by protracted conflicts and longstanding disputes on the continent in innovative ways and at the highest level. Envoys and special representatives of the Secretary-General, including the heads of many special political missions, are engaged in mediation, preventive diplomacy or other peace and security related activities (www.un.org/sg/en/content/africa). The UN also plays a key role in providing support to the African Union (AU) to consolidate peace, security and good governance in Africa.

Great Lakes region

In February 2013, 11 countries signed the Peace, Security and Cooperation (PSC) Framework for the Democratic Republic of the Congo (DRC) and the region, which outlines key national, regional, and international level actions required to end the recurring cycles of violence in eastern DRC and the region. It also aims to help address the root causes of conflict. Kenya and the Sudan became signatories of the PSC Framework in 2014. The **Office of the Special Envoy for the Great Lakes Region** (ungreatlakes.unmissions.org) provides support to the countries that are signatories of the Framework, as well as to its implementation.

Burundi

A decade of civil strife in Burundi (1993–2003) left between 250,000 and 300,000 people dead and several hundred thousand displaced. By mid-2003, ceasefire agreements were signed with three major factional groups. The African Union (AU) authorized deployment of the African Mission in Burundi (AMIB), comprising up to 3,500 troops. By the end of April 2003, midway through the transitional period, President Ndayizeye (Hutu) and Vice-President Alphonse-Marie Kadege (Tutsi) were sworn in. However, deadly attacks continued to take place in Bujumbura, Burundi's capital, and the UN was forced to withdraw its nonessential staff from the city. Sustained efforts by South Africa and other countries in the region resulted in a ceasefire agreement in November. AMIB's presence was instrumental in establishing peace. The Mission suffered from a serious lack of funds and logistics support, however, and the AU requested the UN to take over AMIB's functions. In 2004, the Security Council authorized the deployment of the United Nations Operation in Burundi (ONUB)—to be composed, initially, of more than 2,000 AMIB troops re-branded as UN forces. In 2005, a referendum on Burundi's post-transitional constitution was held, followed by communal elections in June, and the election of the country's first post-transitional president in August. A ceasefire agreement was signed in September, which the UN helped implement.

In January 2007, ONUB was replaced by the United Nations Integrated Office in Burundi (BINUB), to support the peace consolidation process and assist the government. In January 2011, the **United Nations Office in Burundi (BNUB)** replaced BINUB. In February 2013, the Security Council extended the BNUB mandate until 15 February 2014 and asked it to support the government in facilitating dialogue between national actors; strengthening national institutions; fighting impunity; promoting and protecting human rights; supporting the socioeconomic development of women and youth, as well as the reintegration of conflict-affected populations; and increasing Burundi's regional integration. At the request of the Government of Burundi, BNUB closed on 31 December 2014. The **United Nations Electoral Observation Mission in Burundi (MENUB)** was established on 1 January 2015 for a period of one year.

Political discord and violence erupted in April when President Pierre Nkurunziza announced his intention to run for another term. While the crisis crystallized around the elections, it had deeper political roots. In November, the Secretary-General appointed Jamal Benomar (United Kingdom) as his Special Adviser for Conflict Prevention (including Burindi) and deployed a team in Burundi to help find a peaceful settlement to the crisis through support to the regional mediation efforts. He also submitted options on the configuration of a future UN presence in the country. MENUB concluded its mandate on 18 November and its operations drew to a close on 31 December 2015.

In July 2016, the Security Council authorized the deployment of a UN police component of 228 police officers in Burundi, under the authority of the Office of the Special Adviser, to monitor the security and human rights situation in the country for an initial period of one year.

Democratic Republic of the Congo

Following the 1994 genocide in Rwanda and the establishment of a new government there, some 1.2 million Rwandan Hutus—including elements that had taken part in the genocide—fled to the neighbouring Kivu provinces of the Democratic Republic of the Congo (DRC), formerly Zaïre. A rebellion began in those provinces in 1996. Forces led by Laurent Désiré Kabila, aided by Rwanda and Uganda, took the capital city of Kinshasa in 1997 and renamed the country the Democratic Republic of the Congo. In 1998, a rebellion against the Kabila government, led by the Congolese Rally for Democracy (RCD), started in the Kivu regions. The rebels, supported by Rwanda and Uganda, seized large areas of the country. Angola, Chad, Namibia and Zimbabwe promised President Kabila military support, but the rebels maintained their grip on the eastern regions. The Security Council called for a ceasefire and the withdrawal of foreign forces. In early 1999, the DRC, along with Angola, Namibia, Rwanda, Uganda and Zimbabwe, signed the Lusaka Ceasefire Agreement, which provided for the holding of an inter-Congolese dialogue. The RCD and the Mouvement de Libération du Congo signed it in August. The Council subsequently established the United Nations Mission in the Democratic Republic of the Congo (MONUC) to assist in implementing the agreement.

In January 2001, President Kabila was assassinated and was succeeded by his son Joseph. In October, the inter-Congolese dialogue began in Addis Ababa, Ethiopia. In July 2002, an agreement was signed by the DRC and Rwanda on the withdrawal of Rwandan combatants from the DRC. In September, a similar agreement was reached between the DRC and Uganda. By the end of the year, the parties to the conflict, under UN and South African mediation, agreed to form a transitional government. The Security Council enlarged MONUC to 8,700 military personnel and expanded its presence eastward, but fighting erupted in South Kivu, generating massive refugee flows. Finally, in May 2003, the parties signed a ceasefire agreement for the Ituri region. Following the ceasefire, the Council authorized deployment of an Interim Emergency Multinational Force (IEMF) to Bunia, the capital city of the Ituri province, to help stabilize the situation. In June 2003, the government and the country's main opposition factions signed an agreement on military and security arrangements, and subsequently, a power-sharing government of national unity and transition was installed—led by President Kabila. The Council increased MONUC's military strength to 10,800. Acting under Chapter VII of the *Charter of the United Nations*, it authorized the mission to use force to fulfil its mandate in Ituri and North and South Kivu. In September, IEMF handed over its security responsibilities to MONUC.

The country's first free and fair elections in 46 years were held in July 2006, with voters electing a 500-seat National Assembly. Joseph Kabila won a run-off election for the presidency in October. The electoral process represented one of the most complex votes the UN had ever helped organize.

Through MONUC, the UN remained actively involved in trying to resolve the conflict in North Kivu between the army and dissident forces. In July 2010, MONUC became the **United Nations Organization Stabilization Mission in the Democratic Republic of the Congo (MONUSCO)** (monusco.unmissions.org), reflecting the new phase reached in the country. The Council decided that MONUSCO would comprise, in addition to its civilian and judiciary components, a maximum of 19,815 military personnel, 760 military observers, 391 police personnel and 1,050 members of formed police units. Future reconfigurations of MONUSCO would be determined as the situation evolved, including: the completion of military operations in North and South Kivu as well as the Orientale provinces; improved government capacity to protect the population; and the consolidation of state authority throughout the DRC. In June 2012, the Council decided that the Mission would provide technical and logistical support for the organization and holding of provincial and local elections.

On 20 November 2012, after intense fighting involving the DRC armed forces and MONUSCO, the former National Congress for the Defence of the People (CNDP)—later known as the Mouvement du 23 mars (M23)—occupied Goma; it withdrew from the city on 2 December. The situation in the eastern DRC remained fragile, as M23 elements further consolidated their control over a significant portion of North Kivu.

In February 2013, the Peace, Security and Cooperation (PSC) Framework for the DRC and the region was signed in Addis Ababa, Ethiopia, by representatives of 11 countries in the region, the AU, the International Conference on the Great Lakes Region, the Southern African Development Community and the UN Secretary-General. In March, the Security Council extended MONUSCO's mandate until 31 March 2014 and created an "intervention brigade" to strengthen the peacekeeping operation. The brigade would be set up for an initial period of one year within the Mission's authorized troop ceiling.

In 2015 and 2016, in support of reform, dialogue and electoral processes, the Council strengthened MONUSCO's political mandate, stressing the use of its good offices to encourage dialogue among Congolese stakeholders and create conditions conducive to the holding of peaceful, credible and transparent elections. It also extended the mandate until 31 March 2017 and underlined that the protection of civilians should remain a priority.

West Africa

In 2001, the Secretary-General decided to establish the **Office of the Special Representative of the Secretary-General for West Africa (UNOWA)** to promote an integrated, subregional strategy, involving the UN and its partners, to address the interlinked political, economic and social problems faced by West African countries. Based in Dakar, Senegal, UNOWA became operational in 2002. It was the first UN regional peacebuilding office. In January 2016, following the strategic review of the Office of the Special Envoy for the Sahel, the Security Council requested the merger of the two offices. The new entity, the **United Nations Office for West Africa and the Sahel (UNOWAS)** (unowas.unmissions.org), is headed by the Secretary General's Special Representative for West Africa and the Sahel. It works with the UN system in West Africa and the Sahel to support the efforts of regional and sub-regional organizations—Economic Community of West African States (ECOWAS), AU, Lake Chad Basin Commission, the G-5 Sahel, Gulf of Guinea Commission and Mano River Union—to promote peace, stability and good governance, including gender mainstreaming in conflict prevention initiatives. UNOWAS also helps countries in West Africa and the Sahel to address a broad range of peace and stability challenges, such as growing socioeconomic inequalities, increased transnational organized crime, illicit drug trafficking, and continued insecurity in the Lake Chad Basin due to the activities of Boko Haram, and in the Sahel due to the activities of armed and terrorist groups. The Special Representative encourages further collaboration between the concerned member states and regional organizations, with UN support, to help address the underlying drivers of conflict related to lack of development, social exclusion, and weak governance. As the Secretary General's High Representative to Nigeria, the Special Representative continues to mobilize international and regional partners to support the Nigerian authorities in finding a lasting solution to the Boko Haram menace.

The Special Representative also serves as chairperson of the **Cameroon-Nigeria Mixed Commission (CNMC)** (unowas.unmissions.org/cameroon-nigeria-mixed-commission), established by the Secretary-General at the request of the Presidents of Nigeria and Cameroon, to consider all aspects of the implementation of an October 2002 ruling by ICJ on the boundary between the two countries. Achievements to date include the withdrawal of Nigeria and transfer of authority to Cameroon in the Lake Chad area (2003), along the land boundary (2004) and in the Bakassi Peninsula (a process completed in 2008); the end of the special transitional regime of five years (2006); the delineation of the maritime boundary (2007); and the exercise by Cameroon of full rights of sovereignty over the Bakassi zone (2013). The CNMC is currently focused on completing the remaining demarcation activities, such as pillar construction, final mapping of the boundary and the implementation of confidence-building measures for the affected population.

Boko Haram attacks. In April 2014, the Security Council condemned the terrorist attacks committed in Nigeria on 13 and 14 April by an Islamic extremist group, Jama'atu Ahlis Sunna Lidda'awati Wal-Jihad (known as "Boko Haram"), causing numerous deaths and injuries. Based in northeastern Nigeria, yet also active in northern Cameroon, Chad and Niger, as at November 2016, the group was estimated to have killed at least 20,000 people and displaced 2.6 million from their homes in its six-year insurgency. Territorial advances by the governments of Cameroon, Chad, Niger and Nigeria against Boko Haram, including through the Multinational Joint Task Force (MNJTF) were commended by the Council in May 2016. As at January 2017, although 10.7 million people were in need of humanitarian assistance, and 2.4 million people were displaced, there was hope that 2017 would prove to be a turning point for the people affected by the crisis. The nature of the conflict was changing and more areas were coming under Government control. In Cameroon, UNHCR was ensuring protection and assistance to some 370,000 refugees and asylum-seekers, mainly from the Central African Republic and Nigeria.

Côte d'Ivoire

In September 2002, military personnel attempted a coup in Côte d'Ivoire and occupied the northern part of the country. The coup failed in Abidjan, but succeeded elsewhere resulting in a de facto partition of the country, with the government of President Laurent Gbagbo controlling only the south. The fighting caused massive displacements. The Economic Community of West African States (ECOWAS) established a peace-keeping force in Côte d'Ivoire (ECOMICI) to monitor a ceasefire agreement between the government and one of the country's rebel groups. In May 2003, the government and the remaining rebel groups agreed to a ceasefire. The same month, the Security Council established the United Nations Mission in Côte d'Ivoire (MINUCI) to facilitate implementation of the agreement. A peace agreement was reached and President Gbagbo established a national reconciliation government in March 2004. Two months later, the army and the Forces nouvelles—comprising three rebel groups—signed a ceasefire agreement.

Responding to this situation, the Security Council, in early 2004, established the **United Nations Operation in Côte d'Ivoire (UNOCI)** (onuci.unmissions.org), asking the Secretary-General to transfer authority from MINUCI and the ECOWAS forces to UNOCI, and authorizing the French troops in the country to use all necessary means to support the new Mission, which had an authorized maximum strength of 6,240 military personnel and a wide-ranging mandate.

In April 2005, the government and the rebel Forces nouvelles began a withdrawal of weapons from the "zone of confidence" on both sides of the frontline—an area held by peacekeepers of UNOCI and the UN-authorized French forces. President Gbagbo and Forces nouvelles secretary-general Guillaume Soro signed the "Ouagadougou Political Agreement" in March 2007. It called for the creation of a new transitional government; free and fair presidential elections; merging the Forces nouvelles with the national defence forces; dismantling the militias; and replacing the zone of confidence separating the government-controlled south and rebel-controlled north with a "green line" to be monitored by UNOCI.

Presidential elections were held in November 2010 and the Independent Electoral Commission declared Alassane Ouattara the winner. The President of the Constitutional Council, however, stated that the results were invalid, and declared Mr. Gbagbo the winner. Both candidates claimed victory and took the presidential oath of office. The UN, AU, ECOWAS, EU and most states recognized Mr. Ouattara as President-elect and called for Mr. Gbagbo to step down. Mr. Gbagbo refused and ordered UN peacekeepers to leave the country. The Security Council extended UNOCI's mandate until the end of June 2011, and decided to send 2,000 supplementary peacekeepers. The World Bank halted loans to the country and travel restrictions were placed on Mr. Gbagbo and his allies.

In April 2011, following military operations conducted by forces loyal to President-elect Ouattara, UNOCI and French troops, Mr. Gbagbo was arrested and placed in government custody. The Constitutional Council ratified the results of the presidential election showing that Mr. Ouattara had won, reversing its 2010 decision in favour of Mr. Gbago. In May 2011, Mr. Ouattara was sworn in as President. In November, the International Criminal Court (ICC) issued an arrest warrant against Mr. Gbagbo for crimes against humanity, and he was transferred by Ivorian authorities to the ICC detention centre at The Hague.

In April 2016, the Security Council extended UNOCI's mandate for a final period until 30 June 2017.

Guinea-Bissau

In June 2009, the **United Nations Integrated Peacebuilding Office in Guinea-Bissau (UNIOGBIS)** (uniogbis.unmissions.org) was established. It succeeded the United Nations Peacebuilding Support Office in Guinea-Bissau, which was launched in March 1999 following a period of conflict in the country. Unrest occurred again in April 2010, when the Prime Minister and the Army Chief of Staff were briefly detained by soldiers, and in April 2012, when a military coup d'état gave rise to a transitional period. Since the legislative and presidential elections of 2014, governance has continued to be paralyzed as the President, the Speaker of the National Assembly and four succeeding Prime Ministers have sparred over the separation of powers under the country's semi-presidential constitutional system. In this critical context, the Special Representative of the Secretary-General in Guinea-Bissau and Head of UNIOGBIS has facilitated and supported a mediation process led by ECOWAS. ECOWAS mediated a six-point roadmap, which was signed by the key political stakeholders in September 2016, and an October accord (Conakry Agreement) aimed at implementing the roadmap. The agreements call for the appointment of a Prime Minister and formation of an inclusive government, and foresee the conduct of a national dialogue and the adoption of constitutional, electoral, justice and security sector reforms to be implemented before the general elections in 2018. Beyond their support for implementation of the roadmap, UNIOGBIS and the UN Peacebuilding Commission work to strengthen the capacity of national institutions to maintain constitutional order and respect for the rule of law; support the establishment of law enforcement and criminal justice systems; support the development and implementation of the security sector reform strategy; and promote human rights in general and women's rights in particular. UNIOGBIS cooperates with AU, the Community of Portuguese-language Countries (CPLP), ECOWAS, the EU, and other partners.

In February 2017, the Security Council extended the UNIOGBIS mandate until 28 February 2018.

Liberia

After eight years of civil strife, a democratically elected government was installed in Liberia in 1997, and the United Nations Peacebuilding Support Office in Liberia (UNOL) was established. In 1999, however, fighting broke out between government forces and the Liberians United for Reconciliation and Democracy (LURD). In early 2003, a new armed group emerged—the Movement for Democracy in Liberia (MODEL). By May, rebel forces controlled 60 per cent of the country. As the parties gathered on 4 June in Accra, Ghana, for peace talks sponsored by ECOWAS, the Special Court for Sierra Leone jointly established by the Government and the United Nations unsealed its indictment of Liberian President Charles Taylor for war crimes in Sierra Leone during its 10-year civil war. Subsequently, the President agreed to step down and leave Liberia. Two weeks later, the government, LURD and MODEL signed a ceasefire accord, aiming to reach a comprehensive peace agreement within 30 days and the formation of a transitional government without President Taylor. Despite that promising development, the fighting escalated, and ECOWAS deployed a vanguard force of over 1,000 troops (ECOMIL).

President Taylor resigned in mid-August and left the country for asylum in Nigeria; Vice-President Moses Blah succeeded him, heading an interim government. A few days later, the Secretary-General's special representative secured an agreement by the parties to ensure unimpeded access of humanitarian aid to all territories under their control, and to guarantee the security of aid workers. The parties also signed a comprehensive peace agreement.

In September 2003, the Security Council established the **United Nations Mission in Liberia (UNMIL)** (unmil.unmissions.org)—with up to 15,000 military personnel and over 1,000 civilian police officers—to take over from the ECOWAS force, and replace UNOL. Its mandate included: monitoring the ceasefire; assisting in the disarmament, demobilization, reintegration and repatriation of armed parties; providing security at key government installations and vital infrastructure; protecting UN staff, facilities and civilians; assisting in humanitarian aid and human rights; and helping the transitional government consolidate its institutions with a view to holding free and fair elections by October 2005. In October 2003, 3,500 ECOWAS soldiers were "rehatted" under UNMIL and the national transitional government was installed, led by Chairman Gyude Bryant. Former President Blah turned over a large quantity of arms to UN peacekeepers. In late 2004, Liberia's warring militias formally disbanded in a ceremony at UNMIL headquarters.

In October 2005, after 15 years of conflict, the people of Liberia, with UN assistance, held their first post-war elections, electing Ellen Johnson-Sirleaf as President—the first female president of an African country—who took office in January 2006. By the end of February, more than 300,000 internally displaced Liberians had returned to their home villages. In 2007, Liberia became eligible to receive assistance from the UN Peacebuilding Fund and was placed on the agenda of the Peacebuilding Commission in 2010. The funding was allocated to projects that consolidated peace, addressed insecurity and catalyzed the nation's broader development.

In December 2016, the Security Council extended the mandate of UNMIL for a final period until 30 March 2018; ordered a reduction of its remaining military component to a ceiling of 434 personnel and its police strength to 310 police officers by 28 February 2017; and requested the Secretary-General to withdraw all uniformed and civilian UNMIL components other than those required to complete the Mission's liquidation by 30 April 2018.

Mali

In 2012, Mali became a significant source of international concern. In mid-January, the Tuareg Mouvement national pour la libération de l'Azawad (MNLA), along with Islamic armed groups including Ansar Dine, Al-Qaida in the Islamic Maghreb (AQIM) and the Mouvement pour l'unicité et le jihad en Afrique de l'Ouest (MUJAO), as well as deserters from the Malian armed forces, attacked government forces in the north of the country. In March, a mutiny by disaffected soldiers from defeated units resulted in a military coup d'état. A military junta took power, suspended the Constitution and dissolved Government institutions. On 27 March, ECOWAS appointed President Blaise Compaoré of Burkina Faso to mediate in the crisis. On 6 April, the military junta and ECOWAS signed a framework agreement that led to the resignation of President Amadou Toumani Touré on 8 April, and the appointment of Dioncounda Traoré as interim President on 12 April. On 17 April, Cheick Modibo Diarra was appointed interim Prime Minister.

MNLA overran government forces in the Kidal, Gao and Timbuktu regions and proclaimed an independent state of Azawad in April. Ideological tensions later emerged among the armed groups in the north and, by 18 November, Ansar Dine and MUJAO had driven MNLA out of the main towns of Kidal, Gao, and Timbuktu. Those groups then controlled two thirds of Malian territory. Some 430,000 people were displaced as a result of the crisis.

In December 2012, the Security Council authorized the deployment of an African-led International Support Mission in Mali (AFISMA) to, among other tasks, support the Malian defence forces in protecting the population and assist with stabilization activities. The Secretary-General was asked to establish a multidisciplinary UN presence in Mali to support the political and security processes underway. However, in January 2013, when Ansar Dine, AQIM and MUJAO advanced southwards and captured Konna, the transitional authorities requested French assistance.

The **United Nations Office in Mali (UNOM)** began its deployment to the Malian capital, Bamako, on 21 January. UNOM assisted Malians to achieve a broad-based, national dialogue leading to national elections. On 29 January, the Malian Parliament approved a road map for the transition. On 25 April, the Security Council established the **United Nations Multidimensional Integrated Stabilization Mission in Mali (MINUSMA)** (minusma.unmissions.org). On 18 June, the transitional Government and the armed groups signed the Ouagadougou Preliminary Agreement, which provided, among other things, the cessation of hostilities and the launch of an inclusive dialogue. UNOM was subsumed into MINUSMA and the Mission took over AFISMA operations on 1 July, retaining many of its personnel. Mali held presidential elections later that month and Ibrahim Boubacar Keïta was elected in a run-off in August.

In May 2014, following violent clashes in Kidal in the context of a visit by the Malian Prime Minister to the town, armed groups repelled the Malian armed forces who subsequently withdrew from northern Mali. Concerted efforts by the President of Mauritania, then Chairman of the African Union, and the Special Representative of the Secretary-General brought both sides to sign a ceasefire agreement on 23 May. In June, in anticipation of peace negotiations, armed groups organized themselves in two coalitions – the Coordination des mouvements de l'Azawad (CMA) and the Plateforme préliminaire d'Alger en vue du dialogue inclusif inter-malien (Plateforme). Starting in July 2014, an international mediation team led by the Government of Algeria and comprising Mali's neighbours, together with international organizations, including MINUSMA, mediated the inter-Malian talks between the Government and the two coalitions. MINUSMA was instrumental in brokering cessations of hostilities and defusing tensions on the ground as hostilities broke out several times during the talks. On 20 June 2015, the three parties signed the Agreement for Peace and Reconciliation in Mali, which provided for institutional and security sector reforms, development programmes as well as justice and reconciliation efforts.

Delays in the implementation of the political and institutional provisions of the agreement—notably the establishment of interim administrations, and violations of the ceasefire—stalled the implementation of the Agreement, including the redeployment of Malian Defense and Security Forces. This led to a severe deterioration of the security environment including an increase in the number of asymmetric attacks against peacekeepers. Twenty-seven peacekeepers died as a result of hostile attacks between 1 January and 31 December 2016 compared to 12 in 2015.

In June 2016, the Security Council renewed the mandate of MINUSMA for one year to support implementation of the peace agreement and the gradual restoration and extension of state authority as its strategic priority. It asked the Mission to adopt a more proactive and robust posture and authorized an increase in up to 13,289 military and 1,920 police personnel.

Central and East Africa

The **United Nations Regional Office for Central Africa (UNOCA)** (unoca.unmissions.org) was established in March 2011 in Libreville, Gabon, with an initial two-year mandate to assist member states and subregional organizations in consolidating peace and preventing potential conflicts. UNOCA is headed by the Acting Special Representative of the Secretary-General for Central Africa, François Louncény Fall (Guinea). Based on a strategic review of UNOCA conducted in 2015 and the ensuing recommendations of the Secretary-General, the following objectives were approved by the Security Council for the Office: monitor political developments in Central Africa; carry out good offices and special assignments on behalf of the Secretary-General; enhance subregional capacities for conflict prevention and mediation in countries of the subregion; support UN efforts in the subregion as well as regional and subregional initiatives on peace and security; enhance coherence and coordination of UN work in the subregion on peace and security; and advise the Secretary-General and UN entities in the region on significant developments in Central Africa. In July 2015, the Security Council renewed UNOCA's mandate until 31 August 2018.

Central African Republic

The conflict in the Central African Republic began in the mid-1990s as elements within the armed forces staged a series of mutinies. In 1998, to help improve security, the UN Security Council established the United Nations Mission in the Central African Republic (MINURCA), succeeded in 2000 by the UN Peacebuilding Support Office in the Central African Republic (BONUCA).

In March 2003, a rebel military group ousted the elected president and seized power. The Council condemned the coup, stressing that the authorities had to elaborate a plan for national dialogue, including a timeframe for the holding of elections. A process of national dialogue led to two rounds of legislative and presidential elections in 2005. In the final runoff, François Bozizé, who had led the coup, was elected President. The newly elected National Assembly held its first regular session in mid-2006.

BONUCA played a significant role in encouraging the signing in 2008 of the Global Peace Agreement between the government and three main rebel groups. It also facilitated the holding in December 2008 of the Inclusive Political Dialogue between the government, leaders of rebel groups, exiled political opponents, civil society and other stakeholders.

In 2009, the United Nations Integrated Peacebuilding Office in the Central African Republic (BINUCA) succeeded BONUCA and operated under a mandate from the Security Council to help consolidate peace and national reconciliation, strengthen democratic institutions to promote the rule of law, and mobilize international political support and resources for national reconstruction and economic recovery. It also promoted public awareness of human rights issues.

In late 2012, a rebel coalition known as Séléka seized large parts of the country. Agreements to resolve the crisis were signed in January 2013 in the Gabonese capital Libreville, under the aegis of the Economic Community of Central African States. BINUCA provided logistical and technical support to the talks among the warring parties. In the ensuing months, however, the security situation in the country deteriorated. The Security Council authorized the intervention of French (Sangaris) and African Union (MISCA) forces in December 2013. In April 2014, the Council authorized the establishment of the **United Nations Multidimensional Integrated Stabilization Mission in the Central African Republic (MINUSCA)** (minusca.unmissions.org), which subsumed BINUCA. With the support of the Mission, a Cessation of Hostilities Agreement was signed in July 2014 in Brazzaville under the auspices of the President of the Congo, Denis Sassou Nguesso, in his role as the International Mediator for the Central African Republic. The agreement initiated a process amongst all political stakeholders and armed groups to end the violence and return stability to the country to through peaceful transition. In September 2014, the Council transferred the authority from MISCA to MINUSCA.

The Mission supported the Central African Republic authorities in implementing key milestones of the transition, including: a constitutional referendum on 13 December 2015 in which 93 per cent of voters approved the new Constitution; the first round of presidential and legislative elections on 30 December; and the second round of presidential elections on 14 February 2016. On 30 March, Faustin Archange Touadéra was inaugurated as President, thereby formally ending the transition. MINUSCA's mandate was renewed until 15 November 2017, with the objective of working towards the sustainable reduction of armed groups while maintaining its core tasks of protecting civilians, facilitating the delivery of humanitarian assistance and protecting human rights.

Somalia

The people of Somalia have been living without a functioning state since 1991, when the government was overthrown and civil war broke out, dividing the country into fiefdoms controlled by rival warlords. Arms, ammunition and explosives flowed freely across Somalia's borders in breach of a UN embargo. When talks organized by the Secretary-General led to a ceasefire in the capital, Mogadishu, the Security Council in April 1992 established the United Nations Operation in Somalia (UNOSOM I) to monitor the ceasefire; provide protection and security for UN personnel, equipment and supplies; and escort deliveries of humanitarian supplies. The deteriorating security situation, however, led the Council in December to authorize member states to form a Unified Task Force (UNITAF) to ensure the safe delivery of humanitarian assistance. In March 1993, the Council established UNOSOM II to complete UNITAF's efforts to restore peace, but the escalation of inter-clan fighting led to the withdrawal of the Operation in March 1995.

In April 1995, the Secretary-General established the United Nations Political Office for Somalia (UNPOS) to help him advance peace and reconciliation through contacts with Somali leaders, civic organizations, and concerned states and organizations. UNPOS supported a Djibouti initiative that led, in 2000, to the formation of a Transitional National Government, but its authority was subsequently challenged by Somali leaders in the south, and by regional administrations in "Puntland" in the north-east, and "Somaliland" in the north-west.

In 2002, a national reconciliation conference sponsored by the Intergovernmental Authority on Development (IGAD) led to agreement on a cessation of hostilities and on structures and principles to govern the national reconciliation process. In 2004, Somali leaders agreed on the establishment of a Transitional Federal Government (TFG)—the internationally recognized federal government of Somalia—and a Transitional Federal Parliament (TFP). The TFG and TFP were defined in the Transitional Federal Charter, also adopted in 2004. The Charter outlined a five-year mandate leading to the establishment of a new constitution and a transition to a representative government after the holding of national elections. The President of "Puntland", Abdullahi Yusuf Ahmed, was elected President of the TFG in October 2004, and all 25 presidential candidates promised to support him and to demobilize their militias. By May 2006, however, militias of the Alliance for the Restoration of Peace and Counter-Terrorism and of the Sharia Courts were battling each other in Mogadishu. In July, forces loyal to the Islamic Courts advanced towards the city of Baidoa. During the year, the Islamic Courts Union (ICU) took over much of the south. The TFG, with the assistance of Ethiopian troops and AU peacekeepers, managed to drive out the ICU, which then splintered into factions. Radical elements, including Al-Shabaab, regrouped to resume the insurgency against the TFG and oppose the Ethiopian military presence.

In December 2006, the Security Council authorized IGAD and AU member states to establish a protection and training mission in Somalia. With hundreds of thousands fleeing heavy fighting in Mogadishu, the Council, in February 2007, authorized the AU to establish a wider operation—the African Union Mission in Somalia (AMISOM) (am-isom-au.org)—to replace the IGAD mission. AMISOM was authorized to take all neces-sary measures to fulfil its mandate to create a secure environment. The Council extended AMISOM several times and approved contingency planning for a possible UN operation.

By 2008, Al-Shabab had gained control of key areas, including Baidoa. In Decem-ber 2008, President Abdullahi Yusuf Ahmed resigned. In January 2009, Sharif Ahmad was elected President and Omar Abdirashid Ali Sharmarke was selected as Prime Minis-ter. During that same month, the Ethiopian troops withdrew. The TFG, backed by AU troops, began a counteroffensive in February 2009 to retake control of the south.

Also in January 2009, the United Nations Support Office for AMISOM (UNSOA) was established in Nairobi to provide logistical and technical support to the AU op-eration. Fighting continued throughout 2010. Up to late 2010, Secretary-General Ban Ki-moon maintained that deploying a UN mission was not viable given the security situ-ation. The UN focused, therefore, on encouraging dialogue between the TFG and op-position groups and on strengthening AMISOM.

A consequence of the conflict was an upsurge in piracy off the coast of Somalia. The Security Council adopted resolutions to combat the problem and, in 2008, a multina-tional coalition established a Maritime Security Patrol Area within the Gulf of Aden. Acts of piracy reached unprecedented levels in 2011, but declined sharply in 2012, thanks to the joint efforts of the international community and the private sector.

A major military offensive against Al-Shabaab began in February 2011, and TFG forces, supported by AMISOM, made significant territorial gains in Mogadishu. By mid-August, the TFG had influence over 90 per cent of the capital. As a result of those gains, the Secretary-General's Special Representative for Somalia was able to relocate his office to Mogadishu on 24 January 2012.

Somalia's eight-year political transition ended successfully with the establishment of a new Federal Parliament on 20 August 2012. The Parliament selected the President, Hassan Sheikh Mohamud. UNPOS provided good offices and political support to facili-tate the end of the transition. Despite reports of intimidation and interference, the pro-cess yielded the most transparent and representative election in Somalia's 20-year crisis, and the first to be held inside the country. Nevertheless, the security situation in Moga-dishu, though improved, remained unpredictable. Somali National Security Forces and AMISOM maintained their hold on the city, but Al-Shabaab attacks occurred frequently.

In March 2013, the Security Council authorized AU member states to maintain AMISOM until 28 February 2014 to assist the Federal Government in: reducing the threat posed by Al-Shabaab and other armed opposition groups; extending state authority in areas recovered from Al-Shabaab; providing protection to the Federal Government and those involved with the peace and reconciliation process; and creating security conditions for the provision of humanitarian assistance. The Council agreed with the Secretary-General's assessment that UNPOS had fulfilled its mandate and should be dissolved and replaced by a new, expanded political mission as soon as possible. In May, the Council decided to establish, for an initial period of 12 months, the **United Nations Assistance Mission in Somalia (UNSOM)** (unsom.unmissions.org) by 3 June 2013, following the end of the UNPOS mandate on 2 June. UNSOM's mandate to provide good offices supporting the Federal Government's peace and reconciliation process and to provide strategic policy advice to the Federal Government and AMISOM, has been renewed several times since then, most recently in March 2016. The Mission, with offices in Mogadishu and several regional locations, also assists the Federal Government in coordinating international donor support and helps build its capacity in the areas of human rights and women's empowerment, child protection, conflict-related sexual and gender-based violence, and justice. It also monitors, helps investigate and prevent, and reports to the Council on abuses or violations of human rights or international humanitarian law committed in Somalia, as well as abuses committed against children or women. Meanwhile, in November 2015, the **United Nations Support Office in Somalia (UNSOS)** (unsos.unmissions.org) replaced UNSOA. UNSOS was also responsible for support to AMISOM, UNSOM, the Somali National Army and the Somali Police Force on joint operations with AMISOM.

In October 2016, following the completion of the four year term of the Federal Parliament and Government, Somalia embarked on an electoral process to transfer power to a new Federal Parliament and Government, supported by the UN and international partners (unsom.unmissions.org/electoral-support). Although the security and humanitarian situation continues to be fragile and Al-Shabaab remains undefeated, the peaceful transition of power marks a milestone for Somalia after decades of anarchy and conflict.

Republic of South Sudan

The birth of the Republic of South Sudan was the culmination of a six-year process that began with a peace agreement. In a phase of civil conflict in the Sudan that began in 1983, the Sudanese government and the Sudan People's Liberation Movement/Army (SPLM/A), the main rebel movement in the south of the country, fought over resources, power, the role of religion in the state, and self-determination. Over 2 million people died, 4 million were uprooted and some 600,000 others fled the country until the signing of the Comprehensive Peace Agreement (CPA) in January 2005. Under the Agreement, interim institutions would govern for six-and-a-half years, following which the people would vote for Sudanese unity or secession in an internationally monitored referendum.

In March 2005, the Security Council established the UN Mission in the Sudan (UNMIS) to support implementation of the CPA; facilitate humanitarian assistance and the voluntary return of refugees and IDPs; assist the parties in mine action; protect and promote human rights; and coordinate international efforts to protect civilians. In September 2005, a Government of National Unity was established.

In January 2011, a referendum took place in Southern Sudan on whether the region should remain a part of Sudan or become independent. The Southern Sudan Referendum Commission organized the referendum process, while the United Nations provided technical and logistical assistance in preparation for the referendum. An overwhelming majority of participants—98.8 per cent—voted for independence. On 9 July, with the expiration of the interim period under the CPA, the Republic of South Sudan was formally declared an independent state. The President of South Sudan, Salva Kiir, took the oath of office and signed the country's Transitional Constitution.

Also on 9 July, the UNMIS mandate ended and the Security Council established the **United Nations Mission in South Sudan (UNMISS)** (unmiss.unmissions.org) to help establish the conditions for development in South Sudan, with a view to strengthening the government's capacity to govern effectively and establish good relations with its neighbours. UNMISS would consist of up to 7,000 military personnel, up to 900 civilian police and an appropriate civilian component. On 14 July 2011, the General Assembly admitted South Sudan as the 193rd member state of the United Nations.

While negotiations between South Sudan and the Sudan on outstanding issues continued under the auspices of the AU High-level Implementation Panel, the relationship took a turn for the worse in March 2012 when violence along the border increased substantially. The conflict escalated on 10 April, when SPLA captured and occupied oil-rich Heglig, effectively shutting down more than 50 per cent of the Sudan's oil production. Responding to international pressure, including from the UN, South Sudan announced the unconditional withdrawal of SPLA from Heglig on 20 April.

In the wake of the Heglig crisis, Sudan and South Sudan returned to peaceful dialogue. Clashes on the border significantly reduced. After several months of mediation by the AUHIP—which continued working closely with the Secretary-General's special envoy—the two parties signed nine agreements on 27 September 2012 addressing many of the main issues, including economic arrangements with respect to debt; oil exploitation and the use of existing oil infrastructure; the status of respective nationals of one country in the other; and border security.

On 15 December 2013, violence broke out in South Sudan's capital Juba and spread to other locations in the country resulting in a deep nation-wide political and security crisis. Due to a rift between President Salva Kiir and Vice-President Riek Machar—with the former accusing the latter of plotting a coup d'état—and driven further by ethnic motivations, the Sudan People's Liberation Movement/Army (SPLM/A) split, with SPLM/A in Opposition aligning behind the Vice-President. UNMISS estimated that thousands of people had been killed during the hostilities with both parties to the conflict responsible for ethnically targeted attacks on civilians. The influx of civilians into UN premises and their settlement, presented unique challenges and placed a huge strain on Mission resources.

The Security Council increased the troop level of UNMISS to 12,500 personnel and the police component to 1,323 personnel through temporary transfers from existing peacekeeping operations through inter-mission cooperation. In May 2014, the Council reprioritized the UNMISS mandate towards the protection of civilians, human rights monitoring and support for the delivery of humanitarian assistance. It also authorized the deployment within UNMISS of an Intergovernmental Authority on Development (IGAD) task force to support protection of civilians and the Monitoring and Verification Mechanism (MVM) established pursuant to the Cessation of Hostilities Agreement of 23 January 2014.

In August 2015, after 20 months of conflict, the Agreement on the Resolution of the Conflict in the Republic of South Sudan (ARCSS) mediated by IGAD was signed by the parties. The Agreement provided for a transitional phase of governance, within which a transitional government with power-sharing and key security arrangements were to be put in place, including cantonment and reintegration of the Sudan People's Liberation Army. In March 2016, the Secretary-General appointed Nicholas Haysom (South Africa) as his Special Envoy for Sudan and South Sudan.

Despite the return of SPLM/A in Opposition leader Riek Machar to Juba and the establishment of the Transitional Government of National Unity (TGoNU) at the end of April 2016, the ARCSS was never implemented in earnest. Simmering tensions between the forces of SPLA-in Government and SPLA-in Opposition across the country remained. In July, renewed hostilities in Juba between SPLA and SPLA-in Opposition resulted in a dramatic deterioration of the security, humanitarian and human rights situation with hundreds killed and wounded, widespread sexual violence, thousands of civilians displaced, attacks on aid workers and the killing of two UN peacekeepers. First Vice-President Riek Machar withdrew from Juba, and in his absence, on 25 July,

President Salva Kiir appointed Taban Deng Gai, former SPLM/A-in Opposition chief negotiator and Minister of Mining, as First Vice-President.

On 12 August, the Security Council authorized a 4,000 strong Regional Protection Force (RPF) within UNMISS to increase the Mission's ability to protect civilians in Juba. The overall security situation in South Sudan remained extremely volatile with increasing intercommunal violence and an unpredictable political landscape. In December 2016, the Council extended the UNMISS mandate for one year, maintaining a troop ceiling of 17,000 personnel, including 4,000 for RPF, and increasing the police ceiling to 2,101 police personnel. The resumption of an inclusive and credible political process remains, however, the only solution to bring the crisis to a sustainable end.

The Sudan

The Sudan has endured years of civil conflict since it became independent on 1 January 1956. Civil conflict between the Sudanese government and the Sudan People's Liberation Movement/Army (SPLM/A), the main rebel movement in the south of the country, led to the signing of the Comprehensive Peace Agreement (CPA) in January 2005 and a referendum in January 2011 that resulted in the Republic of South Sudan becoming an independent state. The situation and tensions in the Abyei Area and in the Darfur region of the Sudan remained unresolved.

Abyei. At the end of 2010, tensions increased in the Abyei Area of the Sudan in the lead-up to the referendum on the self-determination of Southern Sudan. Those tensions led to a series of violent incidents in January 2011 and a buildup of armed forces from the North and the South. A simultaneous referendum to be held in Abyei on whether the Area should become part of South Sudan was postponed due to demarcation and residency issues. Although temporary security arrangements were agreed on by the parties to the 2005 Comprehensive Peace Agreement (CPA), in the Kadugli Agreements of January 2011 and the Abyei Agreement of March, the Agreements were not fully implemented and a number of security incidents occurred between the parties or their proxies in April and May. On 19 May, a United Nations Mission in Sudan (UNMIS) convoy transporting a Sudanese Armed Forces (SAF) Joint Integrated Unit was attacked in Dokura, an area controlled by Southern police. On 21 May, following the SAF takeover of Abyei town, the government of the Sudan unilaterally dissolved the Abyei Administration. As the violence unfolded, more than 100,000 civilians fled southward.

On 20 June 2011, the government of the Sudan and SPLM signed the Agreement on Temporary Arrangements for the Administration and Security of the Abyei Area. The Agreement provided for: the establishment of an Abyei Area Administration, led jointly by a Chief Administrator nominated by SPLM and a Deputy nominated by the government of the Sudan, and the Abyei Joint Oversight Committee (AJOC); the total withdrawal of all armed elements from the Area and full demilitarization, to be observed by the new Joint Military Observer Committee; and the establishment of an Abyei Police Service. The UN was asked to deploy an interim security force to support the arrangements and provide security in the Area.

On 27 June 2011, the Security Council established the **United Nations Interim Security Force for Abyei (UNISFA)** (unisfa.unmissions.org) for an initial period of 6 months, with a mandate to monitor and verify the redeployment of SAF and SPLA from the Abyei Area; participate in relevant Abyei Area bodies; provide demining assistance and technical advice; facilitate the delivery of humanitarian aid; strengthen the capacity of the Abyei Police Service; and provide security for oil infrastructure, in cooperation with the police. On 29 June, the parties signed an Agreement on Border Security and the Joint Political and

Security Mechanism, which provided for the establishment of a safe demilitarized border zone, and requested UNISFA to provide protection for an international border monitoring verification mission. In December, the Security Council broadened the UNISFA mandate to include, among other tasks, assistance in the process of border normalization.

The governments of the Sudan and the South Sudan made no further progress in the establishment of the joint interim institutions—the Abyei Area Administration, the Abyei Area Council and the Abyei Police Service—due to disagreements on the Chair of the Legislative Council. The killing of the Ngok Dinka Paramount Chief on 4 May 2013 by Misseriya armed militia marked a turning point. The gains made in fostering trust and building bridges through the holding of AJOC meetings and other mechanisms were lost, leading to a complete rupture between the Ngok Dinka and Misseriya communities.

Since 4 May, the Ngok Dinka have prevented the Misseriya or persons from the Sudan coming into Abyei town or the areas further south. The AJOC stopped meeting. The Ngok Dinka community rejected any joint mechanism, conducted a unilateral community referendum in October 2013, and announced that 99.99 per cent of eligible voters had opted for the Abyei Area to become part of South Sudan and that, from that day forward, the Area would be part of South Sudan. The officials on the South Sudan side continue not only to resist engagement in any discussion on a joint administration for Abyei, but also keep reaffirming their right to self-determination.

UNISFA continues to implement its mandate in a politically difficult environment, compounded by the absence of any governance or rule of law institutions. In the absence of an agreement, UNISFA continues to carry out monitoring and early warning assessments; maintains a disengagement area between the local communities; conducts deterrent day and night patrols, as well as aerial monitoring; and promotes constant engagement with the local communities through joint security committees and with the authorities in the Sudan and South Sudan. UNISFA maintains a zero-tolerance policy on small arms and engages with both communities for an effective mechanism for the disarmament of all individuals. It also continues to consolidate its position as the sole provider of security in the area, taking action against all violations when necessary.

In November 2016, the Security Council extended the UNISFA mandate until 15 May 2017. It noted that despite the stated intention by both sides to hold another AJOC meeting, a meeting had not yet taken place, and urged the holding of more meetings.

Darfur. The Darfur conflict broke out in 2003 as a result of political, economic and social marginalization. After three years of intense fighting between the Government of Sudan forces and allied militias and the armed rebel groups with a severe impact on the civilian population and a series of unsuccessful mediation processes, the Government and the Sudan Liberation Movement/Army signed the Darfur Peace Agreement in 2006. Despite providing for power and wealth-sharing, a comprehensive ceasefire, and security arrangements, the Agreement did not lead to an end to the conflict because of its rejection by other major armed groups.

In July 2007, the UN Security Council authorized the deployment of a joint **African Union-United Nations Hybrid Operation in Darfur (UNAMID)** (unamid.unmissions. org), which would replace the African Union Mission in Sudan (AMIS) and would be mandated to, inter alia, protect civilians, facilitate the delivery of humanitarian assistance and support the implementation of the Agreement. UNAMID was constituted as the first hybrid operation involving the United Nations and another regional entity.

In 2011, the Government and the Liberation and Justice Movement, an umbrella of armed groups, signed the Doha Document for Peace in Darfur under the facilitation of the Government of Qatar, and with the AU and UN support. The Document provided a series of measures to address the root causes of the conflict, including power and wealth-sharing, security arrangements, compensation and the return of IDPs and refugees, justice and reconciliation, as well as an internal dialogue process. Despite its broad provisions, the Document did not end the fighting due to it being rejected by several of the major armed movements in Darfur, in addition to political and funding challenges impeding its implementation.

In 2014, the UN Security Council and the AU Peace and Security Council endorsed the outcome of the strategic review of UNAMID which defined three strategic priorities for the Mission: support the negotiations between the Government of Sudan and the non-signatory armed movements, while taking into account the National Dialogue process; protect civilians; and facilitate the provision of humanitarian assistance. The AU and UN have worked jointly to increase the inclusiveness of the political process through negotiations between the Government and the non-signatory movements and create the conditions for the armed movements to join the National Dialogue process, which was launched in October 2015.

Despite those efforts, an inclusive political solution to the Darfur crisis has yet to be reached. Since early 2014, Government forces have implemented a counter-insurgency military campaign to dislodge armed movements from Darfur resulting in the displacement of civilians. In 2016, these counter-insurgency efforts have been focused exclusively on removing the Sudan Liberation Army/Abdul Wahid from its positions in the mountainous Jebel Marra area. As a consequence of the overall Darfur conflict, inter-communal violence and incidents of attacks against civilians by criminal groups and militias have also persisted. Over 2.6 million civilians have been displaced, while an additional 300,000 refugees remain in Chad.

UNAMID reinforced its presence in nearby team sites where thousands of civilians affected by the fighting in Jebel Marra have sought refuge. It has also engaged key Government and community stakeholders to prevent the escalation of inter-communal violence, bring about the cessation of hostilities and, in conjunction with the United Nations Country Team (UNCT), address the root causes of the conflict. In 2016, the AU and UN Security Councils endorsed recommendations for UNAMID to focus its activities on the protection of IDPs and on addressing the increasing threat of inter-communal violence.

UNAMID and humanitarian actors continue to face considerable challenges in the implementation of their respective mandates, including armed attacks, denials of access and freedom of movement—particularly to conflict areas such as Jebel Marra—and operational restrictions from the Sudanese authorities.

The UNAMID mandate was extended until 30 June 2017. Further to the request of the UN Security Council, UNAMID and the UNCT are in the process of planning for the gradual and phased transfer of mandated tasks to the latter. The AU, UN and Sudanese Government have been engaged in discussions on developing an exit strategy for the Mission based on the Mission's strategic priorities and corresponding benchmarks as endorsed by the two Councils.

North Africa

Libya

In early February 2011, in the context of the wider "Arab Spring", an internal crisis in Libya—then, the Libyan Arab Jamahiriya—escalated into a civil war between forces loyal to Libya's leader Colonel Muammar Qadhafi and those seeking to overthrow his government. The international community launched several diplomatic initiatives to end the crisis. On 26 February, the Security Council referred the situation to the Prosecutor of the International Criminal Court (ICC) and imposed an arms embargo, a travel ban and asset freeze on Colonel Qadhafi and members of his circle. On 1 March, the General Assembly suspended Libya's membership in the Human Rights Council—the first time a sitting member was removed.

On 19 March, two days after the Security Council authorized member states to take all necessary measures to protect civilians, United States and European forces launched an air strike campaign to establish a no-fly zone over the country and protect civilians. Meanwhile, the Secretary-General's Special Envoy for Libya carried out mediation efforts to establish a ceasefire. After months of intense fighting, opposition forces took the city of Sirte in October and Colonel Qadhafi was killed. On 23 October, the National Transitional Council—the political leadership of the anti-Qadhafi movement—declared Libya fully liberated and took charge of the country

The **United Nations Support Mission in Libya (UNSMIL)** (unsmil.unmissions. org) was established by the Council in September to support the country's new transitional authorities in their post-conflict efforts. Violence and instability across the country, however, erupted into a renewed civil war in 2014. A ceasefire in December 2015, led to the signing of the Libyan Political Agreement and the formation of the Government of National Accord. In December 2016, the Council mandated UNSMIL, to exercise mediation and good offices in support of the Libyan political agreement's implementation; the consolidation of governance, security and economic arrangements of the Government; and subsequent phases of the Libyan transition process. The Mission supports key Libyan institutions and provides essential services and humanitarian assistance. The UNSMIL mandate was extended until 15 September 2017.

Americas

The United Nations has been instrumental in bringing peace to the Central American region—including in Costa Rica, El Salvador, Guatemala, Honduras and Nicaragua—where it conducted some of its most complex and successful operations. Its support of peace and security in Colombia and Haiti is ongoing. In response to a 2016 request from the Government of El Salvador, on 16 January 2017, on the occasion of the twenty-fifth anniversary of the Salvadorian Peace Accords, the Secretary-General appointed Benito Andión (Mexico) as his Special Envoy to facilitate dialogue in El Salvador with a view to reach agreements on challenges facing the country.

Colombia

In July 2015, the Government of Colombia and the Revolutionary Armed Forces of Colombia-People's Army (FARC-EP), the parties to the peace talks in Havana, requested UN support in the process. The Secretary-General's Delegate to the Sub-Commission on End of Conflict Issues within the Colombian Peace Process, Jean Arnault (France) appointed in August 2015, and later selected as his Special Representative, worked closely with the negotiating teams of the two parties. In January 2016, in response to another request from the parties, the Security Council established the **UN Mission in Colombia** (colombia.unmissions.org), a political mission of unarmed international observers to monitor and verify both the laying down of arms, and the bilateral ceasefire and cessation of hostilities following the signing of a peace agreement.

On 23 June, the parties signed the Agreement on the Bilateral and Definitive Ceasefire and Cessation of Hostilities and Laying down of Arms, which heralded the end of the longest conflict in the region and provided the parameters for the tasks to be carried out by the Mission. Personnel required for the Mission comprised 450 observers and a civilian component, to be deployed in 40 locations. By 22 July, 80 observers had been deployed to Bogotá. Although the Mission's ceasefire monitoring and verification responsibilities were activated with the 26 September signing of the Final Agreement for Ending the Conflict and Building a Stable and Long Lasting Peace, a "No" vote in the plebiscite of 2 October made it legally impossible for the Colombian Government to implement the agreement. In search of a new peace agreement, President Juan Manuel Santos Calderón, who was awarded the Nobel Peace Prize on 7 October for his efforts to resolve the 50-year conflict, led talks and a national dialogue with various sectors, including leaders of the "No" campaign.

A revised Final Agreement was signed by the parties on 24 November, ratified by the Colombian Congress on 30 November and entered into force on 1 December 2016, thereby initiating the timetable for implementation of its provisions relating to the cease-fire, cessation of hostilities and laying down of arms. The UN Mission in Colombia, along with the parties, intensified efforts to meet the requirements of implementation. A national reintegration council was established and an amnesty law was passed, respectively on 2 and 30 December. As at 18 February 2017, 6,900 armed members of FARC-EP had moved to the 26 agreed zones and points without incident. A major milestone, the process of the laying down of arms, began on 1 March. As at 29 March, the Mission had registered 85 per cent (7,000 weapons) of the weapons in the camps. Implementation of the peace agreement continues and has been unfolding in a political environment increasingly marked by the general elections, which will take place in May 2018.

Haiti

As Haiti celebrated its bicentennial in January 2004, a severe political deadlock threatened the country's stability. Clashes between pro- and anti-government militias led to a spiral of increasing violence, which forced President Jean-Bertrand Aristide, who had been serving a second term since 2001, to resign and leave the country. The Security Council authorized the immediate deployment of a Multinational Interim Force, following a request for assistance by the new President, Boniface Alexandre. A United States-led force was quickly deployed. In April 2004, the Council established the **United Nations Stabilization Mission in Haiti (MINUSTAH)** (minustah.unmissions.org) to support the continuation of a peaceful and constitutional political process in a secure and stable environment. In the following years, the mandate of MINUSTAH, its concept of operations and the authorized strength were adjusted by the Council on several occasions to adapt to the changing circumstances on the ground and to the evolving requirements as dictated by the prevailing political, security and socioeconomic situation.

Following the devastating January 2010 earthquake, the Council increased the overall force levels of MINUSTAH to support recovery, reconstruction and stability efforts. MINUSTAH, together with OCHA and the UN Country Team, provided humanitarian and recovery assistance. It also supported the holding of elections which were won in 2011 by Michel Martelly, whose term came to an end in February 2016 without the election of a successor. Efforts of the interim government to hold the delayed presidential elections, with the President of the National Assembly acting as Head of State, were thwarted by the devastation brought by Hurricane Matthew which struck Haiti in October 2016. The presidential elections were subsequently held on 20 November 2016 and won by Jovenel Moïse of the Parti Haïtien Tèt Kale. He was sworn into office on 7 February 2017. The Security Council extended the MINUSTAH mandate until 15 April 2017, maintaining its force levels at 2,370 and a police component of 2,601 personnel. It is expected to decide on a new UN presence in Haiti by that date.

Asia and the Pacific

The Middle East

From its earliest days, the United Nations has been concerned with the question of the Middle East. It has formulated principles for a peaceful settlement and dispatched various peacekeeping operations. It continues to support efforts towards a just, lasting and comprehensive solution to the underlying political problems.

The question has its origin in the issue of the status of Palestine, one among former Ottoman territories placed under United Kingdom administration by the League of Nations in 1922. All of these territories eventually became fully independent states, except Palestine, where in addition to "the rendering of administrative assistance and advice" the British Mandate incorporated the "Balfour Declaration" of 1917, expressing support for "the establishment in Palestine of a national home for the Jewish people". During the Mandate, from 1922 to 1947, large-scale Jewish immigration, mainly from Eastern Europe took place. Arab demands for independence and resistance to immigration led to a rebellion in 1937, followed by continuing violence from both sides.

In 1947, the United Kingdom turned the question of Palestine over to the UN. Palestine had a population of some 2 million—two thirds Arabs and one third Jews. The 57-member General Assembly, on 29 November 1947, endorsed a plan prepared by the United Nations Special Committee on Palestine for the partition of the territory in May 1948 when the British mandate ended. The plan provided for creating an Arab and a Jewish state, with Jerusalem under a special international regime administered by the Trusteeship Council on behalf of the United Nations. The plan was rejected by the Palestinian Arabs, the Arab states and other states. The Palestine problem quickly widened into a Middle East dispute between those states and Israel. On 14 May 1948, the United Kingdom relinquished its mandate, and the Jewish Agency for Palestine proclaimed the state of Israel. The following day, the Palestinian Arabs, assisted by Arab states, opened hostilities against the new state. The military confrontation was halted through a truce called for by the Security Council and supervised by a mediator appointed by the General Assembly, who was assisted by a group of military observers that came to be known as the **United Nations Truce Supervision Organization (UNTSO)**—the first United Nations observer mission (untso.unmissions.org/).

As a result of the conflict, some 750,000 Palestinian Arabs lost their homes and livelihoods and became refugees. To assist them, the General Assembly in 1949 established the **United Nations Relief and Works Agency for Palestine Refugees in the Near East (UNRWA)** (www.unrwa.org), which has since been a major provider of assistance and a force for stability in the region. Today, 5 million Palestine refugees benefit from UNRWA services in Jordan, Lebanon, the Gaza Strip, the Syrian Arab Republic and the West Bank, including East Jerusalem.

The conflict remaining unresolved, Arab-Israeli warfare erupted again in 1956, 1967 and 1973, each time leading member states to call for UN mediation and peacekeeping missions. The 1956 conflict saw the deployment of the first full-fledged peacekeeping force—the United Nations Emergency Force (UNEF I)—which oversaw troop withdrawals and contributed to peace and stability.

The 1967 war involved fighting between Israel and the Arab states Egypt, Jordan and Syria, during which Israel occupied the Sinai Peninsula, the Gaza Strip, the West Bank of the Jordan River, including East Jerusalem, and part of Syria's Golan Heights. The Security Council called for a ceasefire, and subsequently dispatched observers to supervise the ceasefire in the Egypt-Israel sector.

The Council, by resolution 242(1967), defined principles for a just and lasting peace, namely: "withdrawal of Israel armed forces from territories occupied in the recent conflict"; and "termination of all claims or states of belligerency and respect for and acknowledgement of the sovereignty, territorial integrity and political independence of every state in the area and their right to live in peace within secure and recognized boundaries, free from threats or acts of force". The resolution also affirmed the need for "a just settlement of the refugee problem".

After the 1973 war between Israel and Egypt and Syria, the Security Council adopted resolution 338(1973), which reaffirmed the principles of resolution 242(1967) and called for negotiations aimed at "a just and durable peace". These resolutions remain the basis for an overall settlement in the Middle East.

To monitor the 1973 ceasefire, the Security Council established two peacekeeping forces. One of them was UNEF II, which was deployed to supervise the ceasefire between Egypt and Israel. The other operation, the **United Nations Disengagement Observer Force (UNDOF)** (undof.unmissions.org), established in 1974, is still in place in Golan Heights. UNDOF supervises the disengagement agreement between the Israeli and Syrian forces and its protocol with regard to the areas of separation and limitation; and uses its best efforts to maintain the ceasefire and see that it is observed. Since 2012, the ongoing conflict in Syria has significantly affected UNDOF and the way in which it implements its mandate. Attacks on UNDOF peacekeepers occurred most notably in August and September 2014. UNDOF temporarily relocated the bulk of its troops outside the area of separation and adapted its operations to prevailing circumstances. A planned limited and incremental return to some of the positions vacated by UNDOF was initiated in the fall of 2016. Despite a number of significant violations of the Disengagement of Forces Agreement, both parties repeatedly stated their continued commitment to the Agreement and their support to UNDOF.

In the years following the 1973 ceasefire, the General Assembly called for an international peace conference on the Middle East, under UN auspices. In 1974, the Assembly invited the Palestine Liberation Organization (PLO) to participate in its work as an observer. The following year, it established the **Committee on the Exercise of the Inalienable Rights of the Palestinian People** (unispal.un.org/DPA/DPR/unispal.nsf/com.htm), which continues to work as the Assembly's subsidiary organ to advance the inalienable rights of the Palestinian people and support a peaceful settlement on the question of Palestine. The Committee is composed of 28 member states and 24 observers. Its mandate is renewed by the Assembly annually on 29 November as part of the UN observance of the International Day of Solidarity with the Palestinian People. The Committee also organizes international meetings and conferences, collaborates with civil society organizations, and maintains an extensive collection of publications and information on the question of Palestine.

Middle East peace process (1987–2016). In 1987, the Palestinian uprising (intifada) began in the occupied territories of the West Bank and Gaza Strip with a call for Palestinian independence and statehood. In 1988, the Palestine National Council proclaimed the state of Palestine, which the General Assembly acknowledged. The Assembly also decided to employ the designation "Palestine" when referring to the PLO within the UN system, without prejudice to its observer status.

In September 1993, following talks in Madrid and subsequent Norwegian-mediated negotiations, Israel and the PLO established mutual recognition and signed the *Declaration of Principles on Interim Self-Government Arrangements*. The UN appointed a **Special Coordinator for UN assistance (UNSCO)** (www.unsco.org), whose mandate expanded in 1999 to include good offices assistance to the Middle East peace process.

The Special Coordinator later became the Secretary-General's Envoy to the Middle East Quartet—composed of the European Union, the Russian Federation, the United States and the United Nations—thus further shaping the role of UNSCO.

The transfer of powers from Israel to the Palestinian Authority (PA) in the Gaza Strip and Jericho began in 1994. One year later, Israel and the PLO signed an agreement on Palestinian self-rule in the West Bank, providing for the withdrawal of Israeli troops and the handover of civil authority to an elected Palestinian Council. In 1996, Yasser Arafat was elected President of the PA. An interim agreement in 1999 led to further redeployment of Israeli troops from the West Bank, agreements on prisoners, the opening of safe passage between the West Bank and Gaza, and resumption of negotiations on permanent status issues. High-level peace talks held under United States mediation, however, ended inconclusively in 2000. Unresolved issues included the status of Jerusalem, the Palestinian refugee question, security, borders and Israeli settlements.

In September 2000, a new wave of violence flared up. The Security Council repeatedly called for an end to the violence and affirmed the vision of two states, Israel and Palestine, living side by side within secure and recognized borders. International efforts to bring the two parties back to the negotiating table were increasingly carried out through the Middle East Quartet.

In April 2003, the Quartet presented its "road map" to a permanent two-state solution—a plan with distinct phases and benchmarks, calling for parallel and reciprocal steps by the two parties, to resolve the conflict by 2005. It also envisaged a comprehensive settlement of the Middle East conflict, including the Syrian-Israeli and Lebanese-Israeli tracks. The Council endorsed the road map in resolution 1515(2003) and both parties accepted it. Nevertheless, the last half of 2003 saw a sharp escalation of violence.

In 2005, Israel unilaterally withdrew its military and settlements from the Gaza Strip. In February, Israeli Prime Minister Ariel Sharon and President Mahmoud Abbas met in Egypt and announced steps to halt the violence. They met again in June, and by September, Israel's withdrawal was complete. Despite these positive developments, two significant events in January 2006 changed the political landscape: Prime Minister Sharon suffered a stroke and fell into a coma; and in legislative elections, the Palestinians voted the militant Hamas faction into power.

Despite appeals from the Quartet and others, Hamas did not formally recognize Israel's right to exist. The Israeli government, led by Prime Minister Ehud Olmert, took the position that the entire PA had become a terrorist entity, and imposed a freeze on Palestinian tax revenues. Violence escalated, including the launching of rockets from Gaza into Israel, along with major Israeli counter-operations. International aid donors balked at funding the Hamas-led government as long as it did not renounce violence, recognize Israel's right to exist, and abide by signed agreements. The humanitarian situation in the West Bank and Gaza deteriorated.

In May 2007, intra-Palestinian clashes led to a shift in governance, with the PA governing the West Bank and Hamas governing the Gaza strip. Towards the end of 2008, following a spate of rocket attacks from Gaza, Israel launched a military operation, which culminated in a ground invasion. The operation worsened the humanitarian situation and strengthened the three-year blockade and closure of Gaza. It also led to massive damage to infrastructure, including to UN facilities, and hundreds of civilians died, mostly Palestinians. In 2009, the Council adopted resolution 1860(2009) calling for an immediate ceasefire and withdrawal of Israeli forces from Gaza and condemning violence and acts of terrorism. Following intense diplomatic efforts, Israel announced a unilateral ceasefire in mid-January, followed by a unilateral ceasefire declaration by Hamas. A UN Human

Rights Council investigation into the conflict under South African former judge Richard Goldstone concluded in a September 2009 report that both sides had committed violations amounting to crimes against humanity.

In March 2010, the Quartet urged Israel to freeze all settlement activity and reaffirmed that unilateral action would not be recognized by the international community. It underscored that the status of Jerusalem was an issue that remained to be resolved. In September, the United States launched direct Israeli-Palestinian negotiations in Washington, D.C., with a one-year time limit. The talks ended, however, when an Israeli partial moratorium on settlement construction in the West Bank expired. The Palestinians refused to negotiate if Israel did not extend the freeze.

In September 2011, the Quartet urged resumption of direct bilateral Israeli-Palestinian negotiations without delay or preconditions and proposed concrete steps to re-establish the trust necessary for such a negotiation to succeed.

In October 2011, the UNESCO General Conference admitted Palestine as a member. In April 2012, the Quartet supported exploratory Israeli-Palestinian talks held in early 2012 in Amman. In November, however, a fresh cycle of violence erupted between Israel and Gaza, which concluded with an Egyptian-brokered ceasefire.

On 29 November 2012, the UN General Assembly accepted Palestine as a non-member state with observer status in the UN, without prejudice to the acquired rights, privileges and role of the PLO in the United Nations as the representative of the Palestinian people.

In March 2013, the United States initiated direct talks that were suspended in April 2014 by Israel after the announcement of an intra-Palestinian unity agreement for the formation of a National Consensus Government, coupled with Israel's refusal to release the final tranche of prisoners previously proposed.

In response to a significant increase in rocket and mortar attacks from Gaza towards Israel, on 8 July 2014 Israel launched operation "Protective Edge" which was the longest and most violent of the three military confrontations in Gaza. It took several attempts before an open-ended ceasefire was brokered under Egyptian auspices on 26 August. The operation led to a worsened humanitarian situation. Reconstruction efforts, despite the setting up of the Gaza Reconstruction Mechanism with the United Nations, have been hampered by Israeli and Egyptian closures and slow international donor support.

On 2 January 2015, the Secretary-General deposited 16 instruments of accession signed by President Abbas, including the Rome Statute of the International Criminal Court.

In July 2016, the Quartet reported on threats to the two-state solution and recommended steps the parties should take to enable an eventual return to negotiations to end the occupation and resolve all final status issues.

In December, the Council, by resolution 2334(2016), stated that settlements in the Palestinian territory had no legal validity, constituted a flagrant violation under international law and were a major obstacle to the achievement of the two-state solution. The Council also called for immediate steps to prevent violence against civilians, including acts of terror, as well as all acts of provocation and destruction.

Lebanon

From April 1975 through October 1990, Lebanon was torn by civil war. Early on, southern Lebanon became a theatre of hostilities between Palestinian groups on one hand and, on the other, Israeli forces and their local Lebanese auxiliary. After Israeli forces invaded southern Lebanon in 1978, following a Palestinian commando raid in Israel, the Security Council adopted resolutions 425(1978) and 426(1978), calling on Israel to withdraw and establishing the **United Nations Interim Force in Lebanon (UNIFIL)**

(unifil.unmissions.org). The Force was set up to confirm the Israeli withdrawal, restore international peace and security, and assist Lebanon in re-establishing its authority in the area. In 1982, after intense exchanges of fire in southern Lebanon and across the Israel-Lebanon border, Israeli forces moved into Lebanon, reaching and surrounding Beirut. Israel withdrew from most of the country in 1985, but kept control of a strip of land in southern Lebanon, where Israeli forces and their local Lebanese auxiliary remained, and which partly overlapped UNIFIL's area of deployment. Hostilities between Lebanese groups and Israeli forces continued. In May 2000, Israeli forces withdrew in accordance with the 1978 Security Council resolutions. The Council endorsed the Secretary-General's plan to assist Lebanon in re-establishing its authority. Nevertheless, the situation along the "Blue Line" marking Israel's withdrawal from southern Lebanon remained precarious.

Tensions escalated in February 2005, when former Lebanese Prime Minister Rafiq Hariri was assassinated. In November, the Council supported establishment of a special tribunal to try those allegedly responsible for the assassination. In April 2005, the UN verified the withdrawal of Syrian troops, military assets and intelligence operations from Lebanon. In May and June, parliamentary elections were held with UN assistance. Violations of the Blue Line continued through 2005 and 2006 with intermittent clashes between Israel and Hizbullah. When two Israeli soldiers were seized by Hizbullah in July 2006, Israel responded with air attacks, and Hizbullah retaliated with rocket attacks. The 34-day conflict ended in August, by the terms of Council resolution 1701(2006), which called for an immediate cessation of hostilities, to be followed by deployment of Lebanese troops; a significantly expanded UNIFIL peacekeeping presence across southern Lebanon (from 2,000 troops in August 2006 to a maximum of 15,000); and the withdrawal of Israeli forces from the area. Since 1978, UNIFIL has had 312 fatalities. A significant problem facing UNIFIL was the risk posed by up to 1 million pieces of unexploded ordnance left from the conflict.

Since the adoption of resolution 1701(2006), violations of the Blue Line were reported by Israel and Lebanon. In June 2016, the Secretary-General reported that while the parties continued to affirm their commitment to that resolution, there was no substantive progress in implementation of their respective obligations outstanding under the resolution.

Lebanon and Syria established diplomatic relations in October 2008. Following the peaceful conduct of parliamentary elections in June 2009, newly elected Prime Minister Saad Hariri formed a national unity government in November.

The **Office of the Special Coordinator for Lebanon (UNSCOL)** (unscol.unmissions. org), established in 2007, continued to represent the Secretary-General in political and coordination aspects of UN work in Lebanon. In March 2015, the Special Coordinator briefed the Council on issues, including the possession of arms by Hezbollah, the effects of the Syrian conflict on Lebanon, and the refugee crisis. Lebanon was hosting nearly 1.2 million Syrian registered refugees. Also of concern in May 2016 was the two-year-long vacancy in the presidency of Lebanon that affected its ability to address the growing security, economic, social and humanitarian challenges facing the country. On 1 November, the Council welcomed the election of Michel Aoun as President and urged him and other leaders to swiftly form a new Government and take steps to promote the country's stability. The Council extended the UNIFIL mandate until 30 August 2017.

Syria

A civil war in Syria between government forces and armed rebels erupted in March 2011 setting in motion a devastating six-year conflict in which hundreds of thousands have been killed, 6.5 million displaced and 4.8 million fleeing to other neighbouring countries for refuge. It also produced intensified regional and international polarization and new extremist threats (www.un.org/undpa/en/middleeast-westasia/syria). In April 2012, the United Nations established the UN Supervision Mission in Syria (UNSMIS) to monitor a cessation of armed violence by all parties and to support implementation of the six-point plan to end the conflict, put forth by the United Nations/League of Arab States Joint Special Envoy, former UN Secretary-General Kofi Annan. Intensified armed violence across the country forced UNSMIS to suspend its activities in June 2012. When security conditions stipulated by the Security Council to allow UNSMIS monitors to implement their mandate were not met, the Mission's mandate ended on 19 August 2012.

The Geneva Communique, the outcome document of a June 2012 meeting of key international and regional stakeholders convened by the Secretary-General and Joint Special Envoy Annan provided guidance on implementation of the six-point plan and political transition, including the establishment of a transitional governing body with full executive powers formed on the basis of mutual consent. Following the failure of the Security Council to adopt a resolution endorsing the Communique and the imposition of sanctions on parties violating the six-point plan, in August 2012, the Joint Special Envoy said that he did not intend to continue his work when his mandate expired. The same month, the Secretaries-General of the UN and the League of Arab States (LAS) announced the appointment of Lakhdar Brahimi (Algeria) as their Joint Special Representative for Syria.

Following reports of the alleged use of chemical weapons in the Ghouta area of Damasucs on 21 August 2013, the Secretary-General briefed the Council on the findings of chemical weapons investigations in September, stating that the mission had confirmed, unequivocally and objectively, that chemical weapons were used in Syria. On 27 September, the Council adopted resolution 2118(2013) authorizing a joint UN-Organization for Prohibition of Chemical Weapons (OPCW) mission to eliminate Syria's chemical weapons and endorsed the Geneva Communique.

In January and February 2014, Joint Special Representative Brahimi convened intra-Syrian negotiations in Geneva on implementing the Geneva Communique. The parties agreed on a four-point agenda: violence and terrorism; a transitional governing body; national institutions; and reconciliation. They were unable, however, to agree on the sequence for negotiating these issues, leading Brahimi to suspend the negotiations. He resigned in May. In July 2014, the Secretary-General appointed Staffan de Mistura (Italy/Sweden) as **Special Envoy for Syria**. In August and September, the Security Council adopted resolutions on combatting terrorist groups in Syria, with a particular focus on the Islamic State of Iraq and the Levant (ISIL) and Al-Nusra Front. Between September 2014 and February 2015, the Special Envoy focused on achieving a ceasefire to the fighting in the northern city of Aleppo.

On 30 September 2014, the OPCW-UN Joint Mission announced that it had completed its work to eliminate Syria's declared chemical stockpile while work continued to destroy its remaining production facilities. In November, the Assembly's Third Committee adopted a resolution on Syria encouraging the Council to take appropriate action to ensure accountability, noting the role the International Criminal Court (ICC) could play in that regard.

In May 2015, Special Envoy de Mistura announced the beginning of the Geneva Consultations. In August, the Council adopted resolution 2235(2015) aimed at identifying individuals, entities, groups, or governments involved in the use of chemicals as weapons and requested a joint UN-OPCW investigative mechanism to attribute responsibility for the use of chemical weapons in Syria. In September, the Secretary-General called for the situation in Syria to be referred to ICC.

Meetings of the International Syrian Support Group (ISSG) on how to end the conflict, convened by the United States and Russia, with foreign ministers from 17 countries, the LAS, and the EU, culminated in the adoption in December 2015 of resolution 2254(2015). The Council reiterated past endorsements of the Geneva Communique and set a timeline for the political transition, including negotiations on the establishment of a credible, inclusive, non-sectarian governance; a process and timeline for drafting a new constitution; and the conduct of free and fair elections held under UN supervision within 18 months. A nationwide ceasefire was envisaged to begin once initial steps towards a transition had taken place.

From January to April 2016, Special Envoy de Mistura mediated several rounds of intra-Syrian negotiations between representatives from the Syrian Government and opposition. In February, the ISSG formed a ceasefire task force under the auspices of the UN, co-chaired by Russia and the United States. On 26 February, the Council adopted resolution 2268(2015) demanding that all warring parties comply with the terms of a United States-Russian Agreement on a cessation of hostilities. The listed terrorist organisations of ISIL and Al-Nusra Front were not parties to the cessation and operations against them were permitted under the cessation's regime. After an observed reduction in violence in March and April, violence approached pre-cessation levels by the summer. On 19 September 2016, a UN-Syrian Arab Red Crescent humanitarian convoy came under attack. Roughly 30 people were killed or wounded. The Secretary-General established a UN Headquarters Board of Inquiry to investigate the attack. In October, the Special Envoy briefed the Council, underscoring that eastern Aleppo was at risk of total destruction within months. Separate draft resolutions to establish ceasefires and humanitarian aid in Aleppo failed to be adopted by the Security Council.

After years of conflict and besiegement, the Battle for Aleppo ended on 22 December 2016 with the Syrian Government's announcement that it had retaken full control over the city. The Council requested the UN and other relevant institutions to carry out neutral monitoring and observation of evacuations of formerly opposition-held areas.

On 29 December, Turkey and Russia announced a nationwide ceasefire between the Government of Syria and armed opposition groups in Syria. The Security Council resolution endorsed the ceasefire, called on parties to allow humanitarian agencies access throughout Syria and welcomed a meeting in Astana as an important part of the UN-led political process and a step towards the resumption of negotiations under UN auspices.

On 4 April 2017, reports emerged of alleged use of chemical weapons in an air strike in the Khan Shaykhun residential area of southern Idlib, Syria, that led to the death and injury of many Syrian civilians, including children. The Secretary-General recalled that the Security Council had previously determined that the use of chemical weapons anywhere constituted a threat to international peace and security, and a serious violation of international law.

Yemen

Since the uprisings in Yemen broke out in 2011, the United Nations has been engaged, through the good offices of the Secretary-General, in helping Yemenis to find a peaceful solution. The UN provided support for the negotiations between the Government and the opposition, which resulted in the signing of the Gulf Cooperation Council Initiative and its Implementation Mechanism in Riyadh on 23 November 2011.

The Secretary-General established the **Office of the Special Adviser to the Secretary-General on Yemen (OSESGY)** (osesgy.unmissions.org) to engage with all Yemeni political groups to provide support for the effective implementation of the Initiative and its

Implementation Mechanism. Since the establishment of the Office, the United Nations has provided support for the Yemeni-led political transition process and has promoted inclusive participation, including of previously marginalized groups, such as women, youth, the Houthis and Southern Hirak. A National Dialogue Conference was concluded in January 2014, bringing together 565 delegates from all regions and political groups in Yemen. The outcome document established the foundation for a new federal and democratic Yemen, with support for good governance, the rule of law and human rights.

Despite important progress in the political transition, conflicts between the Houthis, other armed groups and government forces led to an escalation of military violence in mid-2014. The Houthis and allied units of the armed forces seized control of Sana'a and other parts of the country in September 2014 and over the ensuing months.

Numerous rounds of UN-facilitated negotiations to resolve the political impasse were ineffective in halting the escalation of military confrontations that continued into early 2015. At the request of President Abd Rabbuh Mansour Hadi, a coalition of countries led by Saudi Arabia intervened militarily on 26 March to secure the return of Government control. The ensuing conflict triggered a humanitarian emergency. Al-Qaeda in the Arabian Peninsula and other terrorist groups have exploited the chaos, extending their control over significant areas and conducting frequent attacks against government and civilian targets in many areas.

In April 2015, the Security Council requested the Secretary-General to intensify his good offices role in order to enable the resumption of a peaceful, inclusive and orderly Yemeni-led transition. That same month, the Secretary-General appointed Ismail Ould Cheikh Ahmed (Mauritania) as his new Special Envoy for Yemen. The Special Envoy has facilitated successive rounds of consultations to end the conflict and resume the political transition process, including direct talks in Switzerland in June and December 2015, and in Kuwait from April to August 2016. Despite these efforts, fighting continues between various parties throughout the country, including along the Saudi Arabia-Yemen border. Concurrently, attacks claimed by Al-Qaeda in the Arabian Peninsula and Islamic State, as well as counter-insurgency operations against those groups, continue in southern Yemen.

On 25 April 2016, the Security Council, following the launch of peace talks, on 10 and 21 April, called on all Yemeni parties to develop a roadmap for the implementation of interim security measures, withdrawals, handover of heavy weapons, restoration of state institutions and the resumption of political dialogue in line with the Gulf Cooperation Council Initiative and its Implementation Mechanism and the outcomes of the National Dialogue Conference. The Council also requested the Secretary-General to present a plan outlining how the **Office of the Special Envoy of the Secretary-General for Yemen (OSE-Yemen)** (osesgy.unmissions.org) could support the next phase of its work with the parties, which was submitted in May 2016. The overall aim of OSE-Yemen is to provide support to the Yemen peace process, the cessation of hostilities and implementation of agreements resulting from the peace process to enable the resumption of a peaceful, Yemeni-led transition.

Afghanistan

In September 1995, the Taliban faction in Afghanistan's civil war took Kabul, its capital, after having seized most of the country. President Burhannudin Rabbani fled and joined the "Northern Alliance", which held territory in the northern part of the country. In August 1998, following the terrorist bomb attacks on United States embassies in Nairobi, Kenya, and Dar-es-Salaam, Tanzania, the Council repeated its concern at the continuing presence of terrorists in Afghanistan. In December, it demanded that the Taliban, which was never recognized as Afghanistan's legitimate government, stop providing sanctuary and training for international terrorists and their organizations. The Taliban failed to respond.

In October 1999, the Council applied broad sanctions under the enforcement provisions of the UN *Charter*. It then demanded that the Taliban turn over to the appropriate authorities Osama bin Laden, who had been indicted by the United States for the embassy bombings.

On 11 September 2001, members of bin Laden's Al-Qaida organization hijacked four commercial jets in the United States, crashing two into the World Trade Center in New York City, one into the Pentagon in the US capital, and the fourth into a field in Pennsylvania when passengers tried to stop the hijacking. Nearly 3,000 people were killed in the attacks. In the days that followed, the US administration issued an ultimatum to the Taliban: turn over bin Laden and close the terrorist operations in Afghanistan or risk a massive military assault. The Taliban refused. In October, forces of the United States and United Kingdom launched missile attacks against Taliban military targets and bin Laden's training camps in Afghanistan. Two weeks of bombings were followed by the deployment of US ground forces. The Security Council supported efforts of the Afghan people to replace the Taliban regime. The United Nations promoted dialogue among Afghan parties aimed at establishing a broad-based, inclusive government. A UN-organized meeting of Afghan political leaders in Bonn, Germany, concluded in December with an agreement on a provisional arrangement, pending re-establishment of permanent government institutions. The Afghan Interim Authority was established and the Security Council authorized the establishment of the International Security Assistance Force (ISAF) to help the Authority maintain security in Kabul and its surrounding areas. Later that month, the internationally recognized administration of President Rabbani handed power over to the new Afghan Interim Authority, headed by Chairman Hamid Karzai, and the first ISAF troops were deployed.

In January 2002, an International Conference on Reconstruction Assistance to Afghanistan garnered pledges of over $4.5 billion. The Council, welcoming the positive changes in Afghanistan as a result of the collapse of the Taliban, adjusted its sanctions to target Al-Qaida and its supporters. In March, the Council established the **United Nations Assistance Mission in Afghanistan (UNAMA)** (unama.unmissions.org) to fulfill the tasks entrusted to the UN under the Bonn Agreement in such areas as human rights, the rule of law and gender issues. Headed by the Secretary-General's special representative, UNAMA would also promote national reconciliation, while managing all UN humanitarian activities in coordination with the Interim Authority and its successors.

In June 2002, a nine-day Emergency Loya Jirga ("Grand Council", a traditional forum in which tribal elders come together and settle affairs) was opened by Zahir Shah, the former King of Afghanistan, who nominated Hamid Karzai to lead the nation. Subsequently, Mr. Karzai was elected as Afghanistan's head of state to lead the transitional government for two years. Following the agreement of the Constitutional Loya Jirga on the text of Afghanistan's Constitution in January 2004, more than 8 million Afghans went to the polls in October of that year, choosing Hamid Karzai as the country's first-ever elected President. In September 2005, the Afghan people voted for the members of their National Assembly and Provisional Councils, despite a series of deadly attacks during the campaign.

The Afghanistan Compact—a five-year agenda to consolidate democratic institutions, curb insecurity, control the illegal drug trade, stimulate the economy, enforce the law, provide basic services to the Afghan people, and protect their human rights—was launched in January 2006 and endorsed by the Security Council as providing a framework for partnership between the Afghan government and the international community. In June 2008, about $20 billion was pledged to finance the Compact's implementation, including support for the preparation of elections in 2009 and 2010, which saw the re-election of President Karzai.

Despite political advances, violence escalated throughout 2008 and 2009. In a Taliban attack on a UN guesthouse in Kabul in October 2009, five foreign UN employees and three Afghans were killed. In 2010 conferences highlighted the need to transfer responsibility for security matters to the Afghan authorities by 2011 and discussed the transition of Afghan provinces from ISAF control to the National Security Forces by 2014. Issues of good governance, fairness of the judicial system, human rights and the continuing problem posed by drug trafficking were also considered.

On 20 September 2011, former President Rabbani was killed by a suicide bomber. Mr. Rabbani's death—the culmination of a series of high-profile assassinations of figures formerly part of or close to the Northern Alliance—intensified internal political maneuvering and weakened trust between factions and ethnic groups. In October 2012, at a meeting of defence ministers of the North Atlantic Treaty Organization (NATO), ISAF was directed to begin planning a post-2014 training mission. On 15 November, Afghanistan and the United States launched negotiations on a bilateral security agreement in line with their strategic partnership agreement. In March 2013, the Security Council called on the United Nations to support Afghanistan's National Priority Programmes covering the issues of security, governance, justice and economic and social development, as well as implementation of the National Drug Control Strategy.

Following presidential and provincial council elections on 5 April 2014—in which the Afghan people participated in record numbers despite threats and intimidation by the Taliban and other extremist and terrorist groups—the Council welcomed the 29 September inauguration of Ashraf Ghani as the new President of Afghanistan, marking the first democratic transition of power in the country's history.

In December 2014, the Council welcomed the Afghanistan-NATO agreement to create the post-2014 Resolute Support Mission (RSM), which was the follow on mission after ISAF completed its mandate on 28 December. In June 2015, although political progress had been achieved with the appointment of all cabinet members, the security situation remained a challenge with the infiltration of foreign terrorist fighters into the country. In September 2015, the UNODC Executive Director stressed that illegal drugs in Afghanistan were supporting instability, insurgency, corruption and organized crime, while weakening state institutions and Afghanistan's overall ability to promote peace and good governance. Counter-narcotics efforts continued.

On 14 September 2016, the Council called on the international community to continue its civilian and development efforts to assist Afghanistan.

The security situation in Afghanistan remains volatile. The head of UNAMA informed the Council in 2013 that while the capability of Afghan security forces was growing, they would need international support for at least five additional years to achieve requisite capacity. Terrorist attacks took place throughout 2014, 2015 and 2016, including a 19 April 2016 terrorist attack in Kabul by the Taliban that killed 28 and injured more than 300 people. In January 2017, the Council condemned attacks in Kabul, Helmand and Kandahar, which resulted in more than 161 people killed or injured. In March, the Council extended the UNAMA mandate until March 2018 by resolution 2344(2017).

Iraq

The United Nations' response to Iraq's invasion of Kuwait in 1990, and the situation following the collapse of Saddam Hussein's regime in 2003, illustrate the scope of the challenges the UN faces in seeking to restore international peace and security. In August 1990, the Security Council demanded Iraq's withdrawal from Kuwait and imposed sanctions, including a trade and oil embargo. On 16 January 1991, multinational forces authorized by the Council, but not under UN direction or control, launched military operations against Iraq. Hostilities were suspended in February after the Iraqi forces withdrew from Kuwait.

The Council decided that Iraq's weapons of mass destruction should be eliminated and established the United Nations Special Commission (UNSCOM) on the disarmament of Iraq, with powers of no-notice inspection, and entrusted the International Atomic Energy Agency (IAEA) with similar verification tasks in the nuclear sphere. UNSCOM and the IAEA uncovered and eliminated large quantities of Iraq's banned weapons programmes and capabilities in the nuclear, chemical and biological field. In 1998, Iraq, after calling on the Council to lift its oil embargo and declaring that there were no more proscribed weapons, suspended cooperation with UNSCOM, which conducted its final mission in December. In the same month, the United States and the United Kingdom launched air strikes on Iraq.

In December 1999, the Security Council established the United Nations Monitoring, Verification and Inspection Commission (UNMOVIC) to replace UNSCOM. In November 2002, the Council adopted resolution 1441(2002), providing for an enhanced inspection regime and offering Iraq a final opportunity to comply with its resolutions. UN inspectors returned to Iraq, and the Council was repeatedly briefed by the UNMOVIC Executive Chairman and the IAEA Director-General. In the midst of negotiations, and outside the framework of the Security Council, Spain, the United Kingdom and the United States presented Iraq with a 17 March 2003 deadline to disarm completely. The Secretary-General ordered the withdrawal of UN international staff on 17 March and the suspension of all operations. Following military action by a coalition headed by the United Kingdom and the United States in March 2003 and the collapse of Saddam Hussein's regime, the Security Council, in May, adopted resolution 1483(2003), stressing the right of the Iraqi people to freely determine their political future. It also recognized the authorities, responsibilities and obligations of the Coalition (the "Authority") until the swearing-in of an internationally recognized government. It lifted international sanctions and provided a legal basis for the UN to resume operations in Iraq.

In August 2003, the Security Council established the **United Nations Assistance Mission for Iraq (UNAMI)** (www.uniraq.org) with a mandate to coordinate humanitarian and reconstruction aid and assist with the establishment of an internationally recognized, sovereign Iraqi government. On 19 August, the UN headquarters in Baghdad was the target of a terrorist attack that resulted in 22 deaths, and more than 150 injured. Fifteen of the dead were UN staff, including the head of the mission, Sergio Vieira de Mello. The Secretary-General withdrew most UN international personnel from Baghdad, maintaining only a small team, principally Iraqis, to provide essential humanitarian assistance, including the delivery of food, water and health care.

When UNAMI returned to the country in 2004 under Council resolution 1546(2004), which also pertained to the United States-led Multi-National Force (MNF) mandate, its mission was to support the transitional assembly elections, which were held on 30 January 2005. The Independent Electoral Commission of Iraq, established in June 2004, conducted with UN support, two national elections and a con-

A student in a UNICEF tent classroom at the Al-Takya Al-Kaznazaniya IDP camp near Baghdad in Iraq. Nearly 1.5 million people had returned to their areas of origin across Iraq by February 2017 (23 August 2015, UNICEF/Khuzaie).

stitutional referendum, despite a serious security situation on the ground. In October 2005, Iraq's draft constitution was adopted in a nation-wide referendum, and parliamentary elections were held in December. By June 2006, the new government had been formed. Despite the successful political transition, sectarian violence worsened. By late 2007, some 2.2 million Iraqis had fled the country and there were nearly 2.4 million IDPs. The United Nations took on a lead role in addressing the refugee and IDP situation. The UN country team, which regroups the 20 UN agencies currently operating in Iraq, plays a critical role in efforts to provide assistance.

In accordance with the 2008 status-of-forces agreement between the United States and Iraq, United States forces completed their withdrawal from Iraq on 18 December 2011.

In June 2007, the Council formally terminated the UNMOVIC and IAEA mandates in Iraq and in August of that year, it expanded UNAMI's mandate and separated it from the MNF mandate. Since then, the UNAMI mandate has been renewed annually; the current extension is until 31 July 2017. Key priorities of the UNAMI engagement in Iraq include, promoting more inclusive and effective governance and fostering national reconciliation. It also supports national development efforts on political, electoral, and humanitarian levels.

India–Pakistan

Relations between India and Pakistan have been troubled by a decades-old dispute over Kashmir. The issue dates back to the 1940s, when the princely state of Jammu and Kashmir became free to accede to India or Pakistan under a partition plan and the India Independence Act of 1947. The Hindu Maharaja of mostly Muslim Jammu and Kashmir signed the state's instrument of accession to India.

The Security Council first discussed the issue of Jammu and Kashmir in 1948, following India's complaint that tribesmen and others, with Pakistan's support and participation, were invading the state, and fighting was taking place. Pakistan denied the charges and declared Jammu and Kashmir's accession to India illegal. The **United Nations Military Observer Group in India and Pakistan (UNMOGIP)** (www.un.org/en/peacekeeping/missions/unmogip) was established in 1949 to super-vise the ceasefire between India and Pakistan and to assist the Military Adviser to the UN Commission for India and Pakistan (UNCIP), established by the Council in 1948. Since the India-Pakistan hostilities at the end of 1971 and a subsequent ceasefire agree-ment of 17 December of that year, the UNMOGIP mandate has been to monitor and report on the ceasefire along the Line of Control (LoC) in Jammu and Kashmir. The UN is also committed to promoting harmonious relations between the two countries.

In 2003, India's Prime Minister and the President of Pakistan began a series of recip-rocal steps to improve bilateral relations. In November, Pakistan offered to implement a unilateral ceasefire along the LoC in Jammu and Kashmir. India responded positively. Those efforts led to a summit meeting in 2004 between Prime Minister Atal Bihari Vajpayee of India and Pakistan's President Pervez Musharraf and its Prime Minister Zafarullah Khan Jamali. A bus service across the ceasefire line was inaugurated in 2005 as a gesture of peace and an opportunity to reunite families divided for nearly 60 years.

An attack on the Delhi-Lahore "Friendship Express" in February 2007, which left 67 people dead and nearly 20 injured, tested relations between the two countries. The Secretary-General and the Security Council, condemned the terrorist bombing and called for the perpetrators to be brought to justice. In November 2008, a wave of coor-dinated attacks by Lashkar-e-Taiba extremists, a terrorist group based in Pakistan, took place across Mumbai, India's financial hub. The attacks lasted three days, killing 173 people and wounding 300. An operation by India's armed forces resulted in the death of the attackers at the Taj Mahal hotel, with one captured alive. Pakistan condemned the attacks, but relations between the two neighbours were once again strained.

The killing of a young separatist militant in Srinagar by the Indian forces in 2016 led to an increase in the frequency and intensity of exchanges of fire between India and Pakistan along the LoC. Nevertheless, the overall security situation along the LoC has remained relatively calm. UNMOGIP continues to monitor and report on the obser-vance of the ceasefire demonstrating that the United Nations has neither forgotten the people of Jammu and Kashmir nor the unresolved conflict in their disputed state.

Central Asia

The **United Nations Regional Centre for Preventive Diplomacy for Central Asia (UNRCCA)** (unrcca.unmissions.org) was inaugurated in December 2007. Based in Ashgabat, Turkmenistan, the Centre was established to help the governments of the region peacefully and cooperatively manage an array of common challenges and threats—including terrorism, drug trafficking, organized crime, the management of transboundary water and environmental degradation. The Centre offers governments of the region support in a number of areas, including: building capacity to prevent conflict; facilitating dialogue; and catalyzing international support for specific projects and initiatives. The Centre cooperates closely with the UN programmes and agencies in Central Asia, as well as with regional organizations and other partners. Its 2015–2017 priorities include: transnational threats and challenges; management of common natural resources; domestic factors affecting regional stability; and building national/regional conflict prevention capacities.

Cambodia

Following Cambodia's emergence from French colonialism in the 1950s, the country suffered the spillover of the Viet Nam war in the 1960s and 1970s, as well as devastating civil conflicts and the totalitarian rule of Pol Pot. Under his "Khmer Rouge" regime, from 1975 to 1979, nearly 2 million people perished of murder, disease or starvation, many in Cambodia's infamous "killing fields". In 1993, with help from the United Nations Transitional Authority in Cambodia, the country held its first democratic elections. Since then, UN agencies and programmes have assisted the government in strengthening reconciliation and development. In 2003, an agreement was reached with the government for the UN to help it set up and run a special court to prosecute crimes committed under the Khmer Rouge.

The **Extraordinary Chambers in the Courts of Cambodia (ECCC)** (www.eccc.gov.kh/en) was established in 2005 and issued its first charges for crimes against humanity in July 2007, taking several persons into provisional detention. In 2008, the Cambodians who suffered under the Khmer Rouge participated for the first time in the court through their lawyers.

In February 2012, the Supreme Court Chamber sentenced Kaing Guek Eav, the first person to stand trial before the ECCC and found guilty in 2010, to life imprisonment, the maximum sentence available under the law. In 2010, the four most senior (surviving) members of the Democratic Kampuchea regime—Ieng Sary, Ieng Thirith, Khieu Samphan and Nuon Chea—were indicted on charges of crimes against humanity; the genocide of the Cham and Vietnamese ethnic groups; grave breaches of the Geneva Conventions; and violations of the 1956 Cambodian criminal code, including murder, torture and religious persecution.

Following the September 2012 Trial Chamber affirmation that Ieng Thirith was unfit to stand trial and her release from provisional detention, she passed away in August 2015 while under a regime of judicial supervision. On 14 March 2013, the proceedings against Ieng Sary were terminated, following his death the same day.

In August 2014, the Trial Chamber found Nuon Chea and Khieu Samphan guilty of crimes against humanity committed between 17 April 1975 and December 1977 and sentenced them to life imprisonment. Although defence appealed the convictions, the Supreme Court Chamber upheld most of them on 23 November 2016 and concluded that the life sentence for each of the accused was appropriate. A second trial against Khieu Samphan and Nuon Chea, with additional charges, was still ongoing with presentation of evidence.

Myanmar

Since Myanmar's military leadership voided the results of democratic elections in 1990, the UN has sought to help bring about a return to democracy and improvements in the human rights situation there through an all-inclusive process of national reconciliation. In 1993, the General Assembly urged an accelerated return to democracy, asking the Secretary-General to assist the government in that process. Using his good offices to that end, the Secretary-General designated successive special envoys to engage in dialogue with all parties.

The Assembly has renewed the Secretary-General's good offices mandate annually since 1993. Through the mandate, the UN seeks to promote progress in four key areas: the release of political prisoners, a more inclusive political process, a halt to hostilities in the border areas, and a more enabling environment for the provision of humanitarian assistance.

During his 2009 visit to the country, the Secretary-General argued for the release of all political prisoners, including the detained opposition leader Aung San Suu Kyi of the National League for Democracy (NLD) party; the resumption of substantive dialogue between the government and the opposition; and the creation of conditions conducive to credible and legitimate elections. In August of that year, however, Aung

San Suu Kyi was sentenced to three years of hard labour, which was commuted to 18 months of house arrest—a verdict criticized by the Secretary-General.

In March 2010, the government approved new laws relating to the elections. The political-parties registration law, which prohibited persons serving a prison term from voting or being a member of a political party, prevented Aung San Suu Kyi from participating in the elections. The Secretary-General said that the new election laws did not meet "international expectations of what is required for an inclusive political process".

In May, Cyclone Nargis devastated the Irrawaddy delta and left tens of thousands dead and missing. An estimated 1.2 million to 1.9 million people were affected, left homeless, and exposed to the risk of disease and possible starvation. UN agencies offered assistance, but the government only allowed in limited aid and restricted the access of foreign aid workers. The Secretary-General expressed concern at the slow response to the crisis and travelled to Myanmar to persuade the government to accept international aid. Subsequently, the government accepted humanitarian personnel, who began to arrive in early June. It was also agreed that the aid effort should be led by the Association of Southeast Asian Nations (ASEAN), which resulted in the formation of an ASEAN-UN-Myanmar tripartite mechanism.

In November 2010, the Secretary-General described the elections held that month—Myanmar's first in 20 years and only the third multiparty poll in more than 60 years since independence—as "insufficiently inclusive, participatory and transparent", and called for the release of all political prisoners. Aung San Suu Kyi was released from house arrest on 13 November.

On 19 August 2011, the new President, U Thein Sein, met with Aung San Suu Kyi in talks aimed at finding common ground. In October, a number of political prisoners were released by the government as part of amnesty granted by the President.

In April 2012, candidates from various political parties, including NLD, participated freely in parliamentary by-elections, in which Aung San Suu Kyi won a seat in Parliament. A UN team witnessed the voting in a number of constituencies. On 30 April, the United Nations and the government signed an agreement on UN assistance in the census to be held in Myanmar in 2014—the first in 30 years. Despite these positive developments, the Secretary-General, in October 2012, called on the Myanmar authorities to bring lawlessness under control in the country, characterizing the recent outbreak of communal violence in the northern Rakhine region as "deeply troubling".

In January 2013, the Secretary-General noted reports of air strikes against targets in Kachin State and called on the authorities to desist from any action that could endanger the lives of civilians living in the area or further intensify the conflict in the region. In March, he welcomed the agreement between the Union Peace Working Committee and the Kachin Independence Organization to work towards ceasefire, and encouraged the parties to redouble their efforts toward a fair, genuine and durable solution.

Myanmar conducted a nationwide census between 30 March and 10 April 2014 and the UN provided technical assistance aimed at providing policymakers the information they need for planning and delivering services, in particular to the poorest and most vulnerable. Myanmar successfully chaired ASEAN in 2014 and worked closely with the UN towards UN-ASEAN cooperation.

On 15 October 2015, the Government went ahead with a formal signing—by eight of 17 armed groups—of the Nationwide Ceasefire Agreement (NCA), which was ratified in Parliament on 8 December 2015. Further steps were taken by both sides towards the implementation of the agreement, including the establishment of a Joint Monitoring Committee and the preliminary articulation of a political dialogue framework.

A Union Peace Dialogue Joint Committee was formed in January 2016 and the first session of the Union Peace Conference formally opened in Nay Pyi Taw on 12 January.

The 8 November 2015 general elections gave a landslide electoral victory to the NLD party. The UN provided material and technical assistance to the Union Election Commission for the conduct of the election. The first civilian President of Myanmar, Htin Kyaw, and civilian government took office on 30 March 2016. Aung San Suu Kyi, prohibited from becoming President due to a clause in the Constitution, became Foreign Minister and on 6 April 2016 also State Counsellor (a role akin to Head of Government). The new Myanmar Government has committed to political dialogue that would bring together the various groups in a unified track and pave the way for more inclusive negotiations.

Rakhine. A large number of voters from minority communities, in particular the Rohingya, were denied the right to vote in the November 2015 elections, and some were disqualified as candidates. Progress in improving their living conditions remains elusive. In an effort to address the Rakhine situation, in August 2016, Aung San Suu Kyi appointed the Rakhine Advisory Commission (www.rakhinecommission.org) headed by former UN Secretary-General Kofi Annan.

On 9 October 2016, groups of Rohingya attacked border posts, killed guards and looted weapons and munitions. A subsequent security operation in the area raised concerns about humanitarian access and respect for human rights. In December, the UN High Commissioner for Human Rights condemned the October attacks on border police posts, yet expressed concern that reprisals against Rohingya Muslims continuing more than two months after the border post attacks had caused some 27,000 people to flee across the border into Bangladesh. He emphasized that OHCHR stood ready to advise the Government and provide training and assistance in improving the human rights situation for all the people of Myanmar.

Also in December 2016, the Special Adviser to the Secretary-General on Myanmar, Vijay Nambiar (India), who completed his mandate at the end of that month, urged authorities to take measures to protect the local civilian population and allow humanitarian access to the areas of conflict. He also appealed to Aung San Suu Kyi to address the root causes affecting the local population, namely that of citizenship and status, and to provide relief to the internally displaced since 2012.

Europe

The United Nations continues to address peace and security related matters in Europe, including through the activities of the Secretary-General's special representatives and envoys (www.un.org/sg/en/srsg/europe.shtml). In addition, the **United Nations Liaison Office for Peace and Security (UNLOPS)** (unlops.unmissions.org), established in 2011 and based in Brussels, Belgium, represents the three UN departments that support member states and the Secretary-General in maintaining peace and security— DPKO, DPA and DFS. UNLOPS supports the UN-EU partnership and other Brussels- and Vienna-based organizations on peace and security matters. It also contributes to strengthening institutional dialogue and improving coordination on policy and the planning and conduct of operations

Cyprus

The **United Nations Peacekeeping Force in Cyprus (UNFICYP)** (unficyp.unmissions. org) was established in 1964 to prevent a recurrence of fighting between the Greek Cypriot and Turkish Cypriot communities and to contribute to the maintenance and restoration of law and order and a return to normal conditions. In 1974, a coup d'état by Greek Cypriot and Greek elements favouring union of the country with Greece was followed by military intervention by Turkey, major population displacement and the de facto division of the island. Since then, UNFICYP has supervised a de facto ceasefire that came into effect on 16 August 1974, and maintained a buffer zone between the ceasefire lines of the Cyprus National Guard and Greek forces to the south and the Turkish and Turkish Cypriot forces to the north.

While UNFICYP has kept the peace, the Security Council designated a mediator to facilitate a solution, a mandate which continues today through the **Office of the Special Adviser to the Secretary-General on Cyprus** (unficyp.unmissions.org/about-good-offices), based in Nicosia. Since 1974, the Cyprus problem grew from one of governance and power-sharing to include property, territory, and security issues. In 1977 and 1979, the outline of a comprehensive settlement took shape through two high level agreements, and remains the target of the current negotiations, namely a bizonal bicommunal federation with political equality, single sovereignty and international personality.

In 1999, the prospect of EU membership for the Republic of Cyprus triggered a renewed effort to re-unite the island. The Secretary-General, once again used his good offices in 1999, 2000 and 2002 to facilitate a peace process, but agreement could not be reached and talks were suspended in 2003. In 2004, resumed negotiations culminated in detailed proposals by the Secretary-General, who presented a plan: the "Comprehensive Settlement of the Cyprus Problem", calling for the creation of a federal bi-zonal bi-communal United Cyprus Republic including a Greek Cypriot constituent state and a Turkish Cypriot constituent state. For the first time, the process brought together the Greek Cypriot and Turkish Cypriot leaders, as well as the guarantor powers of Greece, Turkey and the United Kingdom. Seventy-six per cent of voters in the Greek Cypriot referendum opposed the plan, while 65 per cent of voters in the Turkish Cypriot referendum supported it. Without the approval of both communities, the plan was defeated, and so Cyprus entered the EU as a divided and militarized island.

Following an agreement in March 2008 between the Greek Cypriot and the Turkish Cypriot leaders to restart full-fledged negotiations under UN auspices, the Secretary-General revived his good offices mission and appointed a special adviser, Alexander Downer (Australia). The succeeding Special Adviser on Cyprus, Espen Barth Eide (Norway), appointed in August 2014, facilitates the leader-led and Cypriot-owned talks (www.uncyprustalks.org). After eight years of efforts, in September 2016, the incumbent Greek Cypriot and Turkish Cypriot leaders reiterated their determination to do their utmost to reach a comprehensive settlement in their ongoing talks, as described in the joint statement of 11 February 2014, within 2016.

Against this backdrop, a greater sense of security has prevailed since 2004, along with a certain normalisation. After the Turkish Cypriot authorities began to open crossing points through the UN-patrolled buffer zone, thousands of Greek Cypriots and Turkish Cypriots crossed for the first time in nearly three decades, which continues today through the now seven crossing points across the 180 km buffer zone. The UN has undertaken widespread demining, backed by EU funding, removing more than 27,000 landmines. The Committee on Missing Persons has exhumed the remains of more than 1,200 individuals, and after DNA identification, returned more than 650 to their families.

Despite these positive developments, direct contact between the respective authorities outside of the peace process remains limited. In the absence of a political settlement, UNFICYP's facilitating presence and interceding role remains critical to addressing daily issues arising between the opposing forces, the law and order elements and to liaise for civilian related issues. In the event of a settlement, the peacekeeping operation remains committed to supporting the sides in the implementation of an agreement.

South Caucasus

The United Nations continues to monitor political and conflict-related developments in the South Caucasus. Since the August 2008 six-point agreement between Georgia and the Russian Federation to end the hostilities in South Ossetia and the end of the mandate of the UN Observer Mission in Georgia (UNOMIG) in 2009, the United Nations has been supporting the Geneva International Discussions (GID) on security and stability and the return of IDPs and refugees. The Representative of the Secretary-General (UNRGID) (www.un.org/undpa/en/unrgid), Antti Turunen (Finland) serves as the UN representative in the discussions, which are co-chaired by the Organization for Security and Co-operation in Europe (OSCE), the EU and the United Nations.

Greece–FYROM

Since 1999, the Personal Envoy of the Secretary-General, Matthew Nimetz (United States), has been facilitating the talks between Greece and the former Yugoslav Republic of Macedonia (FYROM) to resolve the dispute over the latter country's name. In the Interim Accord of 13 September 1995, the two countries agreed to continue negotiations under the auspices of the Secretary-General pursuant to relevant Security Council resolutions. While no solution has been reached so far, both parties continue to cooperate in the process, expressing the wish for the Secretary-General and the Personal Envoy's continued engagement.

Kosovo

In 1989, the Federal Republic of Yugoslavia revoked local autonomy in Kosovo, a province in southern Yugoslavia historically important to Serbs that was more than 90 per cent ethnically Albanian. Kosovo Albanians dissented, boycotting Serbian state institutions and authority in a quest for self-rule. Tensions increased, and the Kosovo Liberation Army (KLA) surfaced in 1996, seeking independence through armed rebellion. It launched attacks against Serb officials and Albanians who collaborated with them, and Serb authorities responded with mass arrests. Fighting erupted in March 1998 as Serbian police swept the Drenica region, ostensibly looking for KLA members. The Security Council imposed an arms embargo against Yugoslavia, including Kosovo, but the situation deteriorated into open warfare.

In 1999, following warnings to Yugoslavia, and against the backdrop of a Serbian offensive in Kosovo, the North Atlantic Treaty Organization (NATO) began air strikes against Yugoslavia. Yugoslavia launched a major offensive against the KLA and began mass deportations of ethnic Albanians from Kosovo, causing an unprecedented outflow of 850,000 refugees. UNHCR and other humanitarian agencies rushed to assist them in Albania and The former Yugoslav Republic of Macedonia. Yugoslavia accepted a peace plan proposed by the Group of Eight (seven Western industrialized nations and Russia). The Security Council endorsed the plan and authorized member states to establish a security presence to deter hostilities, demilitarize the KLA and facilitate the return of refugees. It also asked the Secretary-General to establish an interim international civilian administration, under which the people could enjoy substantial autonomy and self-government. Yugoslav forces withdrew, NATO suspended its bombings, and a 50,000-strong multinational Kosovo Force (KFOR) arrived to provide security.

The **United Nations Interim Administration Mission in Kosovo (UNMIK)** (unmik. unmissions.org) immediately established a presence on the ground. The Security Council vested UNMIK with authority over the territory and people of Kosovo, including all legislative and executive powers and administration of the judiciary. Some 841,000 of the 850,000 refugees who fled during the war returned. UNMIK made significant progress towards re-establishing normal life. The KLA was completely demilitarized before the end of 1999 and its members reintegrated in civil society. In the following months, some 210,000 non-Albanian Kosovars left Kosovo for Serbia and Montenegro. Remaining non-Albanian minorities lived in isolated enclaves guarded by KFOR.

In 2001, the International Tribunal for the former Yugoslavia indicted former Yugoslav President Slobodan Milosevic and four others for crimes against humanity during a "systematic attack directed against the Kosovo Albanian civilian population of Kosovo". Milosevic died in 2006 of natural causes while in detention. He was facing 66 counts of genocide, crimes against humanity and war crimes in Bosnia and Herzegovina, Croatia, and Kosovo.

Also in 2001, the Security Council lifted its arms embargo. In November, a Kosovo Assembly was elected which, in 2002, elected the province's first President and Prime Minister. In December, UNMIK completed the transfer of responsibilities to local provisional institutions, though it retained control over security, foreign relations, protection of minority rights, and energy—pending determination of the province's final status.

Following the conduct of four rounds of direct negotiations between the parties in 2006, the first high-level meeting between top Serbian and Kosovar leaders, and the presentation by the Secretary-General's special envoy of his final status plan in 2007, Kosovo's ethnic Albanian government and Serbia remained at odds. The special envoy subsequently reported that the only viable option for Kosovo was independence—which has been consistently opposed by Serbia. Later that year, a troika composed of the EU, Russia and the United States agreed to lead further negotiations on Kosovo's future status; however, the parties have not been able to reach an agreement.

In 2008, the Kosovo Assembly adopted a declaration of independence. In 2010, the International Court of Justice issued an advisory opinion on the declaration that stated it did not violate international law. At the same time, the Secretary-General reaffirmed the UN readiness to contribute to the process of dialogue between Belgrade and Pristina in close coordination with the EU. The dialogue began in 2011 and continued into 2012.

On 19 October 2012, the first high-level meeting in Brussels between Prime Ministers Ivica Dačić of Serbia and Hashim Thaçi of Kosovo was held under EU auspices. As at 22 March 2013, the two Prime Ministers had met for seven rounds of dialogue. On 19 April 2013, the two sides signed the landmark "First Agreement on Principles Governing the Normalization of Relations", cementing their commitment to normalisation. Until September 2015, the dialogue remained on track, with both sides continuing to implement the dialogue agreements. These included the integration of northern Serb-majority municipalities and local Belgrade-financed police and security personnel into Kosovo's administrative framework. The engagement in the dialogue led to the signing of an EU-Kosovo Stabilization and Association Agreement in October 2015 and opening of the first negotiations chapters on Serbia's accession process to the EU in December 2015. In 2016, however, progress slowed down as the sides engaged in difficult discussions concerning the issues of energy, telecommunications and the implementation of the 25 August 2015 agreement on the establishment of the Association/ Community of Serb majority municipalities.

As at July 2016, 113 member states had recognized Kosovo as an independent state.

DISARMAMENT

Since the birth of the United Nations, the goals of multilateral disarmament and arms limitation have been central to its efforts to maintain international peace and security (www.un.org/disarmament). The UN has given highest priority to reducing and eventually eliminating nuclear weapons, destroying chemical weapons and strengthening the prohibition of biological weapons—all of which pose the direst threats to humankind. While these objectives have remained constant over the years, the scope of deliberations and negotiations has changed as political realities and the international situation evolved. The international community continues to consider more closely the excessive and destabilizing proliferation of small arms and light weapons and has mobilized to combat the massive deployment of landmines—instruments that threaten the economic and social fabric of societies and kill and maim civilians, all too many of whom are women and children. The UN is also focusing on the impact of new information, telecommunications technologies and other emerging technologies on international security.

The tragic events of 11 September 2001 in the United States, and subsequent terrorist attacks in a number of countries, underlined the potential danger of non-state actors acquiring weapons of mass destruction. Such attacks could have had even more devastating consequences had the terrorists been able to acquire and use chemical, biological or nuclear weapons. Reflecting these concerns, the General Assembly adopted in 2002, for the first time, a resolution (57/83) on measures to prevent terrorists from acquiring weapons of mass destruction and their means of delivery.

In 2004, the Security Council took its first formal decision on the danger of the proliferation of weapons of mass destruction, particularly among non-state actors. Acting under the enforcement provisions of the *Charter of the United Nations*, the Council unanimously adopted resolution 1540(2004), obliging states to refrain from any support for non-state actors in the development, acquisition, manufacture, possession, transport, transfer or use of nuclear, chemical and biological weapons and their means of delivery. The resolution imposes far-reaching obligations on states to establish domestic measures to prevent the proliferation of such weapons including the establishment of appropriate controls over related materials. Subsequently, the General Assembly adopted the *International Convention for the Suppression of Acts of Nuclear Terrorism*, which entered into force in 2007.

In addition to its role in disarmament and in verifying compliance, the UN assists member states in establishing new norms in multilateral disarmament and in strengthening and consolidating existing agreements.

Disarmament machinery

The *Charter* gives the General Assembly chief responsibility for considering "the general principles of cooperation in the maintenance of international peace and security, including the principles governing disarmament and the regulation of armaments" (Article 11). The Assembly has two subsidiary bodies dealing with disarmament and international security issues: the First (Disarmament and International Security) Committee, which meets during the Assembly's regular session and deals with all disarmament issues on its agenda; and the Disarmament Commission, a specialized deliberative body that focuses on specific issues and meets for three weeks every year.

The **Conference on Disarmament** is the single multilateral disarmament negotiating forum of the international community. The Conference and its predecessors have negotiated the *Biological Weapons Convention*, the *Chemical Weapons Convention, the*

Comprehensive Nuclear-Test-Ban Treaty and the *Treaty on the Non-Proliferation of Nuclear Weapons*. Since 1997, however, the Conference has been unable to adopt and carry out a programme of work due to lack of consensus among its members on disarmament priorities, despite intensive discussions and several proposals for a programme of work during its 2016 session. Since the Conference addresses matters that touch upon the national security interests of states, it works strictly on the basis of consensus. It has a limited membership of 65 states and a unique relationship with the General Assembly. While the Conference defines its own rules and develops its own agenda, it takes into account the recommendations of the Assembly and reports to it annually.

The **Office for Disarmament Affairs (ODA)** (www.un.org/disarmament/) implements the decisions of the Assembly on disarmament matters. The **United Nations Institute for Disarmament Research (UNIDIR)** undertakes independent research on disarmament and related problems, particularly international security issues. The **Advisory Board on Disarmament Matters** advises the Secretary-General on matters relating to arms limitation and disarmament, and serves as the Board of Trustees of UNIDIR. It also advises on implementation of the recommendations of the **United Nations Disarmament Information Programme**.

Multilateral agreements

Important international disarmament and arms regulation measures concluded through negotiations in multilateral and regional forums include:

- 1925 *Geneva Protocol*: prohibits the first use of chemical and biological weapons.
- 1959 *Antarctic Treaty*: demilitarizes the continent and bans the testing of any kind of weapon on the continent.
- 1963 *Treaty Banning Nuclear Weapon Tests in the Atmosphere, in Outer Space and Under Water (Partial Test Ban Treaty)*: restricts nuclear testing to underground sites only.
- 1967 *Treaty for the Prohibition of Nuclear Weapons in Latin America and the Caribbean (Treaty of Tlatelolco)*: prohibits testing, use, manufacture, storage, or acquisition of nuclear weapons by the countries of the region.
- 1967 *Treaty on Principles Governing the Activities of States in the Exploration and Use of Outer Space, including the Moon and Other Celestial Bodies (Outer Space Treaty)*: mandates that outer space be used for peaceful purposes only and that nuclear weapons not be placed or tested in outer space.
- 1968 *Treaty on the Non-Proliferation of Nuclear Weapons*: establishes that the non-nuclear-weapon states agree never to acquire nuclear weapons and, in exchange, are promised access to and assistance in the peaceful uses of nuclear energy. Nuclear-weapon states pledge to carry out negotiations relating to the cessation of the nuclear arms race and to nuclear disarmament, and not to assist in any way in the transfer of nuclear weapons to non-nuclear-weapon states.
- 1971 *Treaty on the Prohibition of the Emplacement of Nuclear Weapons and Other Weapons of Mass Destruction on the Sea-bed and the Ocean Floor and in the Subsoil Thereof (Sea-bed Treaty)*: bans the emplacement of nuclear weapons, or any weapon of mass destruction, on the sea-bed or ocean floor.
- 1972 *Convention on the Prohibition of the Development, Production and Stockpiling of Bacteriological (Biological) and Toxin Weapons and on Their Destruction (Biological Weapons Convention)*: bans the development, production and stockpiling of biological and toxin agents, and provides for the destruction of such weapons and their means of delivery.

- 1980 *Convention on Prohibitions or Restrictions on the Use of Certain Conventional Weapons Which May Be Deemed to Be Excessively Injurious or to Have Indiscriminate Effects* (CCW): prohibits certain conventional weapons deemed excessively injurious or having indiscriminate effects. *Protocol I* bans weapons which explode fragments that are undetectable by X-ray within the human body. Amended *Protocol II* (1995) limits the use of certain types of mines, booby-traps and other devices. *Protocol III* bans incendiary weapons. *Protocol IV* bans the use of blinding laser weapons.
- 1985 *South Pacific Nuclear Free Zone Treaty (Rarotonga Treaty)*: bans the stationing, acquisition or testing of nuclear explosive devices and the dumping of nuclear waste within the zone.
- 1990 *Treaty on Conventional Armed Forces in Europe (CFE Treaty)*: limits the numbers of various conventional armaments in a zone stretching from the Atlantic Ocean to the Urals.
- 1992 *Open Skies Treaty*: enables states parties to overfly and observe the territory of one another, based on principles of cooperation and openness. Has been used for the verification of several arms control agreements and for other monitoring mechanisms.
- 1993 *Convention on the Prohibition of the Development, Production, Stockpiling and Use of Chemical Weapons and on Their Destruction (Chemical Weapons Convention)*: prohibits the development, production, stockpiling and use of chemical weapons and requires their destruction.
- 1995 *Treaty on the Southeast Asia Nuclear Weapon-Free Zone (Bangkok Treaty)*: bans the development or stationing of nuclear weapons on the territories of the states parties.
- 1996 *African Nuclear-Weapon-Free Zone Treaty (Treaty of Pelindaba)*: bans the development or stationing of nuclear weapons on the African continent.
- 1996 *Comprehensive Nuclear-Test-Ban Treaty (CTBT)*: places a worldwide ban on nuclear test explosions of any kind and in any environment.
- 1997 *Convention on the Prohibition of the Use, Stockpiling, Production and Transfer of Anti-Personnel Mines and on Their Destruction (Mine Ban Convention)*: prohibits the use, stockpiling, production and transfer of antipersonnel mines and provides for their destruction.
- 2005 *International Convention for the Suppression of Acts of Nuclear Terrorism (Nuclear Terrorism Convention)*: outlines specific acts of nuclear terrorism, aims to protect a broad range of possible targets, bring perpetrators to justice and promote cooperation among countries.
- 2006 *Treaty on a Nuclear-Weapon-Free Zone in Central Asia*: establishes zone comprising the five Central Asian states—Kazakhstan, Kyrgyzstan, Tajikistan, Turkmenistan and Uzbekistan.
- 2008 *Convention on Cluster Munitions*: prohibits the use, development, production, acquisition, stockpiling, retention or transfer of such munitions.
- 2010 *Central African Convention for the Control of Small Arms and Light Weapons, Their Ammunition and All Parts and Components That Can Be Used for Their Manufacture, Repair and Assembly (Kinshasha Convention)*: restricts the manufacture, transfer between states, and possession by civilians of small arms and light weapons; requires arms to be marked, brokering activities and brokers to be regulated and states to limit the number of entry points of weapons on their national territory.
- 2013 *Arms Trade Treaty*: regulates international trade in conventional weapons.

(For status of ratification of these agreements, see disarmament.un.org/treaties and treaties.un.org/Pages/ParticipationStatus.aspx?clang=_en)

Weapons of mass destruction

Nuclear weapons

Through sustained efforts, the world community has achieved numerous multilateral agreements aimed at reducing nuclear arsenals; excluding their deployment from certain regions and environments (such as outer space and the ocean floor); limiting their proliferation; and ending testing. Despite these achievements, the world stockpile of over 15,000 nuclear weapons and their proliferation remain major threats to peace and a major challenge to the international community. Issues of concern in this area include the need for reductions in nuclear weapons, upholding the viability of the nuclear non-proliferation regime, and preventing the development and proliferation of ballistic missiles and missile defence systems.

Bilateral agreements on nuclear weapons. While international efforts to contain nuclear weapons continue in different forums, it has been generally understood that the nuclear-weapon powers hold special responsibility for maintaining a stable international security environment. During and after the cold war, the two major powers arrived at agreements that have significantly reduced the threat of nuclear war.

Multilateral agreements on nuclear weapons and non-proliferation. The *Treaty on the Non-Proliferation of Nuclear Weapons (NPT)*, the most universal of all multilateral disarmament treaties, was opened for signature in 1968 and came into force in 1970. A total of 191 states have joined. The NPT is the cornerstone of the global nuclear non-proliferation regime and the foundation for the pursuit of nuclear disarmament. The decision by the Democratic People's Republic of Korea (DPRK) to withdraw from the *Treaty* in January 2003—the first such decision since the *Treaty's* entry into force 33 years earlier— was of great concern to the international community.

The 2010 Review Conference of the Parties to the NPT adopted a 22-point Action Plan on Nuclear Disarmament, outlining concrete steps in the areas of nuclear disarmament, security assurances, nuclear testing and fissile materials. The Conference also endorsed the convening of a conference in 2012, attended by all Middle Eastern states, on the establishment of a zone free of nuclear weapons in the region. The meeting was not held due to the political turmoil in the Middle East. In 2015, participants of the NPT Review Conference were unable to reach agreement on a substantive outcome, due primarily to disagreement on the way forward on the establishment of a Middle East zone free of nuclear and all other weapons of mass destruction.

To verify obligations assumed under the NPT, states parties are required to accept the nuclear safeguards of the International Atomic Energy Agency (IAEA). At the end of 2015, there were safeguards agreements in force with 181 states, 173 of which have comprehensive safeguards agreements. Additional protocols are in force in 127 States. In addition to the NPT, the *Treaties of Bangkok, Pelindaba, Rarotonga, Tlatelolco* and on a *Nuclear Weapon-Free Zone in Central Asia* require non-nuclear-weapon states to apply IAEA safeguards.

In 1996, an overwhelming majority of General Assembly members adopted the *Comprehensive Nuclear-Test-Ban Treaty* (CTBT), proscribing any nuclear-test explosions anywhere. Originally proposed in 1954, it took four decades to adopt the *Treaty*, which extended the 1963 partial test ban to all environments. Over 2,000 nuclear explosions were recorded between July 1945 when the first nuclear bomb was tested by the United States and 1996 when the CTBT banning such explosions was opened for signature. The CTBT has not yet entered into force. As at 31 January 2017, 183 states had signed the CTBT, with 166 states ratifying it. The *Treaty* will enter into force 180 days after the 44 states listed in its Annex 2 have ratified it. These "Annex 2" states are countries that participated in the negotiations for the CTBT between 1994 and 1996 and possessed nuclear power reactors or research reactors at that time. As at 31 January 2017, eight Annex 2 states remained outside of the treaty: China, DPRK, Egypt, India, Iran, Israel, Pakistan and the United States. The UN Secretary-General, in his capacity as the Depositary of the *Treaty*, has convened a series of Conferences on Facilitating the Entry into Force of the CTBT—in 1999, 2001, 2003, 2005, 2007, 2009, 2011, 2013 and 2015. Work continues in the Provisional Technical Secretariat, established in 1997, to ensure that an international monitoring system is operational by the time the *Treaty* enters into force. When complete, the monitoring system will consist of 337 monitoring facilities, complemented by an intrusive on-site inspection regime applicable once the *Treaty* has entered into force.

Nuclear-weapon-free zones. In a development that was to herald a new movement in regional arms control, the signing of the 1967 *Treaty for the Prohibition of Nuclear Weapons in Latin America and the Caribbean (Treaty of Tlatelolco)* established for the first time a nuclear-weapon-free zone in a populated area of the world. With the deposit of Cuba's instrument of ratification in 2002, the nuclear-weapon-free zone in Latin America and the Caribbean was consolidated to include all states in the region. Subsequently, four additional zones were established—in the South Pacific (*Treaty of Rarotonga*, 1985), South-East Asia (*Treaty of Bangkok*, 1995), Africa (*Treaty of Pelindaba*, 1996), and Central Asia (*Central Asia Nuclear-Weapon-Free Zone Treaty*, 2006). Proposals have been made for establishing nuclear-weapon free zones in Central Europe and South Asia, as well as for a zone free of nuclear and all other weapons of mass destruction in the Middle East. The concept of an individual country as a nuclear-weapon-free zone was acknowledged by the international community in 1998, when the General Assembly supported Mongolia's self-declaration of its nuclear-weapon-free status.

Preventing nuclear proliferation

The **International Atomic Energy Agency (IAEA)** (www.iaea.org) verifies that states are honoring their international legal obligations to use nuclear material and technology only for peaceful purposes. Its independent verification work allows IAEA to play an indispensable role in preventing the spread of nuclear weapons. Under agreements concluded with states, IAEA inspectors regularly visit nuclear facilities to verify the correctness and completeness of states' reports on their nuclear material and nuclear-related activities. Inspectors audit and compare operating records with reports to the Agency, verify inventories and inventory changes, take environmental samples, apply seals and install surveillance equipment. In 2015, IAEA experts conducted 2,118 field verifications on the implementation of the safeguards agreements in 181 states. Their aim is to ensure that nuclear material held in more than 1,200 facilities is not diverted from peaceful uses to military purposes.

Three types of safeguards agreements can be concluded with IAEA depending on whether a country is party to the *Treaty on the Non-Proliferation of Nuclear Weapons (NPT)* and if it is a non-nuclear weapons state, or a weapons state under the treaty. The agreements can be complemented with an *Additional Protocol* that encompasses countries' complete nuclear-fuel-cycle activities. Safeguards also apply to the nuclear-weapon-free zone treaties of *Bangkok, Central Asia, Pelindaba, Rarotonga* and *Tlatelolco*. IAEA safeguards are an integral part of the international regime for non-proliferation and ensuring the implementation of the NPT.

On 14 July 2015, IAEA and Iran signed a *Road-map for the Clarification of Past and Present Outstanding Issues regarding Iran's Nuclear Program* and the E3/EU+3 and Iran agreed on a *Joint Comprehensive Plan of Action (JCPOA)*. On 20 July 2015, the Security Council requested the IAEA Director General to "undertake the necessary verification and monitoring of Iran's nuclear-related commitments for the full duration of those commitments under the JCPOA".

IAEA has been unable to carry out verification activities in the Democratic People's Republic of Korea (DPRK) since 2009, but continues to closely follow the DPRK nuclear issue. In November 2016, the Council imposed the stricter sanctions on DPRK in response to its repeated nuclear and missile tests.

Chemical and biological weapons

The entry into force of the *Chemical Weapons Convention (CWC)* in 1997 completed a process that began in 1925, when the *Geneva Protocol* prohibited the use of poison gas weapons. The *Convention* created, for the first time in the history of international arms control, a stringent international verification regime involving the collection of information on chemical facilities and routine global inspections to oversee compliance with treaty obligations by states parties to the *Convention*. Established for that purpose at The Hague, the **Organisation for the Prohibition of Chemical Weapons (OPCW)** (www.opcw.org) is very active. Following the accession of Angola and Myanmar in 2015, the OPCW membership, as at October 2016, stood at 192 nations, representing more than 98 per cent of the global population.

Unlike the CWC, the 1972 *Biological and Toxin Weapons Convention* (BTWC or BWC) (*www.opbw.org*), which entered into force in 1975, does not provide for a verification mechanism. States parties exchange, as a confidence-building measure, detailed information each year on such items as their high-risk biological research facilities. In 2006, the Sixth Review Conference of the States Parties to the Biological and Toxin Weapons Convention decided to establish an Implementation Support Unit to help states parties bolster implementation of the *Convention*. Unlike the nuclear non-proliferation and chemical weapons treaties, which are supported by IAEA and OPCW, respectively, there was no institutional support with respect to biological weapons. Meetings of the states parties to the *Convention* take place at the UN on a regular basis, with the Eighth Review Conference held in November 2016.

Conventional weapons, confidence-building and transparency

Small arms, light weapons and practical disarmament. States have an inherent right to individual or collective self-defence and may use armed force in conformity with the *Charter of the United Nations*. Apart from arming their national armed and security forces, most countries allow private security companies and citizens—usually under certain conditions—to own firearms and weapons and use them for lawful purposes. There are hundreds of millions of licensed firearms in the world. Of these, roughly two-thirds are in the hands of civilians. The legal trade in these weapons exceeds several billion dollars a year, while the illicit trade is believed to be worth over $1 billion annually. Controlling the proliferation of illicit weapons is a necessary step towards better international, regional or national control over all aspects of the issue of small arms.

In 2001, an international Conference on the Illicit Trade in Small Arms and Light Weapons in All Its Aspects was held at the United Nations. Under the Conference's resulting *Programme of Action*, member states agreed to improve legislation and controls, and strengthen marking, record-keeping and tracing of small arms. The inclusion in the 2030 Agenda for Sustainable Development of a target on reducing illicit arms trafficking

A member of the MINUSMA Nepalese contingent assesses explosives threat at the Kidal Airstrip in northern Mali (15 September 2015, UN Photo/Marco Dormino).

firmly establishes illicit small arms—and the related armed violence—as an issue relevant for development. Meanwhile, the United Nations has developed a set of International Small Arms Control Standards (ISACS) (www.smallarmsstandards.org), which provide state-of-the-art practical guidance on establishing national controls over the full life-cycle of small arms and light weapons, thereby reducing the risk of their falling into the hands of criminals, armed groups, terrorists and others who would misuse them.

Ammunition. In over 60 countries during the last decade, poorly-stored ammunition stockpiles have inadvertently exploded (www.un.org/disarmament/ammunition). Thousands of people have died and the livelihoods of entire communities were disrupted. Unsecured or poorly-monitored national ammunition stockpiles also lead to massive diversion to illicit markets. Diverted conventional ammunition is increasingly used to assemble improvised explosive devices (IEDs). Following a recommendation by the Security Council to promote stockpile security and the management of arms and ammunition as an urgent priority and the General Assembly request for the United Nations to develop guidelines for ammunition management, the UN SaferGuard Programme (www.un.org/disarmament/un-saferguard) was established. It oversees the dissemination of the International Ammunition Technical Guidelines (IATG): detailed standards for voluntary use by countries that wish to improve the safety and security of their ammunition storage sites. These guidelines assist national authorities, industry and others to enhance the safety and security of ammunition stockpiles and are fully coordinated with ISACS.

Arms Trade Treaty. Virtually all areas of world trade are covered by regulations that bind countries to agreed conduct, but there was no global set of rules governing the trade in conventional weapons. In 2013, the General Assembly adopted the *Arms Trade Treaty* (www.un.org/disarmament/att). Signatories are bound to show responsibility in their decisions regarding arms transfers. This means that before approving any international transfer of weapons, they should assess the risk of the transfer exacerbating conflict or facilitating violations of international humanitarian law and human rights law.

Anti-personnel mines. The proliferation and indiscriminate use of anti-personnel landmines around the world has been a particular focus of the UN attention. In 1995, a review of the *Convention on Certain Conventional Weapons (CCW)*—also known as the *Inhumane Weapons Convention*—produced the *Amended Protocol II*, which entered into force in 1998, strengthening restrictions on certain uses, transfers and types (self-destroying and detectable) of landmines. As at 31 December 2016, 102 states were bound by this *Protocol*. The *Convention* has five protocols that, besides banning landmines and booby-traps, also ban non-detectable fragments, incendiary weapons, blinding lasers and explosive remnants of war. Subsequently, states negotiated an agreement on a total ban on all anti-personnel landmines—the *Convention on the Prohibition of the Use, Stockpiling, Production and Transfer of Anti-personnel Mines and on Their Destruction (Mine-Ban Convention)*, which opened for signature in 1997 and entered into force in 1999. As at 31 December 2016, 162 states had become parties to it.

Implementation of both instruments has led to the destruction of stockpiles, mine clearance in affected countries, and fewer victims. A total of 3,678 casualties by mines, cluster munition remnants, and other explosive remnants of war were recorded in 2014. The incidence rate of 10 casualties per day in 2014, is a significant decrease from 1999 when there were approximately 25 casualties per day. On the ground, 12 UN departments and offices, specialized agencies, programmes and funds are active in mine action programmes in 30 countries and three territories.

The **United Nations Mine Action Service (UNMAS)** (www.mineaction.org) collaborates with 11 UN entities to ensure a proactive and coordinated response to the problems of landmines and explosive remnants of war, including cluster munitions. Once restricted to "demining", UNMAS activities encompass three broad categories: risk mitigation and landmine clearance; weapons and ammunition management; and improvised explosive devices (IED) threat mitigation. UNMAS carries out efforts to mitigate these threats when mandated by the Security Council, or when requested by the Secretary-General or an affected country, often in response to a humanitarian emergency. It sets up and manages mine-action coordination centres in countries as part of peacekeeping operations and humanitarian emergencies or crises. In these situations, UNMAS plans and carries out mine-action projects, orchestrates the work of local and international mine-action service providers, and sets priorities for mine clearance, mine-risk education and other aspects of mine action. UNMAS also coordinates UN advocacy in support of treaties and international legal instruments related to landmines and explosive remnants of war.

Register of Conventional Arms. In order to contribute to building confidence and security among states, the General Assembly in 1991 established the *United Nations Register of Conventional Arms* (www.un.org/disarmament/register). This voluntary reporting arrangement enables participating governments to provide information on the export and import of major conventional weapons systems, from warships and battle tanks to combat aircraft—and on small arms. Member states are also invited to provide data on procurement through national production, and military holdings. Such data are compiled and published annually by the UN as official documents available to the general public, as well as through the UN website. It is estimated that the *Register* captures more than 95 per cent of the global trade in major conventional weapons.

Transparency of military expenditures. Another global mechanism designed to promote transparency in military matters is the United Nations Report on Military Expenditures (www.un.org/disarmament/milex), introduced in 1980. This voluntary instrument covers national expenditures on military personnel, operations and maintenance, procurement and construction, and research and development. The UN collects this information and makes it public.

Explosive remnants of war (ERW) and mines other than anti-personnel mines (MOTAPM). While significant steps have been taken to address anti-personnel landmines, many civilians are killed or injured by other explosive munitions. They pose a potential hazard to populations through inadvertent contact or deliberate tampering, especially if the danger is not well understood. They can cause severe damage even in small numbers; when placed in strategic locations, a single mine can cause entire roads to be closed and can disrupt normal activities. Combined with other possible characteristics of MOTAPM, such as anti-handling devices and minimum metal content, their humanitarian impact can be quite serious.

Under *Protocol V* to the CCW, states parties to armed conflict are required to take action to clear, remove or destroy ERW, and record, retain and transmit information related to the use or abandonment of explosive ordnance. They are also obligated to take all feasible precautions for the protection of civilians and humanitarian missions and organizations. States parties in a position to do so should provide cooperation and assistance for marking, clearance, removal, destruction, and victim assistance. *Protocol V* entered into force in 2006.

The *Convention on Cluster Munitions*, which prohibits all use, stockpiling, production and transfer of cluster munitions, entered into force in 2010. In addition, it establishes a framework for cooperation and assistance to ensure adequate care and rehabilitation to victims and their communities, for clearance of contaminated areas, for risk reduction education and for the destruction of stockpiles.

Prevention of an arms race in outer space. Matters related to outer space have been pursued in international forums along two separate lines: those related to peaceful applications of space technology, and those related to the prevention of an arms race in that environment. These issues have been discussed in the General Assembly, the Committee on the Peaceful Uses of Outer Space and its subsidiary bodies, and the Conference on Disarmament. To increase access to the benefits of current space applications, and develop new technologies which may offer further benefits, there is a need to preserve and protect the outer space environment for use by future generations. To this end, the Committee established in 2010 a Working Group on the Long Term Sustainability of Outer Space Activities, which has intensified its activities during the biennium.

In accordance with the recommendations contained in the 2013 report of the Group of Governmental Experts (GGE) on Transparency and Confidence-Building Measures in Outer Space Activities to promote in various fora the practical implementation of transparency and confidence-building measures in outer space activities, China, the Russian Federation and the United States proposed a related agenda item at the 2016 substantive session of the UN Disarmament Commission.

The First Committee, at its seventieth session, remained divided on broader issues of preventing an arms race in outer space, including on the non-placement of weapons in outer space. Nevertheless, the three most prominent space-faring states—China, Russia and the United States—displayed renewed unity on the implementation of transparency and confidence-building measures.

Regional approaches to disarmament. The United Nations supports both regional and subregional initiatives towards disarmament, promoting security and confidence-building measures among states within a region. It also assists them in implementing the international guidelines and standards for disarmament, arms control and non-proliferation. To foster regional disarmament, the UN works with governmental organizations and regional arrangements—such as the African Union, the European Union, the League of Arab States, the Organization of American States, the Organisation of Islamic Cooperation, the Organisation for Security and Co-operation in Europe, the Association of Southeast Asian Nations, the Pacific Island Forum and the Caribbean Community—as well as with international, regional and local NGOs. In addition, the three regional centres for disarmament and peace in Africa (unrec.org), Asia and the Pacific (unrcpd.org), and in Latin America and the Caribbean (www.unlirec.org) support member states in their effort to promote regional security and disarmament.

Disarmament information and education activities. The UN undertakes information and education activities on disarmament and non-proliferation in the framework of its Disarmament Information Programme—through publications, special events, seminars, panel discussions, exhibits and a comprehensive website on disarmament and non-proliferation issues (www.un.org/disarmament/education). Since its inception in 1979, the UN Programme of Fellowship on Disarmament has trained nearly 960 public officials from over 160 countries—many of whom are now in positions of responsibility in the field of disarmament within their own governments.

Gender perspective in disarmament. Conflict and armed violence affect genders differently. The UN promotes understanding of the importance of gender perspectives in all aspects of disarmament, including collecting and destroying weapons, demining, conducting fact-finding missions, training and participating in decision-making and peace processes. Gender perspectives are required across the disarmament spectrum—from the gendered social and economic impacts of the illicit arms trade to the gendered biological impacts of nuclear weapons. In October 2000, the Security Council, in its landmark resolution 1325(2000), encouraged "all those involved in the planning for disarmament, demobilization and reintegration to consider the different needs of female and male ex-combatants". The Global Study on UNSC resolution 1325 (wps.unwomen), released in 2015, highlighted the connections between small arms, violence and gender; recognized the link between gender-based violence and the arms trade; and called for all states to accede to the *Arms Trade Treaty*, which, in Article 7 (4) requires states parties to consider the risk of arms being used to commit acts of gender-based violence.

PEACEFUL USES OF OUTER SPACE

The United Nations works to ensure that outer space is used for peaceful purposes and that the benefits from space activities are shared by all nations. This concern with the peaceful uses of outer space began soon after the launch of Sputnik—the first artificial satellite—by the Soviet Union in 1957, and has kept pace with advances in space technology. The UN has played an important role by developing international space law and by promoting international cooperation in space science and technology. The main intergovernmental body in the space field is the **United Nations Committee on the Peaceful Uses of Outer Space (COPUOS)** (www.unoosa.org/oosa/en/ourwork/copuos/). Established by the General Assembly in 1959, the Committee reviews the scope of international cooperation in peaceful uses of outer space, devises programmes and directs UN technical cooperation, encourages research and dissemination of information, and contributes to the development of international space law. The Committee comprises 84 member states, and a number of international organizations, both intergovernmental and non-governmental, have observer status. It has two subcommittees. The Scientific and Technical Subcommittee is the focal point of international cooperation in space technology and research, and the Legal Subcommittee works to develop a legal framework concomitant with the rapid technological advances of space activities. The Committee and its subcommittees meet annually to consider questions put forth by the General Assembly, reports submitted to them and issues raised by member states. Working on the basis of consensus, the Committee makes recommendations to the Assembly.

Legal instruments

The work of the Committee and its Legal Subcommittee has resulted in the adoption by the General Assembly of five legal instruments, all of which are in force:

- The 1966 *Treaty on Principles Governing the Activities of States in the Exploration and Use of Outer Space, including the Moon and Other Celestial Bodies* (Outer Space Treaty) provides that space exploration shall be carried out for the benefit of all countries, irrespective of their degree of development. It seeks to maintain outer space as the province of all humankind, free for exploration and use by all states, solely for peaceful purposes, and not subject to national appropriation.
- The 1967 *Agreement on the Rescue of Astronauts, the Return of Astronauts and the Return of Objects Launched into Outer Space* (Rescue Agreement) provides for aiding the crews of spacecraft in case of accident or emergency landing, and establishes procedures for returning to the launching authority a space object found beyond the territory of that authority.
- The 1971 *Convention on International Liability for Damage Caused by Space Objects* (Liability Convention) provides that the launching state is liable for damage caused by its space objects on the Earth's surface, to aircraft in flight, and to space objects of another state or persons or property on board such objects.
- The 1974 *Convention on Registration of Objects Launched into Outer Space* (Registration Convention) provides that launching states maintain registries of space objects and share that information with the United Nations. Under the Convention, the Office for Outer Space Affairs maintains a register of such objects. Information has been provided by all launching states and organizations. A searchable index of launched objects is available at www.unoosa.org.
- The 1979 *Agreement Governing Activities of States on the Moon and Other Celestial Bodies* (Moon Agreement) elaborates the principles relating to the moon and other celestial bodies set out in the 1966 Treaty, and sets up the basis to regulate the future exploration and exploitation of natural resources on those bodies.

On the basis of the work of the Committee and its Legal Subcommittee, the General Assembly has adopted the following sets of principles on the conduct of space activities:

- The *Declaration of Legal Principles Governing the Activities of States in the Exploration and Uses of Outer Space* (1963) lays down the fundamental principles on the exploration and use of outer space for the benefit and in the interests of all humankind.
- The *Principles Governing the Use by States of Artificial Earth Satellites for International Direct Television Broadcasting* (1982) recognize that such use has international political, economic, social and cultural implications. Such activities should promote the dissemination and exchange of information and knowledge, foster development, and respect the sovereign rights of states, including the principle of non-intervention.
- The *Principles Relating to Remote Sensing of the Earth from Outer Space* (1986) state that such activities are to be conducted for the benefit of all countries, respecting the sovereignty of all states and peoples over their natural resources, and for the rights and interests of other states. Remote sensing is to be used to preserve the environment and to reduce the impact of natural disasters.
- The *Principles Relevant to the Use of Nuclear Power Sources in Outer Space* (1992) recognize that such sources are essential for some space missions, but that their use should be based on a thorough safety assessment. The *Principles* provide guidelines for the safe use of nuclear power sources and for notification of a malfunction of a space object where there is a risk of re-entry of radioactive material to the Earth.

- The *Declaration on International Cooperation in the Exploration and Use of Outer Space for the Benefit and in the Interest of All States, Taking into Particular Account the Needs of Developing Countries* (1996) provides that states are free to determine all aspects of their participation in international space cooperation on an equitable and mutually acceptable basis, and that such cooperation should be conducted in ways that are considered most effective and appropriate by the countries concerned.

Office for Outer Space Affairs

The Vienna-based **United Nations Office for Outer Space Affairs** (www.unoosa.org) serves as the secretariat for the Committee on the Peaceful Uses of Outer Space and its subcommittees, promotes international cooperation in the peaceful uses of outer space and facilitates the use of space science and technology for sustainable economic and social development. The Office disseminates space-related information to member states and discharges the Secretary-General's responsibilities under international space law, including maintaining the UN register on objects launched into outer space. Through its United Nations Programme on Space Applications (www.unoosa.org/oosa/en/ourwork/psa/), the Office works to improve the use of space science and technology for the development of all nations, in particular developing countries. Under this programme, it also provides technical advisory services to member states in conducting pilot projects, and undertakes training and fellowship programmes in such areas as remote sensing, satellite communication, satellite meteorology, satellite navigation, basic space science and space law.

The Office is a cooperating body of the *International Charter "Space and Major Disasters"*—a mechanism through which UN agencies can request satellite imagery to support their response to disasters. It also serves as executive secretariat to the International Committee on Global Navigation Satellite Systems—an informal body that promotes cooperation on civil satellite-based positioning, navigation, timing and value-added services, as well as on the compatibility and interoperability of global navigation satellite systems, while increasing their use to support sustainable development, particularly in developing countries. The Office is also the secretariat to the Space Mission Planning Advisory Group (www.cosmos.esa.int/web/smpag), an international group whose primary purpose is to prepare for a response to a near-Earth object threat.

The Office manages the **United Nations Platform for Space-based Information for Disaster Management and Emergency Response (UN-SPIDER)** (www.un-spider.org). Established by the General Assembly in December 2006, UN-SPIDER aims to provide all countries and relevant international and regional organizations with universal access to all types of space-based information and services supporting the full disaster-management cycle. It helps increase the number of countries that receive assistance with respect to disaster-management planning, risk reduction and emergency response using space-based information, and advises them on the use of space-based technologies.

The Office provides technical assistance to the regional centres for space science and technology education and to the network of space science and technology education affiliated with the United Nations. The centres work with member states to enhance their capability in space science and technology. They also help scientists and researchers develop skills and knowledge in using space science and technology for sustainable development. There are six regional centres: two African regional centres in Morocco and Nigeria; two Asia and the Pacific regional centres in China and India; the Western Asia regional centre in Jordan; and the joint Latin America and Caribbean centre in Mexico and Brazil.

The Office also serves as secretariat to the Inter-Agency Meeting on Outer Space Activities (UN-Space), which has met annually since 1975 to increase space-related cooperation among UN bodies, coordinate activities, build synergies, and consider new initiatives. The Meeting produces the Secretary-General's report on the coordination of space-related activities of the UN system.

Conferences. The United Nations has organized three major conferences on the exploration and peaceful uses of outer space, all held in Vienna. The first, held in 1968, examined the practical benefits deriving from space research and exploration, and the extent to which non-spacefaring countries might enjoy them. The second conference (UNISPACE '82) assessed the state of space science and technology, considered the applications of space technology for development and discussed international space cooperation. UNISPACE III, held in 1999, outlined actions to: protect the global environment and manage natural resources; increase use of space applications for human security, development and welfare; protect the space environment; increase developing countries' access to space science and its benefits; and enhance training and education opportunities, especially for young people. It also called for a global system to manage natural disaster mitigation, relief and prevention; the improvement of educational programmes and satellite-related infrastructure to promote literacy; and international coordination of activities related to near-Earth objects. In June 2018, the international community will commemorate the fiftieth anniversary of the first UNISPACE conference with UNISPACE+50, a special segment of the annual COPUOS session in Vienna to set out the pathway for future international space cooperation.

DECOLONIZATION

Nearly 100 nations whose peoples were formerly under colonial rule or a trusteeship arrangement have joined the United Nations as sovereign, independent states since the Organization was founded in 1945. Additionally, many other Territories have achieved self-determination through political association or integration with an independent state. The United Nations has played a crucial role in that historic change by encouraging the aspirations of people in dependent territories and by setting goals and standards to accelerate their attainment of independence. UN missions have supervised elections leading to independence in Togoland (1956 and 1968), Western Samoa (1961), Namibia (1989) and in Timor-Leste (2002). Despite the great progress made against colonialism, nearly 2 million people still live under colonial rule, and the United Nations continues its efforts to help achieve self-determination in the remaining Non-Self-Governing Territories (www.un.org/en/decolonization).

The decolonization efforts of the United Nations derive from the *Charter* principle of "equal rights and self-determination of peoples", as well as from three specific chapters in the *Charter*—Chapters XI, XII and XIII—which are devoted to the interests of dependent peoples. Since 1960, the United Nations has also been guided by the General Assembly's *Declaration on the Granting of Independence to Colonial Countries and Peoples*, also known as the *Declaration on Decolonization*, by which member states proclaimed the necessity of bringing colonialism to a speedy end.

According to General Assembly resolution 1541(XV) of 1960, a Non-Self-Governing Territory can be said to have reached "a full measure of self-government" by:

- Emergence as a sovereign independent state;
- Free association with an independent state;
- Integration with an independent state.

International Trusteeship System

Under Chapter XII of the *Charter*, the United Nations established the International Trusteeship System for the supervision of Trust Territories placed under it by individual agreements with the states administering them. The System applied to: Territories held under mandates established by the League of Nations after the First World War; Territories detached from "enemy states" as a result of the Second World War; and Territories voluntarily placed under the system by states responsible for their administration. The goal of the Trusteeship System was to promote the political, economic and social advancement of the Territories and their development towards self-government and self-determination.

The **Trusteeship Council** was established under Chapter XIII of the *Charter* to supervise the administration of Trust Territories and to ensure that governments responsible for their administration took adequate steps to prepare them for the achievement of the *Charter* goals.

In the early years of the United Nations, 11 Territories were placed under the trusteeship system. Over the years, all 11 Territories either became independent states or voluntarily associated themselves with a state. The last one to do so was the Trust Territory of the Pacific Islands (Palau), administered by the United States. The Security Council in 1994 terminated the United Nations Trusteeship Agreement for that Territory after it chose free association with the United States in a 1993 plebiscite. Palau became independent in 1994, joining the United Nations as its 185th member state. With no Territories left on its agenda, the Trusteeship System had completed its historic task.

Non-Self-Governing Territories

Chapter XI of the *Charter*—the *Declaration regarding Non-Self-Governing Territories*—provides that member states administering such Territories recognize "that the interests of the inhabitants of these Territories is paramount" and accept the obligation to promote their well-being as a "sacred trust". To this end, administering powers, in addition to ensuring the political, economic, social and educational advancement of those peoples, undertake to assist them in developing self-government and democratic political institutions. Administering powers have an obligation to transmit regularly to the Secretary-General information on the economic, social and educational conditions in the Territories under their administration.

In 1946, eight member states—Australia, Belgium, Denmark, France, the Netherlands, New Zealand, the United Kingdom and the United States—identified the Non-Self-Governing Territories under their administration. There were 72 such Territories in all, of which eight became independent before 1959. In 1963, the Assembly approved a revised list of 64 Territories to which the 1960 *Declaration on Decolonization* applied. Today, 17 such Non-Self-Governing Territories remain, with France, New Zealand, the United Kingdom and the United States as administering powers (www.un.org/en/decolonization/nonselfgovterritories.shtml).

In 2005, Tokelau's national representative body, the General Fono, approved a draft treaty of free association between Tokelau and New Zealand, and then a draft constitution. In a 2006 referendum, 60 per cent of registered Tokelauans voted in favour of free association, falling short of the required two-thirds majority. A second referendum, held in 2007, fell just 16 votes short of the required majority, with 446 votes in favour out of 692 votes cast. Both referendums to determine the future status of Tokelau were monitored by the United Nations. The UN General Assembly has acknowledged the

2008 decision of the General Fono that consideration of any future act of self-determination by Tokelau would be deferred; and that New Zealand and Tokelau would
enhance essential services and infrastructure on the atolls of Tokelau, thereby ensuring
better quality of life for the people.

Declaration on the Granting of Independence to Colonial Countries and Peoples

The desire of the peoples of dependent Territories to achieve self-determination, and the
international community's perception that principles of the *Charter of the United Nations* were being too slowly applied, led the General Assembly to proclaim in 1960 the
Declaration on the Granting of Independence to Colonial Countries and Peoples (resolution
1514(XV)). The *Declaration* states that subjecting peoples to alien subjugation, domina-
tion and exploitation constitutes a denial of fundamental human rights; is contrary to
the *Charter*; and is an impediment to the promotion of world peace and cooperation.

*Territories to which the Declaration on the Granting of Independence
to Colonial Countries and Peoples continues to apply*

Territory	Administering power	Population
Africa		
Western Sahara[1]	—	586,000
Atlantic Ocean and Caribbean		
Anguilla	United Kingdom	15,700
Bermuda	United Kingdom	65,187
British Virgin Islands	United Kingdom	28,200
Cayman Islands	United Kingdom	58,238
Falkland Islands (Malvinas)[2]	United Kingdom	2,500
Montserrat	United Kingdom	5,000
Saint Helena	United Kingdom	5,765
Turks and Caicos Islands	United Kingdom	36,689
United States Virgin Islands	United States	105,080
Europe		
Gibraltar	United Kingdom	33,140
Pacific Ocean		
American Samoa	United States	55,170
French Polynesia	France	271,800
Guam	United States	159,358
New Caledonia	France	268,767
Pitcairn	United Kingdom	39
Tokelau	New Zealand	1,411

[1] **Western Sahara.** On 26 February 1976, Spain informed the Secretary-General that as of that date it had
terminated its presence in the Territory of the Sahara and deemed it necessary to place on record that Spain
considered itself thenceforth exempt from any responsibility of any international nature in connection its
administration, in view of the cessation of its participation in the temporary administration established for
the Territory. In 1990, the General Assembly reaffirmed that the question of Western Sahara was a question
of decolonization which remained to be completed by the people of Western Sahara.
[2] **Falkland Islands.** A dispute exists between the Governments of Argentina and the United Kingdom concerning sovereignty over the Falkland Islands (Malvinas).

It adds that "immediate steps shall be taken, in Trust and Non-Self-Governing Territories or all other Territories which have not yet attained independence, to transfer all powers to the peoples of those Territories, without any conditions or reservations, in accordance with their freely expressed will and desire, without any distinction as to race, creed or colour in order to enable them to enjoy complete independence and freedom". In resolution 1541(XV), the Assembly also defined the three legitimate political status options offering full self-government—free association with an independent state, integration into an independent state, or independence.

In 1961, the Assembly established a special committee to examine the application of the *Declaration* and recommendations on its implementation. Commonly referred to as the Special Committee on Decolonization or C-24, its full title is the **Special Committee on the Situation with Regard to the Implementation of the Declaration on the Granting of Independence to Colonial Countries and Peoples** (www.un.org/en/decolonization/specialcommittee.shtml). It meets annually, reviews the list of Territories to which the *Declaration* applies, hears petitioners and representatives of the Territories, dispatches visiting missions to the Territories, and organizes annual seminars on the political, social, economic and educational situations in the Territories.

In the years following the adoption of the *Declaration*, some 60 colonial Territories, inhabited by more than 80 million people, attained self-determination through independence, and joined the United Nations as sovereign members. The Assembly has called upon the administering powers to take all necessary steps to enable the peoples of the Non-Self-Governing Territories to exercise fully as soon as possible their right to self-determination, including independence, on a case-by-case basis. It has also reaffirmed its determination to continue to take all steps necessary to bring about the complete and speedy eradication of colonialism and the faithful observance by all states of the relevant provisions of the *Charter*, the *Declaration on the Granting of Independence to Colonial Countries and Peoples* and the *Universal Declaration of Human Rights*.

At the end of the first International Decade for the Eradication of Colonialism (1990–2000), the General Assembly declared the period 2001–2010 the Second International Decade for the Eradication of Colonialism, and called upon member states to redouble their efforts to achieve complete decolonization. By resolution 65/119 of 10 December 2010, the Assembly declared the period 2011–2020 the **Third International Decade for the Eradication of Colonialism** calling upon member states to intensify their efforts to continue to implement the plan of action for the Second Decade.

In 2016, the UN Department of Public Information, in collaboration with the Department of Political Affairs, published an informational booklet *What the UN Can Do To Assist Non-Self Governing Territories*.

Namibia

The United Nations helped bring about the independence of Namibia in 1990 (www. un.org/en/peacekeeping/missions/past/untagS.htm).

Formerly known as South West Africa, Namibia was the only one of seven African Territories under the League of Nations mandate system not placed under the UN trusteeship system. In 1946, the General Assembly recommended South Africa to do so. South Africa refused and in 1949 informed the United Nations that it would no longer transmit information on the Territory. The General Assembly terminated the mandate in 1966 and placed the Territory under the responsibility of the UN Council for South West Africa, renamed the Council for Namibia in 1968. It thus became the only Territory which the United Nations, rather than a member state, assumed direct responsibility. In 1976, the Security Council demanded that South Africa accept elections for the Territory under UN supervision. The Assembly expressed support for the armed liberation struggle of the Namibian people in 1978, stating that any settlement must be in agreement with the South West Africa People's Organization (SWAPO)—the sole representative of the Namibian people. A settlement proposed that year by Canada, France, the Federal Republic of Germany, the United Kingdom and the United States providing for elections for a constituent assembly under UN auspices, was endorsed by the Security Council. A special representative for Namibia was appointed and the United Nations Transition Assistance Group (UNTAG) was established. Following years of negotiations by the Secretary-General and his special representative, as well as United States mediation, in 1988 South Africa agreed to cooperate with the Secretary-General to ensure Namibia's independence through elections.

The operation that led to Namibia's independence started in 1989. UNTAG supervised and controlled the entire electoral process, which was conducted by the Namibian authorities. It monitored the ceasefire between SWAPO and South Africa and the demobilization of all military forces, and ensured a smooth electoral process.

The elections for the constituent assembly were won by SWAPO and were declared "free and fair" by the Secretary-General's special representative. Following the elections, South Africa withdrew its remaining troops. The constituent assembly drafted a new constitution, approved in February 1990, and elected SWAPO leader Sam Nujoma as President for a five-year term. In March, Namibia became independent, with the Secretary-General administering the oath of office to Namibia's first President. In April 1990, Namibia joined the United Nations.

Timor-Leste

Another United Nations success story is the process that led to the independence of Timor-Leste—formerly known as East Timor. A major UN operation oversaw its transition towards independence, after the East Timorese people voted in favour of independence in a popular consultation conducted by the UN in 1999.

The island of Timor lies to the north of Australia, in the south-central part of the chain of islands forming Indonesia. Its western part had been a Dutch colony, and became part of Indonesia when that country attained independence. East Timor was a Portuguese colony.

In 1960, the General Assembly placed East Timor on the list of Non-Self-Governing Territories. In 1974, recognizing its right to self-determination, Portugal sought to establish a provisional government and popular assembly to determine East Timor's status. In 1975, however, civil war broke out between the Territory's newly formed political parties. Portugal withdrew, stating it could not control the situation. One East Timorese side declared independence as a separate country, while another proclaimed independence and integration with Indonesia.

In December, Indonesian troops landed in East Timor, and a provisional government was formed. Portugal broke off relations with Indonesia and brought the matter before the Security Council, which called on Indonesia to withdraw its forces and urged all states to respect the right of the East Timorese people to self-determination. In 1976, the provisional government held elections for an assembly, which then called for integration with Indonesia. When Indonesia issued a law supporting that decision, the pro-independence movement began an armed resistance. In 1983, the Secretary-General started talks with Indonesia and Portugal, but it was only in 1999, through the good offices of the Secretary-General, that agreements were reached, paving the way for a popular consultation.

On the basis of those agreements, the United Nations Mission in East Timor (UNAMET) organized and conducted voter registration and an official ballot. In August 1999, when 78.5 per cent of 450,000 registered voters rejected autonomy within Indonesia, militias opposing independence unleashed a campaign of systematic destruction and violence, killing many and forcing more than 200,000 East Timorese to flee their homes. After intensive talks, Indonesia accepted the deployment of a UN-authorized multinational force. In September, the Security Council authorized the dispatch of the International Force in East Timor (INTERFET), which helped restore peace and security. In October, the Council established the UN Transitional Administration in East Timor (UNTAET), giving it full executive and legislative authority during the country's transition to independence.

In August 2001, more than 91 per cent of East Timor's eligible voters went to the polls to elect an 88-member constituent assembly, tasked with writing and adopting a new constitution and establishing the framework for future elections and the transition to full independence. In March 2002, the constituent assembly signed into force the Territory's first constitution. The following month, after winning 82.7 per cent of the vote, Xanana Gusmão was appointed president-elect. On 20 May 2002, the Territory attained independence. The constituent assembly was transformed into the national parliament, and the new country adopted the name Timor-Leste. In September 2002, it became the 191st member state of the United Nations.

Western Sahara

The United Nations has been dealing with an ongoing dispute concerning Western Sahara—a Territory on the north-west coast of Africa bordering Algeria, Mauritania and Morocco—since 1963.

Western Sahara became a Spanish colony in 1884. In 1963, both Mauritania and Morocco laid claim to it. The International Court of Justice, in a 1975 opinion requested by the General Assembly, rejected the claims of territorial sovereignty by Mauritania and Morocco.

The United Nations has been seeking a settlement in Western Sahara since the withdrawal of Spain in 1976 and the ensuing fighting between Morocco—which had "reintegrated" the Territory—and the Popular Front for the Liberation of Saguia el-Hamra and Río de Oro (Frente Polisario), supported by Algeria. In 1979, the Organization of African Unity (OAU) called for a referendum to enable the people of the Territory to exercise their right to self-determination. By 1982, 26 OAU member states had recognized the "Sahrawi Arab Democratic Republic" (SADR) proclaimed by Polisario in 1976. When SADR was seated at the 1984 OAU summit, Morocco withdrew from the OAU.

A joint good offices mission by the Secretary-General and the OAU Chairman led to settlement proposals in 1988 calling for a ceasefire and referendum to choose between independence and integration with Morocco, to which the parties agreed in principle. By resolution 690(1991), the Security Council created the **United Nations Mission for the Referendum in Western Sahara (MINURSO)** (minurso.unmissions.org) in 1991 to assist the Secretary-General's special representative in the organization and conduct of a referendum of self-determination for the people of Western Sahara. All Western Saharans aged 18 and over counted in the 1974 Spanish census would have the right to vote. An identification commission would update the census list and identify voters. Refugees living outside the Territory would be identified with the assistance of the Office of the United Nations High Commissioner for Refugees (UNHCR).

In September 1991, the ceasefire came into effect. It has been observed ever since by MINURSO's military observers, with no major violations. However, the parties have continued to differ on implementation of the settlement plan—particularly with respect to voter eligibility for the referendum. In 1997, a compromise was brokered by the Secretary-General's personal envoy for Western Sahara, and the identification process was completed at the end of 1999. Although consultations continued, disagreements persisted over implementation of the plan.

In 2004, Morocco rejected a proposal put forward by the personal envoy, as well as the settlement plan itself. Despite the continuing stalemate, there were some positive developments. Frente Polisario released all the remaining Moroccan prisoners of war in August 2005 and in 2004, a UNHCR-sponsored "family visits" programme was established between Western Saharan refugees living in the camps in Tindouf, Algeria, and their relatives in Western Sahara Territory—some of whom had not seen each other for 30 years.

In 2007, the Secretary-General's personal envoy observed that there were two options left: indefinite prolongation of the impasse or direct negotiations. The Security Council called for good faith negotiations without preconditions. The envoy then facilitated meetings with the parties in New York, also attended by Algeria and Mauritania. At the second meeting, the parties acknowledged that the status quo was unacceptable and committed themselves to continuing the negotiations in good faith. This renewed dialogue marked the first direct negotiations between the parties in more than seven years.

A third round of negotiations was held in 2008, and the parties came together for five more informal meetings in 2009, 2010, 2011 and 2012. However, no progress was registered on the core issues of the future status of Western Sahara and the means by which the self-determination of the people of Western Sahara is to occur.

In 2013, 2014 and 2015, the personal envoy used a new approach, engaging in bilateral consultations with the parties and neighbouring states to gauge whether the parties were prepared to be flexible in developing the elements of a compromise solution and how the neighbouring states could be of assistance. While some insights were gained, the divergence in positions remained.

In March 2016, following the Secretary-General's visit to the region, the Government of Morocco announced measures affecting the ability of MINURSO to carry out its functions, including a significant reduction of the civilian component, in particular the political segment, and the cancellation of Morocco's voluntary contribution to the functioning of the Mission. To prevent a rupture of the ceasefire and a resumption of hostilities, and given the continuing efforts of his personal envoy, the Secretary-General recommended the extension of the MINURSO mandate for 12 months. He also urged further engagement with regard to the human rights situation in Western Sahara and the refugee camps, including by supporting human rights entities operating there and augmenting the provision of humanitarian aid in the camps. The Security Council extended the MINURSO mandate until 30 April 2017.

Chapter III
ECONOMIC AND SOCIAL DEVELOPMENT

Ahead of the United Nations Sustainable Development Summit from 25–27 September, a 10-minute film introducing the SDGs was projected onto two of the façades at UN Headquarters, bringing to life each of the 17 goals to raise awareness about the 2030 Agenda for Sustainable Development (22 September 2015, UN Photo/Cia Park).

Many people associate the United Nations with the issues of peace and security, but most of the Organization's resources are devoted to advancing the pledge of its *Charter* to "promote higher standards of living, full employment, and conditions of economic and social progress and development". UN development efforts have profoundly affected the lives and well-being of millions of people throughout the world. These endeavours are guided by the conviction that lasting international peace and security are possible only if the economic and social well-being of people everywhere is assured.

Many of the economic and social transformations that have taken place since 1945 have been significantly affected in their direction and shape by the work of the United Nations. As the global centre for consensus-building, the UN has set priorities and goals for international cooperation to assist countries in their development efforts and to foster a supportive global economic environment. The United Nations provides a platform for formulating and promoting new objectives on the development agenda through international conferences, including the need to incorporate specific issues such as the advancement of women, human rights and good governance into the development paradigm. Over the years, the world view of development has changed. Today, countries agree that sustainable development—development that promotes prosperity and economic opportunity, greater social well-being, and protection of the environment—offers the best path forward for improving the lives of people everywhere.

At the Millennium Summit in 2000, member states adopted the *UN Millennium Declaration*, which was translated into a road map for achieving eight time-bound and measurable goals by 2015, known as the **Millennium Development Goals (MDGs)**. The MDGs aimed to eradicate extreme poverty and hunger; achieve universal primary education; promote gender equality and the empowerment of women; reduce child mortality; improve maternal health; combat HIV/AIDS, malaria and other diseases; ensure environmental sustainability; and develop a global partnership for development.

A high-level panel established in 2012 to make recommendations on the post-2015 development agenda considered the achievements since 2000, such as half a billion fewer people in extreme poverty and about 3 million children's lives saved each year. It also consulted with a wide range of people, including 5,000 civil society organizations in 120 countries, 250 CEOs in 30 countries, farmers, migrants, traders, young people, faith-based groups, trade unions, academics, philosophers and many more. In May 2013, the panel reported that the unprecedented progress had been driven by a combination of economic growth, better policies and global commitment to the MDGs. It concluded that the new development agenda should carry forward the spirit of the *Declaration* and the best of the MDGs, with a practical focus on poverty, hunger, water, sanitation, education and health care. In September 2015, world leaders adopted the 17 **Sustainable Development Goals (SDGs)** of the 2030 Agenda for Sustainable Development. The 2030 Agenda officially came into force on 1 January 2016, marking a new course for the Organization towards ending poverty, protecting the planet and ensuring prosperity for all by 2030. Three other accords adopted in 2015 play critical roles in the global development agenda: the Addis Ababa Action Agenda on financing for development, the Paris Agreement on climate change and the *Sendai Framework* on disaster risk reduction.

COORDINATING DEVELOPMENT ACTIVITIES

International debate on economic and social issues has increasingly reflected the commonality of interests among all countries, rich and poor, in solving the problems that transcend national boundaries. Issues related to refugee populations, organized crime, drug trafficking, HIV and AIDS and climate change are seen as global challenges requiring coordinated action. The impact of persistent poverty and unemployment in one region can be quickly felt in others, not least through migration, social disruption and conflict. Similarly, in the age of a global economy, financial instability in one country can affect the markets of others. There is also growing consensus on the role played by democracy, human rights, good governance and the empowerment of people, including women, youth, older persons, persons with disabilities, indigenous peoples, and people living in poverty, in fostering economic and social development. Despite advances on many fronts, gross disparities in income, wealth and well-being continue to characterize the world's economic and social structure. Reducing poverty and redressing inequalities, both within and between countries, remain fundamental goals of the United Nations.

The UN development system is composed of the entities that receive contributions for operational activities for development. It works in a variety of ways to promote common economic and social goals by providing policy analysis and addressing ongoing and emerging global challenges; advising governments on their development plans and strategies; setting international norms and standards; reviewing trends and progress in international development cooperation; and mobilizing funds for development programmes. Through the work of its various funds and programmes, and its family of specialized agencies, the UN touches the lives of people everywhere, in fields as diverse as education, air safety, environmental protection and labour conditions.

The **Economic and Social Council (ECOSOC)** (www.un.org/ecosoc) is the principal body coordinating the economic and social work of the United Nations and its operational arms. It is also the central forum for discussing international economic and social issues and for formulating policy recommendations. The Council's responsibilities include promoting higher standards of living, full employment, and economic and social progress; identifying solutions to economic, social and health problems; facilitating cultural and educational cooperation; and encouraging universal respect for human rights and fundamental freedoms.

The **Commission for Social Development**, as a preparatory and advisory body of ECOSOC in the area of social policy and development, reports on social aspects related to the agreed annual main theme of the Council. It will also contribute to the follow-up to the 2030 Agenda for Sustainable Development, by supporting the thematic reviews of the high-level political forum.

Under ECOSOC, the **Committee for Development Policy**, made up of 24 experts working in their personal capacity, acts as an advisory body on emerging economic, social and environmental issues. It also sets the criteria for the designation of least developed countries (LDCs) and reviews the list of those countries.

The biennial Development Cooperation Forum, established by the 2005 World Summit, is convened by ECOSOC and mandated to review trends and progress in international development cooperation, with the participation of all relevant stakeholders. The Forum is tasked with providing policy guidance and recommendations to improve development cooperation.

The **United Nations Development Group** (www.undg.org) unites the 32 UN funds, programmes, agencies, departments and offices that play a role in the management and coordination of development work within the Organization. This executive body works to enhance cooperation between policymaking entities and the distinct operational programmes.

The **Executive Committee on Economic and Social Affairs** (www.un.org/development/desa/ecesa/), composed of Secretariat bodies and including the regional commissions, is also an instrument for policy development and management. It aims to bring coherence among UN entities engaged in normative, analytical and technical work in the economic and social field under the leadership of DESA.

Within the United Nations Secretariat, the **Department of Economic and Social Affairs (DESA)** (www.un.org/esa/desa) helps countries address their economic, social and environmental challenges. It operates within a framework of internationally agreed goals known as the UN development agenda. Within this framework, DESA provides analytical support, as well as substantive and technical support to member states in the social, economic and environmental spheres, and carries out policy analysis and coordination. It also provides support in setting norms and standards, and in agreeing on common courses of action in response to global challenges. DESA serves as a crucial interface between global policies and national action, and among research, policy and operational activities.

Five regional commissions facilitate similar exchanges of economic and social information and policy analysis in Africa (ECA) (www.uneca.org), Asia and the Pacific (ESCAP) (www.unescap.org), Europe (ECE) (www.unece.org), Latin America and the Caribbean (ECLAC) (www.eclac.org) and Western Asia (ESCWA) (www.unescwa.org). Many UN funds and programmes deal with operational activities for development in programme countries, and several UN specialized agencies provide support and assistance for countries' development efforts. In a time of increasingly limited resources, both human and financial, enhanced coordination and cooperation among the various arms of the UN system are vital if development goals are to be realized.

The General Assembly, through the **Quadrennial Comprehensive Policy Review (QCPR)** (www.un.org/ecosoc/en/oas-qcpr), establishes key system-wide policy orientations for the development cooperation and country-level modalities of the UN. Adopted every four years, it is the primary policy instrument to define the way the UN development system operates to support programme countries in their development efforts. The most recent QCPR took place in 2016 and culminated in General Assembly resolution 71/243, which guides the UN development system's support to the implementation of the 2030 Agenda. The QCPR focuses, in particular, on cross-cutting and coordination issues on the operational side of the UN development system and is applicable to all funds, programmes and other entities under the direct mandate of the Assembly.

SUSTAINABLE DEVELOPMENT

In the first decades of the United Nations, environmental concerns rarely appeared on the international agenda. The related work of the Organization emphasized the exploration and use of natural resources, while seeking to ensure that developing countries in particular would maintain control over their own resources. During the 1960s, agreements were made concerning marine pollution, especially oil spills. Since then, there has been increasing evidence of the deterioration of the environment on a global scale, and the international community has shown increasing alarm over the impact of development on the ecology of the planet and on human well-being. The United Nations has played a leading role as an advocate for environmental concerns and as a proponent of sustainable development.

The relationship between economic development and environmental degradation was first placed on the international agenda in 1972, at the United Nations Conference on the Human Environment, held in Stockholm, Sweden. After the Conference, governments set up the **United Nations Environment Programme (UNEP)** (web.unep.org), which has become the world's leading environmental agency.

In 1973, the United Nations Sudano-Sahelian Office—now the Drylands Development Centre of UNDP—was set up to spearhead efforts to reverse the spread of desertification in West Africa. The Centre later took on a greater mandate. In 1996, the entry into force of the *UN Convention to Combat Desertification in those Countries Experiencing Serious Drought and/or Desertification, Particularly in Africa* gave added impetus to the Centre's work.

The 1980s witnessed landmark negotiations among member states on environmental issues, including treaties protecting the ozone layer and controlling the movement of toxic wastes. The former World Commission on Environment and Development, established in 1983 by the General Assembly, brought a new understanding and sense of urgency to the need for development that would ensure economic well-being for present and future generations, while protecting the world's environmental resources. The Commission's 1987 report to the Assembly put forward the concept of sustainable development as an alternative to development based simply on unconstrained economic growth. After considering the report, the Assembly called for the United Nations Conference on Environment and Development—the Earth Summit—held in Rio de Janeiro, Brazil, in 1992. Unprecedented in its size, scope and influence, the Earth Summit linked sustainable development with issues of human rights, population, social development and human settlements.

Sustainable development, defined as development that meets the needs of the present without compromising the ability of future generations to meet their own needs, calls for building an inclusive, sustainable and resilient future for people and the planet. To this end, it is crucial to harmonize three core elements—economic growth, social inclusion and environmental protection—as the necessary elements for the well-being of individuals and societies. The United Nations has taken action to integrate the concept of sustainable development in all of its relevant policies and programmes. More than ever, development assistance programmes are directed towards women, in view of their roles as producers of goods, services and food, and as caretakers of the environment. The moral and social imperatives for alleviating poverty are given additional urgency by the recognition that poverty eradication and environmental quality go hand-in-hand.

Summits and conferences

At the 1992 Earth Summit, governments adopted *Agenda 21,* a comprehensive plan for global action in all areas of sustainable development (sustainabledevelopment.un.org/content/documents/Agenda21.pdf). Its implementation and related commitments were reaffirmed at the World Summit on Sustainable Development held in Johannesburg, South Africa, in 2002 and the UN Conference on Sustainable Development—or Rio+20—that took place in Rio de Janeiro, Brazil, in June 2012.

Agenda 21 outlines actions for moving the world away from an unsustainable model of economic growth towards activities to protect and renew the environmental resources on which growth and development depend. Areas for action include protecting the atmosphere; combating deforestation, soil loss and desertification; preventing air and water pollution; halting the depletion of fish stocks; and promoting the safe management of toxic wastes. *Agenda 21* also addresses patterns of development that cause stress to the environment, including poverty and external debt in developing countries; unsustainable patterns of production and consumption; demographic stress; and the structure of the international economy. The action programme recommends ways to strengthen the parts played by major groups—women, trade unions, farmers, children and young people, indigenous peoples, the scientific community, local authorities, business, industry and NGOs—in achieving sustainable development.

Rio+20 marked the twentieth anniversary of the 1992 Earth Summit and the tenth anniversary of the 2002 World Summit. The conference adopted an outcome document, *The Future We Want*, containing practical measures for implementing sustainable development. Rio+20 resulted in over 700 voluntary commitments to deliver concrete results for sustainable development—initiating a new bottom-up approach to advancing sustainable development. Member states also launched a process to develop a set of sustainable development goals.

2030 Agenda

At the UN Millennium Summit held in September 2000 in New York, 189 world leaders endorsed the *Millennium Declaration*. The **Millennium Development Goals (MDGs)** (www.un.org/millenniumgoals), eight time-bound and measurable goals to be reached by 2015, represented a road map for the implementation of the *Declaration*. The MDGs served as a framework for collective action to reduce poverty and improve the lives of poor people. Across eight clear goals, the MDGs included 21 time-bound targets to measure progress in eradicating poverty and hunger, as well as improvements in health, education, living conditions, environmental sustainability and gender equality.

By 2015, significant progress had been made across all goals and millions of lives were improved due to concerted global, regional, national and local efforts. The data and analysis presented in the *Millennium Development Goals Report, 2015* (www.un.org/millenniumgoals/2015_MDG_Report/pdf/MDG 2015 rev (July 1).pdf) proved that, with targeted interventions, sound strategies, adequate resources and political will, even the poorest countries could make dramatic and unprecedented progress. It also acknowledged, however, uneven achievements and shortfalls in many areas. As such, the work on the MDGs was not complete, and needed to continue in the new development era.

Building upon the achievements and lessons learned from the MDGs and the Earth Summit, at the UN summit for the adoption of the post-2015 development agenda held 25–27 September 2015, member states adopted General Assembly resolution 70/1, Transforming our World: the 2030 Agenda for Sustainable Development. The 2030 Agenda seeks to address the unfinished business of the MDGs while committing to achieving sustainable development in its three dimensions—economic, social and environmental—in a balanced and integrated manner. It is the first agreement of its kind that integrates goals from the three pillars of the Organization's work—peace and security, human rights, and sustainable development—into a single agenda. It reflects a paradigm shift from previous approaches to development that focus on the economic or social structure separately. It is also stronger on environment compared to the MDGs.

Bold and transformative, the 2030 Agenda seeks to end poverty by 2030 and pursue a sustainable future. It stands as a universal agenda, consisting of a *Declaration*; 17 goals to be reached by 2030 (see below); the means of its implementation, including through a revitalized global partnership; and a framework for review and follow-up. The world faces immense challenges ranging from widespread poverty, rising inequalities and disparities of wealth, opportunity and power, to environmental degradation and the risks posed by climate change. The 2030 Agenda provides a plan of action for ending poverty in all its dimensions, leaving no one behind and reaching the furthest behind first. It also builds on the outcomes adopted at three other conferences in 2015 on climate change, disaster risk reduction and financing for development.

High-level political forum

In 2012, at the Rio+20 conference, member states agreed to establish a forum to replace the Commission on Sustainable Development, a functional commission of ECOSOC set up in 1992 to ensure full support for *Agenda 21*, which monitored implementation of the agreements and outcomes of the 1992 and 2002 summits. The **High-level political forum on sustainable development** (HLPF) (sustainabledevelopment.un.org/hlpf), established by the General Assembly in 2013, is the main platform for follow-up and review of the 2030 Agenda and the SDGs, working coherently with the General Assembly, ECOSOC and other relevant organs and forums. It provides political leadership and guidance; enhances the integration of economic, social and environmental dimensions of sustainable development in a holistic and cross-sectoral manner at all levels; and addresses new and emerging sustainable development challenges.

The voluntary national reviews (VNRs) by developed and developing countries, in which they share experiences on SDGs implementation, including successes, challenges and lessons learned, represent the mainstay of the forum. The forum aims to attract and engage world leaders, the UN system, and major groups and other stakeholders (MGoS) (sustainabledevelopment.un.org/aboutmajorgroups.html), including civil society and the private sector, keeping sustainable development high on national, regional and global agendas.

Each year, the forum considers a number of key documents, including a global SDGs progress report, a summary of the multi-stakeholder forum on science technology and innovation, the outcome of the financing for development forum, and inputs by MGoS.

The forum meets every four years at the level of heads of state and government under the auspices of the General Assembly, and every year under the auspices of ECOSOC. The theme of the forum's 2017 meeting, to be held 10–19 July, will be "Eradicating poverty and promoting prosperity in a changing world". As at 30 November 2016, 31 countries had volunteered to be part of the VNRs for the 2017 meeting.

Sustainable Development Goals

The 17 time-bound and measurable goals, known as the **Sustainable Development Goals** (**SDGs**) (sustainabledevelopment.un.org/sdgs), represent the core of the 2030 Agenda. Comprising 169 targets and 230 indicators, they may be considered a "to-do list" for people and the planet, and a blueprint for a sustainable future. The goals integrate the social, economic, and environmental dimensions of sustainable development. They are not independent from each other, and need to be implemented in an integrated manner.

The SDGs are also universal, inasmuch as they are valid for all countries, developed, developing, and middle-income, while taking into account different levels of national development and capacities. The SDGs acknowledge that ending poverty necessitates strategies that build economic growth and address a range of social needs including education, health, social protection, and job opportunities, while tackling climate change and environmental protection. The 2030 Agenda emphasizes national ownership of the *Agenda* and its implementation, yet is also inclusive. To be successful, action needs to be taken on the global, national, regional and local levels, by all people and stakeholders. The SDGs unite everyone in the effort to make positive change.

The 17 Sustainable Development Goals

Goal 1.   End poverty in all its forms everywhere
Goal 2.   End hunger, achieve food security and improved nutrition and promote sustainable agriculture
Goal 3.   Ensure healthy lives and promote well-being for all at all ages
Goal 4.   Ensure inclusive and equitable quality education and promote lifelong learning opportunities for all
Goal 5.   Achieve gender equality and empower all women and girls
Goal 6.   Ensure availability and sustainable management of water and sanitation for all
Goal 7.   Ensure access to affordable, reliable, sustainable and modern energy for all
Goal 8.   Promote sustained, inclusive and sustainable economic growth, full and productive employment and decent work for all
Goal 9.   Build resilient infrastructure, promote inclusive and sustainable industrialization and foster innovation
Goal 10. Reduce inequality within and among countries
Goal 11. Make cities and human settlements inclusive, safe, resilient and sustainable
Goal 12. Ensure sustainable consumption and production patterns
Goal 13. Take urgent action to combat climate change and its impacts
Goal 14. Conserve and sustainably use the oceans, seas and marine resources for sustainable development
Goal 15. Protect, restore and promote sustainable use of terrestrial ecosystems, sustainably manage forests, combat desertification, and halt and reverse land degradation and halt biodiversity loss
Goal 16. Promote peaceful and inclusive societies for sustainable development, provide access to justice for all and build effective, accountable and inclusive institutions at all levels
Goal 17. Strengthen the means of implementation and revitalize the global partnership for sustainable development

No poverty

End poverty in all its forms everywhere. Since 2000, social protections have expanded throughout the world, as many developing countries adopted policies that afford protection for multiple contingencies. According to *The Sustainable Development Goals Report, 2016*, the proportion of the global population living below the extreme poverty line, defined at $1.90 or below per person per day using 2011 United States dollars purchasing power parity, dropped by half from 26 to 13 per cent between 2002 and 2012. Still, poverty remains widespread in sub-Saharan Africa, where more than 40 per cent of people lived on less than $1.90 a day in 2012.

Despite progress, only one in five people received any type of social assistance or social protection benefits in low-income countries compared with two in three people in upper-middle-income countries.

In 2015, 10 per cent of the world's workers and their families were living on less than $1.90 per person per day, down from 28 per cent in 2000. According to the *2016 SDG Report*, however, young people aged 15 to 24 are most likely to be among the working poor: 16 per cent of all employed youth were living below the poverty line in 2015, compared to 9 per cent of working adults.

World leaders placed poverty reduction at the top of the international agenda by adopting the SDGs, and, in particular, SDG 1, which calls for universal action to end poverty in all its manifestations, including extreme poverty, and ensure peace and prosperity for all. The **United Nations Development Programme (UNDP)** (www.undp.org) has made poverty alleviation its chief priority. It works to strengthen the capacity of governments and civil society organizations to counteract the range of factors that contribute to poverty. These include increasing food security; generating employment opportunities; increasing people's access to land, credit, technology, training and markets; improving the availability of shelter and basic services; and enabling people to participate in the political processes that shape their lives. The heart of UNDP's anti-poverty work lies in empowering the poor.

Agricultural and rural development

About half of the world's population continues to live in rural areas, where most people derive their livelihoods, directly or indirectly, from agriculture. In fact, the vast majority of the world's poorest live in rural areas. In the rush to industrialize and urbanize, insufficient investment has been made in the agricultural sector. The UN addresses this imbalance in a variety of ways.

The **Food and Agriculture Organization of the United Nations (FAO)** (www.fao. org) works toward a world free from hunger, malnutrition and poverty, where food and agriculture contribute to improving the living standards of all in a sustainable manner. Food and agriculture are key to sustainable development and fundamental to the 2030 Agenda. FAO promotes sustainable and inclusive agricultural and rural development that produces more with less. The FAO framework for sustainable food and agriculture features five elements needed to implement the SDGs:

- improve efficiency in the use of resources;
- conserve, protect and enhance natural ecosystems;
- protect and improve rural livelihoods, equity and social well-being;
- enhance the resilience of people, communities and ecosystems; and
- promote responsible and effective governance mechanisms across natural and human systems.

FAO has almost 2,000 field projects operating worldwide at any given time, ranging from integrated land management projects and emergency response to policy and planning advice to governments, in areas as diverse as forestry and marketing strategies.

The FAO Investment Centre assists countries in formulating investment operations in agricultural and rural development, in partnership with international financing institutions (IFIs). Since 1964, the Centre and its IFI partners have facilitated more than $115 billion in agriculture and rural development investment for over 2,100 projects. Of that amount, over $74 billion was financed by IFIs, with the balance coming from beneficiary countries.

The **International Fund for Agricultural Development (IFAD)** (www.ifad.org) finances agricultural development programmes and projects that enable rural people to overcome poverty. It provides loans and grants for programmes and projects that promote economic advancement and food security. IFAD-supported initiatives enable poor rural people to access the land, water, financial resources, and agricultural technologies and services they need to farm productively; and to access markets and opportunities for enterprise to help them increase their incomes.

IFAD-supported programmes and projects benefit the poorest of the world's people: small farmers, landless labourers, nomadic pastoralists, artisanal fishing communities, indigenous peoples and, across all groups, poor rural women. The Fund is particularly committed to achieving the SDGs through its efforts to eradicate rural poverty and food insecurity, which include investing to raise smallholder productivity and incomes; supporting the empowerment of rural women; fostering inclusive, diversified, and productive rural economies; investing in sustainable agriculture and smallholder adaptation capacity to climate change; and strengthening local institutions and natural resource governance.

Since starting operations in 1978, IFAD has mobilized around $25.3 billion in cofinancing and funding from domestic sources for rural development, and contributed an additional $17.6 billion in loans and grants. It has supported 1,013 programmes and projects in partnership with 123 recipient governments, reaching some 459 million people.

Zero hunger

End hunger, achieve food security and improved nutrition and promote sustainable agriculture. The *2016 SDG Report* found that the proportion of the population suffering from hunger declined globally from 15 per cent in 2000-2002 to 11 per cent in 2014-2016. More than 790 million people worldwide, however, still lack access to adequate food. Over half of the adult population in sub-Saharan Africa faced moderate or severe food insecurity in 2015. Worldwide, in 2014, nearly 1 in 4 children under the age of 5—an estimated total of 159 million children—had stunted growth. Another aspect of child malnutrition is the growing share of children who are overweight, a problem affecting nearly every region. Approximately 41 million children under age 5 worldwide were overweight in 2014; with nearly half of them living in Asia. If properly conducted, agriculture, forestry and fishing can provide nutritious food for all and generate decent incomes, while supporting people-centred rural development and protecting the environment.

Fighting hunger

Food production has increased at an unprecedented rate since the United Nations was founded in 1945. Today, enough food is available to feed every child, woman and man on the planet. Between the early 1990s and 2016, the number of hungry people declined by 216 million globally, notwithstanding a 1.9 billion increase in the world's population. A majority of the countries monitored by FAO met the MDG target to halve the proportion of hungry people by 2015. Still, in 2016, about 793 million people did not have enough to eat. Progress is being made, but too often it is hampered by conflict, political instability or natural disasters, resulting in protracted crises. SDG 2 calls for the global community to end hunger and all forms of malnutrition, and achieve sustainable food production by 2030.

Most of the UN entities fighting hunger have social protection programmes to advance food security for the poorer sectors of the population, particularly in rural areas. Since its establishment, FAO has been working to eradicate poverty and hunger by promoting sustainable rural and agricultural development, and improved nutrition and food security— i.e. physical and economic access by all people at all times to sufficient, safe and nutritious food to meet their dietary needs and food preferences for an active and healthy life.

FAO's Committee on World Food Security monitors, evaluates and consults on the international food security situation. The Committee is an international intergovernmental platform for all stakeholders to work together to ensure food security and nutrition for all. It develops and endorses policy recommendations and guidance on a wide range of food security and nutrition topics.

The FAO Global Information and Early Warning System (www.fao.org/giews) uses satellites to monitor food supply and demand and other indicators for assessing the food security situation in all countries of the world. It alerts governments and donors to any potential threat to food supplies. FAO headquarters also hosts the secretariat of the Agricultural Market Information System, an inter-agency platform promoting food market transparency and action in response to market uncertainty, to combat food price crises that hit those who are most vulnerable hardest.

The 2009 World Summit on Food Security, hosted by FAO, adopted a declaration committing all nations to eradicate hunger at the earliest possible date. It also agreed to face up to the challenges that climate change poses to food security.

The International Fund for Agricultural Development (IFAD) provides development funding to combat hunger in the poorest regions of the world. The majority of the world's poorest people—those living on less than $1 a day—live in rural areas of developing countries and depend on agriculture and related activities for their livelihoods. To ensure that development aid reaches those who need it most, IFAD involves poor rural men and women in their own development, working with them and their organizations to develop opportunities that enable them to thrive economically in their own communities.

The **World Food Programme (WFP)** (www.wfp.org) is the UN front-line agency addressing global hunger and nutrition, focusing first on the people in greatest need. In 2015, WFP directly assisted 76.7 million of the world's most vulnerable people in 81 countries. A further 1.6 million people were reached through programmes funded through trust funds, mostly supported by host governments. WFP purchases more than 2 million metric tons of food every year. The WFP policy to buy food as close to where it is needed as possible, means that at least three quarters of such food assistance comes from developing countries. Buying locally, the agency saves time and money on transport costs and also helps sustain local economies.

WFP efforts to combat hunger focus on emergency assistance, relief and rehabilitation, development aid and special operations. In emergencies, WFP is often first on the scene, delivering food assistance to the victims of war, civil conflict, drought, floods, earthquakes, hurricanes, crop failures and natural disasters. When the emergency subsides, WFP helps communities rebuild shattered lives and livelihoods.

Food and food-related assistance are among the most effective ways to break the cycle of hunger and poverty that entraps so many in the developing world. WFP development projects focus on nutrition, especially for mothers and children, through programmes such as school feeding. WFP is the largest humanitarian organization conducting school-feeding programmes worldwide, which it has done for over 50 years. Each year, WFP provides school meals to between 20 and 25 million children across 63 countries, often in the hardest-to-reach areas. In 2015, WFP provided meals to 17.4 million children in almost 63,000 schools in 62 countries. WFP provides cooked meals, snacks, and/or take-home rations to encourage children, especially girls, to consistently attend classes. These school meals, often the only meal a child will receive each day, not only give children the nutrition and energy they need to focus on their lessons, but also encourage parents to send their children to school when they might otherwise keep them home to work. They also increase school attendance, retention and graduation rates, particularly among girls, who might otherwise be subjected to early marriage. Whenever possible, WFP works with the community and local government to source the food used in school meals from local, smallholder farmers.

In 2015, WFP achieved its second highest level of voluntary contributions, some $4.8 billion. Seventy-nine per cent of expenditure was directed to emergencies. Approximately 12.6 billion rations were delivered at an estimated average cost of $0.31 per ration. Cash-based transfers totalling $680 million assisted 9.6 million people—8 per cent more than in 2014.

WFP warehouse in Colombia. The northern department of La Guajira is among the poorest
in the country and home to a significant portion of the country's indigenous peoples.
WFP has been implementing relief and recovery activities in La Guajira since 2010 to meet the urgent
needs of the population (24 February 2015, WFP/Mike Bloem).

Good health and well-being

Ensure healthy lives and promote well-being for all at all ages. Between 2000 and 2015, the global maternal mortality ratio, or number of maternal deaths per 100,000 live births, declined by 37 per cent, to an estimated ratio of 216 per 100,000 live births in 2015. The *2016 SDG Report* indicated that almost all maternal deaths occur in low-resource settings and can be prevented. Worldwide, 3 out of 4 births were assisted by skilled health-care personnel in 2015. Under-five mortality rates fell rapidly from 2000 to 2015, declining by 44 per cent globally. Nevertheless, an estimated 5.9 million children under the age of 5 died in 2015, with a global under-five mortality rate of 43 per 1,000 live births.

The incidence of major infectious diseases, including HIV, tuberculosis and malaria, has declined globally since 2000. In 2015, however, 2.1 million people became newly infected with HIV and an estimated 214 million people contracted malaria. Almost half of the world's population is at risk of malaria, but sub-Saharan Africa accounted for 89 per cent of all cases.

According to estimates from 2012, around 38 million deaths per year, accounting for 68 per cent of all deaths worldwide, were attributable to non-communicable diseases. Almost two thirds of deaths from non-communicable diseases in people under age 70 were attributed to cardiovascular diseases and cancer.

Unhealthy environmental conditions increase the risk of both non-communicable and infectious diseases. In 2012, an estimated 889,000 people died from infectious diseases caused largely by faecal contamination of water and soil and by inadequate hand-washing facilities, and practices resulting from poor or non-existent sanitation services. The same year, household and ambient air pollution resulted in some 6.5 million deaths.

SDG 3 aims to improve reproductive, maternal and child health; end the epidemics of major communicable diseases; reduce non-communicable and environmental diseases; achieve universal health coverage; and ensure access to safe, affordable and effective medicines and vaccines for all.

In most parts of the world, people are living longer, infant mortality is decreasing and illnesses are being kept in check, as more people have access to basic health services, immunization, clean water and sanitation. The UN has been deeply involved in many of these advances by supporting health services, delivering essential drugs, making cities healthier, providing health assistance in emergencies and fighting infectious diseases. Illness, disability and death caused by infectious diseases have a massive social and economic impact. The causes and the solutions for most infectious diseases, however, are known, and illness and death can in most cases be avoided at an affordable cost. The major infectious diseases are HIV/AIDS, malaria and tuberculosis. The **Global Fund to Fight AIDS, Tuberculosis and Malaria** (www.theglobalfund.org) is a major contributor to these efforts.

Although 78 million people have become infected with HIV since the first cases were reported in 1981, and 35 million have died from AIDS-related illnesses, considerable progress has been made. The **Joint United Nations Programme on HIV/AIDS (UNAIDS)** (www.unaids.org) estimated that at the end of 2015, 37 million people worldwide were living with HIV. By June 2016, more than 18 million people living with HIV were accessing life-saving antiretroviral therapy. Efforts to eliminate mother-to-child transmission of HIV have been successful, halving new HIV infections among children, from 290,000 in 2010 to 150,000 in 2015. The majority of people living with HIV, however, are still unable to access treatment, and progress in HIV prevention has slowed. The number of the newly infected in 2015 stood at 2.1 million—35 per cent lower than in 2000—but new HIV infections have declined by only six per cent since 2010. In 2015, 1.1 million people, including more than 100,000 children, died from AIDS-related causes; about one third of those deaths were due to tuberculosis.

UNAIDS is taking a life-cycle approach to HIV, finding HIV solutions for everyone at every stage of their lives. Research investment is still required to find more effective, tolerable and affordable treatments, as well as a cure and a vaccine.

The General Assembly, at its High-level Meeting on Ending AIDS (New York, 8–10 June 2016), adopted the *Political Declaration on Ending AIDS*, in which countries pledged to end AIDS as a public health threat by 2030. They also adopted three interim fast-track targets to be achieved by 2020: reducing new HIV infections to fewer than 500,000; reducing AIDS-related deaths to fewer than 500,000; and eliminating HIV-related stigma and discrimination.

For decades, the UN system has been at the forefront of the fight against disease through the creation of policies and systems that address the social dimensions of health problems. The **United Nations Children's Fund** (**UNICEF**) (www.unicef.org) focuses on child and maternal health, and the **United Nations Population Fund** (**UNFPA**) (www.unfpa.org) deals with reproductive health and family planning. The UN specialized agency coordinating global action against disease is the **World Health Organization** (**WHO**) (www.who.int). WHO has set ambitious goals for achieving health for all, making reproductive health available, building partnerships and promoting healthy lifestyles and environments.

WHO was the driving force behind various historic accomplishments, including the global eradication of smallpox in 1979, achieved after a 10-year campaign. Another UN entity, FAO, led the way in the eradication of rinderpest, achieved in 2010.

WHO's Water, Sanitation and Health team visited two towns close to Kathmandu (Danchi and Sankhu), which were among the worst affected built-up areas close to the Nepalese capital. About 95 per cent of the populations of the towns were living in small shelters after the 2015 earthquake (29 April 2015, WHO/Payden).

The disease, which has remained undetected in the field since 2001, is the first animal disease ever to be eliminated.

Together with its partners, WHO helped eliminate poliomyelitis from the Americas in 1994, the Western Pacific region in 2000, the European region in 2002 and South East Asia in 2014. It remains engaged in a global effort to eliminate this disease entirely. Since the launch of the **Global Polio Eradication Initiative** (www.polioeradication.org) in 1988, polio cases have decreased by over 99 per cent, from an estimated 350,000 cases that year to 66 reported cases in 2015. In 2016, only three countries—Afghanistan, Nigeria and Pakistan—remained polio-endemic, down from more than 125 in 1988. Through the Initiative, more than 2.5 billion children have been immunized against the disease worldwide. The public health savings resulting from polio eradication are estimated to be $40–50 billion.

The **Roll Back Malaria (RBM) Partnership** (www.rollbackmalaria.org) was launched in 1998 by WHO, UNICEF, UNDP and the World Bank to provide a coordinated global response to the disease. The Partnership includes malaria-endemic countries, their bilateral and multilateral development partners, the private sector, NGOs, community-based organizations, foundations, and academic institutions, working together to bring about a world in which malaria is no longer a major cause of mortality or a barrier to economic and social development. RBM's overall strategy aims to reduce malaria morbidity and mortality by reaching universal coverage and strengthening health systems.

The global **Stop TB Partnership** (stoptb.org), founded in 2001, has as its mission to serve every person who is vulnerable to tuberculosis (TB) and ensure that high-quality diagnosis, treatment and care is available to all who need it. It comprises 1,500 partners, including international and technical organizations, government programmes, research and funding agencies, foundations, NGOs, civil society, community groups and the private sector in more than 100 countries.

The **Partnership for Maternal, Newborn and Child Health (PMNCH)** (www.pmnch.org), with its secretariat hosted at WHO, was formed in September 2005, bringing together 80 members from three organizations—the Partnership for Safe Motherhood and Newborn Health, the Healthy Newborn Partnership, and the Child Survival Partnership—with the mandate to strengthen alignment and consensus-building to support the achievement of the MDGs. Today, the Partnership is an alliance of more than 750 organizations in 77 countries from the sexual, reproductive, maternal, newborn, child and adolescent health communities, as well as health influencing sectors. The Partnership contributes to the *Every Woman Every Child* movement and the *Global Strategy for Women's, Children's and Adolescents' Health (2016–2030)*.

Another major UN achievement was the adoption of a ground-breaking public health treaty to control tobacco supply and consumption in 2003. The *WHO Framework Convention on Tobacco Control* covers tobacco taxation, smoking prevention and treatment, illicit trade, advertising, sponsorship and promotion, and product regulation. The *Convention* is a key part of the global strategy to reduce the epidemic use of tobacco, which kills nearly 5 million people every year. WHO also takes a leading role combating obesity, a worldwide health concern. In 2014, more than 1.9 billion adults, 18 years and older, were overweight. Of these, over 600 million were obese.

WHO developed the **Global Action Plan for the Prevention and Control of Noncommunicable Diseases (NCDs) 2013–2020** (www.who.int/nmh/events/ncd_action_plan), which aims to achieve the commitments of the 2011 UN *Political Declaration on Noncommunicable diseases*. NCDs, including heart disease, stroke, cancer, diabetes, chronic lung disease and mental health conditions—together with violence and injuries—are collectively responsible for more than 70 per cent of all deaths worldwide. Eight out of 10 of these deaths occur in low- and middle-income countries. The Global Action Plan will contribute to progress on 9 global NCD targets to be attained by 2025, including the 25 per cent relative reduction in premature mortality from NCDs and a halt in the rise of global obesity to match the rates of 2010.

Between 1980 and 1995, a joint UNICEF-WHO effort raised global immunization coverage against six killer diseases—diphtheria, measles, polio, tetanus, tuberculosis and pertussis (whooping cough)—from 5 to 80 per cent, saving the lives of some 2.5 million children a year. A similar initiative—the **Global Alliance for Vaccines and Immunization (GAVI)** (www.gavialliance.org)—was launched in 1999 with initial funds from the Bill and Melinda Gates Foundation. Since 2000, GAVI has helped prevent 7 million deaths through routine immunization against hepatitis B, *Haemophilus influenzae* type "b" (Hib) and pertussis, and through one-off investments in immunization against measles, polio and yellow fever. The Alliance incorporates WHO, UNICEF, the World Bank and private sector partners.

WHO priorities in the area of communicable diseases are to reduce the impact of malaria and tuberculosis through global partnership; strengthen surveillance, monitoring and response to communicable diseases; intensify routine prevention and control; and generate new knowledge, intervention methods, implementation strategies and research capabilities for use in developing countries. WHO works with countries to increase and sustain access to prevention, treatment and care for HIV, tuberculosis, malaria and neglected tropical diseases and to reduce vaccine-preventable diseases. WHO is also a key player in promoting primary health care, delivering essential drugs, making cities healthier, promoting healthy lifestyles and environments, and tackling health emergencies.

Another WHO priority is universal health coverage. WHO works together with policymakers, global health partners, civil society, academia and the private sector to support countries to develop, implement and monitor solid national health plans. WHO supports countries to assure the availability of equitable integrated people-centred health services at an affordable price; facilitate access to affordable, safe and effective health technologies; and strengthen health information systems and evidence-based policymaking.

WHO also serves as a motor for health research. Working with its partners, WHO gathers data on current conditions and needs, particularly in developing countries. Data gathered range from epidemiological research in remote tropical forests to monitoring the progress of genetic research. The WHO tropical disease research programme has focused on the resistance of the malaria parasite to the most commonly used drugs, and on fostering the development of new drugs and diagnostics against tropical infectious diseases. Such research also helps improve national and international surveillance of epidemics, and develop preventive strategies for new and emerging diseases.

WHO establishes international standards on biological and pharmaceutical substances. It developed the concept of "essential drugs" as a basic element of primary health care. WHO works with countries to ensure the equitable supply of safe and effective drugs at the lowest possible cost and with the most effective use. To this end, it has developed a "model list" of several hundred drugs and vaccines considered essential to help prevent or treat over 80 per cent of all health problems. The list is updated every two years. WHO also cooperates with member states, civil society and the pharmaceutical industry to develop new essential drugs for priority health problems in poor and middle-income countries, and to continue the production of established essential drugs.

Through the international access afforded to the United Nations, WHO oversees the global collection of information on communicable diseases, compiles comparable health and disease statistics, and sets international standards for safe food, and for biological and pharmaceutical products. WHO also provides unmatched evaluation of the cancer-producing risks of pollutants, and has put into place the universally accepted guidance for global control of HIV/AIDS.

Quality education

Ensure inclusive and equitable quality education and promote lifelong opportunities for all. Despite progress, the world failed to meet the MDG of achieving universal primary education by 2015. In 2013, 59 million children of primary-school age were out of school; among those, 1 in 5 children had dropped out. Recent trends suggest that 2 in 5 of out-of-school children will never set foot in a classroom. In 2013, there were still 757 million adults (aged 15 and over) unable to read and write, of whom two thirds were women. To fulfil the promise of universal primary and secondary education, new primary school teachers are needed, with estimates showing a need for nearly 26 million teachers by 2030. Africa faces the greatest challenges in this regard, with nearly 7 in 10 countries experiencing acute shortages of trained primary school teachers.

Research has shown that access to education is closely related to improved social indicators. Schooling has a multiplier effect for women. An educated woman will typically be healthier, have fewer children and attain more opportunities to increase household income. Her children, in turn, will experience lower mortality rates, better nutrition and better overall health. For this reason, girls and women are the focus of the education programmes of numerous UN agencies.

SDG 4 focuses on the acquisition of foundational and higher-order skills; equitable access to technical and vocational training and higher education; training throughout life; and the knowledge, skills and values needed to function well and contribute to society. Because of the multiplicity of factors involved in education, many parts of the UN system are involved in the funding and development of a variety of education and training programmes.

The lead agency in the area of education is the **United Nations Educational, Scientific and Cultural Organization (UNESCO)** (www.unesco.org). Together with other partners, it works to ensure that all children are enrolled in child-friendly schools with trained teachers providing quality education. UNESCO's education sector focuses on providing educational access to all, at all levels; the success of special-needs and marginalized populations; teacher training; developing competencies for work forces; success through education; ensuring opportunities for non-formal and lifelong learning; and using technology to enhance teaching and learning, and to expand educational opportunities. The Organization is the only UN agency with a mandate to cover all aspects of education. Through the *Incheon Declaration* adopted at the World Education Forum in May 2015, UNESCO was entrusted to lead and coordinate the global *Education 2030* agenda with its partners. The road map to achieve the ten targets of SDG 4 is the *Education 2030 Framework for Action* (FFA), adopted in November 2015, which provides guidance to governments and partners on how to turn commitments into action.

In addition to declaring quality education the fourth SDG, the UN has launched a number of education initiatives. Every year, hundreds of Model UN conferences are held at all educational levels and in a variety of configurations, including the **Global Model United Nations Conference** (outreach.un.org/mun/). Through these programmes, students act as diplomats and participate in simulated sessions of the General Assembly and other UN system bodies.

The **United Nations Academic Impact (UNAI)** (academicimpact.un.org/) is an initiative that aligns institutions of higher education with the UN through activities and research in a shared culture of intellectual social responsibility. UNAI members commit themselves to the principles inherent in the UN *Charter*; human rights, including freedom of inquiry, opinion and speech; educational opportunity for all people regardless of gender, race, religion or ethnicity; opportunity for everyone to acquire the skills and knowledge necessary for the pursuit of higher education; building capacity in higher education; encouraging global citizenship; advancing peace and conflict resolution; addressing issues of poverty; promoting sustainability; and promoting intercultural dialogue and understanding. Since its launch in 2010, UNAI has grown to comprise more than 1,200 institutions in some 120 countries.

Gender equality

Achieve gender equality and empower all women and girls. While the world has achieved progress towards gender equality and women's empowerment under the MDGs (including equal access to primary education between girls and boys), women and girls continue to suffer discrimination and violence in every part of the world. Assuring women's rights through legal frameworks is a first step in addressing discrimination against them. As of 2014, 143 countries guaranteed equality between men and women in their constitutions; another 52 countries have yet to make this important commitment. Globally, women's participation in parliament rose to 23 per cent in 2016, representing a 6 per cent increase over a decade.

The proportion of women aged between 20 and 24 who reported that they were married before their eighteenth birthday dropped from 32 per cent around 1990 to 26 per cent around 2015. In 30 countries where the practice of female genital mutilation is concentrated, more than a third of girls aged 15 to 19 have been subjected to the procedure.

In every region, women and girls do the bulk of unpaid work, including caregiving and such household tasks as cooking and cleaning. On average, women report that they spend 19 per cent of their time each day in unpaid activities, versus 8 per cent for men.

SDG 5 aims to eliminate all forms of discrimination and violence against women and girls, including harmful practices, and seeks to ensure that they have sexual, reproductive health and reproductive rights; receive due recognition for unpaid work; have full access to productive resources; and enjoy equal participation with men in political, economic and public life.

Promotion of equality between women and men and the empowerment of women are central to UN work. Achieving gender equality and empowering all women and girls is recognized as a critical means for progress in achieving all the SDGs. Equal access to quality education, as well as equal opportunities for employment, leadership and decision-making at all levels are key factors to their advancement. The United Nations actively promotes women's human rights and works to eradicate violence against women, including in armed conflict and through trafficking. It also adopts global norms and standards for gender equality and the empowerment of women and girls, and supports follow-up and implementation at the national level, including through its development assistance activities.

UN conferences in Mexico City (1975), Copenhagen (1980), Nairobi (1985) and Beijing (1995) galvanized commitment and action towards gender equality and the empowerment of women around the world. At the latter, the Fourth (1995) World Conference on Women, 189 governments adopted the *Beijing Declaration* and *Platform for Action* to address inequality and discrimination and ensure women's empowerment in all spheres of life. In 2015, the Beijing+20 review (beijing20.unwomen.org) welcomed progress made, yet expressed concern about slow, uneven progress and remaining gaps and obstacles.

The **United Nations Entity for Gender Equality and the Empowerment of Women (UN-Women)** (www.unwomen.org) works towards eliminating discrimination against women and girls, empowering women and achieving equality between women and men as partners and beneficiaries of development, human rights, humanitarian action, and peace and security. It supports intergovernmental bodies, such as the Commission on the Status of Women, in formulating policies, global standards and norms; helps member states implement these standards by providing technical and financial support at the national level and forging partnerships with civil society; and holds the UN system accountable for its work on gender equality, including regular monitoring of system-wide progress.

Under the Economic and Social Council, the **Commission on the Status of Women** (www.unwomen.org/en/csw) monitors progress towards gender equality worldwide by reviewing implementation of the 1995 *Platform for Action*, and contributes to the follow-up to the 2030 Agenda. It makes recommendations for further action to promote women's rights and to address discrimination and inequality in all fields. Major accomplishments of the 45-member Commission over its more than 60 years of activity include the preparation of, and follow-up to, four world conferences on women and the development of the treaty on women's human rights: the 1979 *Convention on the Elimination of All Forms of Discrimination against Women* and its 1999 *Optional Protocol*. The Commission's 2015 session reviewed progress since 1995 and the post-2015 development agenda (unwomen. org/en/csw/csw59-2015).

The **Committee on the Elimination of Discrimination against Women (CEDAW)** (www.ohchr.org/en/hrbodies/cedaw) monitors adherence to the *Convention* and exercises the functions conferred to it by the *Optional Protocol*. The 23-member Committee holds constructive dialogues with states parties on their implementation of the *Convention*, based on reports they submit. Its recommendations have contributed to a better under-standing of women's rights, and of the means to ensure the enjoyment of those rights and the elimination of discrimination against women.

Beyond the Secretariat, all the organizations of the UN family address issues relat-ing to women and gender in their policies and programmes; and empowering women is central to the SDGs.

Clean water and sanitation

Ensure availability and sustainable management of water and sanitation for all. Water stress affects more than 2 billion people around the globe, a figure that is projected to rise. Progress was achieved on the MDG tar-gets to reduce by half the proportion of population without access to safe drinking water and basic sanitation. Globally, 147 countries have met the drinking water target, 95 countries have met the sanitation target and 77 countries have met both. In 2015, 6.6 billion people, or 91 per cent of the global population, used an improved drinking water source compared to 82 per cent in 2000, surpassing the MDG target of 50 per cent, which was met in 2010. An estimated 663 million people in 2015, however, were still using unimproved sources or surface water. Between 2000 and 2015, the proportion of the global population using improved sanitation increased from 59 per cent to 68 per cent. However, 2.4 billion were left behind: among them were 946 million people without any facilities at all, who continued to practise open defecation.

SDG 6 goes beyond drinking water, sanitation and hygiene to also address the qual-ity and sustainability of water resources. It involves expanding international coopera-tion and garnering the support of local communities in improving water and sanitation management.

Water resources. Basic access to a sufficient water supply is defined as a source likely to provide 20 litres per person per day at a distance no greater than 1 kilometre (a 30-minute round-trip journey). Such sources would include household connections, public standpipes, boreholes, protected dug wells, protected springs and rainwater col-lections. The United Nations has been addressing the global crisis caused by growing demands on the world's water resources to meet human, commercial and agricultural needs, as well as the need for basic sanitation. The International Drinking Water Supply and Sanitation Decade (1981–1990), the International Conference on Water and the Environment (1992), the Earth Summit (1992) and Rio+20 (2012) all focused on this vital resource. The Decade, in particular, helped some 1.3 billion people in developing countries gain access to safe drinking water.

Causes of inadequate water supply include inefficient use, degradation of water by pollution, and overexploitation of groundwater reserves. Corrective action aims at achieving better management of scarce freshwater resources. UN system activities focus on the sustainable development of fragile and finite freshwater resources, which are un-der increasing stress from population growth, pollution and the demands of agricultural and industrial uses.

To raise public awareness of the importance of intelligent development of freshwater resources, the General Assembly declared 2003 the UN International Year of Fresh-water. Also that year, the UN System Chief Executives Board for Coordination (CEB) established **UN-Water** (www.unwater.org)—an interagency mechanism to coordinate UN system actions to achieve the water-related goals of the *Millennium Declaration* and the 2002 World Summit on Sustainable Development. The Assembly also proclaimed the period 2005–2015 the International Decade for Action, "Water for Life"; the Decade began on 22 March 2005, observed annually as **World Water Day**. In 2016 and 2017, UNESCO published the seventh and eighth editions of the *United Nations World Water Development Report*, entitled, respectively, "Water and Jobs" and "Wastewater: the Untapped Resource".

In September 2016, the High-level Panel on Water (sustainabledevelopment.un.org/ HLPWater), established for a two-year period, called for a fundamental shift in the way the world looks at water. It issued an action plan for a new approach to water management that will help the world to achieve the 2030 Agenda.

Sanitation. According to the *Millennium Development Goals Report 2015*, worldwide, 2.1 billion people have gained access to improved sanitation and the proportion of people practising open defecation has fallen almost by half since 1990. Nevertheless, some 2.4 billion people still lack access to basic sanitation, defined as connection to a public sewer or septic system, a pour-flush latrine, a simple pit latrine or a ventilated and improved pit latrine.

Affordable and clean energy

 Ensure access to affordable, reliable, sustainable and modern energy for all. The proportion of the global population with access to electricity has increased steadily, from 79 per cent in 2000 to 85 per cent in 2012. Still, 1.1 billion people are without this valuable service. The proportion of the world's population with access to clean fuels and technologies for cooking increased from 51 per cent in 2000 to 58 per cent in 2014, although there has been limited progress since 2010. The absolute number of people relying on polluting fuels and technologies for cooking, such as solid fuels and kerosene, however, has increased, reaching an estimated 3 billion people. Modern renewables grew rapidly, at a rate of 4 per cent a year between 2010 and 2012. Energy intensity, calculated by dividing total primary energy supply by gross domestic product (GDP), reveals how much energy is used to produce one unit of economic output. Globally, energy intensity decreased by 1.7 per cent per year from 2010 to 2012. This represented a considerable improvement over the period from 1990 to 2010, when it decreased by 1.2 per cent a year. As energy is the dominant contributor to climate change—accounting for around 60 per cent of total global greenhouse gas emissions—reducing its carbon intensity is critical to long-term climate goals.

Energy. Nearly 15 per cent of the world's population lives without electricity, and even more people lack access to modern fuels for cooking and heating. Yet while an adequate supply of energy is essential to economic advancement and poverty eradication, the environmental and health effects of conventional energy systems are a matter of concern. The increasing demand for energy per capita, coupled with the rising global population, is resulting in consumption levels that cannot be sustained using current energy systems. UN system activities on energy help developing countries in many ways, including through education, training and capacity-building, assistance in policy reforms, and the provision of energy services. Although efforts are being made to move towards renewable sources of energy that are significantly less polluting, additional demand still outpaces the introduction of new capacity.

In 2004, CEB established **UN-Energy** (www.un-energy.org/) as the principal interagency mechanism in the field of energy. Its task is to help ensure coherence in the UN system's response to the global energy challenge, as well as the engagement of major actors from the private sector and the NGO community for implementing energy-related decisions of the 2030 Agenda.

Safe, secure and peaceful uses of nuclear materials

In 2016, almost 450 nuclear power reactors were in operation in 30 countries, providing about 11 per cent of the world's electricity. Energy is essential for sustainable economic growth and improved human welfare. Nuclear energy provides access to clean, reliable and affordable energy, mitigating the negative impacts of climate change. It is a significant part of the world energy mix and its use is expected to grow in the coming decades. The **International Atomic Energy Agency (IAEA)** (www.iaea.org), a member of the UN family, fosters the development of the safe, secure and peaceful uses of atomic energy, playing a prominent role in international efforts to ensure the use of nuclear technology for sustainable development. IAEA serves as the world's central intergovernmental forum for scientific and technical cooperation in the nuclear field.

The Agency is a focal point for the exchange of information and the formulation of guidelines and norms in the area of nuclear safety, as well as for the provision of advice to governments, at their request, on ways to improve the safety of reactors and avoid the risk of accidents. The Agency's role in the area of nuclear safety has increased as nuclear-power programmes have grown. IAEA formulates standards for radiation protection and issues, and provides standards and technical guidelines on specific types of operations, including the safe transport of radioactive materials.

Acting under the *Convention on Assistance in the Case of a Nuclear Accident or Radiological Emergency* and the *Convention on Early Notification of a Nuclear Accident*, both adopted in 1986, the Agency facilitates emergency assistance to member states in the event of a radiation accident. Other international treaties for which IAEA is the depositary include the 1987 *Convention on the Physical Protection of Nuclear Material*, and its 2005 *Amendment*, which entered into force in May 2016; the 1963 *Vienna Convention on Civil Liability for Nuclear Damage;* the 1994 *Convention on Nuclear Safety*, and the 1997 *Joint Convention on the Safety of Spent Fuel Management and on the Safety of Radioactive Waste Management*.

The IAEA technical cooperation programme provides assistance in the form of in-country projects, experts and training in the application of peaceful nuclear techniques with an emphasis on sustainable development. These help countries in such critical areas as water, health, nutrition, medicine and food production. Examples include work related to mutation breeding, through which beneficial varieties of crops have been developed using radiation-based technology, thereby improving food security. The use of isotope hydrology to map underground aquifers, manage ground and surface water, detect and control pollution, and monitor dam leakage and safety, improves access to safe drinking water. The Agency also facilitates the use of radiotherapy equipment for use in medical treatment and trains staff to safely treat cancer patients in developing and middle-income countries.

The Agency collects and disseminates information on virtually every aspect of nuclear science and technology through its International Nuclear Information System (www. iaea.org/inis). IAEA laboratories in Austria and in Monaco conduct research and provide training. IAEA also collaborates with other UN organizations. With UNESCO, it operates the International Centre for Theoretical Physics in Trieste, Italy (www.ictp.it). The Agency works with FAO in research on atomic energy in food and agriculture and cooperates with WHO on radiation in medicine and biology.

The **United Nations Scientific Committee on the Effects of Atomic Radiation (UNSCEAR)** (www.unscear.org), established in 1955, assesses and reports on the levels and effects of exposure to ionizing radiation. Governments and organizations worldwide rely on its estimates as the scientific basis for evaluating radiation risk, establishing radiation protection and safety standards, and regulating radiation sources.

Decent work and economic growth

 Promote sustained, inclusive and sustainable economic growth, full and productive employment and decent work for all. Roughly half the world's population still lives on the equivalent of about $2 a day. In too many places, having a job does not guarantee the ability to escape from poverty. The global annual growth rate of real GDP per capita increased by 1.3 per cent in 2014, a significant slowdown compared to 2010 (2.8 per cent growth) and 2000 (3.0 per cent growth). Developing regions grew far faster than developed regions, with average annual growth rates in 2014 of 3.1 per cent and 1.4 per cent, respectively. While labour productivity increased in the developing regions from 2005 to 2015, the value for developed regions was still more than twice that of any developing region, and around 20 times greater than the values for sub-Saharan Africa and Southern Asia.

The global unemployment rate stood at 6.1 per cent in 2015, down from a peak of 6.6 per cent in 2009, mostly owing to a decline in unemployment in the developed regions. Unemployment affects population groups differently. Globally, women and youth (aged 15 to 24) are more likely to face unemployment than men and adults aged 25 and over. SDG 8 aims to provide opportunities for full and productive employment for all while eradicating forced labour, human trafficking and child labour.

The *Millennium Development Goals Report, 2015* indicated that as the global economy had entered a new period combining slower growth, widening inequalities and turbulence, employment was not expanding fast enough to keep up with the growing labour force. The employment-to-population ratio—the proportion of the working-age population that is employed—has fallen from 62 per cent in 1991 to 60 per cent in 2015, with a significant downturn during the 2008–2009 global economic crisis. According to ILO, more than 204 million people were unemployed in 2015. This was over 34 million more than before the start of the economic crisis and 53 million more than in 1991.

Youth Employment Programme. With 71 million unemployed youth worldwide and 156 million young workers living in poverty, youth employment remains a global challenge and a top policy concern. ILO has had a long-standing commitment to promote decent work for youth (www.ilo.org/global/topics/youth-employment). Its activities on youth employment include advocacy, knowledge development and dissemination, policy and technical advice, and capacity-building services.

In other efforts to address employment, the Secretary-General appointed Werner Faymann (Austria) as his **Special Envoy on Youth Unemployment** in September 2016.

For more on employment see *labour.*

Industry, innovation and infrastructure

 Build resilient infrastructure, promote inclusive and sustainable industrialization and foster innovation. Investments in infrastructure—transport, irrigation, energy and information and communication technology—are crucial to achieving sustainable development and empowering communities in many countries. Manufacturing is a foundation of economic development, employment and social stability. In 2015, the share of manufacturing value added in terms of GDP of developed regions was estimated at 13 per cent, a decrease over the past decade owing largely to the increasing role of services in developed regions. In contrast, the share of manufacturing value added in GDP remained relatively stagnant for developing regions, increasing marginally from 19 per cent in 2005 to 21 per cent in 2015. SDG 9 can be achieved through enhanced financial, technological and technical support; research; and increased access to information and communication technologies (ICTs).

Industrial development

As the structure of world economies shifts to less energy-intensive industries, and countries implement policies for enhanced energy efficiency, almost all regions have shown a reduction in carbon intensity of GDP. Global carbon dioxide emissions per unit of value added showed a steady decline between 1990 and 2013—a decrease of about 30 per cent.

Infrastructure and economic development also rely on ICTs. Mobile cellular services have spread rapidly around the world, allowing people in previously unconnected areas to join the global information society. By 2015, the percentage of the population living in areas covered by mobile broadband networks stood at 69 per cent globally. In rural areas, the share was only 29 per cent.

The globalization of industry has created unprecedented industrial challenges and opportunities for developing countries and countries with economies in transition. The mandate of the **United Nations Industrial Development Organization (UNIDO)** (www.unido.org), as described in the *Lima Declaration* adopted at the fifteenth session of the UNIDO General Conference in 2013, is to promote and accelerate inclusive and sustainable industrial development (ISID) to achieve shared prosperity and environmental sustainability around the world. The concept of ISID is included in SDG 9 and means that:

- every country achieves a higher level of industrialization in their economies, and benefits from the globalization of markets for industrial goods and services;
- no one is left behind in benefiting from industrial growth, and prosperity is shared among women and men, young and old, rural and urban dwellers alike, in all countries; and
- broader economic and social growth is supported within an environmentally sustainable framework.

UNIDO focuses on three programmatic fields of activity to support developing countries and countries with economies in transition to achieve higher levels of ISID: creating shared prosperity, advancing economic competitiveness and safeguarding the environment. Each of these fields of activity contains a number of individual programmes through UNIDO's four enabling functions: technical cooperation; analytical and research functions; standards and quality-related activities; and partnerships for knowledge transfer, networking and industrial cooperation. UNIDO also implements a selected number of cross-cutting programmes, including industrial policy advice, research and statistics; partnership mobilization and South-South cooperation; gender equality and the empowerment of women; and a wide range of regional programmes.

Reduced inequalities

Reduce inequality within and among countries. One of the SDG targets is to ensure that income growth among the poorest 40 per cent of the population in every country is more rapid than its national average. This was true in 56 of 94 countries with data available from 2007 to 2012. This, however, does not necessarily imply greater prosperity, since nine of those countries experienced negative growth rates over that period. Preferential treatment for developing countries and the **least developed countries (LDCs)** in trade can help reduce inequalities by creating more export opportunities. Major developed country markets already offer duty-free market access to LDCs on most of their tariff lines. The share of exports from LDCs and developing regions that benefitted from duty-free treatment increased from 2000 to 2014, reaching 79 per cent for developing countries and 84 per cent for LDCs.

SDG 10 calls for reducing inequalities in income, as well as those based on sex, age, disability, race, class, ethnicity, religion and opportunity—both within and among countries. It also aims to ensure safe, orderly and regular migration.

LDCs, LLDCs and SIDS

LDCs, **landlocked developing countries (LLDCs)** and **small island developing states (SIDS)** refer to segments of the global community that face the most binding constraints to sustainable economic growth and development (www.un.org/ohrlls). Not only are they exposed to significant economic, environmental and health-related shocks, they are also the least equipped to withstand and manage these hazards. As a result, LDCs, LLDCs and SIDS face the possibility of seeing their development achievements reversed when struck by shocks.

LDCs are low-income countries that display the most severe structural handicaps, in particular very low human capital stock and narrow production and export bases. Their weak institutional capacities undermine their ability to formulate, implement and sustain national development policies or fully engage in policy discussions at the international level.

LLDCs and SIDS are also defined in relation to challenges related to their geography. LLDCs are developing countries that do not have direct maritime access. They must rely on the trade and transport systems of neighbouring and coastal countries which, in most cases, are as precarious as theirs. Such dependence, combined with their remoteness from major consumer markets, causes their transport and other trade transaction costs to be prohibitively high. These costs hamper their ability to build competitive production and export bases, compete in global markets, sustain strong investment and economic growth, and promote social and environmental sustainability. SIDS are small in size—either in terms of land mass or population or both. They are also the most exposed to biodiversity loss and disproportionately bear the effects of climate change and natural disasters. They are among the countries with the narrowest production and export bases, and experience high economic growth volatility.

In recognition of the specific development challenges of LDCs, LLDCs and SIDS, the UN organizes once-a-decade conferences dedicated to these countries, which result in compacts in support of their development. The most recent of these frameworks include the *Istanbul Programme of Action for LDCs* (2011–2020), the *Vienna Programme of Action for LLDCs* (2014–2024) and the *SAMOA Pathway for SIDS* (2014). These 10-year programmes of action establish objectives for these groups of countries and identify priorities for action, most of which are supported by goals and targets.

Small islands. Owing to their ecological fragility, small size, limited resources and isolation from markets, SIDS are unable to take advantage of globalization, posing a major obstacle to their socioeconomic development. Previous outcome documents from conferences on the sustainable development of SIDS include the *Barbados Programme of Action* (1994) and *Mauritius Strategy* (2005). The *Strategy* addressed, among others, such issues as climate change and rising sea levels; natural and environmental disasters; waste management; tourism and biodiversity resources; transportation and communication; globalization and trade liberalization; sustainable production and consumption; capacity-building and education for sustainable development; health; and knowledge management and information for decision-making.

The Third International Conference on SIDS was held in Apia, Samoa, in September 2014, with the theme "The sustainable development of small island developing states through genuine and durable partnerships". Nearly 300 partnerships were announced at the conference. The *SIDS Accelerated Modalities of Action Pathway (SAMOA*

Pathway) (www.sids2014.org) adopted at the Conference addresses priority areas for SIDS and calls for urgent action and support for the efforts of SIDS to achieve their sustainable development goals.

Sustainable cities and communities

Make cities and human settlements inclusive, safe, resilient and sustainable. Today more than half the world's population of 7.5 billion lives in cities. By 2030, it is expected that 6 out of 10 people will be urban dwellers. As more people migrate to cities in search of a better life and urban populations grow, however, housing issues intensify. In 2014, 30 per cent of the urban population lived in slum-like conditions. That year, more than 880 million people were living in slums and about half the urban population globally were exposed to air pollution levels at least 2.5 times above the standard of safety set by WHO.

Urban areas generate 70 per cent of the world's gross domestic product and contribute between 39 and 49 per cent of the world's greenhouse gases; a percentage expected to rise to 70 by 2050. Urbanization—the process by which towns and cities are formed and become larger as more people begin living and working in central areas—has become one of the most important global trends of the twenty-first century. It is a transformative force that can be harnessed to enhance economic productivity, inclusive growth and environmental sustainability. SDG 11 aims to renew and plan cities and other human settlements in a way that fosters community cohesion and personal security while stimulating innovation and employment.

Human settlements

The **United Nations Human Settlements Programme (UN-Habitat)** (www.unhabitat. org) is the leading UN system agency for addressing urban issues. It is mandated by the General Assembly to promote socially and environmentally sustainable towns and cities, with the goal of providing adequate shelter for all. In 1996 the Second UN Conference on Human Settlements (Habitat II), adopted the *Habitat Agenda*, a global plan of action in which governments committed themselves to the goals of adequate shelter for all and sustainable urban development. On 20 October 2016, participants at the UN Conference on Housing and Sustainable Urban Development (Habitat III) held in Quito, Ecuador, adopted the **New Urban Agenda (NUA)** (unhabitat.org/new-urban-agenda-adopted-at-habitat-iii), a new framework laying out how cities should be planned and managed to best promote sustainable urbanization. The conference drew some 36,000 people from 167 different countries. As mandated by Habitat III, UN-Habitat is committed to establishing and strengthening mechanisms to promote UN system action to support implementation, follow-up and review of NUA. In December, the General Assembly requested the Secretary-General to report on NUA implementation every four years, beginning in 2018.

UN-Habitat also coordinates the World Urban Campaign (www.worldurbancampaign.org), a global advocacy and partnership platform—comprising 136 partners and networks—that raises awareness about positive urban change in order to achieve productive, safe, inclusive and well planned cities. Other networks and advocacy platforms to facilitate NUA implementation include the World Urban Forum, World Cities Day and World Habitat Day. UN-Habitat has developed programmes and initiatives to address the most common challenges of poor urbanization. Among others, these include:

▪ The City Prosperity Initiative (CPI) assists city authorities and other stakeholders in designing effective policy interventions. CPI provides technical and substantive support to municipalities for innovative solutions.

- The Participatory Slum Upgrading Programme aims to address uneven and unequal urban development represented by slums. It puts key urban stakeholders and concerned communities at the heart of the effort to improve the lives of slum dwellers.
- The Safer Cities Programme is implemented on a community-based, citywide scale, focused on stakeholder inclusion and collaboration to ensure safety and security for all. It is grounded in the instruments of local government as the tools to address crime, violence, conflict and insecurity in cities and human settlements.
- The Urban Planning and Design Lab responds to requests from local, regional and national governments for assistance in sustainable urban planning. It uses spatial planning to coordinate various aspects of urban development and translate them into concrete and implementable projects that generate value, economic development and jobs.
- National Urban Policy is a tool for governments to direct and manage urbanization for the better that encourages a coherent set of decisions towards a long-term common vision that promotes transformative, productive, inclusive and resilient urban development.
- Planned City Extensions define and structure city growth to provide space for better functioning and more livable urban settlements that include public space. They reduce the costs of public basic services and establish connectivity and proximity to the existing city, setting the basis for compact, connected, integrated and inclusive cities that are resilient to climate change.
- Urban Basic Services programmes focus on four programmatic clusters: urban mobility; urban energy; water and sanitation; and urban waste management. The Urban Basic Services Trust Fund was created in December 2013 to support implementation of the SDGs in these four cluster areas.
- Global Land Tool Network (GLTN) is an alliance of global, regional and national partners contributing to poverty alleviation through the promotion of land reform, improved land management and security of tenure by developing and disseminating pro-poor and gender-responsive land tools.

Responsible consumption and production

 Ensure sustainable consumption and production patterns. The material footprint reflects the amount of primary materials required to meet a country's needs. In 2010, the total material footprint in developed regions was significantly higher than that of developing regions, 23.6 kg per unit of GDP versus 14.5 kg per unit of GDP, respectively. The material footprint of developing regions increased from 2000 to 2010, with non-metallic minerals showing the largest increase. Domestic material consumption measures the amount of natural resources used in economic processes. In 2010, domestic material consumption per capita in developed regions was 72 per cent higher than that of developing regions. SDG 12 aims to promote consumption and production patterns through measures such as specific policies and international agreements on the management of materials that are toxic to the environment. One target the goal seeks to achieve by 2020 is the environmentally sound management of chemicals and all wastes throughout their life cycle in order to significantly reduce their release to air, water and soil in order to minimize their adverse impacts on human health and the environment.

Hazardous wastes and chemicals. To regulate the millions of tons of toxic waste that cross national borders each year, member states negotiated the 1989 *Basel Convention on the Control of Transboundary Movements of Hazardous Wastes and their Disposal*

(www.basel.int), administered by UNEP. The *Convention*, which has 185 parties, was strengthened in 1995 to ban the export of toxic waste to developing countries, which often do not have the technology for safe disposal. The *Convention* obligates states parties to reduce shipping and dumping of dangerous wastes across borders and minimize their toxic potential. In 1999, governments adopted the *Basel Protocol on Liability and Compensation* to deal with the question of financial responsibility in the event of the illegal dumping or accidental spill of hazardous wastes.

Ozone depletion

The ozone layer refers to ozone molecules in the stratosphere—thinly spread approximately 15 to 35 kilometers (9 to 20 miles) above the ground—that shield the Earth from the sun's damaging ultraviolet rays. In the mid-1970s, a hypothesis emerged that manmade chemicals, such as chlorofluorocarbons (CFCs) used for refrigeration, air conditioning and industrial cleaning, were destroying the ozone layer. It became a matter of increasing international concern, since greater exposure to ultraviolet radiation results in skin cancer, eye cataracts and suppression of the human immune system, and causes damage to crops, wildlife and ecosystems. Hard evidence of the actual depletion was discovered in the mid-1980s.

In response to the challenge, UNEP helped negotiate the historic 1985 *Vienna Convention for the Protection of the Ozone Layer*, along with the 1987 *Montreal Protocol on Substances that Deplete the Ozone Layer* and its ensuing amendments. Under these agreements, administered by UNEP, CFCs were phased out worldwide in 2010, except for limited essential uses phased out in 2016, and other ozone-depleting substances have been phased out. *Montreal Protocol* parties are now phasing out hydrochlorofluorocarbons (HCFCs). The **UNEP Ozone Secretariat** (ozone.unep.org) has documented a 98 per cent decrease in ozone-depleting substances globally, as well as early signs of the expected ozone recovery of the stratosphere. Continued elimination of all emissions of ozone-depleting substances should help restore the global ozone layer to the benchmark 1980 levels around mid-century.

Climate change mitigation. In October 2016, parties to the *Montreal Protocol* adopted the *Kigali Amendment* to limit the use of hydrofluorocarbons (HFCs). HFC phasedown is expected to prevent the emission of up to 105 million tonnes of carbon dioxide equivalent of greenhouse gases and circumvent up to 0.5 degree Celsius of global temperature rise by 2100, while continuing to protect the ozone layer.

Climate action

Take urgent action to combat climate change and its impacts. Climate change is now affecting every country on every continent. People are experiencing its significant impacts, including changing weather patterns, rising sea levels, and more extreme weather events. Greenhouse gas emissions from human activities are now at their highest levels in history. In April 2016, 175 member states signed the historic Paris Agreement, which sets the stage for ambitious climate action by all to ensure that global temperatures rise no more than 2 degrees Celsius. The new agreement aims to reduce the pace of climate change and to accelerate and intensify the actions and investments needed for a sustainable low-carbon future.

Climate change often exacerbates disasters. Between 1990 and 2013, more than 1.6 million people died in internationally reported disasters, with annual deaths trending upwards. As a result, more countries are acting on the imperative to implement national and local disaster risk reduction strategies. In 2015, 83 countries had legislative and/or regulatory provisions in place for managing disaster risk. SDG 13 calls for urgent action not only to combat climate change and its impacts, but to also build resilience in responding to climate-related hazards and natural disasters.

In March 2015, at the Third UN World Conference on Disaster Risk Reduction in Sendai City, Japan, UN member states adopted the **Sendai Framework for Disaster Risk Reduction 2015–2030** (www.unisdr.org/we/coordinate/sendai-framework). In December 2015, countries adopted the Paris Agreement at the UN Climate Change Conference (COP21) in Paris (unfccc.int/paris_agreement/items/9485.php). In the *Agreement*, which opened for signature in April and entered into force on 4 November 2016, all countries agreed to work to limit global temperature rise to below 2 degrees Celsius, and to strive for 1.5 degrees Celsius.

Weather and climate

From weather prediction to research on climate change and early warning on natural hazards, the **World Meteorological Organization (WMO)** (public.wmo.int) coordinates global scientific efforts to provide timely and accurate information on the state and behaviour of the Earth's atmosphere, its interaction with the oceans, the climate it produces and the resulting distribution of water resources. WMO facilitates international cooperation in operating networks of stations for making meteorological, climatological, hydrological and related observations. It promotes the rapid exchange of meteorological information, standardization of meteorological observations, and uniform publication of observations and statistics. It also extends the application of meteorology to weather-sensitive socioeconomic activities such as aviation, shipping, and agriculture; promotes water resources development; and encourages research and training.

The World Weather Watch (www.wmo.int/pages/prog/www/) is the backbone of WMO activities. It offers up-to-the-minute worldwide weather information delivered through observation systems and telecommunication links operated by its member states and territories. These systems employ satellites, aircraft, land observation stations, ship stations, moored buoys and drifting buoys carrying automatic weather stations. The resulting data, analyses and forecasts are exchanged every day, freely and without restriction, between WMO centres and weather offices in every country. This, along with advances in computing power, has made today's five-day weather forecast as reliable as a two-day forecast was 20 years ago.

WMO programmes help countries apply meteorology to protect life and property and to advance social and economic development. They improve public weather services, increase the safety of sea and air travel, reduce the impact of desertification, and improve agriculture and the management of water, energy and other resources. Prompt meteorological advice can mean a substantial reduction in losses caused by droughts, pests and disease. The Tropical Cyclone Programme helps countries that are vulnerable to cyclones minimize destruction and loss of life by improving forecasting and warning systems and disaster preparedness. The Disaster Risk Reduction Programme ensures the integration of various WMO activities with related activities of international, regional and national organizations, particularly with respect to risk assessment, early warning systems and capacity-building.

The World Climate Programme collects and preserves climate data, helping governments plan for climate variability and change. It can also warn governments of impending climate variations (such as El Niño and La Niña events) and their impact several months ahead of time, and of changes, natural or man-made, that could affect critical human activities. The WMO-led Global Framework for Climate Services (GFCS) guides the development of science-based climate information and services to support decision-making in climate-sensitive sectors.

The World Weather Research Programme coordinates research on the structure and composition of the atmosphere, the physics and chemistry of clouds, weather modification, tropical meteorology, and weather forecasting. It helps member states conduct research projects, disseminate scientific information, and incorporate the results of research into forecasting and other techniques. Under the Global Atmosphere Watch Programme, a network of global and regional monitoring stations and satellites assesses the levels of greenhouse gases, ozone, radionuclides and other traces of gases and particles in the atmosphere.

The Hydrology and Water Resources Programme helps assess, manage and conserve global water resources. It promotes global cooperation in evaluating water resources and developing hydrological networks and services. It facilitates cooperation with respect to water basins shared between countries, and provides specialized forecasting in flood-prone areas, thus helping preserve life and property.

The Education and Training Programme and the Voluntary Cooperation Programme encourage the exchange of scientific knowledge, the development of technical expertise and the transfer of technology. The Information and Public Affairs Programme informs the general public about the work of WMO and the broader issues that WMO addresses.

Since the dawn of the industrial age, there has been a steady—and now dangerously increasing—build-up of greenhouse gases in the Earth's atmosphere, leading to a continuing rise in global temperatures. When fossil fuels are burned to generate energy, or when forests are cut down and burned, carbon dioxide is released. Greenhouse gases, including methane, nitrous oxide and others, have accumulated in the atmosphere to such an extent that the planet now faces the prospect of massive and potentially destructive consequences. The UN system is meeting this challenge head-on through its work on climate change (www.un.org/climatechange).

In 1988, at a time when the best research available was beginning to indicate the possible severity of the problem, two UN bodies—UNEP and WMO—established the **Intergovernmental Panel on Climate Change (IPCC)** (www.ipcc.ch) to assess the science related to climate change, including its impacts and future risks, and provide options for adaptation and mitigation. IPCC assessments provide a scientific basis for governments to develop climate-related policies, and underlie negotiations at the UN Climate Conference—the United Nations Framework Convention on Climate Change. The Panel reviews scientific research on the issue, with a view to developing a legally binding and coordinated approach to the problem. In recognition of its work, the Panel was awarded the 2007 Nobel Peace Prize, together with former United States Vice-President Albert Arnold (Al) Gore, Jr.

Heeding the warnings of scientists worldwide, the nations of the world came together in Rio de Janeiro in 1992 to sign the *United Nations Framework Convention on Climate Change* (www.unfccc.int).

In 1995, evidence presented by IPCC scientists made it clear that the 1992 target would not be enough to prevent global warming and its associated problems. In 1997, countries that had ratified the *Convention* met in Kyoto, Japan, and agreed on a protocol under which developed countries were to reduce their collective emissions of six greenhouse gases by 5.2 per cent between 2008 and 2012. The *Protocol's* first commitment period ended in 2012. Under the *Doha Amendment* to the *Protocol*, adopted in December 2012, 37 industrialized countries and the European Union committed to reduce greenhouse gas emissions to an average of five per cent against 1990 levels. During the

Satellite data can be used for improved climate change adaptation and disaster risk reduction. UN-SPIDER helps developing countries to use space-based information in all phases of the disaster management cycle. The Svalbard Satellite Station in Norway is recognized as the best-located ground station in the world for satellite observations (8 July 2015, UN Photo/Rick Bajornas).

second commitment period, the parties committed to reduce emissions by at least 18 per cent from 2013 to 2020. The 2015 Paris Agreement, which saw nations agree to further strengthen the global response to the threat of climate change, requires all parties to put forward their best efforts through "nationally determined contributions" and to strengthen these efforts in the years ahead.

When the United Nations first began to mobilize world public opinion to address the threat posed by climate change, many people remained unconvinced that such change was taking place. In 2007, however, IPCC reported with 90 per cent certainty that significant global warming was in process and increasing, to a degree that was directly attributable to human activity and that would worsen unless major corrective actions were taken. The Panel's report—*Climate Change 2007*—represents a consensus agreement of climate scientists and experts from 40 countries and has been endorsed by 113 governments. It indicates that the world faces an average temperature rise of around 3 degrees Celsius by the end of this century if greenhouse gas emissions continue to rise at their current pace. The results of such an increase would include more extreme temperatures; heat waves; new wind patterns; worsening drought in some regions and heavier precipitation in others; melting glaciers and Arctic ice; and rising sea levels worldwide. While the number of tropical cyclones (typhoons and hurricanes) is projected to decline, their intensity is expected to increase, with higher peak wind speeds and more intense precipitation due to warmer ocean waters.

The *Hyogo Framework for Action, 2005–2015*, adopted by 168 nations at the 2005 UN World Conference on Disaster Reduction in Kobe, Japan, included recommendations on reducing the disaster risks caused by climate-related hazards. The *Sendai Framework (2015–2030)* adopted in March 2015 continues those efforts. Ultimately, however, the only effective course is to combat the tide of global warming by restoring the sustainability of the atmosphere. Fortunately, the means to do so have been outlined, and the goal can be accomplished if the people of the world come together to make it happen.

Life below water

Conserve and sustainably use the oceans, seas and marine resources for sustainable development. Oceans, along with coastal and marine resources, play an essential role in human well-being and social and economic development worldwide. They are particularly crucial for people living in coastal communities, who represented 37 per cent of the global population in 2010. The proportion of global marine fish stocks within biologically sustainable levels declined from 90 per cent in 1974 to 69 per cent in 2013. In 2014, 8.4 per cent of the marine environment under national jurisdiction (up to 200 nautical miles from shore) was under protection. From 2000 to 2016, the share of marine key biodiversity areas that were completely covered by protected areas increased from 15 per cent to 19 per cent. SDG 14 seeks to sustainably use marine and coastal ecosystems, prevent marine pollution and increase the economic benefits to SIDS and LDCs from the sustainable use of marine resources.

High-seas fishing. Overfishing and the near exhaustion of many species of commercially valuable fish, along with the increasing incidence of illegal, unregulated and unreported fishing, have led governments to call for measures to conserve and sustainably manage fish resources—especially those that migrate across broad areas of the ocean or move through the economic zone of more than one country. The 1995 *Agreement for the Implementation of the Provisions of the United Nations Convention on the Law of the Sea of 10 December 1982 relating to the Conservation and Management of Straddling Fish Stocks and Highly Migratory Fish Stocks* provides a regime for the conservation and management of these stocks, with a view to ensuring their long-term conservation and sustainable use. It has 84 parties, including the European Union.

Protecting the marine environment

Coastal and marine areas cover some 70 per cent of the Earth's surface and are vital to the planet's life support system. Protecting the marine environment has become a primary concern of the United Nations, and UNEP has worked hard to focus the world's attention on oceans and seas. Most water pollution comes from industrial waste, mining, agricultural activities and emissions from motor vehicles; some of these forms of pollution occur thousands of miles inland. The **Global Programme of Action for the Protection of the Marine Environment from Land-based Activities** (web.unep.org/gpa), adopted in 1995 under UNEP auspices, is considered a milestone in international efforts to protect oceans, estuaries and coastal waters from such pollution. To prevent the influx of marine litter in the environment, the Global Partnership on Marine Litter (GPML) was launched in June 2012 at Rio+20. The GPML, besides being supportive of the Global Partnership on Waste Management, seeks to protect human health and the global environment by reducing and managing marine litter.

Under its **Regional Seas Programme** (web.unep.org/regionalseas), which now covers more than 140 countries, UNEP addresses the accelerating degradation of the world's oceans and coastal areas. The Programme works to protect shared marine and water resources through 13 conventions or action plans. Regional programmes, established under the auspices of UNEP, cover the Black Sea, East Asian Seas, Eastern Africa, the Regional Organization for the Protection of the Marine Environment Sea Area, the Mediterranean, the North-East Pacific, the North-West Pacific, the Red Sea and the Gulf of Aden, the South Asian Seas, the Pacific, the South-East Pacific, Western Africa and the Wider Caribbean.

Despite the dramatic expansion of world shipping, oil pollution from ships was reduced by around 60 per cent during the 1980s, and has continued to decline since then.

This has been due partly to the introduction of better methods of controlling the disposal of operational wastes and partly to the tightening of controls through international conventions (oils.gpa.unep.org). The **International Maritime Organization (IMO)** (www. imo.org) is the UN specialized agency responsible for measures to help prevent marine pollution from ships and improve the safety of international shipping. The pioneering *International Convention for the Prevention of Pollution of the Sea by Oil* was adopted in 1954, and IMO took over responsibility for it five years later. Since the 1960s, IMO has developed many measures to help prevent accidents at sea and oil spills; minimize the consequences of accidents and spills; and combat marine pollution, including that generated by land-based activities.

The *International Convention for the Prevention of Marine Pollution from Ships, 1973, as modified by the Protocol of 1978 relating thereto and by the 1997 Protocol (MARPOL Convention)* covers not only accidental and operational oil pollution, but also pollution by chemicals, packaged goods, sewage and garbage. Annex VI addresses the prevention of air pollution from ships and provides for greenhouse gas mitigation through energy efficiency measures adopted in 2011. The *MARPOL Convention* also obliges all tankers to have double hulls, or a design that provides equivalent cargo protection in the event of a collision or grounding. Further treaties provide for states to prepare oil spill response plans and carry out contingency planning for incidents involving other hazardous and noxious substances. IMO has also established a system of liability and compensation to provide for a straightforward process for claiming compensation in the event of a spill of oil, carried as cargo or carried as fuel.

IMO is also responsible for the 1972 *Convention on the Prevention of Marine Pollution by Dumping of Wastes and Other Matter;* and its 1996 *Protocol*, which prohibits the dumping of wastes at sea, except for certain materials on a permitted list.

A key IMO treaty aimed at preventing the spread of potentially invasive aquatic species in the ballast water of ships enters into force in September 2017. The *International Convention for the Control and Management of Ships' Ballast Water and Sediments*, 2004, will require ships to manage their ballast water in order to remove, render harmless, or avoid the uptake or discharge of aquatic organisms and pathogens within ballast water and sediments. IMO has also prohibited the use of anti-fouling paints on ships which may harm the marine environment. Some 15 particularly sensitive sea areas (PSSAs) have been designated around the world, in which special measures to restrict maritime activities have been adopted, such as areas to be avoided and vessel traffic routing and reporting systems.

IMO's technical cooperation programme and capacity-building projects support countries to ratify and implement IMO's environmental treaties in order to protect the marine environment and also to contribute to the fight against climate change.

Life on land

 Protect, restore and promote sustainable use of terrestrial ecosystems, sustainably manage forests, combat desertification, and halt and reverse land degradation and halt biodiversity loss. Between 2000 and 2016, the percentage of global terrestrial, inland freshwater and mountain key biodiversity areas covered by protected areas increased from 16.5 per cent to 19.3 per cent, 13.8 per cent to 16.6 per cent and 18.1 per cent to 20.1 per cent, respectively. Despite those gains, in 2015, over 23,000 species of plants, fungi and animals were known to face a high probability of extinction. Since 1999, at least 7,000 species of animals and plants have been detected in illegal trade affecting 120 countries. The *2016*

SDG Report indicated that human activities are causing species extinctions at rates three orders of magnitude higher than those normal throughout the Earth's history.

Between 1990 and 2015, the world's forest area diminished from 31.7 per cent of the world's total land mass to 30.7 per cent. The loss was mainly attributable to the conversion of forest to other land uses, such as agriculture and infrastructure development. Meanwhile, other areas were transformed into forests through planting, landscape restoration or the natural expansion of forest. As a result of these ongoing processes and efforts to slow deforestation, the global net loss of forest area declined from 7.3 million hectares per year in the 1990s to 3.3 million hectares per year during the period from 2010 to 2015. SDG 15 aims to ensure that livelihoods are preserved for those that depend directly on forests and other ecosystems, that biodiversity will thrive, and that the benefits of these natural resources will be enjoyed for generations to come.

Biodiversity and pollution

Biodiversity—the world's resplendent variety of plant and animal species—is essential to maintain resilient ecosystems and services vital to the well-being of humans. These biological resources are put under tremendous pressure by climate change and human activity. The 1992 *United Nations Convention on Biological Diversity* (www.cbd.int), to which 195 states and the European Union are party, is the main international instrument focusing on the protection and conservation of biodiversity worldwide. The *Convention*, which is administered by the UNEP, obligates states to conserve biological diversity, promote the sustainable use of its components, share the benefits arising from the use of genetic resources with equity, and submit national reports which demonstrate their contribution to the implementation of the *Convention*. Its *Cartagena Protocol on Biosafety* (2000), which entered into force in 2003 and has 170 parties, aims to ensure the safe transport, labelling and handling of genetically modified organisms. Its *Nagoya Protocol on Access and Benefit Sharing*, which aims to guarantee the equitable sharing of benefits, entered into force in 2014 and has 79 parties. The Strategic Plan for Biodiversity 2011–2020 includes 20 time-bound targets, known as the "Aichi targets", to organize and prioritize national and international efforts to fight biodiversity loss.

UNESCO's **Man and the Biosphere Programme** (www.unesco.org/new/en/natural-sciences/environment/ecological-sciences/man-and-biosphere-programme) concerns itself with the sustainable use and conservation of biological diversity, as well as the improvement of the relationship between people and their environment. The Programme combines natural and social sciences, economics and education to improve livelihoods and safeguard natural ecosystems, and to promote innovative approaches to economic development that are socially and culturally appropriate, as well as environmentally sustainable.

Other biodiversity-related conventions include:

- The 2004 *International Treaty on Plant Genetic Resources for Food and Agriculture* (www.fao.org/plant-treaty) aims to ensure the conservation and sustainable use of plant genetic resources for food and agriculture and the fair and equitable sharing of the benefits arising out of their use. The *Treaty* covers all plant genetic resources for food and agriculture, while its Multilateral System of Access and Benefit-sharing covers a specific list of 64 crops and forages. It also includes provisions on farmers' rights.
- The 1979 *Convention on Long-range Transboundary Air Pollution* and its protocols, negotiated under the auspices of the UN Economic Commission for Europe, provide for the control and reduction of air pollution in Europe and North America. Acid rain, caused by emissions of sulphur dioxide from industrial manufacturing processes, has been significantly reduced. The *Convention* has 51 parties.

- The 1979 *Bonn Convention on the Conservation of Migratory Species of Wild Animals* (www.cms.int), administered by UNEP, and a series of associated regional and species specific agreements, aim to conserve terrestrial, marine and avian migratory species and their habitats, especially those threatened with extinction. The *Convention* has 124 parties.
- The 1973 *Convention on International Trade in Endangered Species of Wild Fauna and Flora* (www.cites.org), administered by UNEP, controls international trade in specimens of wild animals and plant species or products through quotas or outright bans to ensure their survival. The *Convention* accords varying degrees of protection to more than 30,000 plant and animal species.
- The 1972 *World Heritage Convention* (whc.unesco.org/en/convention), administered by UNESCO, identifies and conserves the world's cultural and natural heritage by listing sites whose outstanding values should be preserved for all humanity and to ensure their protection through a closer cooperation among nations.
- The 1971 *Ramsar Convention on Wetlands* (www.ramsar.org) provides the framework for national action and international cooperation for the conservation and wise use of wetlands and their resources. The *Convention* covers all aspects of wetland conservation and wise use and recognizes wetlands as ecosystems that are extremely important for biodiversity conservation in general and for the well-being of human communities.
- The 1952 *International Plant Protection Convention* (www.ippc.int) aims to protect world plant resources, including cultivated and wild plants, by preventing the introduction and spread of plant pests and promoting appropriate measures for their control. The *Convention* provides the mechanisms to develop the International Standards for Phytosanitary Measures (ISPMs), and to help countries to implement the ISPMs and the other obligations under the *Convention*. FAO hosts the secretariat of the *Convention*.

The **Intergovernmental Science-Policy Platform on Biodiversity and Ecosystem Services (IPBES)** (www.ipbes.net) is the intergovernmental body that assesses the state of biodiversity and of the ecosystem services it provides to society, in response to requests from decision makers. The Platform operates under the auspices of four UN entities: UNEP, UNESCO, FAO and UNDP and is administered by UNEP. Its secretariat is located on the UN campus, in Bonn, Germany. One thousand scientists from all over the world currently contribute to the work of IPBES on a voluntary basis. Peer review forms a key component of IPBES work to ensure that a range of views is reflected and that the work is complete to the highest scientific standards.

Sustainable forest management

With international trade in forest products generating hundreds of billions of dollars annually, more than 1.6 billion people around the world rely on forests for their livelihoods. As the foundation of indigenous knowledge, forests provide profound sociocultural benefits. As ecosystems, they play a critical role in mitigating the effects of climate change and protecting biodiversity. While the rate of net forest loss is slowing down, thanks to new planting and natural expansion of existing forests, every year some 13 million hectares of the world's forests are lost to deforestation, which accounts for up to 20 per cent of global greenhouse gas emissions. The world's forests and forest soils store more than 1 trillion tons of carbon—twice the amount found in the atmosphere.

The most common causes of deforestation are unsustainable timber harvesting, the conversion of forests to agricultural land, unsound land management practices, and the creation of human settlements. The UN has been at the forefront of the movement towards sustainable forest management since the 1992 Earth Summit, which adopted a non-binding statement of forest principles.

From 1995 to 2000, the Intergovernmental Panel on Forests and the Intergovernmental Forum on Forests were the main intergovernmental forums for the development of forest policy. In 2000, the Economic and Social Council established the **United Nations Forum on Forests** (www.un.org/esa/forests), a high-level intergovernmental body with universal membership charged with strengthening long-term political commitment for sustainable forest management. The secretariat of the Forum provides technical services for capacity development in sustainable forest management, as well as other analytical and information services.

In 2007, the Forum adopted a landmark agreement on international forest policy and cooperation: the *Non-Legally Binding Instrument on All Types of Forests*, adopted by the General Assembly the same year. The instrument includes four global objectives on forests which aim to reduce the loss of forest cover: prevent forest degradation, promote sustainable livelihoods for all forest-dependent peoples, increase sustainably managed forests and mobilize additional financing for forests. In 2015, the Assembly in its resolution 70/199 renamed the instrument the "United Nations forest instrument", and extended the timeline of the global objectives on forests to 2030, in line with the timeline of the 2030 Agenda.

In January 2017, the special session of the Forum adopted the **UN Strategic Plan on Forests (2017–2030)** and the quadrennial programme of work for the period 2017–2020.

Desertification

Desertification means land degradation in arid, semi-arid and dry, sub-humid areas— "drylands" in general—resulting from various factors, including climatic variations and human activities. In the context of sustainable development, the term excludes hyper-arid areas (deserts). Drylands, which cover about 41 per cent of the Earth's land area, are characterized by low rainfall and high rates of evaporation. They are home to more than 2 billion people, including half of all those living in poverty worldwide, with 1.8 billion living in developing countries.

Land degradation in drylands is the reduction or loss of biological or economic productivity in such areas. Its main human causes are overcultivation, overgrazing, deforestation and poor irrigation. UNEP has estimated that land degradation affects one third of the Earth's surface and more than 1 billion people in more than 110 countries. Sub-Saharan Africa, where two thirds of the land is either desert or dryland, is particularly at risk.

Drought is a naturally occurring phenomenon that occurs when precipitation has been significantly below normal, causing serious desertification. It is a complex and slowly encroaching natural hazard with significant and pervasive socioeconomic and environmental impacts. The consequences of desertification and drought include food insecurity, famine and poverty. Ensuing social, economic and political tensions can create conflicts, cause more impoverishment and further increase land degradation. Growing desertification threatens to increase by millions the number of poor people forced to seek new homes and livelihoods.

The *United Nations Convention to Combat Desertification in those Countries Experiencing Serious Drought and/or Desertification, Particularly in Africa* (www.unccd.int) seeks to address this problem. It focuses on rehabilitation of land, improving productivity, and the conservation and management of land and water resources. It also supports countries in the development of national drought policies based on the principles of risk reduction. Two billion hectares of degraded land worldwide have the potential for land rehabilita-

A severe drought threatens famine in Somalia where the UN estimates 5.5 million people are at risk. In March 2017, IOM launched a $24.6 million drought appeal. Young girls line up at a feeding centre in Mogadishu (9 March 2017, UN Photo/Tobin Jones).

tion and forest restoration. The *Convention* emphasizes the establishment of an enabling environment for local people to help reverse land degradation on terrestrial ecosystems with a focus on land degradation neutrality. It also sets out criteria for the preparation by affected countries of national action programmes and gives an unprecedented role to NGOs in preparing and carrying out such programmes. The *Convention*, which was adopted by the General Assembly in 1994 and entered into force in 1996, has 195 parties (194 countries and the European Union).

Many UN entities, including IFAD, FAO, UNEP and the World Bank, assist in the efforts to combat desertification. UNDP funds anti-desertification activities through its Nairobi-based Global Policy Centre on Resilient Ecosystems and Desertification.

Peace, justice and strong institutions

Promote peaceful and inclusive societies for sustainable development, provide access to justice for all and build effective, accountable and inclusive institutions at all levels. Peace, justice and effective, accountable and inclusive institutions are at the core of sustainable development. Many countries still face protracted armed conflict and violence, and far too many people struggle as a result of weak institutions and the lack of access to justice, information and other fundamental freedoms. The number of victims of intentional homicide worldwide remained relatively stable from 2008 to 2014. Yet during that period, the homicide rate in developing countries was twice that in developed countries, and increased in the least developed countries. In 2011, 34 per cent of the victims of human trafficking at the global level were children, up from 13 per cent in 2004.

Progress with respect to the rule of law and access to justice is mixed. Globally, the proportion of people held in detention without sentencing decreased slightly, from 32 per cent of total detainees in 2003–2005 to 30 per cent in 2012–2014. The proportion of countries with national human rights institutions has doubled over the past 15 years, reaching 35.5 per cent by the end of 2015. SDG 16 seeks to ensure that all people are supported by strong, effective institutions and have access to justice, information and other fundamental freedoms.

The United Nations has defined a broad range of internationally accepted rights and established mechanisms to promote and protect these rights, including those on the rights of vulnerable persons, such as women, children, persons with disabilities, migrants and indigenous peoples. Special rapporteurs have also been appointed to address specific issues such as violence against women and girls and trafficking in persons.

Partnerships for the goals

 Strengthen the means of implementation and revitalize the Global Partnership for Sustainable Development. Target areas for strengthening partnerships to implement the 2030 Agenda, include finance, trade, technology and capacity-building. Official development assistance totalled $131.6 billion in 2015, which was 6.9 per cent higher in real terms than in 2014 and represents the highest level ever reached. The debt service to export ratio fell significantly over the period 2000–2012, dropping from 11.7 in 2000 to under 2.7 in 2012. In 2015, fixed-broadband Internet penetration reached 29 per cent in developed regions, but only 7.1 per cent in developing regions and 0.5 per cent in LDCs. Ninety per cent of all countries and 88 per cent of developing countries conducted a population and housing census over the period 2006–2015, a key source of essential data. SDG 17 aims to revitalize partnerships that mobilize all available resources from Governments, civil society, the private sector, the UN system and other actors.

As the UN specialized agency for information and communication technologies (ICTs), the **International Telecommunication Union (ITU)** (www.itu.int) has the leading role in facilitating the part ICTs will play in meeting the SDGs by 2030. To that end, much of the work at ITU is done in study groups comprised of experts in their fields. Many of these experts represent competing commercial interests, yet within the walls of ITU, they collaborate to develop systems, share best practices, and formulate principles and guidelines that will serve the interests of the industry and consumers as a whole. The main output of a study group is the establishment of technical standards or guidelines known as "Recommendations", which are made freely available for industry and governments to implement and operationalize. By providing a neutral platform, ITU offers a vital and efficient facility to an ecosystem that is a primary driver for socioeconomic development and empowerment.

Financing sustainable development

At the 1992 Earth Summit, it was agreed that most financing for *Agenda 21* would come from each country's public and private sectors. Additional external funds, however, were deemed necessary to support developing countries' efforts to implement sustainable development practices and protect the global environment. The holistic approach to financing sustainable development is rooted in the financing for development process, embodied in the 2002 *Monterrey Consensus*, the 2008 *Doha Declaration* on financing for development, and the 2015 Addis Ababa Action Agenda on financing for development.

The third International Conference on Financing for Development (Addis Ababa, 13–16 July 2015) resulted in the adoption of the Addis Ababa Action Agenda, which provides a strong foundation to support implementation of the 2030 Agenda. It includes a new global framework for financing sustainable development by aligning all financing flows and policies with economic, social and environmental priorities. Member states and other stakeholders also agreed on a set of policy actions, with more than 100 concrete measures that draw upon all sources of finance, technology, innovation, trade, debt and data in order to support achievement of the SDGs. All of the means of implementation of the 2030 Agenda are included in the Addis Ababa Action Agenda.

On 27 July, the General Assembly decided to establish an annual ECOSOC forum on financing for development, with universal, intergovernmental participation, as a follow-up process to the Addis Ababa Action Agenda. The forum consists of up to five days, including the special high-level meeting with the Bretton Woods institutions, WTO and UNCTAD.

The **Global Environment Facility (GEF)** (www.thegef.org/gef), established in 1991, helps developing countries fund projects that protect the global environment and promote sustainable livelihoods in local communities. By its twenty-fifth anniversary in 2016, GEF had provided some $14.5 billion in grants and generated $75.4 billion in co-financing from recipient governments, international development agencies, private industry and NGOs to support nearly 4,000 projects in 165 developing countries and economies in transition. Its original three partners—the World Bank, UNDP and UNEP—have grown into a network of 18 implementing and executing agencies, including FAO, IFAD and UNIDO.

Official development assistance

Official development assistance (ODA) totalled $131.6 billion in 2015. This represents 0.3 per cent of gross national income of the 28 member countries of the Development Assistance Committee (DAC) of the Organization for Economic Co-operation and Development (OECD), which is less than half of the 0.7 per cent target set by the General Assembly. The UN development system is currently the largest channel for direct multilateral funding from OECD/DAC countries.

In terms of directing aid to the poorest and most vulnerable people, ODA and funding for UN operational activities for development can have significant impact, as these flows are generally more targeted towards development objectives such as the MDGs and SDGs. This is especially true for the least developed countries (LDCs)—48 nations whose extreme poverty and indebtedness have marginalized them from global growth and development. These nations, 34 of which are in Africa, are given priority attention by the UN development system. Roughly 50 per cent of annual country-level expenditures on UN operational activities for development are spent in LDCs. Small island developing states (SIDS), landlocked developing countries (LLDCs) and countries with economies in transition also suffer from critical problems and are given priority attention in assistance programmes and ODA.

UN operational activities are those that entities of the UN development system carry out with the primary objective of promoting the advancement and welfare of developing countries. In 2014, donors contributed a total of $28.4 billion for UN operational activities, which was the highest volume ever and represented over 20 per cent of total ODA that year.

United Nations ODA is derived from grant assistance from UN system agencies, funds and programmes; and support from lending institutions, such as IFAD and the World Bank. The World Bank Group committed $64.2 billion in loans, grants, equity investments and guarantees to help promote economic growth and overcome poverty in developing countries in fiscal year 2016. Since starting operations in 1978, IFAD has invested $14.8 billion in over 900 projects and programmes, reaching some 400 million rural people. Governments and other financing sources in recipient countries contributed $12.2 billion, and multilateral, bilateral and other donors provided approximately $9.6 billion in co-financing.

South-South cooperation

South-South cooperation, a distinctive element of international cooperation, is recognized as a complement to North-South cooperation. The Addis Ababa Action Agenda welcomed the increased contributions of South-South cooperation to poverty eradication and sustainable development. In line with the provisions contained in the 2009 Nairobi outcome document of the High-level UN Conference on South-South cooperation, developing countries were encouraged to step up their efforts to strengthen South-South cooperation. The sharing of development strategies, priorities, resources and solutions among developing countries that are facing largely common challenges is a key catalyst in capacity building and in the realization of sustainable development.

Partial data suggest that in 2014, South-South cooperation surpassed the $20 billion reached in 2013. There has been growing diversification of financing sources for South-South cooperation beyond government revenues. National development banks, including in Africa, have taken a more prominent role in financing regional and subregional infrastructure. It is estimated that the New Development Bank has the ability to reach an annual lending capacity of $3.4 billion by 2024 and almost $9 billion by 2034. The Asian Infrastructure Investment Bank, which became operational in January 2016, is projected to provide $10 billion to $15 billion in loans annually over the next 15 years. Participants at the second High-level meeting of the Global Partnership for Effective Development Co-operation (28 November–1 December 2016) held in Nairobi, Kenya reaffirmed their commitment to effective development co-operation as a means to achieve the SDGs.

Trade and development

The **United Nations Conference on Trade and Development (UNCTAD)** (www.unctad.org) is tasked with ensuring the integration of all countries in global trade. As the UN focal point for dealing with development-related issues in the areas of trade, finance, technology, investment and sustainable development, UNCTAD works to maximize the trade, investment and development opportunities of developing countries. It helps them face the challenges arising from globalization and integrate into the world economy on an equitable basis. While globalization has helped lift millions out of poverty, tremendous challenges remain. UNCTAD provides research and policy analysis, consensus-building, and technical assistance, which helps developing countries to use trade, investment, finance, and technology as vehicles for inclusive and sustainable development. Working at the national, regional, and global level, UNCTAD efforts help countries to:

- diversify economies to make them less dependent on commodities;
- limit their exposure to financial volatility and debt;
- attract investment and make it more development friendly;
- increase access to digital technologies;
- promote entrepreneurship and innovation;
- help local firms move up value chains;
- speed up the flow of goods across borders;
- protect consumers from abuse;
- curb regulations that stifle competition; and
- adapt to climate change and use natural resources more effectively.

UNCTAD assists developing countries and economies in transition to promote foreign direct investment (FDI) and improve their investment climate. It also helps governments understand the policy implications of FDI and formulate and implement policies accordingly. Global trends in FDI are presented in UNCTAD's annual *World Investment Report, Investment Policy Reviews, World Investment Directory* and other studies.

UNCTAD promotes enterprise development, particularly for small and medium-sized enterprises, through regular intergovernmental discussions and technical cooperation. Its technical cooperation activities include:

- the Automated System for Customs Data (www.asycuda.org), which uses state-of-the-art technology; helps governments modernize customs procedures and management; and is also an instrument for improving economic governance; and
- the EMPRETEC Programme (empretec.unctad.org), which promotes small and medium-sized enterprise development.

UNCTAD measures progress by the SDGs, as set out in the 2030 Agenda. It also supports implementation of the Addis Ababa Action Agenda on financing for development together with four other institutional stakeholders: IMF, the World Bank, WTO and UNDP. Although UNCTAD works mainly with governments in efforts to achieve the SDGs, it also recognizes that partnerships and closer cooperation with the private sector and civil society are essential.

The **International Trade Centre (ITC)** (www.intracen.org) is the joint agency of WTO and the United Nations. ITC is the only development agency that is fully dedicated to supporting the internationalization of small and medium-sized enterprises (SMEs), as engines of inclusive growth, job creation, and innovation.

ITC's mission is to foster inclusive and sustainable economic development in developing countries and transition economies and contribute to achieving the SDGs. It works with policymakers, the private sector and trade and investment support institutions to make businesses more competitive in regional and global markets and to better connect them to the global trading system. The Centre's objectives are to strengthen the integration of SMEs into the global economy; improve trade and investment support for the benefit of SMEs; and improve the international competitiveness of SMEs.

ITC work is structured under six focus areas: providing trade and market intelligence; building a conducive business environment; strengthening trade and investment support institutions; connecting to international value chains; promoting and mainstreaming inclusive and green trade; and supporting regional economic integration and South-South links.

ITC prioritizes support to LDCs, LLDCs, SIDS, sub-Saharan Africa, post-conflict countries and small, vulnerable economies. Economic empowerment of women, young entrepreneurs and support of poor communities as well as fostering sustainable and green trade are priorities.

The **World Trade Organization (WTO)** (www.wto.org) is the international organization whose primary purpose is to open trade for the benefit of all. WTO provides a forum for negotiating agreements aimed at reducing obstacles to international trade and ensuring a level playing field for all, thus contributing to economic growth and development. WTO also provides a legal and institutional framework for the implementation and monitoring of these agreements, as well as for settling disputes arising from their interpretation and application. The current body of trade agreements comprising WTO consists of 16 different multilateral agreements (to which all 164 WTO members are parties) and two different plurilateral agreements (to which only some WTO members are parties). Since its establishment in 1995, WTO and its predecessor organization GATT have helped to create a strong and prosperous international trading system, thereby contributing to unprecedented global economic growth.

Global statistics

Governments, public institutions and the private sector rely heavily on relevant, accurate, comparable and timely statistics at national and global levels, and the United Nations has served as a focal point for statistics since its founding. The UN **Statistical Commission**, an intergovernmental body composed of 24 member states, is the highest decision-making body for international statistical activities. It oversees the work of the **Statistics Division** of DESA (unstats.un.org/unsd), which compiles and disseminates global statistical information, develops standards and norms for statistical activities, and supports countries' efforts to strengthen their national statistical systems.

The Division also facilitates the coordination of international statistical activities, supports the functioning of the Commission and offers a broad range of services for producers and users of statistics, including the following: the UN-data portal (data.un.org), the *Statistical Yearbook*, the *Monthly Bulletin of Statistics*, the *World Statistics Pocketbook*, the *Global Sustainable Development Goals Indicators* database, the *Demographic Yearbook* and *UN Comtrade*. Its specialized publications cover such matters as demographic, social and housing statistics, national accounts, economic and social classifications, energy, international trade, the environment and geospatial information.

The Division aims to strengthen national capabilities in developing countries by providing technical advisory services, training programmes and workshops organized throughout the world on various topics.

Geospatial data and geographical names

Governments, the private sector and citizens increasingly recognize that place and location is a vital component of effective decision-making and authoritative geospatial information is critical. In 2011, the Economic and Social Council established the **UN Committee on Global Geospatial Information Management (UN-GGIM)** (ggim.un.org) as the peak inter-governmental mechanism for all member states. In 2016, the Council strengthened the UN-GGIM mandate, acknowledging in particular its role in implementing the 2030 Agenda, and stressed the continued need to strengthen the coordination and coherence of global geospatial information management. UN-GGIM promotes international cooperation, knowledge sharing, capacity development and norm-setting, further strengthening global geospatial information management capacities.

The **Group of Experts on Geographical Names (UNGEGN)** promotes the recording, standardization and use of locally-used place names reflecting local languages and traditions. Member states confer and disseminate information on standardization activities at the **UN Conference on the Standardization of Geographical Names**. The eleventh conference will be held in August 2017.

Public administration

Effective, accountable and inclusive public institutions are critical for realizing the 2030 Agenda. Achieving the SDGs requires far-sighted, holistic and participatory decision-making by governments. An unprecedented level of policy integration and institutional coordination and expertise is required so that progress is made on all the SDGs at the same time, building on the interrelations and synergies between them. Managing the public sector to address these complex issues is a demanding challenge for national decision makers, policy developers and public administrators.

The United Nations, through its **Programme in Public Administration**, which is implemented by DESA (publicadministration.un.org), assists governments in addressing those challenges and promotes public administration and institutions at all levels to achieve the SDGs. Its work focuses on mobilizing public institutions for implementing the 2030 Agenda; supporting public integrity and transparency; facilitating participation and inclusiveness, participatory decision making; mobilizing innovation and ICTs for SDGs; and galvanizing partnerships for delivering public services. DESA supports countries by conducting analysis, supporting an exchange of experiences among governments, providing advisory services and capacity-building, including close partnerships with other organizations; and knowledge-sharing platforms such as the UN Public Administration Network (UNPAN) (www.upan.org).

United Nations Office for Partnerships (UNOP)

The United Nations Office for Partnerships (UNOP) (www.un.org/partnerships) functions as a gateway for partnership building between the private sector, foundations and other non-state actors and the UN system in furtherance of the SDGs. It serves as the operational interface between the UN Foundation (unfoundation.org) and the UN system in support of high-impact projects implemented by UN system agencies worldwide; as well as the administrative hub for the UN Democracy Fund (www.un.org/democracy-fund.org). UNOP also guides and facilitates partnership events and initiatives between the United Nations and non-state actors in support of the SDGs. As at 31 December 2015, the cumulative allocations approved by the UN Foundation for UNFIP projects for implementation by UN partners reached approximately $1.4 billion. Since its inception, 592 projects have been implemented or are under implementation by 43 UN entities in 124 countries. During 2016, the Foundation disbursed $37.1 million in funding, focusing on polio eradication, malaria, HIV/AIDS and measles prevention, humanitarian relief, disease surveillance, reproductive health care, girls empowerment, sustainable energy development and protection of the environment, and other issues.

Action for the environment

The entire UN system is engaged in environmental protection in diverse ways. Its lead agency in this area is the **United Nations Environment Programme (UNEP)** (web.unep.org). UNEP assesses the state of the world's environment and identifies issues requiring international cooperation. It helps formulate international environmental law and integrate environmental considerations into the social and economic policies and programmes of the UN system, including the SDGs. It helps solve problems that cannot be handled by countries acting alone and provides a forum for building consensus and forging international agreements. In doing so, it strives to enhance the participation of business and industry, the scientific and academic communities, NGOs, community groups and others in achieving sustainable development. UNEP's seven priority areas are: climate change; ecosystem management; environmental governance; chemicals, waste and air quality; disasters and conflicts; resource efficiency; and environment under review.

Scientific research promoted and coordinated by UNEP has generated a variety of reports on the state of the environment—such as the *Global Environment Outlook*, and the annual *Emissions Gap Report* and *Marine Litter: A Global Challenge*—which have created worldwide awareness of ongoing and emerging environmental problems and have even triggered international negotiations on environmental conventions. UNEP has a growing network of centres of excellence, including the UNEP World Conservation Monitoring Centre, the Global Resource Information Database and the International Resource Panel.

UNEP's **Economy Division** encourages decision makers in government, industry and business to adopt policies, strategies and practices that are cleaner and safer, use natural resources more efficiently, and reduce pollution risks to people and the environment. The Division facilitates the transfer of safer, cleaner and environmentally sound technologies; helps countries build capacities for the management of chemicals and the improvement of chemical safety; supports the phase-out of ozone-depleting substances; assists decision makers to make better, more informed energy choices; and works with governments and the private sector to integrate environmental considerations into activities, practices, products and services.

The global report of the UNEP Inquiry into the Design of a Sustainable Financial System (web.unep.org/inquiry), *The Financial System We Need*, describes a "quiet revolution" as sustainability factors are incorporated into the rules that govern the financial system.

UNEP Chemicals (www.unep.org/chemicalsandwaste)—the Division's chemicals branch—provides countries with access to information about toxic chemicals; assists countries in building their capacities to produce, use and dispose of chemicals safely; and supports international and regional actions for reducing or eliminating chemical risks. In 2001, UNEP facilitated the completion of the Stockholm *Convention on Persistent Organic Pollutants*, a treaty to reduce and eliminate releases of certain chemicals that remain intact in the environment for long periods, become widely distributed geographically, collect in the fatty tissue of living organisms and are toxic to humans and wildlife. These include pesticides, industrial chemicals and by-products.

Over the years, UNEP has been the catalyst for the negotiation of other international agreements that form the cornerstone of UN efforts to halt and reverse damage to the planet. The historic 1987 *Montreal Protocol* and its subsequent amendments seek to preserve the ozone layer in the upper atmosphere. In 2016, the *Kigali Amendment* to the *Montreal Protocol* saw nearly 200 countries agree to phase down the use of hydrofluorocarbons (HFCs), which could prevent up to 0.5 degrees Celsius of global warming by the end of this century. The 1989 *Basel Convention on the Control of Hazardous Wastes and their Disposal* has reduced the danger of pollution from toxic waste. In collaboration with FAO, UNEP facilitated the negotiation of the 1998 *Rotterdam Convention on the Prior Informed Consent Procedure for Certain Hazardous Chemicals and Pesticides in International Trade*, which gives importing countries the power to decide which chemicals they want to receive and to exclude those they cannot manage safely.

In January 2013, over 140 nations agreed on the text of a legally binding treaty to prevent emissions and releases of mercury, the *Minamata Convention on Mercury*.

In regard to wildlife and biological diversity, the 1973 *Convention on International Trade in Endangered Species, or CITES,* is universally recognized for its contribution to controlling trade in wildlife products. UNEP assisted African governments in developing the 1994 *Lusaka Agreement on Cooperative Enforcement Operations Directed at Illegal Trade in Wild Fauna and Flora*. The 1992 *Convention on Biological Diversity* and the 2000 *Cartagena Protocol on Biosafety* seek to conserve and encourage the sustainable and equitable use of the planet's wide variety of plants, animals and micro-organisms. UNEP has also helped negotiate and implement conventions on desertification and climate change.

ECONOMIC DEVELOPMENT

One of the founding principles of the United Nations is the conviction that economic development for all peoples is the surest way to achieve political, economic and social security. It is a central concern of the Organization that 13 per cent of the world's population—mostly in Africa and Asia—lived below the extreme poverty line, defined at $1.90 or below per person per day. It was estimated that more than 197 million workers were unemployed worldwide in 2011, and more than 868 million earned less than $2 a day in 2012. The number of undernourished people in the world was estimated at approximately 800 million in 2014–2016.

The UN continues to be the sole institution dedicated to ensuring that economic expansion and globalization are guided by policies promoting human welfare, sustainable development, the eradication of poverty, fair trade and the reduction of immobilizing foreign debt. It urges the adoption of macroeconomic policies that address current imbalances—particularly the growing gap between the North and South—as well as the persistent problems of the least developed countries (LDCs) and the unprecedented needs of countries in transition from centralized to market economies. UN programmes of assistance promote poverty reduction, child survival, environmental protection, women's progress and human rights. For millions of people in poor countries, these programmes *are* the United Nations.

Promoting development worldwide

The **United Nations Development Programme (UNDP)** (www.undp.org) is committed to contributing to the eradication of poverty and the reduction of inequalities and exclusion. UNDP provides sound policy advice and helps build institutional capacity that generates equitable economic growth. UNDP works on the ground in 170 countries to help people help themselves. It focuses on assisting countries in building and sharing solutions to challenges such as poverty reduction; democratic governance; crisis prevention and recovery; environment and sustainable development; and the achievement of the SDGs. In each of these areas, UNDP advocates for the protection of human rights and the empowerment of women.

Most of UNDP's core programme funds go to those countries that are home to the world's extreme poor. During 2014–2015, about 90 per cent of core funds went to low-income countries and 70 per cent went to LDCs. Between 1990 and 2015, the number of people living in extreme poverty was cut by more than half. Progress, however, was uneven across regions. Approximately one in five persons in developing regions lives on less than $1.25 per day, the overwhelming majority of them in Southern Asia and sub-Saharan Africa. A total of 836 million people still live in extreme poverty.

Contributions to UNDP are voluntary and come from a large majority of UN member states. In 2015, UNDP received total contributions of $4.5 billion, composed of $703 million in regular resources and $3.8 billion in other resources. Countries that receive UNDP-administered assistance contribute to project costs through personnel, facilities, equipment and supplies.

To ensure maximum impact from global development resources, UNDP coordinates its activities with other UN funds and programmes and international financial institutions, including the World Bank and the International Monetary Fund (IMF). In addition, UNDP's country and regional programmes draw on the expertise of developing country nationals and NGOs. The vast majority of all UNDP-supported projects are implemented by local organizations.

At the country level, UNDP promotes an integrated approach to the provision of UN development assistance. In several developing countries, it has established a **United Nations Development Assistance Framework** made up of UN teams under the leadership of the local UN resident coordinator, who is in many instances the resident representative of UNDP. The frameworks articulate a coordinated response to the main development challenges identified for the United Nations by governments. Resident coordinators serve as coordinators of humanitarian assistance in cases of human disasters, natural disasters and complex emergency situations.

In addition to its regular programmes, UNDP administers various special-purpose funds. The **UN Capital Development Fund (UNCDF)** (www.uncdf.org) offers a combination of investment capital, capacity-building and technical advisory services to promote microfinance and local development in the least developed countries.

The **United Nations Volunteers (UNV)** programme (www.unv.org) is the UN organization that mobilizes volunteers to make an impact in UN peace and development programmes, and promotes the value and global recognition of volunteerism. Nearly 6,800 UNVs from 153 countries were deployed worldwide in 2015.

Lending for development

The **World Bank Group** (www.worldbank.org) comprises two unique institutions—the International Bank for Reconstruction and Development and the International Development Association—and works in more than 100 developing countries, bringing finance and/or technical expertise to help them reduce poverty. Its portfolio of projects covers Latin America and the Caribbean, the Middle East and North Africa, Europe and Central Asia, East Asia and the Pacific, Africa, and South Asia.

The Bank is currently involved in more than 1,678 projects in virtually every sector and developing country. One of the world's largest sources of development assistance, the Bank supports the efforts of developing country governments to build schools and health centres, provide water and electricity, fight disease and protect the environment. It does this through the provision of loans, which are repaid. In fiscal year 2016, the World Bank Group provided $64.2 billion in loans, grants, equity investments, and guarantees to partner countries and private businesses.

There are two types of World Bank lending. The first type is for higher-income developing countries that are able to pay near-market interest rates or can borrow from commercial sources. These countries receive loans from the **International Bank for Reconstruction and Development (IBRD)** (www.worldbank.org/en/who-we-are/ibrd), which aims to reduce poverty in middle-income and creditworthy poorer countries by promoting sustainable development through loans, guarantees, risk management products, and analytical and advisory services. IBRD loans allow countries more time to repay than if they borrowed from a commercial bank: 15 to 20 years with a three-to-five-year grace period before the repayment of principal begins. Funds are borrowed for specific programmes in support of poverty reduction, delivery of social services, environmental protection and economic growth. In fiscal year 2016, new IBRD loan commitments amounted to $29.7 billion, covering 114 operations. IBRD, with its AAA credit rating, raises nearly all its money through the sale of its bonds in the world's financial markets.

The second type of loan goes to the poorest countries, which are usually not creditworthy in the international financial markets and are unable to pay near-market interest rates on the money they borrow. The **International Development Association (IDA)** (ida.worldbank.org) makes loans to the world's poorest countries and aims to reduce poverty by providing grant financing and credits for programmes that boost economic growth, reduce inequalities and improve people's living conditions. IDA lends money on concessional terms, with credits of zero or very low interests charge and repayments stretched over 25 to 40 years, including a 5- to 10-year grace period. It also provides grants to countries at risk of debt distress, as well as significant levels of debt relief. IDA assistance is largely funded by contributions from its richer member countries. In 2016, new IDA commitments amounted to $16.2 billion for 161 operations, including $14.4 billion in credits, $1.3 billion in grants and $500 million in guarantees. Under its regulations, the Bank can lend only to governments, but it works closely with local communities, NGOs and private enterprise. Its projects are designed to assist the poorest sectors of the population. Successful development requires that governments and communities have ownership of their development projects. The Bank encourages governments to work closely with NGOs and civil society to strengthen participation by people benefiting from Bank-financed projects. NGOs based in borrowing countries collaborate in about half of these projects.

The Bank advocates stable economic policies, sound government finances, and open, honest and accountable governance. It supports many areas in which private-sector development is making rapid inroads—finance, power, telecommunications, information technology, oil and gas, and industry. The Bank's regulations prohibit it from lending directly to the private sector, but a Bank affiliate—the **International Finance Corporation (IFC)** (www.ifc.org)—exists expressly to promote private sector investment by supporting high-risk sectors and countries. Another affiliate, the **Multilateral Investment Guarantee Agency (MIGA)**, provides political risk insurance (guarantees) to those who invest in or lend to developing countries.

In addition to lending money, the World Bank routinely includes technical assistance in the projects it finances. This may include advice on such issues as the overall size of a country's budget and where the money should be allocated, or how to set up village health clinics, or what sort of equipment is needed to build a road. The Bank funds a few projects each year devoted exclusively to providing expert advice and training. It also trains people from borrowing countries on how to create and carry out development programmes.

IBRD supports sustainable development projects in such areas as reforestation, pollution control and land management; water, sanitation and agriculture; and conservation of natural resources. It is the main funder of the **Global Environment Facility (GEF)**, which is itself the largest funder of projects to improve the global environment. IBRD and IDA also support the **Heavily Indebted Poor Countries (HIPC) Initiative**, which aims to reduce the external debt of the world's poorest, most heavily indebted countries. At their July 2005 summit, the leaders of the 'Group of Eight' developed nations proposed 100 per cent cancellation of debt owed to IDA, IMF and the African Development Fund by some of the world's poorest countries, mostly in Africa and Latin America. The cost of debt relief under the resulting **Multilateral Debt Relief Initiative (MDRI)** amounted to an estimated $74.8 billion as at March 2016, while the costs to the four multilateral creditors providing relief under the MDRI was estimated at $41.6 billion in end-2014 present value terms. With 36 countries—most recently Chad in April 2015—having reached their HIPC completion point, the HIPC Initiative and MDRI were nearly complete.

Lending for stability

Many countries turn to the **International Monetary Fund (IMF)** (www.imf.org), a UN specialized agency, when internal or external factors seriously undermine their balance-of-payments position, fiscal stability or capacity to meet debt service commitments. IMF offers advice and policy recommendations to overcome these problems, and often makes financial resources available to member countries in support of economic reform programmes.

Members with balance-of-payments problems generally avail themselves of IMF's financial resources by purchasing reserve assets—in the form of other members' currencies and Special Drawing Rights (SDRs)—with an equivalent amount of their own currencies. IMF levies charges on these loans and requires that members repay the loans by repurchasing their own currencies from IMF over a specified time.

In 2010, IMF upgraded its support for low-income countries (LICs) to reflect the changing nature of economic conditions in those countries and their increased vulnerability due to the effects of the global economic crisis. As part of a broader reform to make the Fund's financial support more flexible and better tailored to the needs of LICs, IMF established the **Poverty Reduction and Growth Trust** with three concessional lending windows: extended, standby and rapid credit facilities, which became effective in January 2010. In April 2013, these instruments were refined to improve the flexibility of Fund support.

The main IMF financing facilities are:

- *Stand-By Arrangements*, designed to help countries address short-term balance of payments problems;
- *Flexible Credit Line*, designed for countries with very strong fundamentals, policies, and track records of policy implementation. Disbursements under the FCL are not conditional on implementation of specific policy understandings as is the case under the SBA because FCL-qualifying countries have a demonstrated track record of implementing appropriate macroeconomic policies;
- *Precautionary and Liquidity Line*, designed for countries with sound fundamentals and policies, and a track record of implementing such policies. PLL-qualifying countries may face moderate vulnerabilities and may not meet the FCL qualification standards, but they do not require the substantial policy adjustments normally associated with SBAs;
- *Extended Fund Facility*, designed to help countries address medium- and longer-term balance of payments problems reflecting extensive distortions that require fundamental economic reforms;
- *Extended Credit Facility*, designed for medium-term support to LICs facing protracted balance of payments problems. Financing under the ECF currently carries a zero interest rate, a grace period of 5½ years, and a final maturity of 10 years;
- *Standby Credit Facility*, provides financial assistance to LICs with short-term or potential balance of payments needs. The SCF can be used in a wide range of circumstances, including on a precautionary basis. Financing under the SCF currently carries a zero interest rate, with a grace period of 4 years, and a final maturity of 8 years;
- *Rapid Credit Facility*, provides rapid financial assistance with limited conditionality to LICs facing an urgent balance of payments need. The RCF streamlines the Fund's emergency assistance for LICs, and can be used flexibly in a wide range of circumstances. Financing under the RCF currently carries a zero interest rate, has a grace period of 5½ years, and a final maturity of 10 years;
- *Rapid Financing Instrument*, providing rapid financial assistance with limited conditionality to all members facing an urgent balance of payments need.

To provide debt relief to heavily indebted poor countries following sound policies, IMF and the World Bank jointly provide, under the Heavily Indebted Poor Countries (HIPC) Initiative, exceptional assistance to eligible countries to reduce their external debt burdens to sustainable levels. They have also joined in supporting the Multilateral Debt Relief Initiative developed to supplement the HIPC Initiative.

To maintain stability and prevent crises in the international monetary system, IMF reviews country policies and national, regional, and global economic and financial developments through a formal system known as surveillance. IMF advises its 189 member countries, encouraging policies that foster economic stability, reduce vulnerability to economic and financial crises, and raise living standards. It also provides regular assessments of global prospects in its *World Economic Outlook*, of financial markets in its *Global Financial Stability Report*, and of public finance developments in its *Fiscal Monitor*, and publishes a series of regional economic outlooks.

IMF provides technical assistance to its members in several broad areas: the design and implementation of fiscal and monetary policy; institution-building; and the collection and refinement of statistical data. Its regional approach to capacity development allows for better tailoring of assistance to the particular needs of a region, closer coordination with other assistance providers, and an enhanced ability to respond quickly to emerging needs. IMF also provides training to member country officials at its headquarters in Washington, D.C., and its regional centres worldwide.

Investment and development

As foreign direct investment (FDI) has continued to expand dramatically, developing countries have increasingly opened up their economies to such investment. At the same time, they also are investing more in other developing countries. Various parts of the UN system, such as FAO, UNDP and the United Nations Industrial Development Organization (UNIDO), monitor and assess developments and assist developing country governments in attracting investment.

Two affiliates of the World Bank—the International Finance Corporation and the Multilateral Investment Guarantee Agency—help promote investment in developing countries. Through its advisory work, the **International Finance Corporation (IFC)** (www.ifc.org) helps governments create conditions that stimulate the flow of both domestic and foreign private savings and investment. It also mobilizes private investment in the developing world by demonstrating that investments there can be profitable. In fiscal year 2016, IFC long-term investment commitments totalled about $18.8 billion, including $7.7 billion mobilized from investment partners. IFC investments in fragile and conflict-affected areas climbed to nearly $1 billion, an increase of more than 50 per cent over the previous year.

The **Multilateral Investment Guarantee Agency (MIGA)** is an investment insurance affiliate of the Bank. Its goal is to facilitate the flow of private investment for productive purposes to developing member countries, by offering investors long term political risk insurance—coverage against the risks of expropriation, currency transfer, war and civil disturbance—and by providing advisory services. MIGA carries out promotional programmes, disseminates information on investment opportunities, and provides technical assistance that enhances the investment promotion capabilities of countries. In fiscal year 2016, MIGA issued a record $4.3 billion in political risk and credit enhancement guarantees underpinning various investments, with 45 per cent of its active portfolio in IDA-eligible countries and 10 per cent in countries affected by conflict and fragility.

Labour

Concerned with both the economic and social aspects of development, the **International Labour Organization (ILO)** (www.ilo.org) is the only tripartite UN agency bringing together representatives of governments, employers and workers to shape policies and programmes promoting decent work for all. ILO is guided by the principle that social stability and integration can be sustained only if they are based on social justice—particularly the right to employment with fair compensation in a healthy workplace. Its four main goals are to promote rights at work, encourage decent employment opportunities, enhance social protection and strengthen dialogue on work-related issues. ILO is responsible for drawing up and overseeing international labour standards aimed at promoting opportunities for women and men to obtain decent and productive work, in conditions of freedom, equity, security and dignity. Its tripartite structure ensures that these standards are backed by governments, employers, and workers alike. International labour standards therefore lay down the basic minimum social standards agreed upon by all players in the global economy.

Over the decades, ILO has helped create such landmarks as the eight-hour work day, maternity protection, anti-child-labour laws, legislation protecting domestic workers and seafarers, and a wide range of policies that promote safety in the workplace and peaceful industrial relations. Specifically, ILO engages in:

- the formulation of international policies and programmes to promote basic human rights, improve working and living conditions and enhance employment opportunities;
- the creation of international labour standards to serve as guidelines for national authorities in putting sound labour policies into practice;
- an extensive programme of technical cooperation, formulated and carried out in partnership with beneficiaries, to help countries make these policies effective; and
- training, education, research and information activities to help advance all these efforts.

ILO's work covers a range of issues such as child labour; safety and health at work; employment security; promoting small and medium-sized enterprises; social protection; developing skills, knowledge and employability; youth employment; labour migration; eliminating discrimination and gender inequality; social dialogue, and promoting the *ILO Declaration on Fundamental Principles and Rights at Work* adopted by the International Labour Conference in 1998.

As ILO moves towards its 100th anniversary in 2019, it is implementing activities to equip the organization to take up the challenges of its social justice mandate in the future. These 'centenary initiatives' focus on: the future of work, poverty, women at work, international labour standards, enterprises, the green economy and ILO governance.

On development cooperation, ILO has 630 programmes and projects in more than 100 countries—with the support of 120 development partners. ILO has integrated many of its existing technical projects into five flagship programmes to enhance the efficiency and impact of its development cooperation with constituents on a global scale. These include: **Better Work**—labour standards in the global garment and footwear industry; **Social Protection**—extending social protection for all; **International Programme on the Elimination of Child Labour (IPEC+)**—working to eliminate forced- and child labour; **Occupational Safety and Health**—in small and medium-sized enterprises; and **Jobs for peace and resilience**—employment generation, especially for young people, in conflict and disaster prone countries.

The ILO Research Department, located in Geneva, promotes policy research and public discussion of emerging issues of concern to ILO. Its Global Research Agenda identifies policy approaches that help improve employment and social outcomes, support recovery from the global financial crisis and boost sustainable economic growth.

The ILO Department of Statistics provides users inside and outside ILO with relevant, timely and reliable labour statistics for the development and evaluation of policies designed to achieve the goal of decent work. Its work includes gathering and disseminating labour statistics; setting international standards for labour statistics; and providing technical cooperation, assistance and training in labour statistics.

The **ILO International Training Centre** (www.itcilo.org), located in Turin, Italy, carries out training for senior and mid-level managers in private and public enterprises, leaders of workers' and employers' organizations, government officials and policymakers. It runs more than 450 programmes and projects each year for some 11,000 people from over 180 countries.

International civil aviation

In 2015, an estimated 3.5 billion passengers flew via civil aviation services, 51 million tonnes of freight were shipped by air, and the number of aircraft departures reached a record 34 million. The **International Civil Aviation Organization (ICAO)** (www.icao. int) is a UN specialized agency that serves as the global forum for cooperation among its member states and with the world aviation community. ICAO's ongoing mission is to foster a global civil aviation system that consistently and uniformly operates at peak efficiency and provides optimum safety, security and sustainability. ICAO activities are guided by its strategic objectives: safety, security, capacity and efficiency, economic development, and environmental protection.

To meet those objectives, ICAO:

- adopts international standards and recommendations applied to the design and performance of aircraft and much of their equipment; the performance of airline pilots, flight crews, air traffic controllers and ground and maintenance crews; and the security requirements and procedures at international airports;
- formulates visual and instrument flight rules, as well as the aeronautical charts used for international navigation, and is responsible for aircraft telecommunications systems, radio frequencies and security procedures;
- works towards minimizing the impact of aviation on the environment through reductions in aircraft emissions and through noise limits;
- facilitates the movement of aircraft, passengers, crews, baggage, cargo and mail across borders by standardizing customs, immigration, public health and other formalities;
- highlights aviation's critical contributions to socioeconomic development and assists states with the development of policies and regulations that foster the development of international air connectivity; and
- prepares global strategic plans to support and foster the sustainable development of the civil aviation network.

ICAO pursues policies and programmes designed to prevent acts of unlawful interference, which pose a serious threat to the safety and security of international civil aviation. In response to the terrorist attacks of 11 September 2001 in the United States, ICAO developed an aviation security plan of action, including a universal audit programme to evaluate the implementation of security standards and recommend remedial action where necessary. ICAO's work in this area is linked to several Security Council resolutions.

During its thirty-ninth Assembly in 2016, ICAO produced new agreements and declarations on air transport's challenges and priorities. The meeting attracted a record 2,500 delegates, who adopted an historic resolution on reducing the impact of aviation emissions on climate change and endorsed enhancements to ICAO's Global Aviation Safety Plan and Global Air Navigation Plan, and the conception of an ICAO Global Aviation Security Plan. The fortieth Assembly session will take place in September and October 2019.

ICAO meets requests from developing countries for assistance in improving air transport systems and training for aviation personnel. It has helped to establish regional training centres in several developing countries. The criteria for ICAO assistance are based on what countries need to make civil aviation safe and efficient, in accordance with ICAO's Standards and Recommended Practices.

ICAO works in close cooperation with other UN specialized agencies such as IMO, ITU, UNWTO and WMO. The International Air Transport Association, the Airports Council International, the International Federation of Air Line Pilots' Associations and other organizations also participate in ICAO meetings.

International shipping

When the **International Maritime Organization (IMO)** (www.imo.org) held its first Assembly in 1959, it had less than 40 member states. Today it has 171 members (170 UN member states plus the Cook Islands) and three associate members. More than 99 per cent of the world's merchant fleets (by tonnage) adhere to the key international shipping conventions developed by IMO, covering safety, training of seafarers, prevention of pollution, load lines, tonnage measurement, collision prevention, search and rescue and facilitation of maritime traffic.

The adoption of maritime legislation is IMO's best-known responsibility. It has developed and adopted more than 50 international conventions and protocols, supported by more than 1,000 codes and recommendations that govern nearly every facet of the shipping industry.

The IMO mandate initially focused on safety-related issues, but was subsequently expanded to include environmental considerations, legal matters, technical cooperation, security and maritime crime, including piracy and armed robbery against ships, as well as issues that affect shipping efficiency.

Safety of life at sea remains a key concern for IMO. The 1974 *International Convention for the Safety of Life at Sea* (SOLAS), includes regulations relating to all aspects of maritime safety and security, from ship construction, fire protection and life-saving appliances to safety management and carriage of cargoes. The Global Maritime Distress and Safety System (GMDSS), which is currently being reviewed and modernized, is mandatory under SOLAS and makes it possible for a ship's distress alert to be received and responded to, anywhere in the world. On 1 January 2017, two new mandatory codes entered into force: one addresses the safety of ships that use gases or other low flash-point fuels, which are increasingly being used as they are cleaner for the environment. The second—the *International Code for Ships Operating in Polar Waters* (Polar Code)—sets additional safety and environmental standards for the increasing number of ships transiting the Arctic and Antarctic waters. The Polar Code is also mandatory under the *International Convention for the Prevention of Pollution from Ships* (MARPOL), which is the key environmental treaty addressing operational discharges and preventing accidental pollution. MARPOL regulations cover the prevention of pollution from oil or chemicals carried in bulk, packaged goods, sewage, garbage, and air pollution from ships, as well as energy efficiency. Under MARPOL, IMO adopted mandatory energy efficiency requirements for international shipping in 2011, which entered into force in 2013, representing the first such mandatory measures for an international transport sector.

IMO's ongoing efforts in the environmental area include measures that will make shipping's environmental footprint a lighter one, such as the use of cleaner fuels, the reduction in harmful exhaust emissions, and action taken to improve ships' energy efficiency. In September 2017, the *Ballast Water Management Convention* (2004) enters into force, setting requirements for ballast water management to prevent the spread of potentially invasive aquatic species in the ballast water of ships.

IMO's technical cooperation activities support implementation of IMO treaties and the UN sustainable development goals. The IMO Member State Audit Scheme, which became mandatory for all member states in 2016, supports the enhanced implementation of IMO instruments and provides member states with an overview of how well they are carrying out their duties as flag, coastal and port states, under the relevant IMO treaties. The process also enables IMO to provide targeted assistance and capacity-building to states.

Two academic institutes operate under ILO auspices, which offer training at the post-graduate level, particularly to students from developing countries: the World Maritime University in Malmö, Sweden and the International Maritime Law Institute in Msida, Malta.

Telecommunications and ICTs

Information and communication technologies (ICTs) have become a key to the global delivery of services. Banking, tourism, transportation and the information industry all depend on quick and reliable access to the digital world. The sector is being revolutionized by powerful trends, including the proliferation of mobile devices, deregulation, ICT services and applications, value-added network services, and intelligent networks. In the process, ICTs are revolutionizing how society functions, including the growth of e-health, e-education and e-government platforms.

The **International Telecommunication Union** (www.itu.int) serves as a global forum through which government and industry work towards consensus on issues affecting the future of ICTs and the role they play in sustainable development. ITU's mission is to enable the growth of, and universal and affordable access to ICTs, so people everywhere can benefit from all digital opportunities such as Smart Cities and the knowledge-sharing economy, as well as to reduce the gap in access to digital technology between women and men. A key priority lies in striving for full digital inclusion—erasing the divide between people with effective access to digital and information technology and those with very limited or no access. In that regard, ITU collects and collates ICT data and publishes its key findings in its annual *Measuring the Information Society Report*, together with the ICT Development Index, which ranks countries in terms of their ICT capacity and readiness.

To achieve its goals, ITU facilitates the public and private sectors to provide global telecommunications networks and services using common standards for the long-term benefit of the planet. Specifically, ITU:

- develops standards that foster the interconnection of national communications infrastructures into global networks, allowing the seamless exchange of information around the world, including nascent technologies like 5G, the Internet of Things, Green Energy and Intelligent Transport Systems;
- works to integrate new technologies into the global telecommunications network, allowing for the development and interoperability of new applications;
- adopts international regulations and treaties governing the sharing of the radio frequency spectrum and satellite orbital positions—finite resources that are used by a wide range of equipment, including television and radio broadcasting, mobile telephones, satellite-based communications systems, aircraft and maritime navigation and safety systems, and wireless computer systems; and
- strives to expand and improve ICTs and broadband, and shrink the gender digital divide in the developing world by providing policy advice, technical assistance, project management and training, and by fostering partnerships between technology ministries, companies, funding agencies and private organizations.

In other activities, ITU convenes focus groups to address urgent, market-oriented industry issues, such as digital finance, as well as seminars, workshops and other events. ITU Telecom World (telecomworld.itu.int), a global platform for high-level debate and knowledge-sharing across the ICT community, brings together representatives of government and industry, with a specific emphasis on small-to-medium sized enterprises (SMEs) from emerging economies, to collaborate, network and innovate for the benefit of all. The 2016 Telecom World was held in Bangkok. The ITU Academy programme trains technicians, regulators, administrators and local communities in how best to use the power of ICTs. An important aspect of ITU's development work is to support least developing countries in ICT uptake and bridging the digital divide. ITU also provides disaster management and emergency communications support to its member states.

International postal service

Each year, more than 5 million postal employees worldwide process and deliver 327 billion letter-posts and 7.4 billion parcels, domestically and internationally, and offer a range of electronic and financial services. Some 680,000 post offices are in operation throughout the world. The **Universal Postal Union** (**UPU**) (www.upu.int) is the UN specialized agency regulating international postal services.

UPU forms a single postal territory of countries for the reciprocal exchange of postal items and postal payment services. Every member state agrees to transmit the mail of all other members by the best means used for its own mail. UPU works to improve international postal services, provide postal customers in every country with harmonized and simplified procedures for their international mail, and make available a universal network of up-to-date products and services.

Thanks to UPU, new products and services are integrated into the international postal network. In this way, such services as registered letters, international reply coupons, small packets, postal parcels and expedited mail services have been made available to most of the world's inhabitants. The agency has taken a leadership role in certain activities, such as the application of electronic data interchange technology by the postal operators of member countries, and the monitoring and improvement of the quality of public postal services worldwide and e-services.

The Universal Postal Congress, the supreme authority of UPU, meets every four years to decide on a new world postal strategy and set the future rules for international mail exchanges. Achievements of the Doha Postal Strategy for 2012–2016 included, among others, the establishment of the Integrated Index for Postal Development (2IPD) methodology, the launch of PosTransfer, UPU's first global trademark for postal remittances, the connection of 23,000 rural post offices in Asia-Pacific to the UPU financial network and the start of a $7 million project to increase access to postal financial services in rural areas in 11 African countries. Some 2,000 representatives from 155 countries participated in the twenty-sixth UPU Congress in Istanbul, Turkey, from 20 September to 7 October 2016 and adopted the Istanbul World Postal Strategy, which sets the course for UPU's work for 2017–2020. The strategy—based on integration, innovation and inclusion—strives to improve interoperability of postal network infrastructure, ensure sustainable and modern products, and foster market and sector functioning.

Intellectual property

Intellectual property (IP) is generally described as referring to "creations of the mind." These include inventions; literary and artistic works; designs; and symbols, names and images used in commerce. IP is protected in law by, among others, patents, copyright and trademarks, which enable innovators to earn recognition or financial benefit from what they invent or create. The IP system aims to foster an environment in which creativity and innovation can flourish. IP plays a central role in today's knowledge-based economy, as reflected in the increasing number of patents, trademarks and industrial designs filed around the world every year.

A UN specialized agency, the **World Intellectual Property Organization (WIPO)** (www.wipo.int), is the global forum for IP services, policy, information and cooperation. WIPO assists its member states in developing a balanced international IP legal framework to meet society's evolving needs; provides business services for obtaining IP rights in multiple countries and for resolving disputes; delivers capacity-building programs to help developing countries benefit from using IP; and provides free access to IP information. WIPO member states meet regularly in committees dealing with copyright; patent law; the law of trademarks, industrial designs and geographical indications; and genetic resources, traditional knowledge and traditional cultural expressions (folklore). WIPO administers 26 international treaties covering all aspects of IP. The most recent, the *Marrakesh Treaty to Facilitate Access to Published Works for Persons Who Are Blind, Visually Impaired or Otherwise Print Disabled* was adopted in 2013 with the goal of increasing access to books, magazines and other printed materials in formats suitable for people with visual impairments.

WIPO international IP filing services (the PCT, Madrid, Hague and Lisbon Systems) provide businesses and innovators with a cost-effective way to protect their inventions, brands and designs in multiple countries by filing a single application or registration. The WIPO Arbitration and Mediation Centre provides a range of alternative dispute resolution services, including for Internet domain name disputes, as an alternative to litigation.

WIPO also works with IP offices to develop worldwide interoperable tools and technical standards that make it easier to share work, data and knowledge. This technical infrastructure provides universal access to the wealth of technology information generated by the IP system. WIPO is the world's most comprehensive source of data on the IP system, as well as of empirical studies, reports, statistics and factual information on IP. WIPO publications and data collections are available online.

WIPO seeks to ensure that all countries can participate equally in the benefits of the IP system. Its cross-cutting Development Agenda ensures that development considerations are integrated into all areas of the organization's work. To help build capacity in developing and least-developed countries, WIPO provides advice on integrating innovation and IP policies into national development strategies, and on developing balanced, appropriate legislative frameworks. It assists IP offices in updating their patent and trademark processing systems and provides training to help build IP skills, including through the WIPO Academy (www.wipo.int/academy).

With a strong focus on innovation as a driver of economic progress and the means to address global challenges, such as climate change, public health and education, WIPO is committed to the SDGs. It has also established a variety of multi-stakeholder, public-private partnerships to develop practical solutions to global issues, such as WIPO Re-Search to combat neglected tropical diseases, and WIPO Green to promote the diffusion of green technologies.

Science and technology for development

The United Nations has been promoting the application of science and technology for the development of its member states since the 1960s. The 43-member **Commission on Science and Technology for Development** (www.unctad.org/cstd) was established in 1992 to examine science and technology questions and their implications for development; promote the understanding of science and technology policies in respect of developing countries; and formulate recommendations on science and technology matters within the UN system.

The Commission also serves as a focal point for the Economic and Social Council, its parent body, in the system-wide follow-up to the World Summit on the Information Society (WSIS). At its 2016 session, the Commission highlighted the instrumental role of science, technology, innovation and ICTs in achieving several of the SDGs; and considered two priority themes: "Smart cities and infrastructure" and "Foresight for digital development". UNCTAD provides substantive and secretariat support for the Commission. It also promotes policies favouring technological capacity-building, innovation and technology flows to developing countries. UNCTAD helps these countries review their science and technology policies, promotes South-South scientific networking, and provides technical assistance on information technologies.

FAO, IAEA, ILO, UNDP, UNIDO and WMO all address scientific and technological issues within their specific mandates. Science for development is also an important element in the work of UNESCO.

SOCIAL DEVELOPMENT

Over the decades, the United Nations has emphasized the social aspects of development to ensure that the aim of better lives for all people remains at the centre of development efforts. The Organization has been at the forefront of supporting government efforts to extend social services relating to health, education, family planning, housing and sanitation to all people. Its evolving policies and programmes have stressed that the three dimensions of sustainable development—social, economic, environmental—are interconnected and cannot be pursued in isolation.

Globalization and liberalization are posing new challenges to social development. There is a growing desire to see a more equitable sharing of the benefits of globalization. The UN takes a people-centred approach to social issues, promoting development strategies that focus on individuals, families and communities. It addresses such issues as health, education and population, and the situation of vulnerable groups, including women, children and youth, indigenous peoples, persons with disabilities, older persons and others marginalized from society and development.

Many UN global conferences have focused on these issues, including the 1995 World Summit for Social Development, which marked the first time the international community came together to advance the struggle against poverty, unemployment and social disintegration. The resulting *Copenhagen Declaration for Social Development* and its 10 commitments represent a social contract at the global level.

The diverse issues of social development represent a challenge for developing and developed countries alike. All societies are confronted by the problems of unemployment, social fragmentation and persistent poverty. A growing number of social issues—from forced migration to drug abuse, organized crime and the spread of diseases—can be successfully tackled only through concerted international action.

The United Nations addresses social development issues through the General Assembly and the Economic and Social Council (ECOSOC), where system-wide policies and priorities are set and programmes endorsed. One of the Assembly's six main committees—the **Social, Humanitarian and Cultural Committee**—takes up agenda items relating to the social sector. Under ECOSOC, the main intergovernmental body dealing with social development concerns is the **Commission for Social Development** (www.un.org/esa/socdev/csd). Composed of 46 member states, the Commission advises ECOSOC and governments on social policies and on the social aspects of development. The priority theme for the Commission's 2017 session (1–10 February) was "**Strategies for eradicating poverty to achieve sustainable development for all**".

Within the Secretariat, the **Division for Social Policy and Development** (www.un.org/esa/socdev) of DESA services these intergovernmental bodies, providing research, analysis and expert guidance. Throughout the UN system, there are also many specialized agencies, funds, programmes and offices that address different aspects of social development.

Research and training

A number of UN specialized organizations conduct academic work in the form of research and training. This work aims to enhance understanding of global problems, as well as foster the human resources required for the more technical aspects of economic and social development and the maintenance of peace and security.

The **United Nations University (UNU)** (www.unu.edu) contributes, through research and capacity-building, to efforts to resolve the pressing global problems that are the concern of the United Nations, its peoples and member states. UNU is a bridge between the United Nations and the international academic community, acting as a think-tank for the UN system; a builder of capacities, particularly in developing countries; and a platform for dialogue and new creative ideas. UNU partners with over 40 UN entities and hundreds of cooperating research institutions around the world.

UNU's 2015–2019 academic activities will focus on three interdependent thematic clusters, including peace and governance; global development and inclusion; and environment, climate and energy. The global UNU system is coordinated by the UNU Centre in Tokyo and includes the following:

- Programme for Biotechnology for Latin America and the Caribbean, Caracas, Venezuela (UNU-BIOLAC)
- Institute on Comparative Regional Integration Studies, Bruges, Belgium (UNU-CRIS)
- Institute on Computing and Society, Macao, China (UNU-CS)
- Institute for Environment and Human Security, Bonn, Germany (UNU-EHS)
- Institute for Integrated Management of Material Fluxes and Resources, Dresden, Germany (UNU-FLORES)
- Institute on Globalization, Culture and Mobility, Barcelona, Spain (UNU-GCM)
- Institute for the Advanced Study of Sustainability, Tokyo, Japan (UNU-IAS)
- International Institute for Global Health, Kuala Lumpur, Malaysia (UNU-IIGH)
- Institute for Natural Resources in Africa, Accra, Ghana (UNU-INRA)
- Institute for Water, Environment and Health, Hamilton, Canada (UNU-INWEH)
- Institute for Sustainable Development in Algiers, Algeria (UNU-IRADDA)
- Maastricht Economic and Social Research Institute on Innovation and Technology, Maastricht, The Netherlands (UNU-MERIT)
- World Institute for Development Economics Research, Helsinki, Finland (UNU-WIDER)
- Iceland-based Programmes on Geothermal Energy (UNU-GTP), Fisheries (UNU-FTP), Land Restoration (UNU-LRT), and Gender Equality (UNU-GEST)
- Centre for Policy Research, Tokyo, Japan (UNU-CPR)
- Operating Unit on Policy-Driven Electronic Governance, Guimarães, Portugal (UNU-EGOV)
- Vice-Rectorate in Europe, Bonn, Germany (UNU-ViE)
- UNU Office at the United Nations, New York, USA

The Geneva-based **United Nations Institute for Training and Research (UNITAR)** (www.unitar.org) works to enhance the effectiveness of the United Nations through training and research. It conducts training and capacity development programmes in support of the 2030 Agenda, thereby strengthening multilateralism, advancing environmental sustainability and green development, improving resilience and humanitarian assistance, promoting sustainable peace, and promoting economic development and social inclusion. UNITAR conducts research on training methodologies and knowledge systems, as well as applied research to address critical issues such as disaster risk reduction and humanitarian emergencies. It also develops pedagogical tools, including e-Learning training packages, workbooks, manuals and training booklets.

The **United Nations System Staff College (UNSSC)** (www.unssc.org), headquartered in Turin (Italy) and with a second campus in Bonn (Germany), is the UN organization mandated to provide staff learning, training and knowledge at an inter-agency level to promote a cohesive management culture. It offers residential courses, distance-learning, seminars and strategic exchanges, ranging from leadership and management development, to the development of those technical and functional competences that are needed to effectively serve as an international civil servant. Since 2015, all of the Staff College learning and training activities are geared towards enabling the UN system and its partners to address the challenges posed by the adoption of the 2030 Agenda.

The **United Nations Research Institute for Social Development (UNRISD)** (www.unrisd.org), located in Geneva, engages in interdisciplinary research on the social dimensions of contemporary development issues. Working through a global network of researchers and institutes, UNRISD provides governments, development agencies, civil society organizations and scholars with a better understanding of how development policies and processes affect different social groups. Recent research themes have included gender equality, social policy, poverty reduction, governance and politics, and social and solidarity economy.

Population and development

The United Nations estimates that the world's population numbered 7.3 billion as at mid-2015, having grown at an annual rate of 1.2 per cent from 2010 to 2015. By 2030, the global population is expected to reach 8.5 billion and increase to 9.7 billion in 2050, with most of this growth expected to occur in Africa and Asia. There is a great diversity in recent population trends and in their future trajectories across countries and regions, driven primarily by differences in levels and trends of fertility. Some countries will experience a decline in population size between 2015 and 2050, while the population will continue to increase in others. Much of the population growth between 2015 and 2030 will be concentrated in countries facing the largest challenges for ending poverty and hunger and ensuring health, education and equality for all. Demographic patterns continue to differ by country and region and shifting patterns are creating new and emerging needs for society. For example, the global number of persons aged 60 or over—the fastest growing segment of the population—is projected to increase from 901 million in 2015 to 2.1 billion by 2050, when all regions of the world except Africa will have nearly a quarter or more of their populations aged 60 years or older.

Sustainable development is linked closely to patterns of human settlement and mobility. Almost all of the increase in global population will take place in urban areas. Responding to rapid urban growth presents an opportunity to implement an ambitious urban development agenda to make cities and human settlements inclusive, safe, resilient and sustainable. Similarly, the migration of persons, both within countries and across borders, presents opportunities and challenges for sustainable development. In 2015, there were 244 million international migrants. Of these, nearly 58 per cent lived in the developed regions, while the developing regions hosted 42 per cent of the total. Migration can be a transformative force, lifting millions of people out of poverty and creating opportunities for a better life.

The UN assists countries in building national capacity for the collection, compilation, dissemination and analysis of population data, including information from censuses and for the production of national population projections. The pioneering quantitative and methodological work of the United Nations, particularly its authoritative estimates and projections of the global population, urban and rural populations, and the stock of international migrants, has helped countries plan ahead, incorporate population policies into national development planning, and make sound economic and social decisions.

The **Commission on Population and Development**, (www.un.org/en/development/desa/population/commission) composed of 47 member states, is charged with studying and advising ECOSOC on population changes and their effects on economic and social conditions. It holds primary responsibility for reviewing the implementation of the programme of action of the 1994 International Conference on Population and Development.

The **Population Division of DESA** (www.unpopulation.org) serves as the secretariat of the Commission and also supports the work of the Second Committee of the General Assembly in its discussions of international migration and development. It also provides the international community with timely, high-quality, comparable, reliable and scientifically objective data and information on population and development, contributing to the monitoring of internationally agreed development goals, including the SDGs. It undertakes studies on population levels, trends, estimates and projections, as well as on population policies and the link between population and development. The Division maintains major databases, among them *World Population Prospects; World Population Policies; World Urbanization Prospects* and *Trends in International Migrant Stock*. The Division is also engaged in capacity-building and training, including on the dissemination and use of population research and demographic data.

The **United Nations Population Fund (UNFPA)** (www.unfpa.org) leads the operational activities of the UN system in this field, helping developing countries and those with economies in transition address their population opportunities and challenges. It assists states in improving reproductive health and family planning services on the basis of individual choice, and in formulating population policies in support of sustainable development. In line with its mission statement, UNFPA works toward a world where every pregnancy is wanted, every childbirth is safe and every young person's potential is fulfilled. Its primary role in fulfilling this mission is as a funding organization for reproductive health, youth, and emergency-related programmes carried out by governments, UN agencies and NGOs.

- *Reproductive health.* UNFPA assists governments in delivering sexual and reproductive health care, including family planning, with a focus on improving maternal health. The ability of parents to choose the number and spacing of their children is an essential component of reproductive health. An estimated 225 million women want to use safe and effective family planning methods, but are unable to do so because they lack access to information and services or the support of their husbands and communities. UNFPA works with governments, the private sector and NGOs to meet family planning needs. It does not provide support for abortion services and seeks to prevent abortion by increasing access to family planning. UNFPA also addresses the reproductive health needs of adolescents with programmes to prevent teenage pregnancy, HIV/AIDS and other sexually transmitted infections; prevent and treat fistulas; and improve access to services and information.

- *Young people.* A large number of the world's 1.8 billion young people (ages 10–24) find it challenging to participate fully in society due to limited opportunities for a quality education, health services and decent work. In about 60 countries, mainly in Africa and South Asia, the window for a demographic dividend is opening. Fertility has started to fall and a proportionately large population of young people is about to reach working age. If sub-Saharan Africa makes the right investments in young people, the region could realize a demographic dividend of about $500 billion a year, for 30 years. UNFPA works with governments and partners to make such investments in young people's health, education and training for work and life.
- *Emergencies.* During conflicts, natural disasters and other emergencies, sexual and re-productive health needs are easily overlooked—yet these needs are often staggering. In crisis situations, one in five women of childbearing age is likely to be pregnant and faces an increased risk of life-threatening complications. Six in ten women are dying in childbirth in countries in humanitarian or fragile situations. Women and young people also become more vulnerable to sexual violence, exploitation and HIV infec-tion. UNFPA works with governments, UN agencies and other partners to ensure that reproductive health is integrated into emergency responses.

The **International Organization for Migration (IOM)** (www.iom.int) works to en-sure the orderly and humane management of migration, promote international coopera-tion on migration issues, assist in the search for practical solutions to migration problems and provide humanitarian assistance to migrants in need, including refugees and IDPs. In 2015, nearly 1 in 5 migrants lived in the top 20 largest cities. Women constituted 48 per cent of international migrants. The year also saw the highest levels of forced displace-ment globally recorded since World War II, with an increase in the number of refugees, asylum-seekers and IDPs. The 45 per cent increase in refugees compared to 2012 was largely due to the ongoing conflict in Syria. IOM works in four broad areas of migration management: migration and development; facilitating migration; regulating migration; and forced migration.

Promoting the rights and well-being of children

The number of children who died before turning 5 fell by more than 50 per cent world-wide between 1990 and 2015. Despite the gain, an estimated 5.9 million children still did not live to see their fifth birthday during 2015, with children from the poorest house-holds nearly twice as likely to die as those from the wealthiest. Of the 2.6 million chil-dren under age 15 living with HIV, just one in three was receiving treatment, and AIDS remains the leading cause of death among adolescents in Africa—with adolescent girls facing especially high risks of infection. Approximately 250 million children of primary school age still could not read, write or do basic arithmetic, despite advances in school enrolment, while 75 million children and adolescents had their education disrupted by crisis. Girls were still 2.5 times more likely than boys to be out of school in conflict situ-ations. In addition, millions of children around the world remain subject to violence, exploitation, abuse and neglect.

The **United Nations Children's Fund (UNICEF)** (www.unicef.org) promotes the rights of every child and takes action to ensure that all children have an opportunity to survive, develop and reach their full potential regardless of their place of birth, fam-ily of origin, race, ethnicity or gender; or if they live in poverty or with a disability. It advocates for full implementation of the *Convention on the Rights of the Child* along with the *Convention on the Elimination of All Forms of Discrimination against Women*. In 190

Children walk home after school at the Minawao refugee camp in Northern Cameroon.
The conflict in North-East Nigeria prompted by Boko Haram resulted in 2.7 million people fleeing
the violence during the six-year insurgency (5 April 2016, UNICEF/Karel Prinsloo).

countries and territories, UNICEF works in partnership with governments, international organizations and civil society to overcome obstacles faced by children, including poverty, violence, disease and discrimination.

The SDGs incorporate objectives that are specific to the health and well-being of every child and highlight the critical importance of access to child and maternal health care, early childhood development, birth registration, quality learning and school completion, gender equality, ending child marriage, and integrating humanitarian action and development work. In line with the commitment of world governments to a pledge "that no one will be left behind" and to "endeavor to reach the furthest behind first", UNICEF programmes are informed by a commitment to position children at the centre of development. The organization works to reach the most vulnerable children, at greatest risk and in greatest need.

In collaboration with its partners, UNICEF contributes to seven outcomes: health; HIV and AIDS; water, sanitation and hygiene; nutrition; education; child protection; and social inclusion. Its advocacy efforts focus on issues ranging from the impact of climate change on children to the need for greater investment in adolescent health and well-being. It also encompasses efforts to promote quality education and gender equality, and to end child marriage, child labour, violence against children and other abuses. In 2015, UNICEF and its partners supplied individual learning materials for 14.9 million children and education materials for more than 348,000 classrooms. It also procured $2.27 billion in health-related supplies—including 2.8 billion doses of vaccines that reached 45 per cent of the world's children under age 5 in 95 countries.

UNICEF is also a knowledge leader on children's issues, contributing to achieving results for children through global and regional research initiatives.

Social integration

The United Nations has come to recognize several social groups as deserving special attention, including youth, older persons, the impoverished, persons with disabilities, minorities and indigenous populations. Their concerns are addressed by the General Assembly, ECOSOC and the Commission for Social Development. Specific programmes for these groups are carried out within the UN Department of Economic and Social Affairs (undesadspd.org). The UN has been instrumental in defining and defending the human rights of such vulnerable groups. It has helped formulate international norms, standards and recommendations for policies and practices regarding these groups, and strives to highlight their concerns through research and data gathering, as well as through the declaration of special years and decades aimed at increasing awareness and encouraging international action.

Families

The United Nations recognizes the family as the basic unit of society. Families have been substantially transformed over the past 60 years as a result of changes in their structure (smaller-sized households, delayed marriage and childbearing, increased divorce rates and single parenthood); global trends in migration; the phenomenon of demographic ageing; the HIV/AIDS pandemic; and the impact of globalization. These dynamic social forces have had a manifest impact on the capacities of families to perform such functions as socializing children and caregiving for younger and older family members. The **International Day of Families**, commemorated each year on 15 May, aims at increasing awareness of issues relating to the family and encouraging appropriate action.

The **UN Focal Point on the Family** (undesadspd.org/Family.aspx) provides substantive servicing to UN intergovernmental bodies in the areas of family and family policy. Its programme on family promotes the realization of the objectives of the International Year of the Family (1994), along with the integration of a family perspective into national, regional and international policymaking; acts as an exchange for expertise and experiences, disseminating information and supporting networking on family issues; supports family research and diagnostic studies; encourages and supports coordination on family policies and programmes within governments and the UN system; provides technical assistance and capacity-building support to developing country governments; and liaises with governments, civil society and the private sector on family issues.

Youth

The General Assembly has adopted several resolutions and campaigns specific to youth—defined as those between 15 and 24 years of age—and the Secretariat has overseen related programmes and information campaigns. The UN **programme on youth** (www.un.org/development/desa/youth) of DESA, which serves as the focal point on youth within the United Nations, aims to build awareness of the global situation of young people; promote their rights and aspirations; and increase participation of young people in decision-making as a means of achieving peace and development. DESA coordinates the participation of youth delegates to the General Assembly and ECOSOC system, where Governments regularly include young people in their official delegations.

The Secretary-General appointed his **Envoy on Youth** (www.un.org/youthenvoy) in January 2013 and a **Special Envoy on Youth Unemployment** in September 2016. Together the youth envoys work to increase youth accessibility to the United Nations;

promote stronger youth participation in setting, implementing and evaluating development frameworks; increase international awareness of, and attention to, youth issues; engage member states, the private sector, academic institutions, media and civil society and facilitate partnerships on youth issues; and work to enhance the coordination and harmonization of youth programming among UN agencies.

In 1999, the General Assembly declared that **International Youth Day** be commemorated each year on 12 August. It also recommended that public information activities be organized to support the Day as a way to enhance awareness of the *World Programme of Action for Youth*, adopted in 1995 as a policy framework and set of practical guidelines for national action and international support to improve the situation of young people around the world.

DESA prepares the *World Youth Report* (www.unworldyouthreport.org), a biennial publication shining a spot light on key areas of youth development.

The **ECOSOC Youth Forum** (www.un.org/ecosoc/en/ecosoc-youth-forum) is a yearly event that aims to provide a platform for young people to voice their needs and concerns through informal dialogue with other stakeholders, in particular member states, and to explore possible ways for promoting youth development at all levels. The Forum represents the most institutionalised venue for youth participation in UN deliberations and is an important vehicle to mobilize support among young people for the implementation of the 2030 Agenda.

Older persons

The world is in the midst of a historically unique and irreversible process of demographic transition due to falling birth rates and rising life expectancy, which is resulting in growing older populations everywhere. The world community has come to recognize the need to integrate the process of global ageing into the larger context of development, and to design policies within a broader 'life-course' and socially inclusive framework. The focus of the UN **programme on ageing** (www.un.org/development/desa/ageing) of DESA is to facilitate and promote the three priority directions of the *Madrid International Plan of Action on Ageing (MIPAA)*, which are older persons and development; advancing health and well-being into old age; and ensuring enabling and supportive environments.

The United Nations has taken several initiatives in response to the challenges and opportunities of global ageing:

- The first World Assembly on Ageing (Vienna, 1982) adopted the *Vienna International Plan of Action on Ageing*, which recommended measures in such areas as employment and income security, health and nutrition, housing, education and social welfare. It saw older persons as a diverse and active population group with wide-ranging capabilities and particular health-care needs.
- The *United Nations Principles for Older Persons,* adopted by the General Assembly in 1991, established universal standards pertaining to the status of older persons in five areas: independence, participation, care, self-fulfillment and dignity.
- The Second World Assembly on Ageing (Madrid, 2002) designed international policy on ageing for the 21st century. It adopted the *Madrid International Plan of Action on Ageing,* by which member states committed themselves to action in three priority areas: older persons and development; advancing health and well-being into old age; and ensuring the existence of enabling and supportive environments.

In May 2014, the Human Rights Council appointed the first Independent Expert on the enjoyment of all human rights by older persons.

Indigenous issues

There are more than 370 million indigenous peoples living in some 90 countries world-wide, where they often face discrimination and exclusion from political and economic power. Indigenous peoples are overrepresented among the poorest, the illiterate and the destitute of the world. They have often been displaced by wars and environmental disasters, removed from their ancestral lands, and deprived of resources needed for physical and cultural survival. Indigenous peoples have also seen their traditional knowledge marketed and patented without their consent or participation. The **International Day of the World's Indigenous Peoples** is commemorated on 9 August each year to promote and endorse the rights of the world's indigenous peoples.

The **Permanent Forum on Indigenous Issues** (www.un.org/indigenous), established by the Economic and Social Council in 2000, considers indigenous issues relating to economic and social development, culture, education, environment, health and human rights. It provides expert advice and recommendations to ECOSOC and, through it, to the programmes, funds and agencies of the United Nations. The aim is to raise awareness, promote the integration and coordination of activities relating to indigenous issues within the UN system, and disseminate information on indigenous issues. The Forum also addresses ways in which indigenous issues may best be pursued in meeting the SDGs, given the fact that, in many countries, attention to indigenous communities will directly contribute to achieving the goals by 2030.

In 2007, the General Assembly adopted the *United Nations Declaration on the Rights of Indigenous Peoples*, setting out the individual and collective rights of indigenous peoples, including their rights to their lands, territories and resources, culture, identity, language, employment, health and education. The *Declaration* emphasizes the rights of indigenous peoples to maintain and strengthen their own institutions, cultures and traditions, and to pursue their development in keeping with their own priorities and aspirations. It prohibits discrimination against them, and promotes their full and effective participation in all matters that concern them, as well as their right to retain their distinct identity and to pursue their own visions of economic and social development. The *Declaration* also reflects global consensus and provides the minimum standards for the survival, dignity and well-being of the indigenous peoples of the world.

In September 2014, the General Assembly held a high-level event known as the **World Conference on Indigenous Peoples**. The outcome document, adopted by consensus, contains a series of commitments to achieve the ends of the *Declaration*.

Persons with disabilities

Persons with disabilities are often excluded from the mainstream of society. Discrimination takes various forms, ranging from invidious discrimination, such as the denial of educational opportunities, to more subtle forms of discrimination, such as segregation and isolation because of the imposition of physical and social barriers. Society also suffers, since the loss of the enormous potential of persons with disabilities impoverishes humankind. Changes in the perception and concepts of disability involve both changes in values and increased understanding at all levels of society. Since its inception, the United Nations has sought to advance the status of persons with disabilities and improve their lives. The Organization's concern for the well-being and rights of such persons is rooted in its founding principles, which are based on human rights, fundamental freedoms and the equality of all human beings.

Following three decades of advocacy and standard-setting for equal opportunities, treatment and access to services for persons with disabilities, the General Assembly, in

2006, adopted the *Convention on the Rights of Persons with Disabilities* and its *Optional Protocol*. The *Convention*, which entered into force in 2008, codified all categories of human rights and fundamental freedoms to be applied to all persons with disabilities. It is based on the following principles: respect for inherent dignity and individual autonomy; non-discrimination; full and effective participation and inclusion in society; respect for differences and acceptance of persons with disabilities as part of human diversity; equal opportunity; accessibility; equality of men and women; and respect for the evolving capacities of children with disabilities and their right to preserve their identities. The *Convention* focuses particularly on areas where rights have been violated, where protections must be reinforced, and where adaptations are needed to enable such persons to exercise their rights. It requires states to monitor its implementation through national focal points, as well as independent monitoring mechanisms.

The **Committee on the Rights of Persons with Disabilities**, composed of 18 expert members, monitors implementation of the *Convention*. Under the *Convention's Optional Protocol*, states parties recognize the Committee's competence to examine individual complaints with regard to alleged violations of the *Convention* by parties to the *Protocol*.

The normative frameworks and international commitments to mainstreaming the perspectives, rights and needs of persons with disabilities were further strengthened with the adoption of the 2030 Agenda in 2015 and the outcome of the General Assembly's high-level meeting on disability and development in 2013. Within the UN system, DESA serves as the **focal point on persons with disabilities** (www.un.org/disabilities) and also as the secretariat for the Conference of states parties to the *Convention*.

Uncivil society: crime, illicit drugs and terrorism

Transnational organized crime, illicit drug trafficking and terrorism have become social, political and economic forces capable of altering the destinies of entire countries and regions. Such practices as the large-scale bribery of public officials, the growth of 'criminal multinationals', trafficking in persons, and the use of terrorism to intimidate communities large and small and to sabotage economic development are threats that require effective international cooperation. The United Nations is addressing these threats to good governance, social equity and justice for all, and is orchestrating a global response.

The Vienna-based **United Nations Office on Drugs and Crime** (UNODC) (www.unodc.org) leads the international effort to combat drug trafficking and use, organized crime and international terrorism—what have been called the 'uncivil' elements of society. The Office is composed of a crime programme, which also addresses terrorism and its prevention, and a drug programme. It has more than 60 field and project offices, and liaison offices in Brussels and New York.

Drug control

An estimated five per cent of the adult population, or nearly 250 million people between the ages of 15 and 64, use illicit drugs at least once a year, with over 29 million people in this category classified as drug dependent. In addition, some 12 million people inject drugs with 14 per cent of these living with HIV. Drug use is responsible for lost wages, soaring health-care costs, broken families and deteriorating communities. In particular, injecting drug use is fueling the spread of HIV, AIDS and hepatitis in many parts of the world. A direct link exists between drugs and an increase in crime and violence. Drug cartels undermine governments and corrupt legitimate businesses, while revenues from illicit drugs fund some of the deadliest armed conflicts. The financial toll is staggering.

Enormous sums are spent to strengthen police forces, judicial systems and treatment and rehabilitation programmes. The social costs are equally high: street violence, gang warfare and urban decay.

The United Nations is tackling the global drug problem on many levels. UNODC provides leadership for all UN drug control activities, working with civil society, including through community-based programmes in prevention, treatment and rehabilitation, as well as the provision of new economic opportunities to economies dependent on illicit crops.

The **Commission on Narcotic Drugs** (www.unodc.org/unodc/en/commissions/CND), a functional commission of ECOSOC, is the main intergovernmental policy-making and coordination body on international drug control. Made up of 53 member states, it analyses the world drug use and trafficking problem and develops proposals to strengthen drug control. It monitors implementation of international drug control treaties, as well as the guiding principles and measures adopted by the General Assembly.

The **International Narcotics Control Board (INCB)** (www.incb.org) is a 13-member, independent, quasi-judicial body that monitors and assists in governments' compliance with international drug control treaties. It strives to ensure that drugs are available for medical and scientific purposes and to prevent their diversion into illegal channels. The Board sends investigative missions and makes technical visits to drug-affected countries. It also conducts training programmes for drug control administrators, particularly those from developing countries.

A series of treaties, adopted under UN auspices, require that governments exercise control over the production and distribution of narcotic and psychotropic substances; combat drug use and illicit trafficking; and report to international organs on their actions.

- The *Single Convention on Narcotic Drugs* (1961) seeks to limit the production, distribution, possession, use and trade in drugs exclusively to medical and scientific purposes, and obliges states parties to take special measures for particular drugs, such as heroin. Its 1972 *Protocol* stresses the need for treatment and rehabilitation of drug users.
- The *Convention on Psychotropic Substances* (1971) establishes an international control system for psychotropic substances. It stands as a response to the diversification and expansion of the drug spectrum, and introduces controls over a number of synthetic drugs.
- The *United Nations Convention against Illicit Traffic in Narcotic Drugs and Psychotropic Substances* (1988) provides comprehensive measures against drug trafficking, including provisions against money laundering and the diversion of precursor chemicals. States parties commit to eliminating or reducing drug demand.

In April 2016, the General Assembly convened a special session on the world drug problem—the first in 18 years and only the third such meeting held by the Assembly on global drug policy. The outcome document adopted by member states reaffirmed their commitments to undertake innovative approaches to drug control within the framework of the three international drug control conventions.

Crime prevention

Crime threatens the safety of people worldwide and hampers the social and economic development of countries. Globalization has opened up new forms of transnational crime. Multinational criminal syndicates have expanded the range of their operations from drug and arms trafficking to money laundering. Criminals smuggle millions of migrants each year, generating billions in illicit profits. A country plagued by corruption is likely to attract less investment than a relatively uncorrupt country, and lose economic growth as a result.

The **Commission on Crime Prevention and Criminal Justice** (www.unodc.org/unodc/en/commissions/CCPCJ), made up of 40 member states, is a functional body of ECOSOC. It formulates international policies and coordinates activities in crime prevention and criminal justice. UNODC carries out the mandates established by the Commission, and is the UN office responsible for crime prevention, criminal justice and criminal law reform. It pays special attention to combating transnational organized crime, corruption, terrorism and trafficking in persons. The UNODC strategy is based on international cooperation and the provision of assistance for those efforts. It fosters a culture based on integrity and respect for the law, and promotes the participation of civil society in combating crime and corruption.

UNODC supports the development of international legal instruments on global crime, including the *United Nations Convention against Transnational Organized Crime* and its three *Protocols* (on trafficking in persons, smuggling of migrants, and illicit manufacturing and trafficking in firearms), which entered into force in 2003; and the *United Nations Convention against Corruption,* which entered into force in 2005. It helps states put those instruments into effect and provides technical cooperation to strengthen the capacity of governments to modernize their criminal justice systems. The UNODC Anti-Organized Crime and Law Enforcement Unit assists states in taking steps, in line with the *Convention,* to fight organized crime.

UNODC cultivates the application of UN standards and norms in crime prevention and criminal justice as cornerstones of humane and effective criminal justice systems— basic requisites for fighting national and international crime. Countries across the globe have relied on these standards for elaborating national legislation and policies. The Office also analyses emerging trends in crime and justice; develops databases; issues global surveys; gathers and disseminates information; and undertakes country-specific needs assessments and early warning measures with regard to issues, such as the escalation of terrorism.

UNODC global programmes. Through a series of thematic global programmes, UNODC assists governments worldwide in tackling threats from a range of issues, including firearms; money laundering; trafficking in persons; smuggling of migrants; wildlife and forest crime; maritime crime; and criminal investigations and criminal justice cooperation. The *Doha Declaration,* which emerged from the 2015 UN Congress on Crime Prevention and Criminal Justice, resulted in the formation of a cross-discipline global programme. It covers issues such as strengthening judicial integrity, fostering prisoner rehabilitation and social integration, preventing youth crime through sports, and encouraging a culture of the rule of law in schools and universities through an 'education for justice' initiative.

The **United Nations Interregional Crime and Justice Research Institute (UNICRI)** (www.unicri.it), the interregional research body that works in close association with UNODC's crime programme, undertakes and promotes research aimed at preventing crime, treating offenders and formulating improved policies. As decided by the General Assembly, an international congress on the prevention of crime and the treatment of offenders is held every five years as a forum to exchange policies and stimulate progress in the fight against crime. Participants include criminologists, penologists and senior police officers, as well as experts in criminal law, human rights and rehabilitation. The Thirteenth Crime Congress, which marked its sixtieth anniversary, met in Doha, Qatar, in April 2015 on the theme "Integrating crime prevention and criminal justice into the wider UN agenda to address social and economic challenges and to promote the rule of law at the national and international levels, and public participation". The next congress will be held in Japan in 2020.

Terrorism prevention

In 2003, UNODC expanded its technical cooperation activities to strengthen the legal regime against terrorism (www.unodc.org/unodc/en/terrorism/index.html). The Office's Terrorism Prevention Branch provides legal technical assistance to countries for becoming party to and implementing the universal anti-terrorism instruments. The Branch also administers the *Global Project on Strengthening the Legal Regime against Terrorism*, which provides the operational framework for UNODC's specialized legal and capacity-building assistance related to terrorism.

UNODC also collaborates with the **Counter-Terrorism Implementation Task Force**, established by the Secretary-General in 2005 to enhance coordination and coherence of the UN system's counter-terrorism efforts. The Task Force consists of 38 international entities and the international criminal police organization (INTERPOL), which by virtue of their work have a stake in multilateral counter-terrorism efforts. They deal with preventing and resolving conflict; supporting victims of terrorism; preventing and responding to terrorist attacks involving weapons of mass destruction; tackling the financing of terrorism; countering the use of the Internet for terrorist purposes; strengthening the protection of vulnerable targets; and protecting human rights while countering terrorism.

Science, culture and communication

The United Nations sees cultural and scientific exchanges, as well as communication, as instrumental in the advancement of international peace and development. Several UN entities concern themselves with activities in these areas. In addition to its central work on education, for example, the **United Nations Educational, Scientific and Cultural Organization (UNESCO)** (www.unesco.org) carries out activities in the fields of science and culture, fostering the advancement, transfer and sharing of knowledge.

Natural and social and human sciences

UNESCO's international and intergovernmental programmes in the natural sciences include the Man and the Biosphere Programme; the Intergovernmental Oceanographic Commission; the Management of Social Transformations Programme; the International Hydrological Programme; the International Basic Sciences Programme; and the International Geoscience Programme. Through science education and capacity-building initiatives, UNESCO helps increase the scientific capacity of developing countries for sustainable development.

In the wake of the 1997 *Universal Declaration on the Human Genome and Human Rights*—the first international text on the ethics of genetic research and practice— UNESCO's General Conference adopted the *International Declaration on Human Genetic Data* in 2003, and the *Universal Declaration on Bioethics and Human Rights* in 2005.

In its efforts to facilitate social transformations conducive to the universal values of justice, freedom and human dignity, UNESCO focuses on philosophy and social sciences research, including the ethics of science and technology; promotes and teaches human rights and democracy; combats all forms of discrimination, including those related to illnesses such as HIV/AIDS; and improves the status of women. Central to the work of UNESCO on these issues is its intergovernmental programme on the Management of Social Transformations. In 2005, the UNESCO General Conference adopted the *International Convention against Doping in Sport*, which seeks the elimination of doping in sport as a means to promote education, health, development and peace.

Through its natural science programmes, UNESCO contributes to the overall implementation of the SDGs by providing policy assistance to support developing countries in strengthening their scientific and technological capacity, and helping member states design effective policies, based on the best available knowledge. UNESCO's Social and Human Sciences Programme aims to firmly entrench **universal values and principles,** such as global solidarity, inclusion, anti-discrimination, gender equality and accountability, in the implementation of the post-2015 development agenda.

Culture and development

UNESCO's cultural activities are concentrated on promoting tangible and intangible heritage to help achieve sustainable development and social cohesion; protecting and promoting the diversity of cultural expressions and the dialogue of cultures, to foster a culture of peace; and building upon cultural factors for reconciliation and reconstruction in post-conflict and post-natural disaster countries.

In 2003, the UNESCO General Conference adopted the UNESCO *Declaration concerning the Intentional Destruction of Cultural Heritage,* mainly in response to the destruction of the Buddhas of Bamiyan in Afghanistan in 2001. The 2003 *Convention for the Safeguarding of the Intangible Cultural Heritage* covers oral traditions, customs, languages, performing arts, social practices, rituals, festive events, traditional knowledge, traditional crafts, endangered languages and the promotion of linguistic diversity. In 2004, UNESCO launched its Creative Cities Network (UCCN) to promote cooperation with and among cities that have identified creativity as a strategic factor for sustainable urban development. The 116 cities which currently make up this network work together towards a common objective: placing creativity and cultural industries at the heart of their development plans at the local level and cooperating actively at the international level. The 2005 *Convention on the Protection and Promotion of the Diversity of Cultural Expressions* recognizes cultural goods and services as vehicles of identity and values, and seeks to strengthen their creation, production, distribution and enjoyment, particularly by supporting related industries in developing countries. In 2015, the *Unite4Heritage initiative*—a global movement and social media campaign powered by UNESCO—was launched to celebrate and safeguard cultural heritage and diversity around the world.

Implementation of UNESCO joint programmes with other UN agencies and strong cooperation with the national authorities will be key for the implementation of the 2030 Agenda.

Alliance of Civilizations

The **Alliance of Civilizations (UNAOC)** (www.unaoc.org) was launched by the Secretary-General in 2005 as a coalition to advance mutual respect for religious beliefs and traditions, and to reaffirm humanity's increasing interdependence in all areas. Its primary mission is to forge collective political will and mobilize concerted action to improve cross-cultural understanding and cooperation among countries, peoples and communities. UNAOC focuses on strengthening relations within and between Western and Muslim societies and addressing persistent tensions and divides in order to reject violent extremism in all its forms. The High Representative for the Alliance of Civilizations is appointed by the Secretary-General. UNAOC works predominantly in four priority areas: education, youth, media and migration. In April 2016, the Alliance held its seventh Global Forum in Baku, Azerbaijan, on the theme "Living in inclusive societies: a challenge and a goal". UNAOC also contributes to anti-terrorism efforts as a member of the Counter Terrorism Implementation Task Force (CTITF) and an advocate of the UN Counter Terrorism Strategy, with a particular emphasis on the prevention of violent extremism (PVE).

Sport for development and peace

The **United Nations Office on Sport for Development and Peace (UNOSDP)** (www.
un.org/sport), based in Geneva with a liaison office in New York, assists the Special Adviser to the UN Secretary-General on Sport for Development and Peace in the Adviser's
worldwide activities as an advocate, facilitator and representative in this field. The Office
brings the worlds of sport and development together through the engagement of governments, sport organizations, athletes, civil society, community leaders and the private
sector. Through dialogue, knowledge-sharing and partnerships, UNOSDP encourages
cross-cutting and interdisciplinary exchanges between all stakeholders interested in using
sport as a tool for education, health, development and peace. The Office and the Special Adviser support and raise awareness about the use of sport to advance development
and peace objectives, including the SDGs, gender equality, youth development, inclusion of persons with disabilities, health education, conflict resolution and peacebuilding.
UNOSDP runs the **Youth Leadership Programme**, which is a platform that empowers
and strengthens the skills of youth leaders who use sport to improve their communities.
The Office also provides technical assistance and facilitates financial support to Sport
for Development and Peace projects. In the lead-up to and during major sport events,
UNOSDP fosters UN-wide coordination and representation.

Communication and information

UNESCO promotes press freedom and pluralistic, independent media. It works in favour
of the free flow of ideas, especially strengthening the communication capacities of developing countries and their access to information and knowledge. It assists member states in
adapting their media laws to democratic standards, and in pursuing editorial independence in public and private media. When violations of press freedom occur, UNESCO's
Director-General intervenes through diplomatic channels or public statements.

At UNESCO's initiative, 3 May is observed annually as **World Press Freedom Day**.
World Telecommunication and Information Society Day is celebrated each year on
17 May, at the initiative of ITU, to promote the vision of a people-centred, inclusive and
development-oriented information society.

With the aim of reinforcing developing countries' communication infrastructures
and human resources, UNESCO provides training and technical expertise and helps
develop national and regional media projects, especially through its International Programme for the Development of Communication (IPDC). The IPDC Special Initiative
on Knowledge-Driven Media Development contributes to SDG 16 by highlighting the
importance of generating and sharing of knowledge to advance media development,
and has special relevance to an inclusive approach to strengthening journalism education worldwide. UNESCO work on the promotion of universal access to information,
including through its Open Solutions Programme, directly contributes to the achievement of SDG 9 on building resilient infrastructure and fostering innovation, particularly
through increasing access to ICT. The **Youth Mobile Initiative** aims to teach young people to directly mitigate hyper-local issues of sustainable development by developing relevant mobile app solutions in local languages.

A member of the Civil Affairs Division of the UN Mission in South Sudan, at a camp near Rumbek in the Lakes State, facilitates a conflict resolution meeting for groups in the region following a recent clash (21 April 2015, UN Photo/JC McIlwaine).

One of the most significant achievements of the United Nations is the creation of a comprehensive body of human rights law (www.un.org/en/sections/universal-declaration/human-rights-law)—a universal and internationally protected code to which all nations can subscribe and all people aspire. The United Nations has defined a broad range of internationally accepted rights, including civil, cultural, economic, political and social rights. It has also established mechanisms to promote and protect these rights and to assist states in carrying out their responsibilities.

The foundations of this body of law are the *Charter of the United Nations* and the *Universal Declaration of Human Rights,* adopted by the General Assembly in 1945 and 1948, respectively. In 1966, the Assembly adopted the *International Covenant on Economic Social and Cultural Rights* and the *International Covenant on Civil and Political Rights*. Together with the *Declaration*, they are known as the *International Bill of Human Rights*. Since then, the United Nations has gradually expanded human rights law to encompass specific standards for women, children, persons with disabilities, migrant workers and their families, refugees, minorities and other groups who are vulnerable to discrimination and violations of human rights in many societies and require special protection for the enjoyment of their human rights.

The United Nations High Commissioner for Human Rights works to strengthen and coordinate UN efforts to promote and protect the human rights of all people. As human rights plays a central role in the Organization's work in key areas such as peace and security, humanitarian assistance, and development, every UN body and specialized agency is involved to some degree in the protection of human rights.

HUMAN RIGHTS INSTRUMENTS

At the San Francisco Conference in 1945 that established the United Nations, some 40 non-governmental organizations representing women, trade unions, ethnic organizations and religious groups joined forces with government delegations, mostly from smaller countries, and pressed for more specific language on human rights than had been proposed by other states. Their determined lobbying resulted in the inclusion of some provisions on human rights in the *Charter of the United Nations*, laying the foundation for the post-1945 era of international lawmaking.

Thus, the Preamble to the *Charter* explicitly reaffirms "faith in fundamental human rights, in the dignity and worth of the human person, in the equal rights of men and women and of nations large and small". Article 1 establishes that one of the four principal tasks of the United Nations is to promote and encourage "respect for human rights and for fundamental freedoms for all without distinction as to race, sex, language, or religion". Other provisions commit states to take action in cooperation with the United Nations to achieve universal respect for human rights.

International Bill of Human Rights

Three years after the United Nations was created, the General Assembly laid the cornerstone of contemporary human rights law: the *Universal Declaration of Human Rights* (www.ohchr.org/EN/UDHR/Pages/UDHRIndex.aspx*),* intended as a "common standard of achievement for all peoples". It was adopted on 10 December 1948, the day now observed worldwide as **International Human Rights Day**. Its 30 articles spell out basic civil, cultural, economic, political and social rights that all human beings in every country must enjoy.

Articles 1 and 2 state that "all human beings are born equal in dignity and rights" and are entitled to all the rights and freedoms set forth in the *Declaration* "without distinction of any kind such as race, colour, sex, language, religion, political or other opinion, national or social origin, property, birth or other status".

Articles 3 to 21 set forth the civil and political rights to which all human beings are entitled, including:

- the right to life, liberty and security;
- freedom from slavery and servitude;
- freedom from torture or cruel, inhuman or degrading treatment or punishment;
- the right to recognition as a person before the law, the right to judicial remedy;
- freedom from arbitrary arrest, detention or exile; the right to a fair trial and public hearing by an independent and impartial tribunal; the right to be presumed innocent until proved guilty;
- freedom from arbitrary interference with privacy, family, home or correspondence;
- freedom from attacks upon honour and reputation; the right to protection of the law against such attacks;
- freedom of movement; the right to seek asylum; the right to a nationality;
- the right to marry and to found a family; the right to own property;
- freedom of thought, conscience and religion; freedom of opinion and expression;
- the right to peaceful assembly and association;
- the right to take part in government and to equal access to public service.

Articles 22 to 27 set forth the economic, social and cultural rights to which all human beings are entitled, including:

- the right to social security;
- the right to work; the right to equal pay for equal work; the right to form and join trade unions;
- the right to rest and leisure;
- the right to a standard of living adequate for health and well-being;
- the right to education;
- the right to participate in the cultural life of the community.

Finally, Articles 28 to 30 recognize that everyone is entitled to a social and international order in which the human rights set forth in the *Declaration* may be fully realized; that these rights may only be limited for the sole purpose of securing recognition and respect of the rights and freedoms of others and of meeting the requirements of morality, public order and the general welfare in a democratic society; and that each person has duties to the community in which she or he lives.

The provisions of the *Universal Declaration* are considered by scholars to have the weight of customary international law because they are so widely accepted and used to measure the conduct of states. Newly independent countries have cited the *Universal Declaration* or included its provisions in their basic laws or constitutions.

The broadest legally binding human rights agreements negotiated under UN auspices are the *International Covenant on Economic, Social and Cultural Rights* and the *International Covenant on Civil and Political Rights*. These agreements, adopted by the General Assembly in 1966, take the provisions of the *Universal Declaration* a step further by translating these rights into legally binding commitments, while committees of experts (treaty bodies) monitor compliance of states parties. Together, the *Universal Declaration*, the *International Covenants* and the *First* and *Second Optional Protocols to the International Covenant on Civil and Political Rights* constitute the **International Bill of Human Rights**.

Economic, social and cultural rights

The *International Covenant on Economic, Social and Cultural Rights* entered into force in 1976, and had 164 states parties as at 31 December 2016. The human rights that the *Covenant* seeks to promote and protect include:

- the right to work in just and favourable conditions;
- the right to social protection, to an adequate standard of living and to the highest attainable standards of physical and mental well-being; and
- the right to education and the enjoyment of benefits of cultural freedom and scientific progress.

The *Covenant* provides for the realization of these rights without discrimination of any kind. The **Committee on Economic, Social and Cultural Rights** (www2.ohchr.org/english/bodies/cescr) was established in 1985 by the Economic and Social Council to monitor implementation of the *Covenant* by states parties. This 18-member body of experts studies reports periodically submitted by states parties in accordance with article 16 of the *Covenant* and discusses them with representatives of the states concerned. The Committee makes recommendations to states based on its review of their reports. It also adopts general comments which seek to outline the meaning of human rights or cross-cutting themes.

In 2008, the General Assembly unanimously adopted an *Optional Protocol* to the *Covenant*, which provides the Committee on Economic, Social and Cultural Rights, with regard to individual complaints, competence to receive and consider communications. The *Optional Protocol* entered into force on 5 May 2013 and had 22 states parties and 45 signatories as at 31 December 2016.

Civil and political rights

The *International Covenant on Civil and Political Rights* and its *First Optional Protocol* entered into force in 1976. The *Covenant* had 168 states parties as at 31 December 2016.

The *Covenant* deals with such rights as freedom of movement; equality before the law; the right to a fair trial and presumption of innocence; freedom of thought, conscience and religion; freedom of opinion and expression; peaceful assembly; freedom of association; participation in public affairs and elections; and protection of minority rights. It prohibits arbitrary deprivation of life; torture, cruel or degrading treatment or punishment; slavery and forced labour; arbitrary arrest or detention; arbitrary interference with privacy; war propaganda; discrimination; and advocacy of racial or religious hatred.

The *Covenant* has two optional protocols. The *First Optional Protocol* (1966) provides the right of petition to individuals who claim to be victims of a violation of a right contained in the *Covenant*; it had 115 states parties as at 31 December 2016. The Second *Optional Protocol* (1989) establishes substantive obligations towards abolition of the death penalty; it had 83 state parties as at 31 December 2016.

The *Covenant* established an 18-member **Human Rights Committee** (www2.ohchr.org/english/bodies/hrc/index.htm) which considers reports submitted periodically by states parties on measures to implement the provisions of the *Covenant*. For states parties to the *First Optional Protocol*, the Committee also considers communications from individuals who claim to be victims of violations of any of the rights set forth in the *Covenant*. The Committee considers such communications in closed meetings; all related communications and documents remain confidential. The findings of the Committee, however, are made public and are reproduced in its annual report to the General Assembly. The Committee also publishes its interpretation of the content of human rights provisions, known as "general comments", on thematic issues or its methods of work.

Spanish artist Cristóbal Gabarrón conducts a painting session with children
at an event marking Human Rights Day (10 December) at the Palais des Nations in Geneva.
Gabarrón created the "Enlightened Universe", a sculpture commemorating
the 70th anniversary of the UN (9 December 2016, UN Photo/Violaine Martin).

Other conventions

The *Universal Declaration of Human Rights* has served as the inspiration for some 80 conventions and declarations that have been concluded within the United Nations on a wide range of issues. Among the earliest of these were conventions on the crime of genocide and on the status of refugees called for at the time, as the world had just emerged from the horrors of the Second World War, the Holocaust and the uprooting of millions of people. They have remained just as pertinent in the new millennium.

- The *Convention on the Prevention and Punishment of the Crime of Genocide* (1948), a direct response to the atrocities of the Second World War, defines the crime of genocide as the commission of certain acts with intent to destroy a national, ethnic, racial or religious group, and commits states to bringing to justice alleged perpetrators. It had 147 states parties and 41 signatories as at 31 December 2016.
- The *Convention relating to the Status of Refugees* (1951), which had 145 states parties and 19 signatories as at 31 December 2016, defines the rights of refugees, especially their right not to be forcibly returned to countries where they are at risk. It also provides for their everyday lives, including their right to work, education, public assistance and social security, and their right to travel documents. The *Protocol relating to the Status of Refugees* (1967) ensures the universal application of the *Convention*, which

was originally designed for people who became refugees as a result of the Second World War. As at 31 December 2016, the *Protocol* had 146 states parties.

In parallel to the *International Covenants*, seven more so-called "core" international human rights treaties (www.ohchr.org/EN/ProfessionalInterest/Pages/CoreInstruments. aspx) are monitored for compliance by states parties. Each of the treaties described below has established a committee of experts—usually referred to as a "treaty body"—to monitor implementation of treaty provisions. Some of these treaties are supplemented by optional protocols dealing with specific concerns, including the possibility for individual persons to file a complaint if they believe they have been a victim of a human rights violation.

- The *International Convention on the Elimination of All Forms of Racial Discrimination* (1966) is accepted by 177 states parties as at 31 December 2016. Based on the premise that any policy of superiority based on racial differences is unjustifiable, scientifically false, and morally and legally condemnable, it defines "racial discrimination" and commits states parties to take measures to abolish it in both law and practice. The *Convention* established a treaty body, the **Committee on the Elimination of Racial Discrimination**, to consider reports from states parties, as well as petitions from individuals alleging a violation of the *Convention*, if the state concerned has accepted this optional procedure of the *Convention*.
- The *Convention on the Elimination of All Forms of Discrimination against Women* (1979), with 189 states parties as at 31 December 2016, guarantees women's equality before the law and specifies measures to eliminate discrimination against women with respect to political and public life, nationality, education, employment, health, financial credit, rural development, marriage and family relations. The **Committee on the Elimination of Discrimination against Women** is the treaty body that monitors implementation and considers reports from states parties. The *Optional Protocol* to the *Convention* (1999), with 108 states parties as at 31 December 2016, allows individuals to submit to the Committee complaints on violations and provides the Committee with a mandate to conduct inquiries if information indicates grave or systematic violations of the *Convention*.
- The *Convention against Torture and Other Cruel, Inhuman or Degrading Treatment or Punishment* (1984), with 160 states parties, defines torture as an international crime, holds states parties accountable for preventing it and requires them to punish perpetrators. No exceptional circumstances may be invoked to justify torture, nor may a torturer offer a defence of having acted under orders. The *Convention*'s monitoring treaty body is the **Committee against Torture**. It reviews reports of states parties, receives and considers petitions from individuals whose states have accepted this procedure, and initiates investigations regarding countries where it believes that torture is serious and systematic. The *Optional Protocol* to the *Convention* (2002) created the **Subcommittee on Prevention of Torture** and allows in-country inspections of places of detention. The *Protocol* also provides for the establishment of national preventive mechanisms. As at 31 December 2016, it had 83 states parties.
- The *Convention on the Rights of the Child* (1989) recognizes children, defined as persons up to the age of 18 years, as right holders. The *Convention* establishes in international law that states must ensure that all children—without discrimination in any form—benefit from special protection measures and assistance. It brings together in one comprehensive code protections for children in all categories of human rights. The *Convention* guarantees non-discrimination and recognizes that the best

interests of the child must guide all actions. Special attention is paid to children who are refugees or members of minorities. States parties are to provide guarantees for children's survival, development, protection and participation. The *Convention* is the most broadly ratified treaty, with 196 states parties as at 31 December 2016. The **Committee on the Rights of the Child**, established by the *Convention*, oversees implementation and considers reports submitted by states parties. The *Convention* has three optional protocols: one on the involvement of children in armed conflict; another on the sale of children, child prostitution and child pornography; and another on a communications procedure that allows children to submit complaints regarding violations of their rights under the *Convention* and permit the undertaking of inquiries if information indicates grave or systematic violations of the *Convention* and its first two *Optional Protocols*. These three optional protocols had, respectively, 166, 173 and 29 states parties as at 31 December 2016.

- The *International Convention on the Protection of the Rights of All Migrant Workers and Members of Their Families* (1990) defines basic rights of, and measures to protect, migrant workers, whether documented or undocumented, throughout the process of migration. It entered into force in 2003 and had 49 states parties as at 31 December 2016. Its monitoring treaty body is the **Committee on Migrant Workers.**

- The *Convention on the Rights of Persons with Disabilities* (2006) recognizes all human rights and dignity of persons with disabilities. The *Convention* outlaws discrimination against the world's 650 million persons with disabilities, in all areas of life, including employment, education, health services, transportation and access to justice. It entered into force in 2008 and, as at 31 December 2016, 171 states and the European Union (EU) were parties to the *Convention*. Its monitoring body is the **Committee on the Rights of Persons with Disabilities.** An *Optional Protocol* to the *Convention* gives individuals recourse to that Committee when all national options have been exhausted. The *Optional Protocol* had 92 parties as at 31 December 2016.

- The *International Convention for the Protection of All Persons from Enforced Disappearance* (2006) prohibits the practice of enforced disappearance and calls on states parties to make it an offence under law. It also affirms the right of victims and their families to know the circumstances of such disappearances and the fate of the disappeared person, as well as to claim reparations. It entered into force in 2010 and had 54 states parties as at 31 December 2016.

The *Universal Declaration* and other UN instruments have also formed part of the background to several regional agreements, such as the *European Convention on Human Rights*, the *American Convention on Human Rights* and the *African Charter of Human and Peoples' Rights*.

Other standards

The United Nations has adopted many other standards and rules on the protection of human rights. These declarations, codes of conduct and principles are not treaties to which states become party. Nevertheless, they have a profound influence, not least because they are carefully drafted by states and adopted by consensus. Some of the most important of these are described.

- The *Declaration on the Elimination of All Forms of Intolerance and of Discrimination Based on Religion and Belief* (1981) affirms the right of everyone to freedom of thought, conscience and religion and the right not to be subject to discrimination on the grounds of religion or other beliefs.

- The *Declaration on the Right to Development* (1986) establishes that right as "an inalienable human right by virtue of which each person and all peoples are entitled to participate in, contribute to and enjoy economic, social, cultural and political development, in which all human rights and fundamental freedoms can be fully realized". It adds that "equality of opportunity for development is a prerogative both of nations and of individuals".
- The *Declaration on the Rights of Persons Belonging to National or Ethnic, Religious and Linguistic Minorities* (1992) proclaims the right of minorities to enjoy their own culture; to profess and practice their own religion; to use their own language; and to leave any country, including their own, and to return to their country.
- The *Declaration on Human Rights Defenders* (1998) seeks to recognize, promote and protect the work of human rights activists all over the world. It enshrines the right of everyone—individually and in association with others—to promote and strive to protect human rights at the national and international levels, and to participate in peaceful activities against human rights violations. States are to take all necessary measures to protect human rights defenders against any violence, threat, retaliation, pressure or other arbitrary action.
- The *Durban Declaration and Programme of Action* (DDPA) (2001) describes the sources, causes, forms and contemporary manifestations of racism, racial discrimination, xenophobia and related intolerance, and identifies various groups which are victims of such racism and related phenomena. It sets out, at the national, regional and international levels measures of prevention, education and protection aimed at the eradication of racism and related intolerance; as well as provisions for effective remedies, recourse and compensatory measures. The DDPA also designed strategies to achieve full and effective equality.

Other important non-treaty standards include the *Standard Minimum Rules for the Treatment of Prisoners* (1957), the *Basic Principles on the Independence of the Judiciary* (1985), the *Body of Principles for the Protection of All Persons under Any Form of Detention or Imprisonment* (1988) and the *Basic Principles on the Role of Lawyers* (1990), among many others.

HUMAN RIGHTS MACHINERY

Human Rights Council

The **Human Rights Council** (www.ohchr.org/EN/HRBodies/HRC) is the main United Nations intergovernmental body responsible for promoting and protecting all human rights and fundamental freedoms. It was established by the General Assembly in 2006 to replace the 60-year-old Commission on Human Rights. The Council addresses human rights violations and makes corresponding recommendations. It responds to human rights emergencies, works to prevent abuses, provides overall policy guidance, develops new international norms, monitors the observance of human rights around the world, and assists states in fulfilling their human rights obligations. It provides an international forum where states (members and observers), intergovernmental organizations, national human rights institutions and NGOs can voice their concerns about human rights issues.

The Council's 47 members are elected directly and individually by secret ballot by the majority of the 193 members of the UN General Assembly. They serve for a three-year renewable term and cannot seek immediate re-election after two consecutive terms. The membership is based on equitable geographical distribution. Thirteen seats each are devoted to the Group of African States and the Group of Asia-Pacific States; eight to the Group of Latin American and Caribbean States; seven to the Group of Western European and other States; and six to the Group of Eastern European States.

The Council meets regularly throughout the year. It holds no fewer than three sessions per year, for no less than 10 weeks in total. Special sessions can be requested at any time by a member state with the support of one third of the Council's members. In 2016, two special sessions were held: one on the deteriorating human rights situation in Syria, and another on the human rights situation in South Sudan.

The Council can rely on the independence and expertise of a wide range of experts and working groups. It can set up commissions of inquiry and fact-finding missions to investigate alleged violations of human rights, provide assistance to states, engage in dialogue with governments to bring about needed improvements and condemn abuses. Through its complaint procedure, the Council can be seized of gross and systematic human rights violations by individuals, groups or NGOs. The procedure is the only universal complaint procedure covering all human rights and fundamental freedoms in all states.

The work of the Human Rights Council is also supported by the **Human Rights Council Advisory Committee**. Composed of 18 experts, the Committee serves as the Council's "think-tank" and provides it with expertise and advice on human rights issues such as missing persons, the right to food, leprosy-related discrimination, and human rights education and training. In the performance of its mandate, the Committee interacts with states, intergovernmental organizations, national human rights institutions, NGOs and other civil society entities.

Universal periodic review. The most innovative feature of the Human Rights Council is the universal periodic review (UPR). This unique mechanism involves a review of the human rights records of all 193 UN member states once every four years. The UPR is a cooperative, state-driven process, under the auspices of the Council, which provides the opportunity for each state to present measures taken and challenges to be met to improve the human rights situation in their country and to meet their international obligations. It is designed to ensure universality and equality of treatment for every country.

UN High Commissioner for Human Rights

The **United Nations High Commissioner for Human Rights** exercises principal responsibility for UN human rights activities. Appointed for a four-year term, the High Commissioner is tasked with, among others, promoting and protecting the effective enjoyment by all of all human rights; making recommendations to UN system bodies to improve human rights; providing advice and assistance for human rights activities; coordinating UN human rights education and public information programmes; working to remove obstacles to the realization of human rights and prevent the continuation of human rights violations; engaging in dialogue with governments; promoting international cooperation for human rights; and stimulating and coordinating human rights activities throughout the UN system. Under the direction and authority of the Secretary-General, the High Commissioner reports to the Human Rights Council and the General Assembly.

The **Office of the High Commissioner for Human Rights** (OHCHR) (www.ohchr. org) is the focal point for UN human rights activities. It serves as the secretariat for the Human Rights Council, the treaty bodies (expert committees that monitor treaty compliance) and other UN human rights organs. It monitors and reports on human rights, provides advisory services, implements technical cooperation programmes, and promotes the global and national adoption of and adherence to human rights norms and standards. OHCHR also works with international human rights mechanisms and bodies in developing and monitoring international human rights standards, while contributing to national efforts to implement those standards on the ground.

Special procedures

The special procedures of the Human Rights Council (www.ohchr.org/EN/HRBodies/SP/Pages/Introduction.aspx) are on the front lines in the protection of human rights. They investigate violations and intervene in individual cases and emergency situations. They are independent human rights experts with mandates to report and advise on human rights from a thematic or country-specific perspective.

Special procedures are either an individual (called "special rapporteur" or "independent expert") or a working group composed of five members, one from each of the five UN regional groupings: Africa, Asia, Latin America and the Caribbean, Eastern Europe and the Western group. Special procedures are appointed by the Human Rights Council and serve in their personal capacities. The independent status of the mandate-holders is crucial for them to be able to fulfil their functions in all impartiality. The tenure of special procedures is limited to a maximum of six years.

Special procedures make country visits, act on individual cases of alleged violations and concerns of a broader nature by sending communications to states, conduct thematic studies and convene expert consultations, engage in advocacy and raise public awareness, and provide advice for technical cooperation. They report annually to the Human Rights Council; the majority of the mandates also report to the General Assembly. As at 31 December 2016, there were 43 thematic and 14 country-specific special procedure mandates.

Country-specific special rapporteurs, independent experts and representatives currently report on Belarus, Cambodia, the Central African Republic, Côte d'Ivoire, the Democratic People's Republic of Korea, Eritrea, Haiti, Iran, Mali, Myanmar, Palestinian territories occupied since 1967, Somalia, the Sudan and Syria.

Thematic special rapporteurs, representatives and working groups currently report on people of African descent; albinism; arbitrary detention; business and human rights; cultural rights; disability; enforced or involuntary disappearances; right to development; education; environment; summary executions; the right to food; foreign debt; freedom of peaceful assembly and association; freedom of opinion and expression; freedom of religion or belief; physical and mental health; adequate housing; human rights defenders; independence of judges and lawyers; indigenous peoples; internally displaced persons; international order; international solidarity; mercenaries; migrants; minority issues; older persons; poverty; privacy; sale of children; sexual orientation and gender identity; slavery; racism and racial discrimination; countering terrorism; torture; hazardous substances and wastes; trafficking in persons; truth, justice, reparation and guarantees of non-recurrence; unilateral coercive measures; violence against women; water and sanitation; and discrimination against women.

PROMOTING AND PROTECTING HUMAN RIGHTS

The role and scope of UN action in promoting and protecting human rights continue to expand. The central mandate of the Organization is to ensure full respect for the human dignity of the "peoples of the United Nations", in whose name the *Charter of the United Nations* was written.

Through human rights education, the UN seeks to advance a universal culture of human rights by building knowledge, skills, attitudes and behaviours which uphold human rights. The World Programme for Human Rights Education (2005-ongoing) (www.ohchr.org/EN/Issues/Education/Training/Pages/Programme.aspx) provides a common platform for action, particularly at the national level, and fosters participatory and learner-centered methodologies in formal and non-formal settings. Programmes for children and adults and related tools and resources have been increasingly developed through cooperation among governmental institutions, academia, national human rights institutions and non-governmental organizations. Human rights education also plays a fundamental role in the implementation of the 2030 Agenda for Sustainable Development, as a specific constituent of the goal to ensure quality education for all, and is a key force for realizing all goals.

Through its international machinery, the UN is working on many fronts.

- As *global conscience*—setting the pace in establishing international standards of acceptable behaviour by nations; it has kept the world's attention focused on practices that threaten to undermine human rights standards. The General Assembly, through a wide range of declarations and conventions, has underscored the universality of human rights principles.
- As *lawmaker*—giving impetus to an unprecedented codification of international law; human rights pertaining to women, children, prisoners, detainees and persons with mental disabilities, as well as to such violations as genocide, racial discrimination and torture, are now a major feature of international law, which once focused almost exclusively on inter-state relations.
- As *monitor*—playing a central role in ensuring that human rights are not only defined, but also protected; the *International Covenant on Civil and Political Rights* and that on *Economic, Social and Cultural Rights* (1966) are among the earliest examples of treaties that empower international bodies to monitor how states live up to their commitments. Treaty bodies and special procedures of the Human Rights Council each have procedures and mechanisms to monitor compliance with international standards and to investigate alleged violations. Their decisions on specific cases carry a moral weight that few governments are willing to defy.
- As *nerve centre*—OHCHR receives communications from groups and individuals claiming violations of their human rights. More than 100,000 complaints are received every year. OHCHR refers these communications to the appropriate UN bodies and mechanisms, taking into account the implementation procedures established by conventions and resolutions. Requests for urgent intervention can be addressed to OHCHR by fax (41 22 917 9022) and e-mail (petitions@ohchr.org).
- As *defender*—when a rapporteur or the chairman of a working group learns that a serious human rights violation, such as torture or imminent extrajudicial execution, is about to occur, he or she may address an urgent message to the state concerned, requesting clarification and seeking guarantees that the alleged victim's rights will be protected.
- As *researcher*—compiling data that is indispensable to the development and application of human rights law; studies and reports prepared by OHCHR at the request of UN bodies point the way towards new policies, practices and institutions to enhance respect for human rights.
- As *forum of appeal*—under the *First Optional Protocol to the International Covenant on Civil and Political Rights*, as well as the *International Convention on the Elimination of All Forms of Racial Discrimination*, the *Convention Against Torture*, the *Optional Protocol to the Convention on the Elimination of All Forms of Discrimination against Women*, the *Optional Protocol to the Convention on the Rights of Persons with Disabilities*, the

International Convention for the Protection of All Persons from Enforced Disappearance, the *Optional Protocol* to the *International Covenant on Economic, Social and Cultural Rights*, and the *Optional Protocol* to the *Convention on the Rights of the Child* on a communications procedure, individuals can bring complaints against states that have accepted the relevant complaint procedure, once all domestic remedies have been exhausted. In addition, the special procedures of the Human Rights Council, as well as its complaint procedure deal with numerous complaints submitted annually by NGOs or individuals.

- As *fact-finder*—the Human Rights Council has mechanisms to monitor and report on the incidence of certain kinds of abuses, as well as on violations in a specific country. The special procedures mandate holders are entrusted with this politically sensitive, humanitarian and sometimes dangerous task. They gather facts, keep contact with local groups and government authorities, conduct on-site visits when governments permit, and make recommendations on how respect for human rights might be strengthened.

- As *discreet diplomat*—the Secretary-General and the UN High Commissioner for Human Rights raise human rights concerns with member states on a confidential basis on such issues as the release of prisoners and the commutation of death sentences. The Human Rights Council may ask the Secretary-General to intervene or send an expert to examine a specific human rights situation, with a view to preventing flagrant violations. The Secretary-General may also undertake quiet diplomacy in the exercise of his good offices to communicate the legitimate concerns of the United Nations and curb abuses.

The right to development

The principle of equality of opportunity for development is deeply embedded in the *Charter of the United Nations* and the *Universal Declaration on Human Rights*. The *Declaration on the Right to Development*, adopted by the General Assembly in 1986, marked a turning point by proclaiming this an inalienable human right, by which each person and all peoples are entitled to participate in, contribute to and enjoy economic, social, cultural and political development. The right to development is given prominence in the 1993 *Vienna Declaration and Programme of Action* of the Second World Conference on Human Rights, and is cited in the outcomes of other major UN summits and conferences, including the 2030 Agenda for Sustainable Development. In 1998, the Commission on Human Rights established a working group to monitor progress, analyze obstacles and develop strategies for implementing the right to development. On 22 September 2016, the General Assembly convened a high-level segment meeting to commemorate the thirtieth anniversary of the *Declaration* (www.ohchr.org/EN/Issues/Development).

The right to food

The right to food is a particular focus of the **Food and Agriculture Organization of the United Nations (FAO)** (www.fao.org). In support of that right, in 2004, the FAO Council adopted its *Voluntary Guidelines to Support the Progressive Realisation of the Right to Adequate Food in the Context of National Food Security*. These "Right to Food Guidelines" cover actions governments can consider to create an environment that enables people to feed themselves with dignity and to establish safety nets for those who are unable to do so. They also recommend measures to strengthen government accountability and promote integration of the human rights dimension in the work of agencies dealing with food and agriculture. The guidelines have transformed principles into practice; the right to food is now part of the constitutions and legal frameworks of over 30 countries.

Labour rights

The **International Labour Organization (ILO)** (www.ilo.org) is the UN specialized agency entrusted with defining, protecting and promoting decent work for all men and women, including workers' rights. Its tripartite **International Labour Conference**— made up of government, employer and worker representatives—had adopted 189 conventions and 204 recommendations as at 10 June 2016 on all aspects of work life, comprising a system of international labour laws. While its recommendations provide guidance on policy, legislation and practice, its conventions create binding obligations for those states that ratify them.

Conventions and recommendations have been adopted on such matters as labour administration, industrial relations, employment policy, working conditions, social security, occupational safety and health. Some seek to ensure basic human rights in the workplace, while others address such issues as the employment of women and children, and special categories such as migrant workers and persons with disabilities (www.ilo.org/global/standards).

ILO's supervisory procedure to ensure that its conventions are applied both in law and in practice is based on objective evaluations by independent experts, and on the examination of cases by the ILO tripartite bodies. There is also a special procedure for investigating complaints of infringement of the freedom of association.

ILO has brought about many landmark conventions, including the following:

- on *forced labour* (1930): requires the suppression of forced or compulsory labour in all its forms. The *Protocol* to the *Convention*, adopted by the International Labour Conference in 2014, requires governments to take new measures tackling forced labour in all its forms;
- on *freedom of association and protection of the right to organize* (1948): establishes the right of workers and employers to form and join organizations without prior authorization, and lays down guarantees for the free functioning of such organizations;
- on *the right to organize and collective bargaining* (1949): provides for protection against anti-union discrimination, protection of workers' and employers' organizations, and measures to promote collective bargaining;
- on *equal remuneration* (1951): calls for equal pay and benefits for work of equal value;
- on *discrimination* (1958): calls for national policies to promote equality of opportunity and treatment, and to eliminate discrimination in the workplace on grounds of race, colour, sex, religion, political opinion, extraction or social origin;
- on *minimum age* (1973): aims at the abolition of child labour, stipulating that the minimum age for employment shall not be less than the age of completion of compulsory schooling;
- on *the worst forms of child labour* (1999): prohibits child slavery, debt bondage, prostitution and pornography, dangerous work, and forcible recruitment for armed conflict;
- on *maternity protection* (2000): provides standards for maternity leave, employment protection, medical benefits and breaks for breastfeeding;
- on *maritime labour* (2006): establishes minimum working and living standards for all seafarers and provides a level playing field for ship owners; and
- on *domestic workers* (2011): addresses exclusions of domestic workers from labour and social protection.

In 2010, the ILO Conference adopted a groundbreaking international labour standard on HIV/AIDS, the first international human rights instrument to focus specifically on this issue in the world of work. It provides for antidiscrimination measures and emphasizes the importance of employment and income-generating activities for workers and people living with HIV.

The General Assembly has also taken a number of measures to protect the rights of migrant workers.

THE STRUGGLE AGAINST DISCRIMINATION

Apartheid

One of the great successes of the United Nations was the abolition of apartheid in South Africa, which demonstrated ways in which it can bring an end to major injustices in the world. Practically from its inception, the UN was involved in the struggle against apartheid, a system of institutionalized racial segregation and discrimination imposed by the South African government from 1948 until the early 1990s.

Apartheid was condemned by the UN in 1966 as a "crime against humanity" incompatible with the *Charter* and the *Universal Declaration of Human Rights*, and it remained on the General Assembly's agenda until its demise:

- During the 1950s, the General Assembly repeatedly appealed to the South African government to abandon apartheid in light of the principles of the *Charter*.
- In 1962, it established the United Nations Special Committee against Apartheid, to keep the racial policies of South Africa under review. The Special Committee became the focal point of international efforts to promote a comprehensive programme of action against apartheid.
- In 1963, the Security Council instituted a voluntary arms embargo against South Africa.
- The Assembly refused to accept South Africa's credentials to its regular sessions from 1970 through 1974. Following this ban, South Africa did not participate in further proceedings of the Assembly until the end of apartheid in 1994.
- In 1971, the Assembly called for a sports boycott of South Africa, a move that had strong impact on public opinion within the country and abroad.
- In 1973, the Assembly adopted the *International Convention on the Suppression and Punishment of the Crime of Apartheid*.
- In 1977, the Council made its arms embargo against South Africa mandatory, after determining that the country's aggressions against its neighbours and its potential nuclear capability constituted a threat to international peace and security. This was the first such action by the Council against a member state.
- In 1985, the Assembly adopted the *International Convention Against Apartheid in Sports*.
- Also in 1985, when the South African government proclaimed a state of emergency and escalated repression, the Security Council, for the first time, called on governments to take significant economic measures against South Africa under Chapter VII of the *Charter*.
- In 1990, the transition from the apartheid government to a non-racial democracy was facilitated by a national peace accord between the government and major political parties, with the full support of the UN.

In 1992, the Security Council deployed the United Nations Observer Mission in South Africa (UNOMSA) to strengthen the structures of the accord. UNOMSA observed the 1994 elections that led to the establishment of a non-racial, democratic government. With the installation of that government and the adoption of the country's first non-racial, democratic constitution, apartheid came to an end.

When the newly elected President, Nelson Mandela, addressed the General Assembly in 1994, he noted that it was the first time in its 49 years that the Assembly had been addressed by a South African head of state drawn from among the African majority. Welcoming the vanquishing of apartheid, he observed: "That historic change has come about not least because of the great efforts in which the United Nations engaged to ensure the suppression of the apartheid crime against humanity."

Racism

In 1963, the General Assembly adopted the *United Nations Declaration on the Elimination of All Forms of Racial Discrimination*. The *Declaration* affirms the fundamental equality of all persons and confirms that discrimination between human beings on the grounds of race, colour or ethnic origin is a violation of the human rights proclaimed in the *Universal Declaration* and an obstacle to friendly and peaceful relations among nations and peoples. Two years later, the Assembly adopted the *International Convention on the Elimination of All Forms of Racial Discrimination*, which obliges states parties to adopt legislative, judicial, administrative and other measures to prevent and punish racial discrimination. The **Committee on the Elimination of Racial Discrimination** monitors the implementation of the *Convention* by its state parties, including examining the regular reports which states parties must submit to the Committee on how the rights are being implemented. The Committee reviews each report and addresses its concerns and recommendations to the state party in the form of "concluding observations".

In 1993, the General Assembly proclaimed the Third Decade to Combat Racism and Racial Discrimination (1993–2003) and called on all states to take measures to combat new forms of racism, especially through laws, administrative measures, education and information. Also in 1993, the Commission on Human Rights appointed a special rapporteur on contemporary forms of racism, racial discrimination, xenophobia and related intolerance. Since then, four persons have fulfilled this mandate, which has been regularly extended by the Human Rights Council.

The third World Conference against Racism, Racial Discrimination, Xenophobia and Related Intolerance, held in 2001, focused on practical measures to eradicate racism, including measures of prevention, education and protection; and adopted the *Durban Declaration and Programme of Action*. In 2009, the Durban Review Conference evaluated progress towards the goals set by the World Conference and adopted the Durban Review Conference outcome document. On 22 September 2011, the General Assembly held a one-day high-level meeting at UN Headquarters in New York to commemorate the tenth anniversary of the adoption of the *Declaration and Programme of Action*. In a political declaration adopted at the meeting, world leaders proclaimed their determination to make the fight against racism, racial discrimination, xenophobia and related intolerance a high priority for their countries.

There are three mechanisms mandated to follow up the *Declaration and Programme of Action*: the Intergovernmental Working Group on the Effective Implementation of the Durban Declaration and Programme of Action, the Ad Hoc Committee on the Elaboration of Complementary Standards, and the Working Group of Experts on People of African Descent.

In previous years, people of African descent have received particular attention. In 2011, the UN observed the *International Year for People of African Descent*. In 2013, the

General Assembly proclaimed the *International Decade for People of African Descent*, which is being observed from 2015 to 2024. It provides a framework for UN member states, civil society and all other relevant actors to join together with people of African descent and take measures to implement the *Decade's* programme of activities and to improve their human rights situation.

The rights of women

Equality for women has been a focus of the work of the United Nations since its founding in 1945. The UN has played a leading role in the global effort for the promotion and protection of the human rights of women; the elimination of all forms of discrimination and violence against women; and efforts to ensure that women have full and equal access to, and opportunities for participation in, politics and public life, including all aspects of economic and social development and decision-making.

The General Assembly created **UN-Women** (www.unwomen.org), the **United Nations Entity for Gender Equality and the Empowerment of Women** in 2010 as part of the UN reform agenda, bringing together resources and mandates for greater impact. UN-Women aims to boost efforts to expand opportunities for women and girls and to tackle discrimination worldwide. Support to intergovernmental bodies in the formulation of global standards and norms on gender equality is one of UN-Women's three principal functions. UN-Women runs a number of public advocacy campaigns to advance women's empowerment, rights and gender equality. Its **Planet 50-50 by 2030: Step It Up for Gender Equality** campaign supports implementation of the SDGs (www.unwomen.org/en/get-involved/step-it-up). By late 2016, nearly 100 Governments had made concrete commitments to advance women's empowerment in the context of the campaign. UN-Women also manages the **UNiTE to End Violence against Women** campaign (www.un.org/en/women/endviolence/index.shtml), which works to raise public awareness and increase political will and resources for preventing and ending all forms of violence against women and girls in all parts of the world. **HeForShe** (www.heforshe.org) is UN-Women's solidarity movement for gender equality, targeting men and boys in particular. Signed by 1.1 million people in late 2016, the campaign has also engaged 10 heads of state and government, 10 global CEOs and 10 university presidents to drive change from the top.

The **Commission on the Status of Women** has elaborated international treaties and recommendations for women's equality and non-discrimination—notably, the 1979 *Convention on the Elimination of All Forms of Discrimination against Women* and its 1999 *Optional Protocol*. It also prepared the *Declaration on the Elimination of All Forms of Violence against Women*, adopted by the General Assembly in 1993, which, among other things, defined violence against women as physical, sexual or psychological violence occurring in the family or the community and perpetrated or condoned by the state. The Commission issues agreed conclusions at its annual sessions that provide guidance to Governments and other stakeholders aimed at the accelerated implementation of the *Declaration* and *Platform for Action*.

The **Committee on the Elimination of Discrimination against Women**, a body made up of 23 independent experts, monitors implementation of the *Convention* by states parties. It considers reports submitted by states parties to assess their progress in achieving the principle of equality of women and men. It also makes general recommendations on issues affecting women to which it believes states parties should devote more attention. The Committee can also examine individual petitions and carry out inquiries under the provisions of the *Convention's Optional Protocol*.

The rights of children

Millions of children die every year from malnutrition and disease. Countless others become victims of war, natural disaster, HIV/AIDS and extreme forms of violence, exploitation and abuse. Millions of children, especially girls, do not have access to quality education. The **United Nations Children's Fund (UNICEF)**, as well as OHCHR and other UN agencies, strive to sustain global commitment to the *Convention on the Rights of the Child*, which embodies universal ethical principles and international legal standards of behaviour towards children. UNICEF supports programmes providing education, counselling and care to children working in very hazardous or abusive conditions, and vigorously advocates against the violation of their rights.

The **Committee on the Rights of the Child**, established under the *Convention*, is a body of 18 independent experts that meets regularly to monitor the progress made by states parties in fulfilling their obligations under the *Convention* and its first two *Optional Protocols*. It makes recommendations to governments on ways to meet those obligations. The Committee also issues its interpretation of the *Convention*'s provisions in the form of general comments.

The General Assembly in 2000 adopted two *Optional Protocols* to the *Convention*: one prohibits the recruitment of children under 18 into armed forces or their participation in hostilities; the other strengthens prohibitions and penalties concerning the sale of children, child prostitution and child pornography. A third *Optional Protocol*, adopted by the Assembly in 2011, entered into force in 2014. It provides a communications procedure that allows individual children to submit complaints regarding violations of their rights under the *Convention* and the first two *Protocols*.

Concerning child labour, the UN seeks to protect children from exploitation and hazardous conditions that endanger their physical and mental development; to ensure children's access to quality education, nutrition and health care; and, in the long term, progressively eliminate child labour. The **International Programme on the Elimination of Child Labour**, an ILO initiative, seeks to raise awareness and mobilize action through the provision of technical cooperation. Direct interventions focus on the prevention of child labour; the search for alternatives, including decent employment for parents; and rehabilitation, education and vocational training for children. UNICEF supports programmes providing education, counselling and care to children working in hazardous or abusive conditions, and advocates against the violation of their rights.

Both the General Assembly and the Human Rights Council have urged governments to take action to protect and promote the rights of children, particularly children in difficult situations. They have called on states to implement programmes and measures that provide children with special protection and assistance, including access to health care, education and social services, as well as (where appropriate) voluntary repatriation, reintegration, family tracing and family reunification, in particular for children who are unaccompanied. The two bodies have also called on states to ensure that the best interests of the child are accorded primary consideration.

The special rapporteur on the sale of children, child prostitution and child pornography, as well as the special representatives of the Secretary-General on violence against children and for children and armed conflict, report regularly to the General Assembly and to the Human Rights Council. The latter also reports to the Security Council.

The post of special representative of the Secretary-General on violence against children was established in 2007, in the wake of the *World Report on Violence against Children*, which was presented to the General Assembly the previous year. The *Report* exposed for the first time the horrendous scale and impact of all forms of violence against children, highlighting the universality and magnitude of the problem in different settings: the home and family; schools; care and justice institutions; the workplace; and the community. Its 12 overarching recommendations and a number of specific recommendations have provided a comprehensive framework for follow-up action. The mandate of the special representative of the Secretary-General for children and armed conflict, established in 1996 by the Assembly for a period of three years, has been renewed ever since, most recently in 2015, for a further three-year period.

The rights of minorities

Some 1 billion people worldwide belong to minority groups, many of which are subject to discrimination and exclusion, and are often the victims of conflict. Meeting the legitimate aspirations of national, ethnic, religious and linguistic groups strengthens the protection of basic human rights, protects and accommodates cultural diversity, and increases the stability of society as a whole. The United Nations has from its inception placed minority rights high on its human rights agenda. The protection of the human rights of members of minority groups is guaranteed specifically in article 27 of the *International Covenant on Civil and Political Rights*, as well as in the principles of non-discrimination and participation, which are basic to all UN human rights law. The adoption of the *Declaration on the Rights of Persons Belonging to National or Ethnic, Religious and Linguistic Minorities* by the General Assembly in 1992 gave new impetus to the UN human rights agenda. Since 2005, OHCHR has organized the Minorities Fellowship Programme. It aims to give national or ethnic, religious and linguistic minorities an opportunity to gain knowledge of the UN system and international human rights mechanisms and learn practical skills on employing these mechanisms in order to protect and promote the rights of persons belonging to their own minority communities.

The **Forum on Minority Issues** (www.ohchr.org/EN/HRBodies/HRC/Minority/Pages/ForumIndex.aspx) was established in 2007 to provide a platform for promoting dialogue and cooperation on issues pertaining to national or ethnic, religious and linguistic minorities, and to provide thematic contributions and expertise to the work of the independent expert on minority issues. The Forum identifies and analyses best practices, challenges, opportunities and initiatives for the further implementation of the *Declaration*. It meets annually for two days of thematic discussions. The independent expert on minority issues guides the work of the Forum and reports its recommendations to the Human Rights Council. The president of the Human Rights Council appoints for each session, on the basis of regional rotation and in consultation with regional groups, a Forum chairperson selected from experts on minority issues.

OHCHR works to raise the visibility of the *Minorities Declaration* through a series of engagements including by leading the UN Network on Racial Discrimination and Protection of Minorities, established in March 2012. The Network enhances dialogue and cooperation between relevant UN departments, agencies, programmes and funds. It also helps member states develop strategies to open opportunities to marginalized minority groups, and to build-in greater protection for their human rights.

Indigenous peoples

The United Nations has increasingly taken up the cause of indigenous peoples, who constitute one of the world's most disadvantaged groups. Indigenous peoples are also called first peoples, tribal peoples, aboriginal peoples and autochthons. There are at least 5,000 indigenous peoples groups, made up of some 370 million individuals living in over 90 countries on five continents. Often excluded from decision-making processes, many have been marginalized, exploited, forcefully assimilated, and subjected to repression, torture and murder when they speak out in defence of their rights. Fearing persecution, they often become refugees and sometimes must hide their identity, abandoning their languages and traditional way of life.

In 1982, the Subcommission on Human Rights established a working group on indigenous populations, which prepared a draft *Declaration on the Rights of Indigenous Peoples*. In 1992, the Earth Summit heard the collective voice of indigenous peoples as they expressed their concerns about the deteriorating state of their lands, territories and environment. Various UN bodies—including UNDP, UNICEF, IFAD, UNESCO, the World Bank and WHO—developed programmes to improve their health and literacy and combat degradation of their ancestral lands and territories. Subsequently, the General Assembly proclaimed 1993 the International Year of the World's Indigenous People, followed by the First (1995–2004) and the **Second International Decade of the World's Indigenous People (2005–2014)**. In 1997, an indigenous fellowship programme was established to assist indigenous peoples wishing to gain experience in the different branches of the Centre for Human Rights and in other parts of the UN system.

This increased focus on indigenous issues led, in 2000, to the establishment of the **Permanent Forum on Indigenous Issues** (www.un.org/development/desa/indigenous-peoples/unpfii-sessions-2.html) as a subsidiary organ of ECOSOC. The 16-expert forum, composed of an equal number of governmental and indigenous experts, advises ECOSOC; helps coordinate related UN activities; and considers indigenous concerns relating to economic and social development, culture, education, the environment, health and human rights. An Inter-Agency Support Group on Indigenous Issues was also established.

In 2007, the General Assembly adopted the landmark *Declaration on the Rights of Indigenous Peoples*. The *Declaration* sets out the individual and collective rights of indigenous peoples, including their rights to culture, identity, language, employment, health, education and other benefits. It emphasizes their rights to maintain and strengthen their own institutions, cultures and traditions, and to pursue their development in keeping with their own needs and aspirations. It also prohibits discrimination against them, and promotes their full participation in public affairs and all matters that concern them, including their right to remain distinct and to pursue their own visions of economic and social development. In 2014, the Assembly held a high level event, the **World Conference on Indigenous Peoples**, and adopted an outcome document containing commitments to achieve the goals of the *Declaration*.

OHCHR has played a pivotal role in the implementation of the *Declaration*, which remains a priority for the Office. It contributes to the UN Inter-Agency Support Group on Indigenous Issues and conducts training on indigenous issues for UN country teams and for OHCHR field presences. OHCHR services the Board of Trustees of the Voluntary Fund for Indigenous Populations. The Fund, composed of five representatives of indigenous communities, supports the participation of indigenous communities and organizations in the annual sessions of the Permanent Forum and the **Expert Mechanism on the Rights of Indigenous Peoples**. Established in 2007, the five-expert mechanism assists the Human Rights Council on indigenous rights issues. OHCHR also supports the Expert Mechanism and assists the special rapporteur on the rights of indigenous peoples. It carries out country-specific and regional activities to advance the rights of indigenous peoples, provides support for legislative initiatives and pursues thematic work on issues such as extractive industries and the rights of isolated indigenous peoples.

Supporters of the *UN Convention on the Rights of Persons with Disabilities* participate in the first Disability Pride parade held in New York (12 July 2015, UN Photo/Devra Berkowitz).

Persons with disabilities

Some 1 billion persons—approximately 15 per cent of the world's population—are estimated to be living with some type of physical, mental or sensory impairment. Around 80 per cent of persons with disabilities live in developing countries. They are often excluded from the mainstream of society. Discrimination takes various forms, ranging from the denial of education or work opportunities to more subtle forms, such as segregation and isolation through the imposition of physical and social barriers. Changing the perception and concept of disability requires changing values and increasing understanding at all levels of society.

Since its inception, the United Nations has sought to advance the status of persons with disabilities and to improve their lives (www.un.org/development/desa/disabilities). Its concern for the well-being and rights of persons with disabilities is rooted in its founding principles of human rights, fundamental freedoms and equality of all human beings.

In the 1970s, the concept of human rights for persons with disabilities gained wider international acceptance. Through its adoption of the *Declaration on the Rights of Disabled Persons* (1975), the General Assembly established standards for equal treatment and equal access to services, thus accelerating the social integration of persons with disabilities. The International Year of Disabled Persons (1981) led to the adoption by the General Assembly of the *World Programme of Action Concerning Disabled Persons*, a policy framework for promoting the rights of persons with disabilities. The programme identifies two goals for international cooperation: equality of opportunity, and full participation of persons with disabilities in social life and development.

A major outcome of the United Nations Decade of Disabled Persons (1983–1992) was the adoption by the General Assembly in 1993 of the *Standard Rules on the Equalization of Opportunities for Persons with Disabilities*, which serve as an instrument for policymaking and provide a basis for technical and economic cooperation. Increased focus on the rights and social situation of persons with disabilities led to the adoption of the *UN Convention on the Rights of Persons with Disabilities* and its *Optional Protocol* in 2006, and a high-level meeting of the General Assembly on disability and development in 2013.

The *Convention* and its *Optional Protocol* opened for signature in 2007. As at 31 December 2016, there were 160 signatories and 172 parties to the *Convention*; and 92 signatories and 92 parties to the *Optional Protocol*. The *Convention* entered into force in 2008. It is the first comprehensive human rights treaty of the 21st century and the first human rights convention to be open for signature by regional integration organizations.

The *Convention* marks a paradigm shift in attitudes and approaches to persons with disabilities. It takes the movement to new heights from viewing persons with disabilities as "objects" of charity, medical treatment and social protection towards viewing them as "subjects" with rights, who are capable of making decisions based on their free and informed consent, as well as being active members of society. The secretariat for the *Convention*'s international monitoring mechanisms, including the **Committee on the Rights of Persons with Disabilities**, lies with OHCHR, while the UN Department for Economic and Social Affairs organizes the conference of states parties in New York.

A growing body of data reveals the need to address disability issues in the context of national development, within the broad framework of human rights. The UN works with governments, NGOs, academic institutions and professional societies to promote awareness and build national capacities for broad human rights approaches to persons with disabilities. In doing so, it links disability issues with the international development agenda, including the Sustainable Development Goals (SDGs). Growing public support for disability action has focused on the need to improve information services, outreach and institutional mechanisms to promote equal opportunity. The UN is involved in helping countries strengthen their national capacities to promote such action in their overall development plans.

Migrant workers

More than 244 million people—including migrant workers, refugees, asylum-seekers, permanent immigrants and others—live and work in a country other than that of their birth or citizenship. Many of them are migrant workers. The term "migrant worker" is defined in article 2 of the *International Convention on the Protection of the Rights of All Migrant Workers and Members of Their Families (Migrant Workers Convention)* as "a person who is to be engaged or has been engaged in a remunerated activity in a state of which he or she is not a national". The *Convention* defines those rights that apply to certain categories of migrant workers and their families, including: frontier workers; seasonal workers; seafarers; workers on offshore installations; itinerant workers; migrants employed for a specific project; and self-employed workers.

The *Migrant Workers Convention* was adopted by the General Assembly in 1990, following 10 years of negotiations. It covers the rights of both documented and undocumented migrant workers and their families. It makes it illegal to expel migrant workers on a collective basis or to destroy their identity documents, work permits or passports. It entitles migrant workers to receive the same remuneration, social benefits and medical care as nationals; to join or take part in trade unions; and, upon ending their employment, to transfer earnings, savings and personal belongings. It also grants children of migrant workers the right to registration of birth and nationality, as well as access to education. The *Convention*, which entered into force in 2003, has 38 signatories and 49 parties as at 31 December 2016. States parties monitor implementation of the *Convention* through the **Committee on Migrant Workers**.

The inter-agency **Global Migration Group** (www.globalmigrationgroup.org) brings together 21 partners (19 UN agencies, the World Bank and the International Organization for Migration) to promote the application of international instruments and norms relating to migration, and to encourage the adoption of coherent, comprehensive and better coordinated approaches to international migration.

ADMINISTRATION OF JUSTICE

The United Nations is committed to strengthening the protection of human rights in the judicial process. When individuals are under investigation by state authorities, or when they are arrested, detained, charged, tried or imprisoned, there is a need to ensure that the law is applied with due regard for the protection of human rights.

The UN has worked to develop standards and codes that serve as models for national legislation. They cover such issues as the treatment of prisoners, the protection of detained juveniles, the use of firearms by police, the conduct of law enforcement officials, the role of lawyers and prosecutors, and the independence of the judiciary. Many of these standards have been developed through the United Nations Commission on Crime Prevention and Criminal Justice and the Centre for International Crime Prevention.

OHCHR has a programme of technical assistance that focuses on human rights training for legislators, judges, lawyers, law enforcement officers, prison officials and the military.

There are a number of international instruments relating to the administration of justice. These include, among others: *Standard Minimum Rules for the Treatment of Prisoners; Basic Principles for the Treatment of Prisoners; Body of Principles for the Protection of All Persons under Any Form of Detention or Imprisonment; United Nations Rules for the Protection of Juveniles Deprived of their Liberty; Safeguards Guaranteeing Protection of the Rights of those Facing the Death Penalty; Code of Conduct for Law Enforcement Officials; Basic Principles on the Use of Force and Firearms by Law Enforcement Officials; Basic Principles on the Role of Lawyers; Guidelines on the Role of Prosecutors; Basic Principles and Guidelines on the Right to a Remedy and Reparation;* and the *International Convention for the Protection of All Persons from Enforced Disappearance. (*For a non-exhaustive list, see www. ohchr.org/EN/ProfessionalInterest/Pages/UniversalHumanRightsInstruments.aspx)

OHCHR PRIORITIES

OHCHR is sharpening its focus around a set of critical human rights challenges that it is well placed to address given its mandate, its independence and the value added it has garnered through experience and lessons learned. The following areas have been identified as the OHCHR thematic priorities for 2014–2017:

- strengthening international human rights mechanisms;
- enhancing equality and countering discrimination;
- combating impunity and strengthening accountability and the rule of law;
- integrating human rights in development and the economic sphere;
- widening the democratic space; and
- early warning and protection of human rights in situations of conflict, violence and insecurity.

OHCHR has developed six thematic strategies built around these priorities.

A national United Nations volunteer (UNV) interviews an elderly,
blind man to assess damage to his home and barn in Kunchok
following the 7.8 magnitude earthquake in Nepal on 25 April 2015.
She was one of 80 UNV civil engineers, and one of 13 women,
helping communities recover through a UNDP debris management
project. The earthquake resulted in 8,790 deaths, 22,300 injuries
and 755,549 houses that were either damaged or completely
destroyed (8 June 2015, UNDP/Lesley Wright).

Since it first coordinated humanitarian relief operations in Europe following the devastation and massive displacement of people in the Second World War, the United Nations has led the international community in responding to natural and man-made disasters that are beyond the capacity of national authorities alone. Today, the Organization is a major provider of emergency relief and longer-term assistance, a catalyst for action by governments and relief agencies, and an advocate for people affected by emergencies (www.un.org/en/sections/priorities/humanitarian-assistance).

The last quarter century has seen an overwhelming shift in frequency, scale and magnitude of humanitarian emergencies. Crises in Afghanistan, Burundi, the Democratic Republic of Congo, Somalia and the Sudan have necessitated humanitarian appeals almost every year. This has also been the case since the turn of the millennium for the Central African Republic, Chad, Iraq and the occupied Palestinian territory. Currently, these same countries and many others are immersed in conflict and urgently require a multidimensional response. About 1.2 million people, 80 per cent of them women and children, have fled from South Sudan, making it the largest refugee movement in Africa.

Humanitarian access has grown in complexity and is severely constrained, preventing humanitarians from carrying out their work and leaving affected people without basic services and protection. Mines, explosive remnants of war and improvised explosive devices impede access and threaten the lives of vulnerable populations in conflict-affected regions. Meanwhile, natural disasters, which are likely to become more frequent, violent and severe owing to climate change, continue to destroy homes and lives, and worsen the impact of any preexisting humanitarian crisis.

Confronted with conflict and the escalating human and financial cost of natural disasters, the UN engages on two fronts. On one hand, it brings immediate relief to those who have been affected, primarily through its operational agencies; on the other hand, it seeks more effective strategies to prevent emergencies from arising in the first place.

When disaster strikes, the UN and its agencies rush to deliver humanitarian assistance. Typhoon Haiyan, one of the most powerful storms ever to make landfall, hit the Philippines in November 2013, resulting in 7,354 deaths or missing persons. An estimated 14 million people were affected, including 5.4 million children. Four million people were displaced and over 1 million homes were damaged. UN emergency relief operations included the airlifting of lifesaving food, health, medical and other supplies. In April 2014, reports indicated that the humanitarian situation had remained stable across the affected regions, shelter cluster partners had provided 120,000 households with assistance enabling them to repair their own homes, and food assistance had been provided to over 4 million people. The distribution of seeds and fertilizer to affected farming families provided livelihoods and produced enough milled rice to feed 800,000 people for a year. Relief assistance was provided for other sudden onset natural disasters, including 7.8 magnitude earthquakes in Nepal and Ecuador, in April 2015 and 2016, as well as for one of the most devastating El Niño-induced droughts in recent history that caused food insecurity in Zimbabwe.

In 2016, action taken by the UN and its humanitarian partners addressed new and ongoing crises. Those efforts resulted in: 130,000 people in Fiji receiving emergency shelter following Tropical Cyclone Winston; 1.9 million people affected by the Syria crisis in Egypt, Iraq, Jordan, Lebanon and Turkey receiving food assistance; 9,500 children displaced from Mosul, Iraq being immunized against polio and measles; 5.1 million patients receiving medical attention in Syria; 1.7 million school children in Ethiopia receiving learning supplies; 78 per cent of refugee households from the Central African Republic living in adequate dwellings; 30,000 litres of water being distributed daily to displaced persons in north and south Gaalkacyo, Somalia; 73 per cent of extremely food insecure people receiving food assistance in regions of Haiti affected by Hurricane Matthew; 27 million square metres of land freed from the threat of mines and explosive remnants of war in South Sudan; and 83 per cent of households in the West Bank, occupied Palestinian territory, whose homes were subject to demolitions or damage receiving immediate shelter and non-food items.

The Central Emergency Response Fund, managed by OCHA, allocated an estimated $289 million for rapid response operations dispatched in 2016. In 2015, the Fund allocated $301 million for rapid response operations. More than $44 million of that amount was allocated to Yemen to address a worsening humanitarian situation due to armed conflict that by year's end resulted in more than 21.2 million Yemenis, or four out of every five people, requiring humanitarian assistance.

Through other means, such as the **United Nations International Strategy for Disaster Reduction (UNISDR)** (www.unisdr.org), the UN works to prevent humanitarian crises and mitigate their effects. On 18 March 2015, at the Third UN World Conference on Disaster Risk Reduction in Sendai City, Japan, UN member states adopted the **Sendai Framework for Disaster Risk Reduction 2015–2030** (www.unisdr.org/we/coordinate/sendai-framework), with seven targets and four priorities for action. The Framework is now the bedrock of policies in the Philippines, one of the most disaster-prone nations in the world. Improved methods for keeping the public risk-informed and ensuring the early dissemination of warnings and efficient evacuations to promote a "zero casualty" approach proved successful in the face of major storms Typhoon Hagupit in December 2014 and Typhoon Koppu in October 2015.

COORDINATING HUMANITARIAN ACTION

Since the 1990s, the world has seen an upsurge in the number and intensity of civil wars. Conflicts in Afghanistan, Iraq and Syria have caused large-scale humanitarian crises—with extensive loss of life, massive displacements of people and widespread damage to societies in complicated political and military environments. In 1991, the General Assembly established an inter-agency standing committee to coordinate the international response to humanitarian crises. The **United Nations Emergency Relief Coordinator**, the Organization's focal point for this endeavor, heads the **Office for the Coordination of Humanitarian Affairs (OCHA)** (www.unocha.org) and serves as the system's principal policy adviser, coordinator and advocate on humanitarian emergencies.

Usually, a number of actors in the international community—including governments, non-governmental organizations (NGOs) and UN agencies—seek to respond simultaneously to complex emergencies. OCHA works with them to ensure that there is a coherent framework within which everyone can contribute promptly and effectively. It determines priorities for action through consultations with member states and the **Inter-Agency Standing Committee (IASC)** (interagencystandingcommittee.org), an umbrella organization that brings together UN and non-UN humanitarian partners, including UN agencies, the Red Cross and Red Crescent Movements, and representatives of NGOs. OCHA also sends emergency response teams to sudden onset crises and coordinates civil-military activities. The **United Nations Disaster Assessment and Coordination (UNDAC)** teams can be dispatched within 12 to 24 hours of a natural disaster or emergency to gather information, assess needs and coordinate international assistance. OCHA field offices provide support for the coordination of needs assessments, contingency planning activities and the formulation of humanitarian response plans. OCHA works to ensure that each humanitarian response element, from food distribution to water provision and protection, are all delivered.

Financing. Funding to support humanitarian response activities has increased from $4.8 billion in 2006 to $22 billion in 2016. Responsible for coordinating the publication of humanitarian needs figures, tracking funding reported by donors, and ensuring that emergency funds are in place when they are needed, OCHA manages the online Financial Tracking System (fts.unocha.org) and the development of the Global Humanitarian Overview. The Office also hosts pledging conferences and manages the infrastructure for two pooled-funding mechanisms that provide rapid access to funding in emergencies.

The **Central Emergency Response Fund (CERF)** (www.unocha.org/cerf) is a global fund that disburses about $450 million annually to ensure a rapid response to sudden onset crises, to rapidly deteriorating conditions in an existing emergency, or to underfunded emergencies. The rapid response window is granted to UN agencies for acute emergencies like natural disasters and rapid escalations of violence that threaten civilians. These included the 2014 Ebola virus outbreak in West Africa, the April 2015 earthquake in Nepal and the conflict and military operations in Iraq in 2016. Some 33 member states and other donors pledged $273 million for 2017 during the annual CERF High-Level Conference in December 2016. Since its establishment in 2006, CERF has allocated over $4.2 billion in funding to humanitarian agencies operating in 94 countries.

Currently, there are 18 country-based pooled funds (CBPFs) around the world that allocate over $500 million annually—from governments and private donors—to UN agencies and NGOs to support humanitarian activity in a specific country. Between CERF and these country-based funds, OCHA coordinates the disbursement of close to $1 billion in humanitarian assistance annually.

Information management. In emergencies, one of the most important factors in ensuring effective response is the collection, storage, and management of humanitarian information and data. On the ground, OCHA's information managers work with partners to determine the most critical humanitarian needs and keep response organizations informed of *who* is implementing *what* relief operations in *which* area. This information is uploaded to global reporting platforms like **Reliefweb** (reliefweb.int) and (unocha.org) where the information can be used to coordinate response. The speed of information collection and dissemination is accelerating. OCHA is at the forefront of this data revolution. It has launched the **Humanitarian Data Exchange** (data.humdata. org) and **KoBoToolbox** (kobotoolbox.org) platforms to more quickly gather and disseminate critical humanitarian information. OCHA and other humanitarian partners are making investments to further increase the speed and effectiveness of information reporting to save more lives and reduce humanitarian need.

World Humanitarian Summit. In May 2016, the Secretary-General convened in Instanbul, Turkey, the first ever World Humanitarian Summit (agendaforhumanity. org/summit), bringing together some 9,000 representatives, including 180 member states, and NGOs, civil society, populations affected by crises, the private sector and international organizations. The humanitarian community resolved to change the way it works in order to adapt to the changing operational context to meet the needs of affected people. Over 3,000 commitments were made in support of the **Agenda for**

Humanity and its five core responsibilities to: prevent and end conflict; respect rules of war and uphold norms to safeguard humanity; work differently to end need; leave no one behind; and invest in humanity.

Advocacy. OCHA launches global campaigns to raise awareness of critical humanitarian issues, such as the challenges faced by internally displaced persons, aid worker security, and the commitments made under the Agenda for Humanity. OCHA also advocates in the national and international press on issues facing local populations, including restrictions on humanitarian access, funding shortfalls, or particular regions or populations that are particularly vulnerable.

HUMANITARIAN ASSISTANCE AND PROTECTION

Four United Nations entities—UNICEF, WFP, UNHCR and UNDP—have primary roles in providing protection and relief assistance in humanitarian crises.

Children and women constitute the majority of refugees and displaced persons. In acute emergencies, the **United Nations Children's Fund (UNICEF)** works alongside other relief agencies to help re-establish basic services such as water and sanitation; set up schools; and provide immunization services, medicines and other supplies to uprooted populations. UNICEF also urges governments and warring parties to act more effectively to protect children. Its programmes in conflict zones have included the negotiation of ceasefires to facilitate the provision of key services such as child immunization. To this end, UNICEF has pioneered the concept of "children as zones of peace" and created "days of tranquility" and "corridors of peace" in war-affected regions. Special programmes assist traumatized children and help reunite unaccompanied children with parents or extended families. In 2015, UNICEF responded to 310 humanitarian situations in 102 countries and organizational spending on humanitarian action totalled $1.685 billion. It provided 25.5 million people with safe drinking water, 7.5 million children with access to basic education and 3.1 million children with psychosocial support. UNICEF also treated 2 million children for severe acute malnutrition and gave 23 million measles vaccinations to children between 6 months and 15 years of age.

The **World Food Programme (WFP)** provides fast, efficient relief to millions of people who are victims of natural or man-made disasters, including most of the world's refugees and internally displaced persons (IDPs). Such crises consume the largest part of WFP's financial and human resources. A decade ago, two thirds of WFP food aid was used to help people become self-reliant. Today, more than three quarters of those resources go to victims of humanitarian crises. In 2015, WFP provided food assistance to 76.7 million people in 81 countries; 79 per cent of expenditures were for emergencies. WFP provided school meals, snacks or take home rations to 6.5 million people in emergencies or post-emergency areas. It also responded to severe, complex emergencies in Iraq, South Sudan, Syria and Yemen, as well as Ebola-affected West Africa; and to major emergencies in the Central African Republic, the Democratic Republic of the Congo, Libya, Mali, Ukraine, Nepal and the Horn of Africa. When war or disaster strikes, WFP responds quickly with emergency relief, then mounts programmes to facilitate recovery aimed at rebuilding lives and livelihoods. WFP provides passenger air transport to the entire humanitarian community through the **UN Humanitarian Air Service (UNHAS)** (www.wfp.org/logistics/aviation), which flies to more than 250 locations worldwide. WFP is also responsible for mobilizing food and funds for all large-scale refugee feeding operations managed by the Office of the UN High Commissioner for Refugees.

Overview of Za'atari refugee camp, the largest for Syrian refugees in Jordan. Set up in 2012 to address the initial mass exodus of refugees, the UNHCR camp has evolved from a collection of tents into a structured settlement and temporary home for 80,000 refugees. UNICEF has established 14 school complexes for the 27,000 school-aged children living there (23 June 2015, UNHCR/Christopher Herwig).

Rural people in the developing world are often the most vulnerable to disasters and crises, with most of these communities dependent on agriculture for their livelihoods, food security and nutrition. With its extensive expertise in sustainable agriculture, the **Food and Agriculture Organization of the United Nations (FAO)** supports countries to increase the resilience of agricultural livelihoods to threats and crises and to respond to crises when they occur.

FAO assists countries in preventing, mitigating, preparing for and responding to disasters. Through a 2016 initiative, its **Early Warning Early Action (EWEA)** system, FAO helps countries translate early warning information into preventions, preparedness and response. Together with WFP, FAO regularly carries out crop and food security assessments in crisis-prone countries to examine the overall food supply and extent to which people can meet their basic food needs. In post-disaster situations, FAO conducts rapid damage and needs assessments with governments and partners to inform the response. FAO works to restore local food production, providing an exit from food aid and other forms of assistance, bolstering self-reliance and reducing the need for relief and coping strategies. Its work in climate-related disasters, food chain crises and complex emergency situations emphasizes the protection and rehabilitation of agricultural livelihoods and the integration of vulnerability reduction measures.

The **World Health Organization (WHO)** focuses on assessing the health needs of those affected by emergencies and disasters, providing health information and assisting in coordination and planning. During emergencies, WHO leads and coordinates the health response in support of countries; undertakes risk assessments; identifies priorities and sets strategies; provides critical technical guidance, supplies and financial resources; and monitors the health situation. WHO also helps countries strengthen their national core capacities for emergency risk management to prevent, prepare for, respond to, and recover from emergencies due to any hazards that pose a threat to human health security. WHO carries out emergency programmes in such areas as nutritional and epidemiological surveillance, control of epidemics, immunizations, management of essential drugs and medical supplies, reproductive health and mental health. It makes special efforts to eradicate polio and to control tuberculosis and malaria in countries affected by emergencies.

The **United Nations Population Fund (UNFPA)**, also moves quickly when emergency strikes. Pregnancy-related deaths and sexual violence soar in times of upheaval, while reproductive health services often become unavailable. Women face greater risk of gender-based violence. Young people become more vulnerable to HIV infection and sexual exploitation, and many women lose access to family planning services. UNFPA ensures that reproductive health is integrated into emergency responses by deploying hygiene supplies, obstetric and family planning supplies, trained personnel, and other support to vulnerable populations. It also works to serve the needs of women and young people through both the emergency and reconstruction phase.

The **United Nations Development Programme (UNDP)** is the agency responsible for coordinating activities for natural disaster mitigation, prevention and preparedness. Governments frequently call on UNDP to help design rehabilitation programmes and to direct donor aid. UNDP and humanitarian agencies work together to integrate concern for recovery and transitional and long-term development in their relief operations. UNDP also supports programmes for the demobilization of former combatants, comprehensive mine action, the return and reintegration of refugees and internally displaced persons, and the restoration of the institutions of governance.

To ensure that resources provided have maximum impact, each project is carried out in consultation with local and national government officials. UNDP offers rapid assistance to entire communities, while helping to establish the social and economic foundations for lasting peace, development, and the alleviation of poverty. This community-based approach has helped provide urgent and lasting relief for hundreds of thousands of victims of war and civil upheaval. Today, many conflict-scarred communities have improved their living standards thanks to UN-led training programmes, credit schemes and infrastructure projects.

Protecting humanitarian workers

United Nations personnel and other humanitarian workers in the field are operating in some of the most dangerous places in the world, delivering life-saving and critical programmes in conflict zones, marked by aerial bombings, heavy weapons or small arms fire, and terrorist attacks. The Organization delivers a large number of programmes in areas with very high residual security risks, in circumstances where activities would normally have been curtailed. Insecurity is expanding to new areas, while conflicts remain unabated in other places. Through a robust security risk management framework, the UN Department of Safety and Security enables UN operations to continue worldwide, while giving the highest priority to the safety and security of UN staff members and their families.

The primary responsibility for the security and protection of UN personnel rests with the host Government. The 1994 *Convention on the Safety of United Nations and Associated Personnel* obliges the governments of countries in which the United Nations is working to safeguard its staff, and to take preventive measures against murders and abductions. Despite these obligations, many UN personnel, as well as peacekeepers and associated personnel, lose their lives each year in service to the world's most vulnerable people. The 2016 annual memorial service (www.un.org/en/memorial) held in October at UN headquarters in New York, honoured the 211 UN personnel who lost their lives in the line of duty during the period 1 January 2015 to 30 June 2016.

PROTECTING AND ASSISTING REFUGEES

At the end of 2015, the **Office of the United Nations High Commissioner for Refugees (UNHCR)** (www.unhcr.org), the UN Refugee Agency, counted 65.3 million forcibly displaced people worldwide. This included 40.8 million internally displaced persons (IDPs), 21.3 million refugees and 3.2 million asylum-seekers. In addition, there were an estimated 10 million stateless people.

More than 53 million people—16.1 million refugees and 37.5 million IDPs—were receiving protection or assistance from UNCHR at the end of 2015—6.9 million more than in 2014. Another 5.2 million Palestinian refugees were assisted under the mandate of the **United Nations Relief and Works Agency for Palestine Refugees in the Near East (UNRWA)**.

Of the 16.1 million refugees under UNHCR's mandate, more than half (54 per cent) came from three countries: the Syrian Arab Republic (4.9 million), Afghanistan (2.7 million) and Somalia (1.1 million). Developing countries were host to 86 per cent of the world's refugees. Turkey hosted the largest number with 2.5 million refugees. Lebanon hosted the largest number in relation to its national population, with almost 1 person in five being a refugee. Children below 18 years of age represented about half of the refugee population. Unaccompanied or separated children—mainly Afghans, Eritreans, Syrians and Somalis—submitted some 98,400 asylum applications in 78 countries.

Refugees are defined as those who have fled their countries because of a well-founded fear of persecution due to their race, religion, nationality, political opinion or membership in a particular social group, and who cannot or do not want to return. It also includes persons who have fled war or other violence. The legal status of refugees is defined in two international treaties, the 1951 *Convention Relating to the Status of Refugees* and its *1967 Protocol*, which spell out their rights and obligations. There are 148 states parties to one or both of these instruments.

UNHCR's core mandate is to provide refugees with international protection—first and foremost access to safety elsewhere—and then with solutions that would eventually lead to their re-establishment as normal citizens back home, in their country of asylum, or in a third country. Although the mandate mentions the provision of assistance and the coordination of activities undertaken by other organizations for the benefit of refugees, the focus of UNHCR when it started in 1951 was on the legal and advocacy aspects of protection. In 1954, UNHCR won the Nobel Peace Prize for its groundbreaking work in this context. A second Nobel Peace Prize was awarded in 1981 for what had become worldwide assistance to refugees.

From the sixties onwards, when large refugee movements started to concentrate in developing countries with few resources to share, emergency and assistance programmes became an increasingly visible aspect of UNHCR work, encompassing activities aimed at ensuring that refugees could enjoy the full range of their rights—from physical security to access to documentation, adequate standards of living, health and education.

In the seventies, UNHCR was asked by the General Assembly to extend its protection, as a part of its regular responsibilities, to stateless people—persons that no state recognizes as its own citizens. Statelessness can deprive a person of most rights we take for granted—from enrolling in school, to finding legal employment and even the right to get married or bury the dead. UNHCR works with states to identify causes of statelessness, prevent their occurrence, and to help stateless persons acquire a legal status and—if possible—citizenship. A global campaign to end statelessness in 10 years

(#IBelong) was launched in 2014 to raise awareness of a situation that affects an estimated 10 million people worldwide. In 2015, there were 3.7 million persons under UNHCR's statelessness mandate.

UNHCR also works with specific groups of persons displaced by conflict who have not crossed an international border, focusing on their protection, shelter and camp management. Today, IDPs comprise the largest group of people of concern to UNHCR. IDPs are people who have been forced to flee their homes to escape war, general violence, human rights violations or natural and man-made disasters, but have not crossed an international border. During 2015, some 2.3 million IDPs were able to return home.

Despite many more refugees finding a durable solution in new countries, the gap between the need and available places has grown. The number of new refugees has increased, and returns to home countries have decreased, due to continuing instability and violence. When returns do happen, they often occur in fragile socioeconomic contexts. To ensure that returnees (former refugees) can rebuild their lives after they return home, UNHCR works with a range of organizations to facilitate their reintegration.

During 2015, only 201,400 refugees returned to their countries of origin. Most returned to Afghanistan (61,400), Sudan (39,500), Somalia (32,300), and the Central African Republic (21,600). At the same time, a record 2 million applications for asylum were submitted. Germany received more requests than any other country (442,000), followed by the United States (173,000) and Sweden (162,877). As the number of refugees and other displaced persons increases, the resources to support them cannot match the needs.

On 19 September 2016, the General Assembly adopted the *New York Declaration*, which contains commitments by member states to address large movements of refugees and migrants. The *Declaration* specifically calls on UNHCR to develop a Framework that will serve as a blueprint for a comprehensive refugee response in each situation involving large movements of refugees. This approach will complement and strengthen the emergency humanitarian response, enhancing the capacity of asylum countries and ensuring the early involvement of a range of actors.

PALESTINE REFUGEES

Since 1950, the **United Nations Relief and Works Agency for Palestine Refugees in the Near East (UNRWA)** (www.unrwa.org) has been providing education, health, relief and social services to Palestine refugees. The General Assembly created UNRWA to provide emergency relief to some 750,000 Palestine refugees who had lost their homes and livelihoods as a result of the 1948 Arab-Israeli conflict. At the end of 2016, UNRWA was providing essential basic services to assist more than 5 million registered Palestine refugees in Jordan, Lebanon, Syria, the Gaza Strip and the West Bank, including East Jerusalem. In the past decade, the need for UNRWA's humanitarian role has been reinforced by recurrent conflicts in the region.

Education is UNRWA's largest area of activity, accounting for nearly 60 per cent of its regular budget. The Agency operates a school system with 692 schools, 21,821 educational staff, 500,698 enrolled pupils (an average of 50.2 per cent female), 8 vocational and technical training centres, 6,855 training sites, 2 educational science faculties and 1,868 teachers in training for the 2015–2016 school year. The Agency's network of 143 primary health care facilities performed 9.5 million medical consultations in 2015. Its environmental health programme controls the quality of drinking water, provides sanitation, and carries out vector and rodent control in refugee camps. From January to September 2016, the UNRWA microfinance programme issued 28,960 loans, valued

Students in a school in Gaza run by UNRWA participate in a meeting of the Gaza central school parliament. Since its establishement, UNRWA has contributed to the welfare and human development of four generations of Palestine refugees (28 June 2016, UN Photo/Eskinder Debebe).

at $29.4 million. Between 1991 and 2015, UNRWA extended 398,154 loans, valued at $440.4 million, across all of its fields of operation.

As at October 2016, UNRWA was providing humanitarian assistance to almost 1.4 million Palestine refugees across its fields of operation. This included 420,000 refugees inside Syria and another 45,000 who had fled to Jordan and Lebanon as a result of the Syria conflict, as well as more than 800,000 in Gaza and 80,000 in the West Bank. Gaza has faced three conflicts in the past eight years and has been under a blockade since 2007. In the West Bank, humanitarian and protection needs result from the continued Israeli occupation and related restrictions on movement and access.

UNRWA continues to help upgrade infrastructure, create employment and improve socioeconomic conditions. Unlike other UN organizations that may work through local authorities or executing agencies, UNRWA provides its services directly to refugees. It plans and carries out its own activities and projects, and builds and administers facilities such as schools and clinics. The international community considers UNRWA a stabilizing factor in the Middle East. The refugees themselves look upon its programmes as a symbol of the international community's commitment to attaining a lasting solution of the Palestine refugee issue.

The Great Hall of Justice of the Peace Palace in the
Hague (the Netherlands) at the delivery of the Court's
Judgment in the case *Marshall Islands v. United Kingdom*
(5 October 2016, UN Photo/ICJ-CIJ/Frank van Beek).

Among the most wide-reaching achievements of the United Nations is its contribution to the development of, and respect for, international law (www.un.org/en/law/). The *Charter of the United Nations* specifically calls on the Organization to encourage the progressive development of international law and its codification (Article 13) and to help in the settlement of international disputes by peaceful means, including judicial settlement (Article 33). While the work of the UN in this area does not always receive attention, it has a daily impact on the lives of people everywhere.

Many of the legal instruments developed under UN auspices, including treaties, resolutions and declarations, form the basis of the law that governs relations among nations. The UN has been at the forefront of efforts to establish a legal framework in such areas as maintaining international peace and security, facilitating international commerce, protecting the environment, regulating the oceans and seas, combating terrorism and prosecuting international crimes. These efforts continue today, as international law, including human rights law and international humanitarian law, assumes a more central role across a wider spectrum of issues. The UN Secretary-General is the depositary of more than 560 multilateral agreements covering a broad range of subject matters (treaties.un.org).

The UN and its organs also play unique roles in the peaceful settlement of disputes. From providing a standing court where states can lawfully resolve their grievances, to establishing ad hoc tribunals in the aftermath of armed conflict, the UN is key to upholding international law and reaffirming its place as a cornerstone of international relations.

JUDICIAL SETTLEMENT OF DISPUTES

The primary United Nations organ for the settlement of disputes is its principal judicial organ, the **International Court of Justice (ICJ)** (www.icj-cij.org). Also known as the "World Court", ICJ is the only court of a universal character with general jurisdiction; this is reflected by the wide range of states parties appearing before it, and of the issues it has been asked to address. Since its founding in 1946, the Court has considered 164 cases, and issued over 120 judgments and over 150 judicial orders on legal disputes brought to it by UN member states. It has also issued 27 advisory opinions in response to requests by UN organizations.

ICJ has become increasingly busy in recent years. As at 12 October 2016, it had 11 active cases on its docket relating to disputes from all corners of the globe. States are increasingly turning to the Court to resolve disputes relating to treaty interpretation, land and maritime frontiers, the environment and the conservation of living resources, and other issues. Consequently, the Court has delivered more judgments in the last 24 years than during the first 44 years of its existence.

ICJ has developed a particularly strong reputation in adjudicating land and maritime boundary disputes, in which tensions between states can escalate into open conflict. Parties to such disputes invariably place their confidence in the prospect of the Court reaching an equitable solution that will in turn normalize relations between them.

Although the most obvious effect of ICJ judgments is the peaceful settlement of disputes, the influence of the Court's jurisprudence is felt more broadly. Its pronouncements are widely perceived as authoritative statements of international law, and are studied closely by other courts and tribunals, legal scholars and advisers to states. Its contribution to the development of international law includes the clarification of specific rules of customary law.

Contentious cases

Contentious cases have represented 80 per cent of ICJ's work since 1946. The Court has delivered judgments on disputes concerning a wide range of issues, including those related to frontiers, maritime boundaries, territorial sovereignty, the non-use of force, violation of international humanitarian law, non-interference in the internal affairs of states, diplomatic relations, hostage-taking, the right of asylum, nationality, guardianship, rights of passage and economic rights.

As to the length of contentious cases, some 75 per cent of cases were dealt with by ICJ within 4 years; 18 per cent were completed within 5–9 years; and 7 per cent (7 cases so far) were completed after 10 years or more. The length of each case varies depending on its complexity, but also on the will of parties to engage in swift proceedings. As the parties to proceedings are sovereign states, ICJ is limited in its ability to expedite its work on cases.

When so requested, the Court can deliver swift decisions. For example, in 1999, it delivered an order for provisional measures 24 hours after an urgent request by Germany in a case against the United States (*LaGrand*) concerning alleged violations of the *Vienna Convention on Consular Relations* in the trial and sentencing for murder of two German nationals. The case itself was dealt with in 28 months.

The procedure followed by the Court in contentious cases includes a written phase as well as an oral phase consisting of public hearings, during which agents and counsels address the Court. Following oral proceedings, the Court deliberates in camera, then delivers its judgment at a public sitting, usually within six months after the end of the oral phase. The judgment is final and without appeal. Should one of the states involved fail to comply, the other party may have recourse to the Security Council. Nearly all ICJ judgments, however, have been implemented.

Recent ICJ cases

In November 2013, in the case concerning the Temple of Preah Vihear, ICJ found that the Judgment of 15 June 1962 had decided that Cambodia had sovereignty over the whole territory of the promontory of Preah Vihear, concluding a long running dispute between Cambodia and Thailand.

In January 2014, in a maritime dispute case between Peru and Chile, the Court decided on the course of the maritime boundary between Chile and Peru without determining the precise geographical coordinates, expecting that the parties would determine those coordinates in accordance with ICJ Judgment, in the spirit of good neighbourliness.

In March 2014, in the case between Australia and Japan concerning whaling in the Antarctic, the Court found that Japan's whaling programme (JARPA II) was not in accordance with three provisions of the schedule to the *International Convention for the Regulation of Whaling* and decided that Japan should revoke any extant authorization permit or license granted in relation to JARPA II, and refrain from granting any further permits in pursuance of that programme.

In February 2015, in the case between Croatia and Serbia concerning application of the *Convention on the Prevention and Punishment of the Crime of Genocide*, the Court rejected both Croatia's claim that Serbia had violated the *Convention* and Serbia's counterclaim that Croatia had violated its obligations under the *Convention* during and after Operation Storm in August 1995.

In December 2015, in the case between Costa Rica and Nicaragua concerning construction of a road in Costa Rica along the San Juan River, and later joined to the case concerning certain activities carried out by Nicaragua in the border areas, the Court found that Costa Rica had violated its obligation to carry out an environmental impact assessment concerning construction of Route 1856, but that it had not breached substantive environmental obligations.

On 17 March 2016, the Court found that it had jurisdiction, on the basis of Article XXXI of the Pact of Bogotá, to entertain the first request put forward by Nicaragua for the Court to determine the precise course of the maritime boundary between Nicaragua and Colombia in the areas of the continental shelf, which appertain to each of them beyond the boundaries determined by the Court in its Judgment of 19 November 2012, and that that request was admissible.

In October 2016, in the three cases brought by the Marshall Islands against India, Pakistan and Great Britain on the obligations concerning negotiations relating to cessation of the nuclear arms race and nuclear disarmament, the Court upheld India, Pakistan and Great Britain's objections to jurisdiction, based on the absence of a dispute between the parties, and decided that it could not proceed to the merits of any of the cases.

The Court removed from its docket, in September 2013 and June 2015, respectively, the case between Ecuador and Colombia concerning aerial herbicide spraying, and the case between Timor-Leste and Australia concerning questions relating to the seizure and detention of certain documents and data, as the parties had come to an agreement or settlement.

As at 31 January 2017, there were 13 pending cases on the Court's docket involving 17 different states: seven involving Central and South American states (Costa Rica and Nicaragua in three cases; Chile and Bolivia in two cases; and Nicaragua and Colombia in two cases); two involving African states (*Democratic Republic of the Congo* v. *Uganda*; *Somalia* v. *Kenya*); two involving European states (*Hungary* v. *Slovakia; Ukraine* v. *Russian Federation*) and two involving states from different regions (*Equatorial Guinea* v. *France*; *Islamic Republic of Iran* v. *United States of America*).

Advisory opinions

Another role of the Court is to respond to any legal questions put to it by certain UN organs and institutions. This procedure culminates in advisory opinions, which represent 20 per cent of the workload of ICJ. Since 1946, the Court has given 27 advisory opinions, of which the majority—55 per cent, or 15 opinions—were requested by the General Assembly.

Unlike judgments, advisory opinions are not binding per se: it is for the UN organs or specialized agencies that request an opinion to give effect to it or not, by the means at their disposal. On occasion, a state and an international organization agree that the organization will request an advisory opinion of the Court in the event of dispute, and that the two parties will treat the opinion as conclusive. The consideration given to the Court's opinions by states and international organizations in their legal practice fosters the development of international law.

ICJ advisory opinions have covered various issues, including the legality of the threat or use of nuclear weapons (1996); the status of human rights rapporteurs (1999); the legal consequences of the construction of a wall in the Occupied Palestinian Territory (2004); and the accordance with international law of the unilateral declaration of independence in respect of Kosovo (2010). Other opinions have addressed admission to UN membership (1948); reparation for injuries suffered in the service of the UN (1949); questions concerning South West Africa (Namibia, in 1950, 1955, 1956 and 1971); the territorial status of Western Sahara (1975); expenses of certain UN operations (1962); and the applicability of the UN Headquarters Agreement (1988). ICJ has also given advisory opinions on judgments rendered by international administrative tribunals, most recently on a request by the Administrative Tribunal of the International Labour Organization in 2012.

So far, the Security Council has only requested one advisory opinion: in July 1970 on the legal consequences for states of the continued presence of South Africa in Namibia. In its advisory opinion of June 1971, the Court found, inter alia, that the continued presence of South Africa in Namibia was illegal and that the former was obligated to withdraw its administration immediately.

DEVELOPMENT AND CODIFICATION OF INTERNATIONAL LAW

The International Law Commission (legal.un.org/ilc) was established by the General Assembly in 1947 to promote the progressive development of international law and its codification. The Commission, which meets annually, is composed of 34 members elected by the General Assembly for five-year terms. Collectively, the members represent the world's principal legal systems and serve as experts in their individual capacity, not as representatives of their governments. They address a wide range of issues relevant to the regulation of relations among states, and frequently consult with relevant international institutions, depending on the subject being examined.

Most of the Commission's work involves the preparation of drafts on aspects of international law. Some topics are chosen by the Commission, others are referred to it by the General Assembly. When the Commission completes work on a topic, the General Assembly sometimes convenes an international conference of plenipotentiaries to incorporate the draft into a convention. The convention is then opened to states to become parties—countries that agree to be bound by the provisions of a convention. Some of these conventions form the foundation of the law governing relations among states. Examples include:

- the *Convention on Diplomatic Relations* and the *Convention on Consular Relations*, adopted at conferences held in Vienna in 1961 and 1963, respectively;
- the *Convention on the Law of Treaties*, adopted at a conference in Vienna in 1969;
- the *Convention on the Prevention and Punishment of Crimes against Internationally Protected Persons, including Diplomatic Agents*, adopted by the General Assembly in 1973;
- the *Convention on the Succession of States in Respect of State Property, Archives and Debts*, adopted at a conference in Vienna in 1983;
- the *Convention on the Law of Treaties between States and International Organizations or between International Organizations*, adopted at a conference in Vienna in 1986; and
- the *Convention on the Non-navigational Uses of International Watercourses*, adopted by the General Assembly in 1997, which regulates the equitable and reasonable utilization of watercourses shared by two or more countries.

Other important instruments developed by the Commission include the draft articles on the responsibility of states for internationally wrongful acts (2001), the prevention of transboundary harm from hazardous activities (2001), diplomatic protection (2006), the responsibility of international organizations (2011), the effects of armed conflicts on treaties (2011), the expulsion of aliens (2014), and the protection of persons in the event of disasters (2016); as well as the draft principles on the allocation of loss in the case of transboundary harm arising out of hazardous activities (2006) and the guide to practice on reservations to treaties (2011).

Topics considered by the Commission in 2016 included immunity of state officials from foreign criminal jurisdiction; subsequent agreements and subsequent practice in relation to the interpretation of treaties, provisional application of treaties, identification of customary international law, protection of the environment in relation to armed conflict, protection of the atmosphere, crimes against humanity and *jus cogens*.

INTERNATIONAL TRADE LAW

The **United Nations Commission on International Trade Law (UNCITRAL)** (www. uncitral.org) facilitates world trade by developing conventions, model laws, rules and legal guides designed to harmonize international trade law. Established by the General Assembly in 1966, UNCITRAL has become the core legal body of the UN system in the field of international trade law. The International Trade Law Division of the UN Office of Legal Affairs serves as its secretariat. The Commission is composed of 60 member state representatives elected by the General Assembly. Membership is structured to represent the world's various geographic regions and its principal economic and legal systems. Members of the Commission are elected for six-year terms. The terms of half the members expire every three years.

In the past 50 years, the Commission has developed texts that are viewed as landmarks in various fields of law. These include the *UNCITRAL Arbitration Rules* (1976); the *UNCITRAL Conciliation Rules* (1980); the *United Nations Convention on Contracts for the International Sale of Goods* (1980); the *UNCITRAL Model Law on International Commercial Arbitration* (1985); the *Model Law on Electronic Commerce* (1996); the *United Nations Convention on Contracts for the International Carriage of Goods Wholly or Partly by Sea* (2008); the *Revisions of the UNCITRAL Arbitration Rules* (2010); the *UNCITRAL Model Law on Public Procurement* (2011); the *UNCITRAL Rules on Transparency in Treaty-based Investor-State Arbitration* (2014); the *United Nations Convention on Transparency in Treaty-based Investor-State Arbitration* (2014); and the *UNCITRAL Model Law on Secured Transactions* (2016). The Commission is also the guardian of the *Convention on the Recognition and Enforcement of Foreign Arbitral Awards* (1958).

At its forty-ninth session in 2016, the Commission considered the issues of micro-small- and medium-sized enterprises; arbitration and conciliation; online dispute resolution; electronic commerce; insolvency law; and security interests. Its work on the compilation and publication of Case Law on UNCITRAL Texts is ongoing.

ENVIRONMENTAL LAW

The UN has pioneered the development of international environmental law, brokering major treaties that have advanced environmental protection worldwide. The **United Nations Environment Programme** (UNEP) (www.unep.org), which administers many of these treaties, has a long history of contributing toward the development and implementation of environmental law. Its current activities are based on the 2009 Montevideo Programme for the Development and Periodic Review of Environmental Law, which formed a strategy for the international legal community and UNEP to formulate environmental law activities for the decade commencing in 2010. UNEP activities include protecting human rights and the environment; improving environmental governance of global commons; preventing transboundary environmental crime; examining the environmental impacts of military activities; helping to build a green economy; strengthening and "greening" water laws; and the progressive development of environmental law. A number of treaties are administered by UNEP or other entities, including treaty secretariats.

- The 1971 *Convention on Wetlands of International Importance Especially as Waterfowl Habitat* obligates states parties to use wisely all wetlands under their jurisdiction (promoted by UNESCO).
- The 1982 *United Nations Convention on the Law of the Sea* regulates numerous maritime issues, including the protection and preservation of coasts and the marine environment; the prevention and control of marine pollution; rights to living and non-living resources; and the management and conservation of living resources.
- The 1985 *Vienna Convention for the Protection of the Ozone Layer* and the 1987 *Montreal Protocol on Substances that deplete the Ozone Layer* and its amendments seek to reduce damage to the ozone layer, that shields life from the sun's harmful ultraviolet radiation (administered by UNEP).
- The 1992 *United Nations Framework Convention on Climate Change* obligates states parties to reduce emissions of greenhouse gases that cause global warming and related atmospheric problems. Its 1997 *Kyoto Protocol* strengthened the international response to climate change by setting legally binding emission targets for the period 2008–2012.
- The 1994 *United Nations International Convention to Combat Desertification in Those Countries Experiencing Serious Drought and/or Desertification, Particularly in Africa* seeks to promote international cooperation to combat desertification and to mitigate the effects of drought.
- The 1998 *Rotterdam Convention on the Prior Informed Consent Procedure for Certain Hazardous Chemicals and Pesticides in International Trade* obligates exporters of hazardous chemicals or pesticides to inform importing states on the potential dangers of these substances.
- The 2001 *Stockholm Convention on Persistent Organic Pollutants* aims to reduce and eliminate releases of certain highly toxic pesticides, industrial chemicals and by-products—such as DDT, PCBs and dioxin—that are highly mobile and accumulate in the food chain.
- The 2003 *Kyiv Protocol on Strategic Environmental Assessment* requires states parties to evaluate the environmental consequences of their draft plans and programmes.
- The 2008 *Agreement on the Conservation of Small Cetaceans of the Baltic, North East Atlantic, Irish and North Seas* aims to promote cooperation among parties for the conservation of small cetaceans and their habitats.
- The 2010 *Agreement on the Conservation of Cetaceans of the Black Sea, Mediterranean Sea and neighbouring Atlantic Area* seeks to reduce the threat to cetaceans and requires that states ban the deliberate capture of cetaceans and create protected zones.
- The 2013 *Minamata Convention on Mercury*, which aims to protect human health and the environment from the adverse effects of mercury, is not yet in force.

For information on additional environmental law treaties, see biodiversity; chemicals; climate change; desertification; environment; ozone depletion; and hazardous wastes.

LAW OF THE SEA

The *United Nations Convention on the Law of the Sea* (www.un.org/depts/los) is one of the most comprehensive instruments of international law. It contains an all-encompassing legal regime for our oceans and seas, establishing rules governing all activities in the oceans and the use of their resources—including navigation and overflight, exploration and exploitation of minerals, conservation and management of living resources, protection of the marine environment, and marine scientific research. It enshrines the notion that all problems of ocean space are interrelated and need to be addressed as a whole. It embodies in one instrument the codification of traditional rules for the use of the oceans, as well as the development of new rules governing emerging concerns.

It is universally accepted that the *Convention* sets out the legal framework within which all activities in the oceans and the seas must be carried out. Its authority resides in its acceptance—as at December 2016, the *Convention* had 168 parties, including the European Union—and recognition as a source of customary international law.

Impact of the Convention

States have consistently upheld the *Convention* as the pre-eminent international legal instrument in the field, which is often referred to as the "constitution for the oceans". It provides the framework and foundation for any future instruments that seek to clarify the rights and obligations of states with regard to the oceans. Some of its principles that have received near-universal acceptance include:

- twelve nautical miles as the limit of the territorial sea;
- coastal states' sovereign rights and jurisdiction in an "exclusive economic zone" up to 200 nautical miles and over the continental shelf extending up to 200 nautical miles or, under certain circumstances, beyond that limit; and
- the general obligation to protect and preserve the marine environment.

The *Convention* has also brought stability in the area of navigation, establishing the rights of innocent passage through the territorial sea; transit passage through narrow straits used for international navigation; sea lanes passage through archipelagic waters; and freedom of navigation in the exclusive economic zone. The *Convention* has also been acknowledged for its provisions on marine scientific research and on the rights of landlocked states and geographically disadvantaged states.

The acceptance of the *Convention* was facilitated in 1994 by the General Assembly's adoption of the *Agreement Relating to the Implementation of Part XI of the Convention*, which removed certain obstacles relating to the international seabed area that had prevented mainly industrialized countries from becoming parties to the *Convention*. As at December 2016, the *Agreement* had 150 parties.

The 1995 *United Nations Agreement on Straddling Fish Stocks and Highly Migratory Fish Stocks* implements provisions in the *Convention* relating to these fish stocks, setting out the legal regime for their conservation and management. It requires states to cooperate in adopting measures to ensure their long-term sustainability and to promote their optimum utilization. States are also required to cooperate to achieve compatibility of measures with respect to these stocks for areas under national jurisdiction and the adjacent high seas. As at December 2016, the *Agreement* had 84 parties.

Bodies established under the Convention

The *Convention* established three bodies to address various aspects of the law of the sea. The UN has concluded relationship agreements with the first two listed below and the secretariat of the third is provided by the UN Secretary-General.

Through the **International Seabed Authority** (www.isa.org.jm), states parties organize and control activities relating to the deep seabed's mineral resources in the International Seabed Area, defined as "the seabed and ocean floor and the subsoil thereof, beyond the limits of national jurisdiction". Inaugurated in 1994, it is located in Kingston, Jamaica. The Authority adopted regulations on prospecting and exploration for polymetallic nodules in the Area (2000, amended 2013); polymetallic sulphides in the Area (2010); and cobalt-rich ferromanganese crusts in the Area (2012). The first 15-year contracts were signed in 2001. To date, ISA has concluded 15-year exploration contracts with 26 contractors. In addition to regulating deep seabed mining and ensuring that the marine environment is protected from any harmful effects of mining activities, ISA carries out seabed area assessments, maintains a database (POLYDAT) on international seabed area resources, and monitors the status of scientific knowledge of the deep sea marine environment.

The **International Tribunal for the Law of the Sea (ITLOS)** (www.itlos.org) was established to settle disputes relating to the interpretation or application of the *Convention*. Composed of 21 judges elected by the states parties, it was inaugurated in 1996, and it is located in Hamburg, Germany. As at November 2016, some 25 cases had been submitted to the Tribunal, several of them seeking the prompt release of vessels and crews allegedly arrested in breach of the *Convention*. Other cases addressed issues like the conservation of living resources (*New Zealand* v. *Japan*; *Australia* v. *Japan*), the protection and preservation of the marine environment (*Ireland* v. *United Kingdom*; *Malaysia* v. *Singapore*) and maritime boundary delimitation (*Bangladesh* v. *Myanmar*; *Ghana* v. *Côte d'Ivoire*). The Tribunal also considered two requests for advisory opinions.

The **Commission on the Limits of the Continental Shelf (CLCS)** (www.un.org/depts/los/clcs_new/clcs_home.htm) was established to facilitate the implementation of the *Convention* with respect to the delineation of the outer limits of the continental shelf beyond 200 nautical miles. Under article 76, a coastal state may establish the outer limits of its continental shelf beyond 200 nautical miles if certain scientific and technical criteria are met. The Commission held its first session at UN Headquarters in 1997. Its 21 members, elected by the states parties, serve in their personal capacity. They are experts in geology, geophysics, hydrography and geodesy. As at November 2016, the Commission had received 82 submissions and had adopted 26 recommendations.

Meetings of states parties and General Assembly processes

The annual meeting of states parties to the *Convention*, which is convened by the UN Secretary-General, addresses administrative matters, such as the election of members of the Tribunal and the Commission, as well as budgetary matters and general issues that arise with respect to the *Convention*. The Secretary-General has also convened informal consultations of the states parties to the *Fish Stocks Agreement* since its entry into force in 2001, as well as the Review Conference in 2006, 2010 and 2016, in order to monitor the implementation of the *Agreement*.

The General Assembly annually reviews developments in ocean affairs and the law of the sea and has established a number of subsidiary bodies to assist in that task. In 2000, it established the UN Open-ended Informal Consultative Process on Oceans and the Law of the Sea, which convenes annually and makes suggestions to the Assembly on specific issues, with an emphasis on areas where coordination and cooperation at the intergovernmental and inter-agency levels should be enhanced. In 2015, the Assembly decided to develop an international legally binding instrument under the *Convention* on the conservation and sustainable use of marine biological diversity in areas beyond national jurisdiction. It established a preparatory committee to meet in 2016 and 2017 and make recommendations on the elements of a draft text of that instrument. In December 2015, the Assembly welcomed the first global integrated marine assessment. The comprehensive report, known as "World Ocean Assessment I", indicates that the world's oceans are facing major pressures simultaneously and that the limits of their carrying capacity are being, or in some cases have been, reached. The report was the output of the first cycle of the Regular Process for Global Reporting and Assessment of the State of the Marine Environment, including Socioeconomic Aspects (www.worldoceanassessment.org), which aims to regularly review the environmental, economic and social aspects of the world's oceans.

INTERNATIONAL HUMANITARIAN LAW

International humanitarian law encompasses the principles and rules that apply in situations of armed conflict and regulate the conduct of the parties to the conflict, with a view to upholding basic principles of humanity in such situations. It provides protection for civilians, the wounded and sick, and detained persons. It also regulates the means and methods by which military operations are conducted. Major instruments include the four *Geneva Conventions* of 1949 and the two *Additional Protocols* concluded in 1977.

The United Nations has taken a leading role in efforts to advance international humanitarian law. The Security Council has taken action to promote and ensure respect for international humanitarian law, including by establishing the **International Tribunal for the former Yugoslavia** (1993) and the **International Criminal Tribunal for Rwanda** (1994), together with their institutional successor, the **International Residual Mechanism for Criminal Tribunals** (2010), to ensure accountability for serious violations of international humanitarian law. The Council regularly calls on parties to conflict to protect civilians, including women, children, journalists and medical and humanitarian personnel, and is increasingly mandating UN peacekeeping operations deployed to situations of armed conflict to protect civilians under imminent threat of physical violence.

The General Assembly has contributed to elaborating a number of instruments that have significantly advanced the scope and application of international humanitarian law, often through its subsidiary organs, such as the International Law Commission and the Conference on Disarmament, or through UN conferences convened by the Assembly. Among them are the *Convention on Certain Conventional Weapons* (1980) and its *Protocols*; the *Convention on the Rights of the Child* (1989) and its *Optional Protocols*; the *Chemical Weapons Convention* (1992); the *Rome Statute of the International Criminal Court* (1998); and the *Arms Trade Treaty* (2013). The Human Rights Council, which is a subsidiary organ of the General Assembly, has mandated a number of fact-finding missions, commissions of inquiry, special rapporteurs and independent experts to report on specific human rights issues, including potential violations of international humanitarian law.

The International Court of Justice has also made important contributions to the interpretation and application of international humanitarian law through its contentious and advisory cases, such as in the *Legality of the Threat or Use of Nuclear Weapons* of 1996.

INTERNATIONAL TERRORISM

The United Nations has consistently addressed the problem of terrorism in both its legal and political dimensions. The UN has also been the target of terrorism. From Afghanistan to Algeria, from Iraq to Pakistan, UN staff members have lost their lives in the line of duty, in the service of peace, human rights and development. In 2015, four of the six UN personnel who lost their lives due to terrorism were killed in a single terrorist attack in Somalia.

Since 1963, the international community—under the auspices of the UN, its specialized agencies and the International Atomic Energy Agency—has elaborated 12 international legal instruments and five amendments to prevent terrorist acts, including:

- *Convention on Offences and Certain Other Acts Committed on Board Aircraft* (1963) and its *Protocol* (2014);
- *Convention for the Suppression of Unlawful Seizure of Aircraft* (1970) and its supplementary *Protocol* (2010);
- *Convention on the Prevention and Punishment of Crimes against Internationally Protected Persons, including Diplomatic Agents* (1973);
- *International Convention against the Taking of Hostages* (1979);
- *Convention on the Physical Protection of Nuclear Material* (1980) and its amendments (2005);
- *Convention for the Suppression of Unlawful Acts against the Safety of Maritime Navigation* (1988) and its *Protocol* (2005);
- *Protocol for the Suppression of Unlawful Acts against the Safety of Fixed Platforms Located on the Continental Shelf* (1988) and its *Protocol* (2005);
- *Convention on the Marking of Plastic Explosives for the Purpose of Detection* (1991).
- *International Convention for the Suppression of Terrorist Bombings* (1997);
- *International Convention for the Suppression of the Financing of Terrorism* (1999);
- *International Convention for the Suppression of Acts of Nuclear Terrorism* (2005);
- *Convention on the Suppression of Unlawful Acts Relating to International Civil Aviation* (2010).

In 1994, the General Assembly adopted a *Declaration on Measures to Eliminate International Terrorism*. In 1996, in a *Declaration to Supplement the 1994 Declaration*, the Assembly condemned all acts and practices of terrorism as criminal and unjustifiable, wherever and by whomever committed. It also urged states to take measures at the national and international levels to eliminate terrorism. An ad hoc committee established by the Assembly in 1996 was tasked with negotiating a comprehensive convention against terrorism to address gaps left by existing treaties.

After the 11 September 2001 terrorist attacks on the United States, the Security Council established its **Counter-Terrorism Committee** (www.un.org/sc/ctc). Among its functions, the Committee monitors implementation of Council resolutions 1373(2001) and 1624(2005), which imposed certain obligations on member states. These include criminalization of terrorism-related activities, including the provision of assistance to carry them out; denial of funding and safe haven to terrorists; and the exchange of information on terrorist groups.

At the 2005 World Summit, world leaders condemned terrorism in all its forms and requested member states to work through the General Assembly to adopt a counter-terrorism strategy based on recommendations from the UN Secretary-General.

The year 2016 marked the tenth anniversary of the **United Nations Global Counter-Terrorism Strategy** (www.un.org/counterterrorism/ctitf/en/un-global-counter-terrorism-strategy), which was launched in 2006, following its unanimous adoption by the Assembly. Based on the fundamental conviction that terrorism in all its forms is unacceptable and can never be justified, the Strategy outlines a range of measures to address terrorism in all its aspects at the national, regional and international levels. In July 2016, following its fifth biennial review of the Strategy, the Assembly adopted a resolution reinforcing global momentum in the fight against terrorism and violent extremism.

The **Counter-Terrorism Implementation Task Force (CTITF)** (www.un.org/counterterrorism/ctitf), established in 2005 to bring system-wide coordination and coherence in UN counter-terrorism work, was institutionalized in the Department of Political Affairs in December 2009. The CTITF Office, which functions as a secretariat, oversees a CTITF membership that extends to 37 UN entities and INTERPOL and organizes its work through 12 inter-agency working groups. The **United Nations Counter-Terrorism Centre (UNCCT)** was established in September 2011 within the CTITF Office to support member states in implementing the Strategy, through jointly funded capacity-building projects.

The Security Council meets to consider the threat to international peace and security posed by ISIL (Da'esh) and the range of UN efforts in support of member states in countering that threat. (7 February 2017, UN Photo/Rick Bajornas)

INTERNATIONAL CRIMINAL COURT

The International Criminal Court (ICC) (www.icc-cpi.int) is an independent, permanent court that investigates and prosecutes persons accused of the most serious crimes of international concern, namely genocide, crimes against humanity and war crimes. It will also have jurisdiction over the crime of aggression subject to a decision to be taken by its states parties in 2017. The Court was established by the *Rome Statute of the International Criminal Court* (www.un.org/law/icc), adopted at a plenipotentiary conference held in Rome on 17 July 1998. The *Statute* entered into force on 1 July 2002. As at November 2016, it had 124 States parties.

ICC is legally and functionally independent of the United Nations, and is not a part of the UN system. Cooperation between the UN and ICC is governed by a 2004 *Negotiated Relationship Agreement*. The Security Council can refer situations to ICC, including those regarding states not party to the Rome Statute. The Court has 18 judges, elected by the states parties for a term limited to nine years. Judges can, however, remain in office to complete any trial or appeal that has already begun. No two judges can be from the same country.

As at November 2016, the ICC was conducting investigations and judicial proceedings in relation to ten situations: the Central African Republic (two situations), Côte d'Ivoire, Darfur (the Sudan), the Democratic Republic of the Congo, Georgia, Kenya, Libya, Mali and Uganda. The ICC Prosecutor was also conducting preliminary examinations in a number of situations. The ICC was seized of 23 cases. In 2016, the landmark decision against Ahmad Al Faqi Al Mahdi, in the situation in Mali, was the first conviction in an international court for destruction of cultural heritage, while the judgment against Jean-Pierre Bemba Gombo, regarding the Central African Republic situation, addressed elements regarding command responsibility and sexual and gender-based violence.

OTHER LEGAL QUESTIONS

The General Assembly has adopted legal instruments on various other questions concerning the international community and the peoples of the world. Among these are the *International Convention against the Recruitment, Use, Financing and Training of Mercenaries* (1989); the *Convention on the Safety of United Nations and Associated Personnel* (1994); and the *United Nations Convention on Jurisdictional Immunities of States and Their Property* (2004).

The Assembly has also adopted international instruments having to do with the work of the UN itself on the recommendation of the **Special Committee on the *Charter of the United Nations* and on the Strengthening of the Role of the Organization**, established by the Assembly in 1974. These include the *Manila Declaration on the Peaceful Settlement of International Disputes* (1982); the *Declaration on the Prevention and Removal of Disputes and Situations Which May Threaten International Peace and Security and on the Role of the United Nations in this Field* (1988); the *Declaration on Fact-finding by the United Nations in the Field of the Maintenance of International Peace and Security* (1991); the *Declaration on the Enhancement of Cooperation between the United Nations and Regional Arrangements or Agencies in the Maintenance of International Peace and Security* (1994); the *United Nations Model Rules for the Conciliation of Disputes between States* (1995); and General Assembly resolutions on *Prevention and peaceful settlement of disputes* (2002) and the *Introduction and implementation of sanctions imposed by the United Nations* (2009).

Under Article 102 of the *Charter of the United Nations*, every treaty and international agreement entered into by any member state shall be registered with the UN Secretariat and published by it. The UN Office of Legal Affairs is responsible for the registration of treaties and their publication in the *United Nations Treaty Series,* which contains the texts of registered treaties and related subsequent actions. It also discharges the functions of the Secretary-General as depositary of more than 560 multilateral treaties adopted within the UN framework or at UN-convened conferences. All relevant information is available online in the United Nations Treaty Collection (treaties.un.org), which contains more than 250,000 entries and is updated daily.

In Bamako, Mali, MINUSMA supports the preservation
of ancient manuscripts. An employee cleans a page
of a manuscript with a brush, part of the third step of the
preservation process. In a later stage, each page
will be digitalized to facilitate access to the manuscripts
and avoid damages due to the usage
(12 January 2016, UN Photo/Marco Dormino).

Appendix I

UNITED NATIONS MEMBER STATES
(Total membership: 193)

Member state	Date of admission	Scale of assessments for 2016 (per cent)	Net contributions* (US dollars)
Afghanistan	19 November 1946	0.006	151,338
Albania	14 December 1955	0.008	201,783
Algeria	8 October 1962	0.161	4,060,886
Andorra	28 July 1993	0.006	151,338
Angola	1 December 1976	0.010	252,229
Antigua and Barbuda	11 November 1981	0.002	50,446
Argentina	24 October 1945	0.892	22,498,825
Armenia	2 March 1992	0.006	151,338
Australia	1 November 1945	2.337	58,945,913
Austria	4 December 1955	0.720	18,160,486
Azerbaijan	2 March 1992	0.060	1,513,374
Bahamas	18 September 1973	0.014	353,120
Bahrain	21 September 1971	0.044	1,109,807
Bangladesh	17 September 1974	0.010	252,229
Barbados	9 December 1966	0.007	176,560
Belarus[1]	24 October 1945	0.056	1,412,482
Belgium	27 December 1945	0.885	22,322,265
Belize	25 September 1981	0.001	25,223
Benin	20 September 1960	0.003	75,669
Bhutan	21 September 1971	0.001	25,223
Bolivia (Plurinational State of)	14 November 1945	0.012	302,675
Bosnia and Herzegovina[2]	22 May 1992	0.013	327,898
Botswana	17 October 1966	0.014	353,120
Brazil	24 October 1945	3.823	96,427,139
Brunei Darussalam	21 September 1984	0.029	731,464
Bulgaria	14 December 1955	0.045	1,135,031
Burkina Faso	20 September 1960	0.004	100,891
Burundi	18 September 1962	0.001	25,223
Cabo Verde	16 September 1975	0.001	25,223
Cambodia	14 December 1955	0.004	100,891
Cameroon	20 September 1960	0.010	252,229
Canada	9 November 1945	2.921	73,676,084
Central African Republic	20 September 1960	0.001	25,223
Chad	20 September 1960	0.005	126,114
Chile	24 October 1945	0.399	10,063,936
China	24 October 1945	7.921	199,790,575
Colombia	5 November 1945	0.322	8,121,773

Member state	Date of admission	Scale of assessments for 2016 (per cent)	Net contributions* (US dollars)
Comoros	12 November 1975	0.001	25,223
Congo	20 September 1960	0.006	151,338
Costa Rica	2 November 1945	0.047	1,185,476
Côte d'Ivoire	20 September 1960	0.009	227,006
Croatia[2]	22 May 1992	0.099	2,497,067
Cuba	24 October 1945	0.065	1,639,489
Cyprus	20 September 1960	0.043	1,084,585
Czech Republic[3]	19 January 1993	0.344	8,676,677
Democratic People's Republic of Korea	17 September 1991	0.005	126,114
Democratic Republic of the Congo[4]	20 September 1960	0.008	201,783
Denmark	24 October 1945	0.584	14,730,173
Djibouti	20 September 1977	0.001	25,223
Dominica	18 December 1978	0.001	25,223
Dominican Republic	24 October 1945	0.046	1,160,254
Ecuador	21 December 1945	0.067	1,689,934
Egypt[5]	24 October 1945	0.152	3,833,881
El Salvador	24 October 1945	0.014	353,120
Equatorial Guinea	12 November 1968	0.010	252,229
Eritrea	28 May 1993	0.001	25,223
Estonia	17 September 1991	0.038	958,470
Ethiopia	13 November 1945	0.010	252,229
Fiji	13 October 1970	0.003	75,669
Finland	14 December 1955	0.456	11,501,641
France	24 October 1945	4.859	122,558,061
Gabon	20 September 1960	0.017	428,789
Gambia	21 September 1965	0.001	25,223
Georgia	31 July 1992	0.008	201,783
Germany[6]	18 September 1973	6.389	161,149,095
Ghana	8 March 1957	0.016	403,567
Greece	25 October 1945	0.471	11,879,985
Grenada	17 September 1974	0.001	25,223
Guatemala	21 November 1945	0.028	706,241
Guinea	12 December 1958	0.002	50,446
Guinea-Bissau	17 September 1974	0.001	25,223
Guyana	20 September 1966	0.002	50,446
Haiti	24 October 1945	0.003	75,669
Honduras	17 December 1945	0.008	201,783
Hungary	14 December 1955	0.161	4,060,886
Iceland	19 November 1946	0.023	580,127
India	30 October 1945	0.737	18,589,275
Indonesia[7]	28 September 1950	0.504	12,712,341,
Iran (Islamic Republic of)	24 October 1945	0.471	11,879,985
Iraq	21 December 1945	0.129	3,253,754
Ireland	14 December 1955	0.335	8,449,670
Israel	11 May 1949	0.430	10,845,846

Member state	Date of admission	Scale of assessments for 2016 (per cent)	Net contributions* (US dollars)
Italy	14 December 1955	3.748	94,535,422
Jamaica	18 September 1962	0.009	227,006
Japan	18 December 1956	9.680	244,157,652
Jordan	14 December 1955	0.020	504,458
Kazakhstan	2 March 1992	0.191	4,817,573
Kenya	16 December 1963	0.018	454,013
Kiribati	14 September 1999	0.001	25,223
Kuwait	14 May 1963	0.285	7,188,526
Kyrgyzstan	2 March 1992	0.002	50,446
Lao People's Democratic Republic	14 December 1955	0.003	75,669
Latvia	17 September 1991	0.050	1,261,145
Lebanon	24 October 1945	0.046	1,160,254
Lesotho	17 October 1966	0.001	25,223
Liberia	2 November 1945	0.001	25,223
Libya	14 December 1955	0.125	3,152,863
Liechtenstein	18 September 1990	0.007	176,560
Lithuania	17 September 1991	0.072	1,816,049
Luxembourg	24 October 1945	0.064	1,614,265
Madagascar	20 September 1960	0.003	75,669
Malawi	1 December 1964	0.002	50,446
Malaysia[8]	17 September 1957	0.322	8,121,773
Maldives	21 September 1965	0.002	50,446
Mali	28 September 1960	0.003	75,669
Malta	1 December 1964	0.016	403,567
Marshall Islands	17 September 1991	0.001	25,223
Mauritania	27 October 1961	0.002	50,466
Mauritius	24 April 1968	0.012	302,675
Mexico	7 November 1945	1.435	36,194,858
Micronesia (Federated States of)	17 September 1991	0.001	25,223
Monaco	28 May 1993	0.010	252,229
Mongolia	27 October 1961	0.005	126,114
Montenegro[2]	28 June 2006	0.004	100,891
Morocco	12 November 1956	0.054	1,362,036
Mozambique	16 September 1975	0.004	100,891
Myanmar	19 April 1948	0.010	252,229
Namibia	23 April 1990	0.010	252,229
Nauru	14 September 1999	0.001	25,223
Nepal	14 December 1955	0.006	151,338
Netherlands	10 December 1945	1.482	37,380,335
New Zealand	24 October 1945	0.268	6,759,736
Nicaragua	24 October 1945	0.004	100,891
Niger	20 September 1960	0.002	50,466
Nigeria	7 October 1960	0.209	5,271,586
Norway	27 November 1945	0.849	21,414,240
Oman	7 October 1971	0.113	2,850,188

Member state	Date of admission	Scale of assessments for 2016 (per cent)	Net contributions* (US dollars)
Pakistan	30 September 1947	0.093	2,345,730
Palau	15 December 1994	0.001	25,223
Panama	13 November 1945	0.034	857,578
Papua New Guinea	10 October 1975	0.004	100,891
Paraguay	24 October 1945	0.014	353,120
Peru	31 October 1945	0.136	3,430,314
Philippines	24 October 1945	0.165	4,161,778
Poland	24 October 1945	0.841	21,212,458
Portugal	14 December 1955	0.392	9,887,376
Qatar	21 September 1971	0.269	6,784,960
Republic of Korea	17 September 1991	2.039	51,429,489
Republic of Moldova	2 March 1992	0.004	100,891
Romania	14 December 1955	0.184	4,641,013
Russian Federation[9]	24 October 1945	3.088	77,888,309
Rwanda	18 September 1962	0.002	50,446
Saint Kitts and Nevis	23 September 1983	0.001	25,223
Saint Lucia	18 September 1979	0.001	25,223
Saint Vincent and the Grenadines	16 September 1980	0.001	25,223
Samoa	15 December 1976	0.001	25,223
San Marino	2 March 1992	0.003	75,669
Sao Tome and Principe	16 September 1975	0.001	25,223
Saudi Arabia	24 October 1945	1.146	28,905,441
Senegal	28 September 1960	0.005	126,114
Serbia[2]	1 November 2000	0.032	807,113
Seychelles	21 September 1976	0.001	25,223
Sierra Leone	27 September 1961	0.001	25,223
Singapore[8]	21 September 1965	0.447	11,274,636
Slovakia[3]	19 January 1993	0.160	4,035,664
Slovenia[2]	22 May 1992	0.084	2,118,723
Solomon Islands	19 September 1978	0.001	25,223
Somalia	20 September 1960	0.001	25,223
South Africa	7 November 1945	0.364	9,181,135
South Sudan[10]	14 July 2011	0.003	75,669
Spain	14 December 1955	2.443	61,619,540
Sri Lanka	14 December 1955	0.031	781,909
Sudan	12 November 1956	0.010	252,229
Suriname	4 December 1975	0.006	151,338
Swaziland	24 September 1968	0.002	50,446
Sweden	19 November 1946	0.956	24,113,090
Switzerland	10 September 2002	1.140	28,754,104
Syrian Arab Republic[5]	24 October 1945	0.024	605,349
Tajikistan	2 March 1992	0.004	100,891
Thailand	16 December 1946	0.291	7,339,863
The former Yugoslav Republic of Macedonia[2]	8 April 1993	0.007	176,560

Member state	Date of admission	Scale of assessments for 2016 (per cent)	Net contributions* (US dollars)
Timor-Leste	27 September 2002	0.003	75,669
Togo	20 September 1960	0.001	25,223
Tonga	14 September 1999	0.001	25,223
Trinidad and Tobago	18 September 1962	0.034	857,578
Tunisia	12 November 1956	0.028	706,241
Turkey	24 October 1945	1.018	25,676,910
Turkmenistan	2 March 1992	0.026	655,795
Tuvalu	5 September 2000	0.001	25,223
Uganda	25 October 1962	0.009	227,006
Ukraine	24 October 1945	0.103	2,597,959
United Arab Emirates	9 December 1971	0.604	15,234,631
United Kingdom of Great Britain and Northern Ireland	24 October 1945	4.463	112,569,794
United Republic of Tanzania[11]	14 December 1961	0.010	252,229
United States of America	24 October 1945	22.000	610,836,578
Uruguay	18 December 1945	0.079	1,992,609
Uzbekistan	2 March 1992	0.023	580,127
Vanuatu	15 September 1981	0.001	25,223
Venezuela (Bolivarian Republic of)	15 November 1945	0.571	14,402,275
Viet Nam	20 September 1977	0.058	1,462,928
Yemen[12]	30 September 1947	0.010	252,229
Zambia	1 December 1964	0.007	176,560
Zimbabwe	25 August 1980	0.004	100,891

Non-member states

The following states are not members of the United Nations but have been invited to participate as observers in the sessions and the work of the General Assembly, and maintain permanent observer missions at Headquarters:

* Holy See
* State of Palestine

The Holy See contributes towards the expenses of the Organization based on a scale of assessment of 0.001 per cent.

* Net contributions are equal to gross contributions less total staff assessment amounts for each country. The staff assessment is an amount deducted from all UN staff members' gross pay and credited to the Tax Equalization Fund, which is used to resolve issues related to staff members' taxes.

Notes

1 On 19 September 1991, the Byelorussian Soviet Socialist Republic informed the United Nations that it had changed its name to Belarus.

2 The Socialist Federal Republic of Yugoslavia was an original member of the United Nations, the *Charter* having been signed on its behalf on 26 June 1945 and ratified 19 October 1945, until its dissolution following the establishment and subsequent admission, as new members, of Bosnia and Herzegovina, the Republic of Croatia, the Republic of Slovenia, The former Yugoslav Republic of Macedonia, and the Federal Republic of Yugoslavia. The Republic of Bosnia and Herzegovina, the Republic of Croatia and the Republic of Slovenia were admitted as members of the United Nations on 22 May 1992. On 8 April 1993, the General Assembly decided to admit as a member of the United Nations the state provisionally referred to for all purposes within the United Nations as "The former Yugoslav Republic of Macedonia" pending settlement of the difference that had arisen over its name. The Federal Republic of Yugoslavia was admitted as a member of the United Nations on 1 November 2000. On 12 February 2003, it informed the United Nations that it had changed its name to Serbia and Montenegro, effective 4 February 2003. In a letter dated 3 June 2006, the President of the Republic of Serbia informed the Secretary-General that the membership of Serbia and

Montenegro was being continued by the Republic of Serbia following Montenegro's declaration of independence from Serbia on 3 June 2006. On 28 June 2006, Montenegro was accepted as a United Nations
member state by the General Assembly.

3 Czechoslovakia, an original member of the United Nations from 24 October 1945, changed its name to the
   Czech and Slovak Federal Republic on 20 April 1990. It was dissolved on 1 January 1993 and succeeded by the
   Czech Republic and Slovakia, both of which became members of the United Nations on 19 January 1993.

4 The Republic of Zaire informed the United Nations that, effective 17 May 1997, it had changed its name to
   the Democratic Republic of the Congo.

5 Egypt and Syria were original members of the United Nations from 24 October 1945. Following a plebiscite on
   21 February 1958, the United Arab Republic was established by a union of Egypt and Syria and continued as
   a single member. On 13 October 1961, Syria, having resumed its status as an independent state, resumed its
   separate membership in the United Nations; it changed its name to the Syrian Arab Republic on 14 September
   1971. On 2 September 1971, the United Arab Republic changed its name to the Arab Republic of Egypt.

6 The Federal Republic of Germany and the German Democratic Republic were admitted to membership
   in the United Nations on 18 September 1973. Through the accession of the German Democratic Republic
   to the Federal Republic of Germany, effective 3 October 1990, the two German states united to form one
   sovereign state. As of that date, the Federal Republic of Germany has acted in the United Nations under the
   designation Germany.

7 By a letter of 20 January 1965, Indonesia announced its decision to withdraw from the United Nations "at
   this stage and under the present circumstances". By a telegram of 19 September 1966, it announced its decision "to resume full cooperation with the United Nations and to resume participation in its activities". On 28
   September 1966, the General Assembly took note of this decision, and the President invited representatives
   of Indonesia to take their seats in the Assembly.

8 The Federation of Malaya joined the United Nations on 17 September 1957. On 16 September 1963, its name
   was changed to Malaysia, following the admission to the new federation of Sabah (North Borneo), Sarawak
   and Singapore. Singapore became an independent state on 9 August 1965 and a member of the United
   Nations on 21 September 1965.

9 The Union of Soviet Socialist Republics was an original member of the United Nations from 24 October
   1945. On 24 December 1991, the President of the Russian Federation informed the Secretary-General that
   the membership of the Soviet Union in the Security Council and all other UN organs was being continued
   by the Russian Federation with the support of the 11 member countries of the Commonwealth of Independent States.

10 The Republic of South Sudan formally seceded from Sudan on 9 July 2011 as a result of an internationally
   monitored referendum held in January 2011, and was admitted as a new United Nations member state on
   14 July 2011.

11 Tanganyika was a member of the United Nations from 14 December 1961 and Zanzibar from 16 December
   1963. Following the ratification on 26 April 1964 of Articles of Union between Tanganyika and Zanzibar,
   the United Republic of Tanganyika and Zanzibar continued as a single member, changing its name to the
   United Republic of Tanzania on 1 November 1964.

12 Yemen was admitted to membership in the United Nations on 30 September 1947 and Democratic Yemen
   on 14 December 1967. On 22 May 1990, the two countries merged and have since been represented as one
   member of the United Nations with the name Yemen.

Appendix II

PEACEKEEPING OPERATIONS: PAST AND PRESENT

UNTSO*	United Nations Truce Supervision Organization (Jerusalem)	May 1948–present
UNMOGIP*	United Nations Military Observer Group in India and Pakistan	January 1949–present
UNEF I	First United Nations Emergency Force (Gaza)	November 1956–June 1967
UNOGIL	United Nations Observation Group in Lebanon	June–December 1958
ONUC	United Nations Operation in the Congo	July 1960–June 1964
UNSF	United Nations Security Force in West New Guinea (West Irian)	October 1962–April 1963
UNYOM	United Nations Yemen Observation Mission	July 1963–September 1964
UNFICYP*	United Nations Peacekeeping Force in Cyprus	March 1964–present
DOMREP	Mission of the Representative of the Secretary-General in the Dominican Republic	May 1965–October 1966
UNIPOM	United Nations India-Pakistan Observation Mission	September 1965–March 1966
UNEF II	Second United Nations Emergency Force (Suez Canal and later Sinai Peninsula)	October 1973–July 1979
UNDOF*	United Nations Disengagement Observer Force (Syrian Golan Heights)	May 1974–present
UNIFIL*	United Nations Interim Force in Lebanon	March 1978–present
UNGOMAP	United Nations Good Offices Mission in Afghanistan and Pakistan	May 1988–March 1990
UNIIMOG	United Nations Iran-Iraq Military Observer Group	August 1988–February 1991
UNAVEM I	United Nations Angola Verification Mission I	December 1988–June 1991
UNTAG	United Nations Transition Assistance Group (Namibia and Angola)	April 1989–March 1990
ONUCA	United Nations Observer Group in Central America	November 1989–January 1992
MINURSO*	United Nations Mission for the Referendum in Western Sahara	April 1991–present
UNIKOM	United Nations Iraq-Kuwait Observation Mission	April 1991–October 2003
UNAVEM II	United Nations Angola Verification Mission II	May 1991–February 1995
ONUSAL	United Nations Observer Mission in El Salvador	July 1991–April 1995
UNAMIC	United Nations Advance Mission in Cambodia	October 1991–March 1992
UNPROFOR	United Nations Protection Force (former Yugoslavia)	February 1992–March 1995
UNTAC	United Nations Transitional Authority in Cambodia	February 1992–September 1993
UNOSOM I	United Nations Operation in Somalia I	April 1992–March 1993
ONUMOZ	United Nations Operation in Mozambique	December 1992–December 1994
UNOSOM II	United Nations Operation in Somalia II	March 1993–March 1995
UNOMUR	United Nations Observer Mission Uganda-Rwanda	June 1993–September 1994
UNOMIG	United Nations Observer Mission in Georgia	August 1993–June 2009
UNOMIL	United Nations Observer Mission in Liberia	September 1993–September 1997
UNMIH	United Nations Mission in Haiti	September 1993–June 1996
UNAMIR	United Nations Assistance Mission for Rwanda	October 1993–March 1996
UNASOG	United Nations Aouzou Strip Observer Group (Chad/Libya)	May–June 1994

UNMOT	United Nations Mission of Observers in Tajikistan	December 1994–May 2000
UNAVEM III	United Nations Angola Verification Mission III	February 1995–June 1997
UNCRO	United Nations Confidence Restoration Operation in Croatia	March 1995–January 1996
UNPREDEP	United Nations Preventive Deployment Force (The former Yugoslav Republic of Macedonia)	March 1995–February 1999
UNMIBH	United Nations Mission in Bosnia and Herzegovina	December 1995–December 2002
UNTAES	United Nations Transitional Administration for Eastern Slavonia, Baranja and Western Sirmium (Croatia)	January 1996–January 1998
UNMOP	United Nations Mission of Observers in Prevlaka	February 1996–December 2002
UNSMIH	United Nations Support Mission in Haiti	July 1996–July 1997
MINUGUA	United Nations Verification Mission in Guatemala	January–May 1997
MONUA	United Nations Observer Mission in Angola	June 1997–February 1999
UNTMIH	United Nations Transition Mission in Haiti	August–November 1997
MIPONUH	United Nations Civilian Police Mission in Haiti	December 1997–March 2000
UNPSG	United Nations Civilian Police Support Group (Croatia)	January–October 1998
MINURCA	United Nations Mission in the Central African Republic	April 1998–February 2000
UNOMSIL	United Nations Observer Mission in Sierra Leone	July 1998–October 1999
UNMIK*	United Nations Interim Administration Mission in Kosovo	June 1999–present
UNAMSIL	United Nations Mission in Sierra Leone	October 1999–December 2005
UNTAET	United Nations Transitional Administration in East Timor	October 1999–May 2002
MONUC	United Nations Observer Mission in the Democratic Republic of the Congo	December 1999–June 2010
UNMEE	United Nations Mission in Ethiopia and Eritrea	July 2000–July 2008
UNAMA**	United Nations Assistance Mission in Afghanistan	March 2002–present
UNMISET	United Nations Mission of Support in East Timor	May 2002–May 2005
MINUCI	United Nations Mission in Côte d'Ivoire	May 2003–April 2004
UNMIL*	United Nations Mission in Liberia	September 2003–present
UNOCI*	United Nations Operation in Côte d'Ivoire	April 2004–present
MINUSTAH*	United Nations Stabilization Mission in Haiti	June 2004–present
UNMIS	United Nations Mission in the Sudan	March 2005–July 2011
ONUB	United Nations Operation in Burundi	May 2004–December 2006
UNMIT	United Nations Integrated Mission in Timor-Leste	August 2006–December 2012
BINUB	United Nations Integrated Office in Burundi	October 2006–December 2010
UNAMID*	African Union/United Nations Hybrid Operation in Darfur	July 2007–present
MINURCAT	United Nations Mission in the Central African Republic and Chad	September 2007–December 2010
MONUSCO*	United Nations Organization Stabilization Mission in the Democratic Republic of the Congo	July 2010–present
UNISFA*	United Nations Interim Security Force for Abyei	June 2011–present
UNMISS*	United Nations Mission in the Republic of South Sudan	July 2011–present
UNSMIS	United Nations Supervision Mission in Syria	April 2012–August 2012
MINUSMA*	United Nations Multidimensional Integrated Stabilization Mission in Mali	April 2013–present

* Current operation.
** Current political mission directed and supported by DPKO.

For the most up-to-date listing of United Nations Peacekeeping Operations, please visit the website: www.un.org/en/peacekeeping.

Appendix III

DECOLONIZATION

Trust and Non-Self-Governing Territories that have achieved independence since the adoption of the *Declaration on the Granting of Independence to Colonial Countries and Peoples* on 14 December 1960

Region/Country	Date of UN admission	Region/Country	Date of UN admission
AFRICA		**CARIBBEAN**	
Algeria	8 October 1962	**Antigua**	
Angola	1 December 1976	**and Barbuda**	11 November 1981
Botswana	17 October 1966	**Bahamas**	18 September 1973
Burundi	18 September 1962	**Barbados**	9 December 1966
Cape Verde	16 September 1975	**Belize**	25 September 1981
Comoros	12 November 1975	**Dominica**	18 December 1978
Djibouti	20 September 1977	**Grenada**	17 December 1974
Equatorial Guinea	12 November 1968	**Guyana**	20 September 1966
Gambia	21 September 1965	**Jamaica**	18 September 1962
Guinea-Bissau	17 September 1974	**Saint Kitts**	
Kenya	16 December 1963	**and Nevis**	23 September 1983
Lesotho	17 October 1966	**Saint Lucia**	18 September 1979
Malawi	1 December 1964	**Saint Vincent**	
Mauritius	24 April 1968	**and the Grenadines**	16 September 1980
Mozambique	16 September 1975	**Suriname**[2]	4 December 1975
Namibia	23 April 1990	**Trinidad and Tobago**	18 September 1962
Rwanda	18 September 1962	**EUROPE**	
Sao Tome and Principe	26 September 1975	**Malta**	1 December 1964
Seychelles	21 September 1976	**PACIFIC**	
Sierra Leone	27 September 1961	**Federated States**	
Swaziland	24 September 1968	**of Micronesia**	17 September 1991
Uganda	25 October 1962	**Fiji**	13 October 1970
United Republic of		**Kiribati**	14 September 1999
Tanzania[1]	14 December 1961	**Marshall Islands**	17 September 1991
Zambia	1 December 1964	**Nauru**	14 September 1999
Zimbabwe	18 April 1980	**Palau**	15 December 1994
ASIA		**Papua New Guinea**	10 October 1975
Brunei Darussalam	21 September 1984	**Samoa**	15 December 1976
Democratic Yemen	14 December 1967	**Solomon Islands**	19 September 1978
Oman	7 October 1971	**Timor-Leste**	27 September 2002
Singapore	21 September 1965	**Tuvalu**	5 September 2000

1 The former Trust Territory of Tanganyika, which became independent in December 1961, and the former Protectorate of Zanzibar, which achieved independence in December 1963, united into a single state in April 1964.
2 By resolution 945(X), the General Assembly accepted the cessation of the transmission of information regarding Suriname following constitutional changes in the relationship between the Netherlands, Suriname and the Netherlands Antilles.

Dependent Territories that have become integrated or associated with independent states since the adoption of the *Declaration on the Granting of Independence to Colonial Countries* and Peoples on 14 December 1960

Territory	
Cameroons (under British administration)	The northern part of the Trust Territory joined the Federation of Nigeria on 1 June 1961 and the southern part joined the Republic of Cameroon on 1 October 1961.
Cook Islands	Fully self-governing in free association with New Zealand since August 1965.
Ifni	Returned to Morocco in June 1969.
Niue	Fully self-governing in free association with New Zealand since August 1974.
North Borneo	North Borneo and Sarawak joined the Federation of Malaya in 1963 to form the Federation of Malaysia.
São Joao Batista de Ajuda	Nationally united with Dahomey (now Benin) in August 1961.
Sarawak	Sarawak and North Borneo joined the Federation of Malaya in 1963 to form the Federation of Malaysia.
West New Guinea (West Irian)	United with Indonesia in 1963.
Cocos (Keeling) Islands	Integrated with Australia in 1984.

Trust Territories that have achieved self-determination

Territory	
Togoland (under British administration)	United with the Gold Coast (Colony and Protectorate), a Non-Self-Governing Territory administered by the United Kingdom, in 1957 to form Ghana.
Somaliland (under Italian administration)	United with British Somaliland Protectorate in 1960 to form Somalia.
Togoland (under French administration)	Became independent as Togo in 1960.
Cameroons (under French administration)	Became independent as Cameroon in 1960.
Tanganyika (under British administration)	Became independent in 1961 (in 1964, Tanganyika and the former Protectorate of Zanzibar, which had become independent in 1963, united as a single state under the name of the United Republic of Tanzania).
Ruanda-Urundi (under Belgian administration)	Voted to divide into the two sovereign states of Rwanda and Burundi in 1962.
Western Samoa (under New Zealand administration)	Became independent as Samoa in 1962.
Nauru (administered by Australia on behalf of Australia, New Zealand and the United Kingdom)	Became independent in 1968.
New Guinea (administered by Australia)	United with the Non-Self-Governing Territory of Papua, also administered by Australia, to become the independent state of Papua New Guinea in 1975.

Trust Territories of the Pacific Islands

Territory	
Federated States of Micronesia	Became fully self-governing in free Association with the United States in 1990.
Republic of the Marshall Islands	Became fully self-governing in free Association with the United States in 1990.
Commonwealth of the Northern Mariana Islands	Became fully self-governing as a Commonwealth of the United States in 1990.
Palau	Became fully self-governing in free Association with the United States in 1994.

Appendix IV

UNITED NATIONS OBSERVANCES

International Decades

2016–2025	United Nations Decade of Action on Nutrition
2015–2024	International Decade for People of African Descent
2014–2024	United Nations Decade of Sustainable Energy for All
2011–2020	Third International Decade for the Eradication of Colonialism
	United Nations Decade on Biodiversity
	Decade of Action for Road Safety
2010–2020	United Nations Decade for Deserts and the Fight against Desertification
2008–2017	Second United Nations Decade for the Eradication of Poverty
2006–2016	Decade of Recovery and Sustainable Development of the Affected Regions (third decade after the Chernobyl disaster)

International Years

2017	International Year of Sustainable Tourism for Development
2016	International Year of Pulses
2015	International Year of Light and Light-based Technologies
	International Year of Soils (FAO)
2014	International Year of Solidarity with the Palestinian People

Annual Weeks

First week of February	World Interfaith Harmony Week
21–27 March	Week of Solidarity with the Peoples Struggling against Racism and Racial Discrimination
19–23 April	Global Soil Week
24–30 April	World Immunization Week (WHO)
25–31 May	Week of Solidarity with the Peoples of Non-Self-Governing Territories
1–7 August	World Breastfeeding Week (WHO)
4–10 October	World Space Week
24–30 October	Disarmament Week
The week of 11 November	International Week of Science and Peace

Annual Days

27 January	International Day of Commemoration in Memory of the Victims of the Holocaust
4 February	World Cancer Day (WHO)
6 February	International Day of Zero Tolerance to Female Genital Mutilation (WHO)
11 February	International Day of Women and Girls in Science
13 February	World Radio Day (UNESCO)
20 February	World Day of Social Justice
21 February	International Mother Language Day (UNESCO)
1 March	Zero Discrimination Day (UNAIDS)
3 March	World Wildlife Day

8 March	International Women's Day
20 March	International Day of Happiness
	French Language Day
21 March	International Day for the Elimination of Racial Discrimination
	World Poetry Day
	International Day of Nowruz
	World Down Syndrome Day
	International Day of Forests
22 March	World Water Day
23 March	World Meteorological Day (WMO)
24 March	International Day for the Right to the Truth concerning Gross Human Rights Violations and for the Dignity of Victims
	World Tuberculosis Day (WHO)
25 March	International Day of Remembrance of the Victims of Slavery and the Transatlantic Slave Trade
	International Day of Solidarity with Detained and Missing Staff Members
2 April	World Autism Awareness Day
4 April	International Day for Mine Awareness and Assistance in Mine Action
6 April	International Day of Sport for Development and Peace
7 April	World Health Day (WHO)
	International Day of Reflection on the Genocide in Rwanda
12 April	International Day of Human Space Flight
20 April	Chinese Language Day
22 April	International Mother Earth Day
23 April	World Book and Copyright Day (UNESCO)
	English Language Day
	Spanish Language Day
25 April	World Malaria Day (WHO)
26 April	International Chernobyl Disaster Remembrance Day
	World Intellectual Property Day (WIPO)
28 April	World Day for Safety and Health at Work (ILO)
29 April	Day of Remembrance for all Victims of Chemical Warfare
30 April	International Jazz Day (UNESCO)
3 May	World Tuna Day
	World Press Freedom Day
8–9 May	Time of Remembrance and Reconciliation for Those Who Lost Their Lives during the Second World War
10 May	World Migratory Bird Day (UNEP)
	"Vesak", the Day of the Full Moon
15 May	International Day of Families
17 May	World Telecommunication and Information Society Day (ITU)
21 May	World Day for Cultural Diversity for Dialogue and Development
22 May	International Day for Biological Diversity
23 May	International Day to End Obstetric Fistula
29 May	International Day of UN Peacekeepers
31 May	World No-Tobacco Day (WHO)
1 June	Global Day of Parents
4 June	International Day of Innocent Children Victims of Aggression
5 June	World Environment Day (UNEP)

6 June	Russian Language Day
8 June	World Oceans Day
12 June	World Day Against Child Labour (ILO)
13 June	International Albinism Awareness Day
14 June	World Blood Donor Day (WHO)
15 June	World Elder Abuse Awareness Day
16 June	International Day of Family Remittances
17 June	World Day to Combat Desertification and Drought
19 June	International Day for the Elimination of Sexual Violence in Conflict
20 June	World Refugee Day
21 June	International Day of Yoga
23 June	International Widows' Day
	United Nations Public Service Day
25 June	Day of the Seafarer (IMO)
26 June	International Day against Drug Abuse and Illicit Trafficking
	United Nations International Day in Support of Victims of Torture
30 June	International Asteroid Day
First Saturday of July	International Day of Cooperatives
11 July	World Population Day
15 July	World Youth Skills Day
18 July	Nelson Mandela International Day
28 July	World Hepatitis Day (WHO)
30 July	International Day of Friendship
	World Day against Trafficking in Persons
9 August	International Day of the World's Indigenous People
12 August	International Youth Day
19 August	World Humanitarian Day
23 August	International Day for the Remembrance of the Slave Trade and Its Abolition (UNESCO)
29 August	International Day against Nuclear Tests
30 August	International Day of the Victims of Enforced Disappearances
5 September	International Day of Charity
8 September	International Literacy Day (UNESCO)
12 September	United Nations Day for South-South Cooperation
15 September	International Day of Democracy
16 September	International Day for the Preservation of the Ozone Layer
21 September	International Day of Peace
26 September	International Day for the Total Elimination of Nuclear Weapons
27 September	World Tourism Day (UNWTO)
28 September	World Rabies Day (WHO)
Last Thursday of September	World Maritime Day (IMO)
1 October	International Day of Older Persons
2 October	International Day of Non-Violence
First Monday in October	World Habitat Day
5 October	World Teachers' Day (UNESCO)
9 October	World Post Day (UPU)
10 October	World Mental Health Day (WHO)
11 October	International Day of the Girl Child
13 October	International Day for Disaster Reduction

15 October	International Day of Rural Women
16 October	World Food Day (FAO)
17 October	International Day for the Eradication of Poverty
20 October (every five years, beginning in 2010)	World Statistics Day
24 October	United Nations Day
	World Development Information Day
27 October	World Day for Audiovisual Heritage (UNESCO)
31 October	World Cities Day
2 November	International Day to End Impunity for Crimes against Journalists
5 November	World Tsunami Awareness Day
6 November	International Day for Preventing the Exploitation of the Environment in War and Armed Conflict
10 November	World Science Day for Peace and Development (UNESCO)
14 November	World Diabetes Day (WHO)
16 November	International Day for Tolerance
Third Thursday in November	World Philosophy Day (UNESCO)
Third Sunday in November	World Day of Remembrance for Road Traffic Victims (WHO)
19 November	World Toilet Day
20 November	Africa Industrialization Day
	Universal Children's Day
21 November	World Television Day
25 November	International Day for the Elimination of Violence against Women
29 November	International Day of Solidarity with the Palestinian People
1 December	World AIDS Day
2 December	International Day for the Abolition of Slavery
3 December	International Day of Persons with Disabilities
5 December	World Soil Day
	International Volunteer Day for Economic and Social Development
7 December	International Civil Aviation Day (ICAO)
9 December	International Anti-Corruption Day
	International Day of Commemoration and Dignity of the Victims of the Crime of Genocide and of the Prevention of this Crime
10 December	Human Rights Day
11 December	International Mountain Day
18 December	International Migrants Day
	Arabic Language Day
20 December	International Human Solidarity Day

For the most up-to-date listing of United Nations Observances, please visit the website: www.un.org/observances.

UN INFORMATION CENTRES, SERVICES AND OFFICES

AFRICA

Accra
Gamal Abdel Nasser/Liberia Roads
(P.O. Box GP 2339)
Accra, Ghana
Tel.: (233) 30 2 665511
Fax: (233) 30 2 701 0943
E-mail: unic.accra@unic.org
Website: http://accra.unic.org
Serving: Ghana, Sierra Leone

Algiers
41 Rue Mohamed Khoudi, El Biar
El Biar, 16030 El Biar, Alger
(Boîte Postale 444, Hydra-Alger 16035)
Algiers, Algeria
Tel.: (213 21) 92 54 42
Fax: (213 21) 92 54 42
E-mail: unic.algiers@unic.org
Website: http://algiers.unic.org
Serving: Algeria

Antananarivo
159, Rue Damantsoa, Ankorahotra
(Boîte Postale, 1348)
Antananarivo, Madagascar
Tel.: (261 20) 22 330 50
Fax: (261 20) 22 367 94
E-mail: unic.antananarivo@unic.org
Website: http://antananarivo.unic.org
Serving: Madagascar

Asmara
Hiday Street, Airport Road
(P.O. Box 5366)
Asmara, Eritrea
Tel.: (291 1) 15 11 66, Ext. 311
Fax: (291 1) 15 10 81
E-mail: dpi.er@undp.org
Website: http://asmara.unic.org
Serving: Eritrea

Brazzaville
Avenue Foch, Case Ortf 15
(Boîte Postale 13210)
Brazzaville, Congo
Tel.: (242) 06 661 20 68
E-mail: unic.brazzaville@unic.org
Website: http://brazzaville.unic.org
Serving: Congo

Bujumbura
13 Avenue de la Révolution
(Boîte Postale 2160)
Bujumbura, Burundi
Tel.: (257) 22 50 18
Fax: (257) 24 17 98

E-mail: unic.bujumbura@unic.org
Website: http://bujumbura.unic.org
Serving: Burundi

Cairo
1 Osiris Street, Garden City
(P.O. Box 262)
Cairo, Egypt
Tel.: (202) 27959816
Fax: (202) 27953705
E-mail: info@unic-eg.org
Website: http://www.unic-eg.org
Serving: Egypt, Saudi Arabia

Dakar
Parcelle N° 20
Route du King Fahd
   (ex. Meridien President)
en face Hotel le LITTORAL
(Boîte Postale 154)
Dakar, Senegal
Tel.: (221) 33 869 99 11
Fax: (221) 33 820 3046
E-mail: unic.dakar@unic.org
Website: http://dakar.unic.org
Serving: Cape Verde, Côte
   d'Ivoire, Gambia, Guinea-Bissau,
   Mauritania, Senegal

Dar es Salaam
182 Mzinga Way, Oysterbay
(P.O. Box 9224)
Dar es Salaam, United Republic
   of Tanzania
E-mail: unic.daressalaam@unic.org
Website: http://daressalaam.unic.org
Serving: United Republic of Tanzania

Harare
Sanders House (2nd floor),
cnr. First Street
Jason Moyo Avenue
(P.O. Box 4408)
Harare, Zimbabwe
Tel.: (263 4) 777 060
Fax: (263 4) 750 476
E-mail: unic.harare@unic.org
Website: http://harare.unic.org
Serving: Zimbabwe

Khartoum
United Nations Compound House
   #7, Blk 5
Gamma'a Avenue
(P.O. Box 1992)
Khartoum, Sudan
Tel.: (249 183) 783 755
Fax: (249 183) 773 772

E-mail: unic.sd@undp.org
Website: http://khartoum.unic.org
Serving: Somalia, Sudan

Lagos
17 Alfred Rewane Road
(formely Kingsway Road), Ikoyi
(P.O. Box 1068), Lagos, Nigeria
Tel.: (234 1) 775 5989
Fax: (234 1) 463 0916
E-mail: lagos@unic.org
Website: http://lagos.unic.org
Serving: Nigeria

Lomé
468, Angle rue Atime
Avenue de la Libération
(Boîte Postale 911)
Lomé, Togo
Tel.: (228) 22 21 23 06
Fax: (228) 22 21 11 65
E-mail: unic.lome@unic.org
Website: http://lome.unic.org
Serving: Benin, Togo

Lusaka
Zambia Revenue Authority
Revenue House (Ground floor)
Kalambo Road
(P.O. Box 32905, Lusaka 10101)
Lusaka, Zambia
Tel.: (260 211) 228 487
Fax: (260 211) 222 958
E-mail: unic.lusaka@unic.org
Website: http://lusaka.unic.org
Serving: Malawi, Swaziland, Zambia

Nairobi
United Nations Office, Gigiri
(P.O. Box 67578-00200)
Nairobi, Kenya
Tel.: (254 20) 762 25421
Fax: (254 20) 762 24349
E-mail: nairobi.unic@unon.org
Website: http://unicnairobi.org
Serving: Kenya, Seychelles, Uganda

Ouagadougou
14 Avenue de la Grande Chancellerie
Secteur no. 4
(Bôite Postale 135, Ougadougou 01)
Ougadougou, Burkina Faso
Tel.: (226) 5030 6076
Fax: (226) 5031 1322
E-mail: unic.ouagadougou@unic.org
Website: http://ouagadougou.unic.org
Serving: Burkina Faso, Chad, Mali,
   Niger

Pretoria
Metropark Building
351 Francis Baard Street
(P.O. Box 12677, Tramshed)
Pretoria, South Africa 0126
Tel.: (27 12) 3548 506
Fax: (27 12) 3548 501
E-mail: unic.pretoria@unic.org
Website: http://pretoria.unic.org
Serving: South Africa

Rabat
13 Avenue Ahmed Balafrej
(Boîte Postale 601), Casier ONU
Rabat-Chellah
Rabat, Morocco
Tel.: (212 537) 75 03 93
Fax: (212 37) 75 03 82
E-mail: cinu.rabat@unic.org
Website: http://www.unicmor.ma
Serving: Morocco

Tunis
41 Bis, Av. Louis Braille
Cité El Khadra
(Boîte Postale 863)
1003 Tunis, Tunisia
Tel.: (216 36) 405235
Fax: (216 36) 405236
E-mail: unic.tunis@unic.org
Website: http://www.unictunis.
org.tn
Serving: Tunisia

Windhoek
UN House, 38–44 Stein Street, Klein
(Private Bag 13351)
Windhoek, Namibia
Tel.: (264 61) 2046111
Fax: (264 61) 2046521
E-mail: unic.windhoek@unic.org
Website: tunis.sites.unicnetwork.org
Serving: Namibia

Yaoundé
Immeuble Tchinda
Rue 2044
Derrière camp SIC TSINGA
(Boîte Postale 836)
Yaoundé, Cameroon
Tel.: (237) 2 221 23 67
Fax: (237) 2 221 23 68
E-mail: unic.yaounde@unic.org
Website: http://yaounde.unic.org
Serving: Cameroon, Central African
Republic, Gabon

THE AMERICAS

Asunción
Avda. Mariscal López esq. Guillermo
Saraví
Edificio Naciones Unidas
(Casilla de Correo 1107)
Asunción, Paraguay
Tel.: (595 21) 614 443
E-mail: unic.asuncion@unic.org
Website: http://asuncion.unic.org
Serving: Paraguay

Bogotá
Calle 100 No. 8A-55 Piso 10
Edificio World Trade Center-Torre "C"
(Apartado, Aéro 058964)
Bogotá 2, Colombia
Tel.: (57 1) 257 6044
Fax: (57 1) 257 6244
E-mail: unic.bogota@unic.org
Website: http://www.nacionesunidas.
org.co
Serving: Colombia,Ecuador,Venezuela

Buenos Aires
Junín 1940, 1er Piso
1113 Buenos Aires, Argentina
Tel.: (54 11) 4803 7671
Fax: (54 11) 4804 7545
E-mail: unic.buenosaires@unic.org
Website: http://www.onu.org.ar
Serving: Argentina, Uruguay

La Paz
Calle 14 esq. S. Bustamante
Edificio Metrobol II, Calacoto
(Apartado Postal 9072)
La Paz, Bolivia
Tel.: (591 2) 262 4512
Fax: (591 2) 279 5820
E-mail: unic.lapaz@unic.org
Website: http://www.nu.org.bo
Serving: Bolivia

Lima
Av. Perez Aranibar 750
Magdalena
(P.O. Box 14-0199)
Lima 17, Peru
Tel.: (511) 625 9140
Fax: (511) 625 9100
E-mail: unic.lima@unic.org
Website: http://www.uniclima.
org.pe
Serving: Peru

Mexico City
Montes Urales 440, 3rd floor
Colonia Lomas de Chapultepec
Mexico City, D.F. 11000, Mexico
Tel.: (52 55) 4000 9717
Fax: (52 55) 5203 8638
E-mail: infounic@un.org.mx
Website: http://www.cinu.mx
Serving: Cuba, Dominican Republic,
Mexico

Panama City
UN House Bldg 128, 1st Floor
Ciudad del Saber, Clayton
(P.O. Box 0819-01082)
Panama City, Panama
Tel.: (507) 301 0035/0036
Fax: (507) 301 0037
E-mail: unic.panama@unic.org
Website: http://www.cinup.org
Serving: Panama

Port of Spain
2nd floor, Bretton Hall
16 Victoria Avenue

(P.O. Box 130)
Port of Spain,
Trinidad and Tobago, W.I.
Tel.: (868) 623 4813
Fax: (868) 623 4332
E-mail: unic.portofspain@unic.org
Website: http://portofspain.
unicnetwork.org
Serving: Antigua and Barbuda,
Aruba, Bahamas, Barbados,
Belize, Dominica, Grenada,
Guyana, Jamaica, Netherlands
Antilles, Saint Kitts and Nevis,
Saint Lucia, Saint Vincent
and the Grenadines, Suriname,
Trinidad and Tobago

Rio de Janeiro
Palácio Itamaraty
Av. Marechal Floriano 196
20080-002 Rio de Janeiro RJ, Brazil
Tel.: (55 21) 2253 2211
Fax: (55 21) 2233 5753
E-mail: unic.brazil@unic.org
Website: http://unicrio.org.br
Serving: Brazil

Washington D.C.
1775 K Street, N.W., Suite 400
Washington, D.C. 20006
United States of America
Tel.: (202) 331 8670
E-mail: unicdc@unic.org
Website: http://www.unicwash.org
Serving: United States of America

ASIA AND THE PACIFIC

Beirut
UN House, Riad El-Sohl Square
(P.O. Box 11-8576)
Beirut, Lebanon
Tel.: (961 1) 981 301
Fax: (961 1) 97 04 24
E-mail: unic-beirut@un.org
Website: http://www.unicbeirut.org
Serving: Jordan, Kuwait, Lebanon,
Syrian Arab Republic, ESCWA

Canberra
Level 1, 7 National Circuit, Barton,
ACT 2600
(P.O. Box 5366, Kingston,
ACT 2604)
Canberra, Australia
Tel.: (61 2) 627 09200
Fax: (61 2) 627 38206
E-mail: unic.canberra@unic.org
Website: http://www.un.org.au
Serving: Australia, Fiji, Kiribati,
Nauru, New Zealand, Samoa,
Tonga, Tuvalu, Vanuatu

Colombo
202/204 Bauddhaloka Mawatha
(P.O. Box 1505, Colombo)
Colombo 7, Sri Lanka
Tel.: (94 112) 580 791

Fax: (94 112) 581 116
E-mail: unic.colombo@unic.org
Website: http://colombo.sites.
  unicnetwork.org
Serving: Sri Lanka

Dhaka
IDB Bhaban (8th floor),
  Sher-e-Banglanagar
(G.P.O. Box 3658, Dhaka-1000)
Dhaka-1207, Bangladesh
Tel.: (880 2) 9183 086 (library)
Fax: (880 2) 9183 106
E-mail: unic.dhaka@undp.org
Website: http://www.unicdhaka.org
Serving: Bangladesh

Islamabad
ILO Building, Sector G-5/2
Near State Bank of Pakistan
(P.O. Box 1107)
Islamabad, Pakistan
Tel.: (0092) 51 9216985
E-mail: unic.islamabad@unic.org
Website: http://www.unic.org.pk/
Serving: Pakistan

Jakarta
Menara Thamrin Building, 3A floor
Jalan MH Thamrin, Kav. 3
Jakarta 10250, Indonesia
Tel.: (62 21) 3983 1011
Fax: (62 21) 3983 1014
E-mail: unic.jakarta@unic.org
Website: http://www.unic-jakarta.
  org
Serving: Indonesia

Kathmandu
Harihar Bhavan Pulchowk
(P.O. Box 107, UN House)
Kathmandu, Nepal
Tel.: (977 1) 55 23 200, Ext. 1600
Fax: (977 1) 55 43 723
E-mail: registry.np@undp.org
Website: http://kathmandu.unic.org
Serving: Nepal

Manama
United Nations House
Bldg. 69, Road 1901, Block 319
(P.O. Box 26004)
Manama, Bahrain
Tel.: (973) 1731 1676
Fax: (973) 1731 1692
E-mail: unic.manama@unic.org
Website: http://manama.unic.org
Serving: Bahrain, Qatar, United Arab
  Emirates

Manila
GC Corporate Plaza (ex Jaka II
  Building)
5th floor, 150 Legaspi Street,
  Legaspi Village
(P.O. Box 7285 ADC (DAPO),
1300 Domestic Road Pasay City)
Makati City
1229 Metro Manila, Philippines

Tel.: (63 2) 336 7720
Fax: (63 2) 336 7177
E-mail: unic.manila@unic.org
Website: http://www.unicmanila.org
Serving: Papua New Guinea,
  Philippines, Solomon Islands

New Delhi
55 Lodi Estate,
New Delhi 110 003, India
Tel.: (91 11) 4653 2242
Fax: (91 11) 2462 0293
E-mail: unic.india@unic.org
Website: http://www.unic.org.in
Serving: Bhutan, India

Sana'a
Street 5, Off Abawnya Area
Handhel Zone, beside Handhal
  Mosque
(P.O. Box 237)
Sana'a, Yemen
Tel.: (967 1) 274 000
Fax: (967 1) 274 043
E-mail: unic.yemen@unic.org
Website: http://www.unicyemen.org
Serving: Yemen

Tehran
No. 8, Shahrzad Blvd., Darrous
(P.O. Box 15875-4557)
Tehran, Iran
Tel.: (98 21) 2 287 3837
Fax: (98 21) 2 287 3395
E-mail: unic.tehran@unic.org
Website: http://www.unic-ir.org
Serving: Iran

Tokyo
UNU Building (8th floor)
53–70 Jingumae 5-Chome,
  Shibuya-Ku
Tokyo 150-0001, Japan
Tel.: (81 3) 5467 4454
Fax: (81 3) 5467 4455
E-mail: unic.tokyo@unic.org
Website: http://www.unic.or.jp
Serving: Japan

Yangon
6 Natmauk Road
Tamwe Township
(P.O. Box 230)
Yangon, Myanmar
Tel.: (95 1) 542 911
Fax: (95 1) 545 634
E-mail: unic.yangon@unic.org
Website: http://yangon@unic.org
Serving: Myanmar

EUROPE AND THE COMMMONWEALTH OF INDEPENDENT STATES

Almaty
67 Tole Bi Street, 050000 Almaty
Republic of Kazakhstan
Tel.: (7 727) 258 2643

Fax: (7 727) 258 2645
E-mail: kazakhstan@unic.org
Website: http://kazakhstan.unic.org
Serving: Kazakhstan

Ankara
Birlik Mahallesi, 415 Cadde No. 11
06610 Cankaya
Ankara, Turkey
Tel.: (90 312) 454-1052
Fax: (90 312) 496-1499
E-mail: unic.ankara@unic.org
Website: http://www.unicankara.
  org.tr
Serving: Turkey

Baku
United Nations Office
UN 50th Anniversary Street, 3
Baku, AZ1001
Azerbaijan
Tel.: (994 12) 498 98 88
Fax: (994 12) 498 32 35
E-mail: un-dpi@un-az.org
Website: http://baku.sites.
  unicnetwork.org
Serving: Azerbaijan

Brussels
Regional United Nations
  Information Centre
Residence Palace
Rue de la Loi/Westraat 155
Quartier Rubens, Block C2
1040 Brussels, Belgium
Tel.: (32 2) 788 84 84
Fax: (32 2) 788 84 85
E-mail: info@unric.org
Website: www.unric.org
Serving: Andorra, Belgium, Cyprus,
  Denmark, Finland, France,
  Germany, Greece, Holy See,
  Iceland, Ireland, Italy, Luxembourg,
  Malta, Monaco, Netherlands,
  Norway, Portugal, San Marino,
  Spain, Sweden, United Kingdom,
  European Union

Geneva
United Nations Information
  Service
United Nations Office at Geneva
Palais des Nations
1211 Geneva 10, Switzerland
Tel.: (41 22) 917 2302
Fax: (41 22) 917 0030
E-mail: press_geneva@unog.ch
Website: www.unog.ch
Serving: Switzerland

Kyiv
United Nations Office
1 Klovskiy Uzviz
Kyiv, Ukraine
Tel.: (380 44) 253 9363
Fax: (380 44) 253 2607
E-mail: registry@un.org.ua
Website: www.un.org.ua
Serving: Ukraine

Minsk
United Nations Office
17 Kirov Street, 3rd Floor
220050 Minsk, Belarus
Tel.: (375 17) 327 3817
Fax: (375 17) 226 0340
E-mail: dpi.staff.by@undp.org
Website: www.un.by
Serving: Belarus

Moscow
9 Leontievsky Pereulok
Moscow 125009, Russian Federation
Tel.: (7 495) 787 2107
Fax: (7 495) 787 2137
E-mail: unic.moscow@unic.org
Website: www.unic.ru
Serving: Russian Federation

Prague
Zeleza 24
11000 Prague 1, Czech Republic
Tel.: (420) 2557 11645
Fax: (420) 2573 16761
E-mail: info.prague@unic.org
Website: www.osn.cz

Serving: Czech Republic

Tashkent
United Nations Office
Mirabad Str. 41/3 Tashkent,
  Uzbekistan 100015
Tel.: (998 71) 1203 450
Fax: (998 71) 1203 485
E-mail: uno.tashkent@undp.org
Website: www.un.uz
Serving: Uzbekistan

Tbilisi
United Nations Office
9, Eristavi Street
0179 Tbilisi, Georgia
Tel.: 995 32 225 11 26
Fax: 995 32 225 02 71
E-mail: uno.tbilisi@unic.org
Website: www.ungeorgia.ge
Serving: Georgia

Vienna
United Nations Information Service
United Nations Office at Vienna
Vienna International Centre
Wagramer Strasse 5

(P.O. Box 500, 1400 Vienna)
1220 Vienna, Austria
Tel.: (43 1) 26060 4666
Fax: (43 1) 26060 5899
E-mail: unis@unvienna.org
Website: www.unis.unvienna.org
Serving: Austria, Hungary, Slovakia,
  Slovenia

Warsaw
ul. Piękna 19
00-549 Warszawa, Poland
Tel.: (48 22) 825 57 84
Fax: (48 22) 825 77 06
E-mail: unic.poland@unic.org
Website: www.unic.un.org.pl
Serving: Poland

Yerevan
United Nations Office
14 Petros Adamyan Street, 1st Floor
0010 Yerevan, Armenia
Tel.: (374 10) 560 212
E-mail: uno.yerevan@unic.org
Website: www.un.am
Serving: Armenia

SELECTED UNITED NATIONS WEBSITES

United Nations	www.un.org
United Nations system	www.unsystem.org

Principal Organs

Economic and Social Council	www.un.org/en/ecosoc
General Assembly	www.un.org/en/ga
International Court of Justice	www.icj-cij.org
Secretariat	www.un.org/en/mainbodies/secretariat
Security Council	www.un.org/en/sc
Trusteeship Council	www.un.org/en/mainbodies/trusteeship

Programmes and Funds

International Trade Center (ITC)	www.intracen.org
Office of the United Nations High Commissioner for Refugees (UNHCR)	www.unhcr.org
United Nations Capital Development Fund (UNCDF)	www.uncdf.org
United Nations Children's Fund (UNICEF)	www.unicef.org
United Nations Conference on Trade and Development (UNCTAD)	www.unctad.org
United Nations Development Programme (UNDP)	www.undp.org
United Nations Entity for Gender Equality and the Empowerment of Women (UN-Women)	www.unwomen.org
United Nations Environment Programme (UNEP)	www.unep.org
United Nations Human Settlements Programme (UN-Habitat)	www.unhabitat.org
United Nations Office on Drugs and Crime (UNODC)	www.unodc.org
United Nations Population Fund (UNFPA)	www.unfpa.org
United Nations Relief and Works Agency for Palestine Refugees in the Near East (UNRWA)	www.unrwa.org
United Nations Volunteers (UNV)	www.unv.org
World Food Programme (WFP)	www.wfp.org

Research and Training Institutes

United Nations Institute for Disarmament Research (UNIDIR)	www.unidir.org
United Nations Institute for Training and Research (UNITAR)	www.unitar.org
United Nations Interregional Crime and Justice Research Institute (UNICRI)	www.unicri.it
United Nations Research Institute for Social Development (UNRISD)	www.unrisd.org
United Nations System Staff College (UNSSC)	www.unssc.org
United Nations University (UNU)	www.unu.edu

Other Entities

Joint United Nations Programme on HIV/AIDS (UNAIDS)	www.unaids.org
United Nations Office for Disaster Risk Reduction (UNISDR)	www.unisdr.org

| United Nations Office for Partnerships (UNOP) | www.un.org/partnerships/ |
| United Nations Office for Project Services (UNOPS) | www.unops.org |

Subsidiary Bodies and Functional Commissions

Commission on Crime Prevention and Criminal Justice	www.unodc.org/unodc/en/commissions/CCPCJ/
Commission on Narcotic Drugs	www.unodc.org/unodc/en/commissions/CND/
Commission on Population and Development	www.un.org/esa/population/cpd/aboutcom.htm
Commission on Science and Technology for Development	www.unctad.org/en/Pages/CSTD.aspx
Commission for Social Development	www.un.org/development/desa/dspd/united-nations-commission-for-social-development-csocd-social-policy-and-development-division.html
Commission on the Status of Women	www.un.org/womenwatch/daw/csw
Counter-Terrorism Committee (CTC)	www.un.org/en/sc/ctc
Disarmament Commission (UNDC)	www.un.org/Depts/ddar/discomm/undc
High-level political forum on sustainable development (HLPF)	sustainabledevelopment.un.org/hlpf/
Human Rights Council (HRC)	www.ohchr.org/EN/HRBodies/HRC/Pages/HRCIndex.aspx
International Tribunal for the former Yugoslavia (ICTY)	www.icty.org
International Law Commission (ILC)	www.un.org/law/ilc
Mechanism for International Criminal Tribunals (MICT)	www.unmict.org
Peacekeeping operations and political missions	www.un.org/en/peacekeeping
Permanent Forum on Indigenous Issues	www.un.org/esa/socdev/unpfii
Statistical Commission	unstats.un.org/unsd/statcom/
United Nations Forum on Forests	www.un.org/esa/forests
United Nations Peacebuilding Commission	www.un.org/en/peacebuilding/

Regional Commissions

Economic Commission for Africa (ECA)	www.uneca.org
Economic Commission for Europe (ECE)	www.unece.org
Economic Commission for Latin America and the Caribbean (ECLAC)	www.cepal.org
Economic and Social Commission for Asia and the Pacific (ESCAP)	www.unescap.org
Economic and Social Commission for Western Asia (ESCWA)	www.unescwa.org

Specialized Agencies

Food and Agriculture Organization of the United Nations (FAO)	www.fao.org
International Civil Aviation Organization (ICAO)	www.icao.int
International Fund for Agricultural Development (IFAD)	www.ifad.org
International Labour Organization (ILO)	www.ilo.org
International Maritime Organization (IMO)	www.imo.org
International Monetary Fund (IMF)	www.imf.org
International Telecommunication Union (ITU)	www.itu.int
United Nations Educational, Scientific and Cultural Organization (UNESCO)	www.unesco.org

United Nations Industrial Development Organization (UNIDO)	www.unido.org
Universal Postal Union (UPU)	www.upu.int
World Bank Group	www.worldbank.org
World Health Organization (WHO)	www.who.int
World Intellectual Property Organization (WIPO)	www.wipo.int
World Meteorological Organization (WMO)	www.wmo.ch
World Tourism Organization (UNWTO)	www.unwto.org

Related Organizations

International Atomic Energy Agency (IAEA)	www.iaea.org
Organization for the Prohibition of Chemical Weapons (OPCW)	www.opcw.org
Preparatory Commission for the Comprehensive Nuclear-Test-Ban Treaty Organization (CTBTO)	www.ctbto.org
World Trade Organization (WTO)	www.wto.org

INDEX